TABLE OF CONTENTS

Chapter 3: **Startup**

Chapter 4: **Navigate**

Chapter 5: **Select**

Chapter 6: **Compositing**

Table of Contents

Table of Contents

Chapter 17: **Filters**

Filter basics

All the filters illustrated

A few filter exercises

Table of Contents

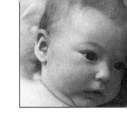

THE BASICS 1

Tool tips

Rest the pointer on a tool icon—without clicking or pressing the mouse button—to learn that tool's name or shortcut **1**. Use the same method to learn the function of a palette option **2**. (Check the Show Tool Tips box in File menu > Preferences > General to access this feature.)

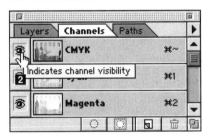

Tool shortcuts

Hide/show the Toolbox and all open palettes	Tab
Cycle through hidden, related tools on same pop-out menu	Shift and shortcut key or Alt-click/Option-click the currently visible tool icon
Cycle through blending modes for current tool (or layer)	Shift + or Shift -

How to use the Toolbox

To **choose** a tool whose icon is currently visible, click once on its icon. Press and drag to choose a hidden tool from a pop-out menu. Or choose a tool using its shortcut (study the next two pages). If you forget a tool's shortcut, just leave the cursor over the tool icon for a moment, and the Tool tip will remind you. **1** Press **Shift** and the same shortcut key to cycle through hidden, related tools, or Alt-click/Option-click the currently visible tool.

Choose **attributes** for a tool—like a blending mode or opacity percentage—from its Options palette **3**. Double-click a tool to bring the Options palette to the front of its group (and also open the palette if it isn't already open) or press Enter/Return if the tool is already highlighted. You can also customize some tools using other palettes, such as Brushes, Swatches, or Color.

Options palette settings will remain in effect for an individual tool until you change them or reset the tool or the Tool palette to its default settings. To restore a **tool's default** settings, click the tool, then choose **Reset Tool** from the Options palette command menu. Choose **Reset All Tools** from the Options palette command menu to restore the default settings for *all* tools. You can choose whether a tool **cursor** looks like its Toolbox icon or a crosshair in File menu > Preferences > Display & Cursors.

If you try to use a tool **incorrectly**, a cancel icon will appear. ⊘ Double-click with the tool in the image window to make an explanation appear. If you choose Current Tool from the Status bar drop-down menu in the lower left corner of the application/image window, the name of the currently selected tool will appear there.

The Toolbox

The Toolbox

Press Shift and a shortcut key to cycle through related tools on the same pop-out menu.

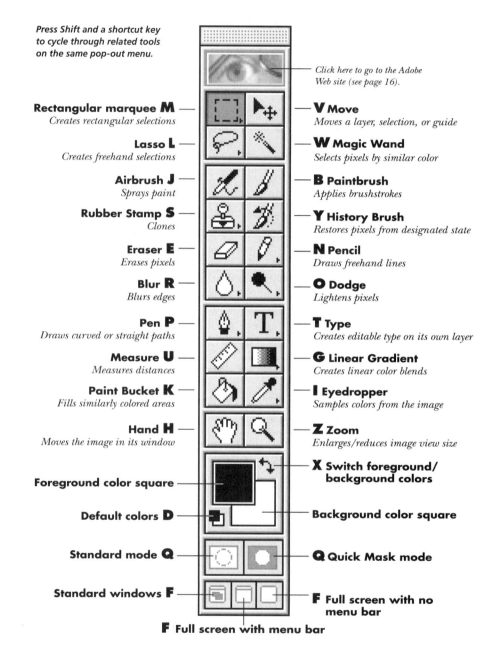

Click here to go to the Adobe Web site (see page 16).

Rectangular marquee M
Creates rectangular selections

V Move
Moves a layer, selection, or guide

Lasso L
Creates freehand selections

W Magic Wand
Selects pixels by similar color

Airbrush J
Sprays paint

B Paintbrush
Applies brushstrokes

Rubber Stamp S
Clones

Y History Brush
Restores pixels from designated state

Eraser E
Erases pixels

N Pencil
Draws freehand lines

Blur R
Blurs edges

O Dodge
Lightens pixels

Pen P
Draws curved or straight paths

T Type
Creates editable type on its own layer

Measure U
Measures distances

G Linear Gradient
Creates linear color blends

Paint Bucket K
Fills similarly colored areas

I Eyedropper
Samples colors from the image

Hand H
Moves the image in its window

Z Zoom
Enlarges/reduces image view size

Foreground color square

X Switch foreground/ background colors

Default colors D

Background color square

Standard mode Q

Q Quick Mask mode

Standard windows F

F Full screen with no menu bar

F Full screen with menu bar

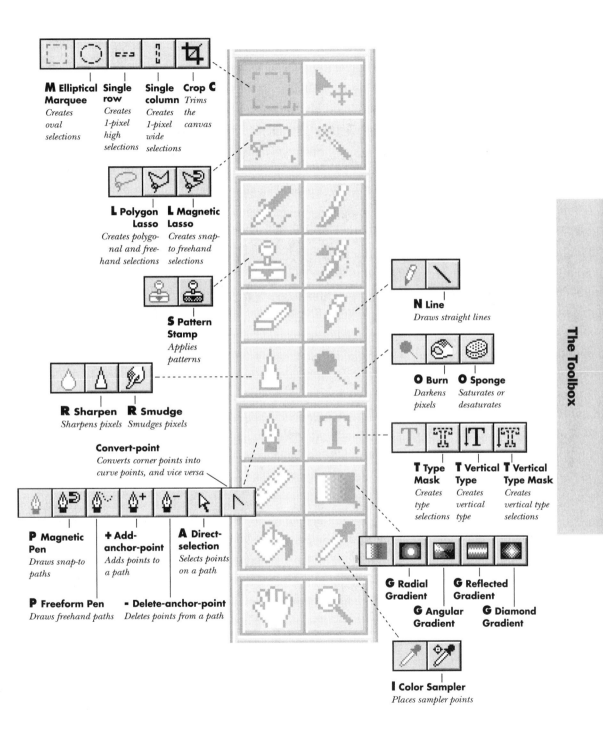

M Elliptical Marquee
Creates oval selections

Single row
Creates 1-pixel high selections

Single column
Creates 1-pixel wide selections

Crop C
Trims the canvas

L Polygon Lasso
Creates polygonal and free-hand selections

L Magnetic Lasso
Creates snap-to freehand selections

S Pattern Stamp
Applies patterns

R Sharpen
Sharpens pixels

R Smudge
Smudges pixels

Convert-point
Converts corner points into curve points, and vice versa

P Magnetic Pen
Draws snap-to paths

+ Add-anchor-point
Adds points to a path

A Direct-selection
Selects points on a path

P Freeform Pen
Draws freehand paths

- Delete-anchor-point
Deletes points from a path

N Line
Draws straight lines

O Burn
Darkens pixels

O Sponge
Saturates or desaturates

T Type Mask
Creates type selections

T Vertical Type
Creates vertical type

T Vertical Type Mask
Creates vertical type selections

G Radial Gradient

G Reflected Gradient

G Angular Gradient

G Diamond Gradient

I Color Sampler
Places sampler points

The Photoshop screen: Macintosh

1 *Menu bar*

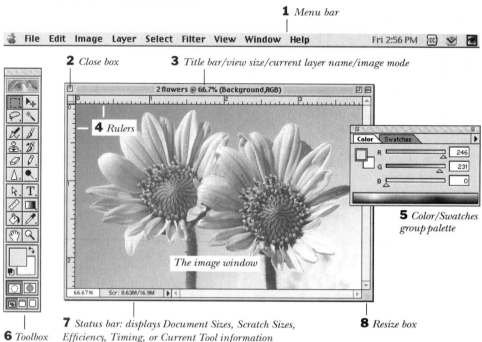

2 *Close box*   **3** *Title bar/view size/current layer name/image mode*

4 *Rulers*

The image window

5 *Color/Swatches group palette*

7 *Status bar: displays Document Sizes, Scratch Sizes, Efficiency, Timing, or Current Tool information*

6 *Toolbox*

8 *Resize box*

Key to the Photoshop screen: Macintosh and Windows

1 *Menu bar*
Press any menu heading to access dialog boxes, submenus, and commands.

2 *Close box (Mac)*
To close an image or a palette, click its close box.

3 *Title bar/view size/current layer/image mode*
Displays the image's title, view size, current layer (or the Background), and image mode.

4 *Rulers*
Choose View menu > Show Rulers to display rulers. The position of the pointer is indicated by a mark on each ruler. Choose ruler units in File menu > Preferences > Units & Rulers.

5 *Palettes*
There are 12 moveable palettes. Their default groupings can be changed. Click a tab (palette name) in a palette group to bring that palette to the front of its group.

6 *Toolbox*
Press Tab to show/hide the Toolbox and all open palettes.

7 *Status bar*
The Status bar displays Document Sizes, Scratch Sizes (the amount of RAM currently available to Photoshop), Efficiency (the percentage of RAM being used), or Current Tool (the name of the current tool) info. Press and hold on the Status bar to display the page preview, which is a thumbnail of the image relative to the paper size. Alt-press/Option-press on the Status bar to display the image's dimensions, number of channels, mode, and resolution.

8 *Resize box*
To resize a window or a palette, drag its resize box diagonally.

The Photoshop screen: Windows

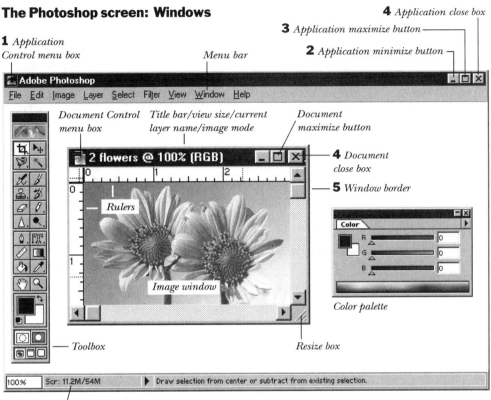

1 *Application Control menu box*

Menu bar

4 *Application close box*

3 *Application maximize button*

2 *Application minimize button*

Document Control menu box

Title bar/view size/current layer name/image mode

Document maximize button

4 *Document close box*

5 *Window border*

Rulers

Image window

Color palette

Toolbox

Resize box

Status bar: displays Document Sizes, Scratch Sizes, Efficiency, or Timing information

Key to the Photoshop screen: Windows

1 *Application (or Document) Control menu box*
The Application Control menu box commands are Restore, Move, Size, Minimize, Maximize, and Close. The Document Control menu box commands are Restore, Move, Size, Minimize, Maximize, Close, and Next.

2 *Application (or Document) minimize button*
Click the Application Minimize button to shrink the document to an icon in the Taskbar. Click the icon on the Taskbar to restore the application window to its previous size.

Click the Document Minimize button to shrink the document to an icon at the bottom left corner of the application window. Click the Restore button to restore the document window to its previous size.

3 *Application (or Document) maximize/restore button*
Click the Application or Document Maximize button to enlarge a window to its largest possible size. Click the Restore button to restore a window to its previous size. When a window is at the restored size, the Restore button turns into the Maximize button.

4 *Application (or Document) close box*
Closes the application (or image).

5 *Window border*
Press and drag a horizontal or vertical border to resize an image window.

The menus

File menu

File menu commands are used to create, open, place, close, save, scan, import, export, or print an image, set preferences, and exit/quit Photoshop.

Windows: You can reopen any of the four most recently opened files via this menu.

> *Choose File menu > Adobe Online to go to the Adobe Web site.*

File menu items:

New...	Ctrl+N
Open...	Ctrl+O
Open As...	Alt+Ctrl+O
Close	Ctrl+W
Save	Ctrl+S
Save As...	Shft+Ctrl+S
Save a Copy...	Alt+Ctrl+S
Revert	
Place...	
Import	▶
Export	▶
Automate	▶
File Info...	
Page Setup...	Shft+Ctrl+P
Print...	Ctrl+P
Preferences	▶
Color Settings	▶
Adobe Online...	
1 D:\...\CachePref.tif	
2 D:\...\WindowMenu.tif	
3 D:\...\StatusBar.tif	
4 D:\...\2flowers2.tif	
Exit	Ctrl+Q

Edit menu

Edit menu commands include Undo, which undoes the last modification made, and the Clipboard commands (Cut, Copy, Copy Merged, Paste, and Paste Into). The Fill, Stroke, Define Pattern, and Transform commands are also executed via the Edit menu. The Purge commands free up memory used by

Edit menu items:

Undo Copy Pixels	⌘Z
Cut	⌘X
Copy	⌘C
Copy Merged	⇧⌘C
Paste	⌘V
Paste Into	⇧⌘V
Clear	
Fill...	
Stroke...	
Free Transform	⌘T
Transform	▶
Define Pattern	
Purge	▶

Image menu

An image can be converted to any of eight image modes via the Mode submenu. The Adjust commands modify an image's hue, saturation, brightness, or contrast. The Image Size command modifies an image's file size, dimensions, or resolution. The Canvas Size dialog box is used to add or subtract from an image's editable canvas area.

Image menu items:

Mode	▶
Adjust	▶
Duplicate...	
Apply Image...	
Calculations...	
Image Size...	
Canvas Size...	
Crop	
Rotate Canvas	▶
Histogram...	
Trap...	

Layer menu

Layer menu commands add, duplicate, delete, modify, add masks to, group, arrange, align, distribute, merge, and flatten layers. Many of these commands can be accessed more quickly via the Layers palette command menu.

Layer menu items:

New	▶
Duplicate Layer...	
Delete Layer	
Layer Options...	
Adjustment Options...	
Effects	▶
Type	▶
Remove Layer Mask	
Disable Layer Mask	
Group Linked	⌘G
Ungroup	⇧⌘G
Arrange	▶
Align Linked	▶
Distribute Linked	▶
Merge Linked	⌘E
Merge Visible	⇧⌘E
Flatten Image	
Matting	▶

The Menus

Select menu

Select	
All	⌘A
Deselect	⌘D
Reselect	⇧⌘D
Inverse	⇧⌘I
Color Range...	
Feather...	⌥⌘D
Modify	▶
Grow	
Similar	
Transform Selection	
Load Selection...	
Save Selection...	

The "All" command on the Select menu selects an entire layer. The Deselect command deselects all selections. The Reselect command restores the last deselected selection. Other Select menu commands enlarge, contract, smooth, or feather selection edges, and save selections to and from channels. The Color Range command creates a selection based on color.

View menu

View	
New View	
Preview	▶
Gamut Warning	⇧⌘Y
Zoom In	⌘+
Zoom Out	⌘-
Fit on Screen	⌘0
Actual Pixels	⌥⌘0
Print Size	
Hide Edges	⌘H
Hide Path	⇧⌘H
Show Rulers	⌘R
Hide Guides	⌘;
✓ Snap To Guides	⇧⌘;
Lock Guides	⌥⌘;
Clear Guides	
Show Grid	⌘"
✓ Snap To Grid	⇧⌘"

The New View command displays the same image in a secondary window. Other View menu commands control view sizes and the display of rulers, guides, and grids. The Gamut Warning highlights colors that won't print on a four-color press. Choose CMYK Preview to see how your image looks in CMYK color without actually changing its mode.

Filter menu

Filter	
Bas Relief	⌘F
Fade Bas Relief...	⇧⌘F
Artistic	▶
Blur	▶
Brush Strokes	▶
Distort	▶
Noise	▶
Pixelate	▶
Render	▶
Sharpen	▶
Sketch	▶
Stylize	▶
Texture	▶
Video	▶
Other	▶
Digimarc	▶

Filters, which perform a wide range of image editing functions, are organized in submenu groups. The Fade command lessens the effect of the last applied filter or Adjust command. The Digimarc filter embeds a copyright watermark in an image.

Window menu

Window
Cascade
Tile
Arrange Icons
Close All
Hide Tools
Show Navigator
Show Info
Show Options
Show Color
Show Swatches
Show Brushes
Show Layers
Show Channels
Show Paths
Show History
Show Actions
Hide Status Bar
1 2 flowers @ 100% (RGB)
✓ 2 Untitled-1 @ 100% (Layer 1,RGB)

Window menu commands display or hide the palettes. Open images are also listed and can be activated via this menu.
Windows: You can also arrange image windows or hide/show the Status bar via Window menu commands.

Help menu

Help	
Contents	F1
Search for Help on...	
Keyboard	
How to Use Help	
About Photoshop...	
About Plug-in	▶
Export Transparent Image...	
Resize Image...	

Use the Help menu commands to read about various Photoshop features, to look up keyboard shortcuts, or to perform tasks via onscreen prompts.

The palettes

How to use the palettes

There are 12 moveable palettes that are used for image editing. To save screen space, the palettes are joined into these default groups: **Navigator/Info/Options**, **History/Actions**, **Color/Swatches/Brushes**, **Layers/Channels/Paths**, and the **Toolbox**.

To **open** a palette, choose Window menu > Show [palette name]. The palette will appear in front within its group. Double-click a tool to display its Options palette.

Press Tab to **hide** or **display** all open palettes, including the Toolbox. Press Shift-Tab to show/hide all open palettes except the Toolbox.

To **display** an open palette at the front of its group, click its tab (palette name).

You can **separate** a palette from its group by dragging its tab (palette name) **1**–**2**. You can **add** a palette to any group by dragging the tab over the group. Use the **resize** box (lower right corner) to widen a palette if you need to make additional tabs visible. You can

resize any palette other than Color, Options, or Info.

To **shrink/expand** a palette, double-click its tab or click the palette minimize/maximize (Win)/zoom box (Mac) in the upper right corner. If the palette is not at its default size, click the minimize/zoom box once to restore its default size, then click a second time to shrink the palette.

If the **Save Palette Locations** box is checked in the File menu > Preferences > General dialog box, palettes that are open when you exit/quit Photoshop will **reappear** in their same location when you re-launch Photoshop.

To restore the palettes' **default** groupings at any time, click **Reset Palette Locations to Default** in the same dialog box.

TIP Quick-change: Click in a field on a palette (or in a dialog box), then press the up or down arrow on the keyboard to change that value incrementally.

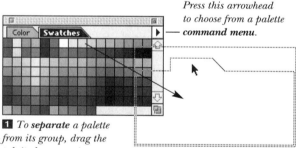

Press this arrowhead to choose from a palette command menu.

1 *To separate a palette from its group, drag the tab (palette name) away from the palette group.*

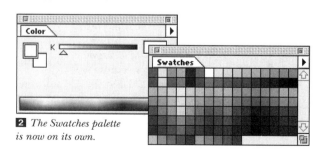

2 *The Swatches palette is now on its own.*

How to Use the Palettes

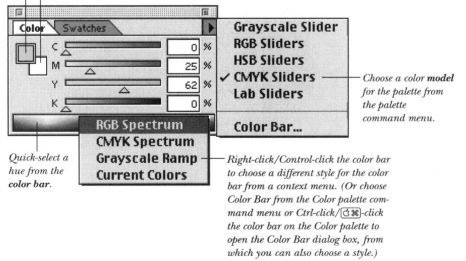

Pop-up sliders

There are two ways to use a pop-up slider **1**. Press an arrowhead and drag the slider in one movement. Or click the arrowhead, then drag the slider. To close a slider, click outside it or press Enter/Return. Press Esc while a slider is open to restore its previous setting.

Color palette

The Color palette is used for mixing and choosing colors. Colors are applied using a painting or editing tool or using a command, such as Fill or Canvas Size. Choose a color model for the palette from the palette command menu. Mix a color using the sliders or quick-select a color by clicking on the color bar at the bottom of the Color palette.

To open the Color Picker, from which you can also choose a color, click once on the Foreground or Background color square if it's already active or double-click a non-active square.

Foreground color square.
The currently active square has a white border.

Background color square.

Choose a color **model** for the palette from the palette command menu.

Quick-select a hue from the **color bar**.

Right-click/Control-click the color bar to choose a different style for the color bar from a context menu. (Or choose Color Bar from the Color palette command menu or Ctrl-click/⌘-click the color bar on the Color palette to open the Color Bar dialog box, from which you can also choose a style.)

9

Swatches palette

The Swatches palette is used for choosing already mixed colors. Individual swatches can be added to or deleted from the palette. Custom swatch palettes can also be loaded, appended, and saved using Swatches palette commands.

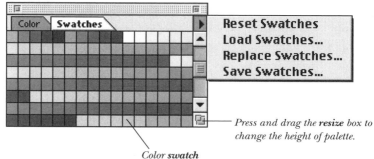

*Press and drag the **resize** box to change the height of palette.*

*Color **swatch***

Channels palette

The Channels palette is used to display one or more of the channels that make up an image. It is also used for creating and displaying alpha channels, which are used for saving selections, and spot color channels, which are used for creating spot color plates.

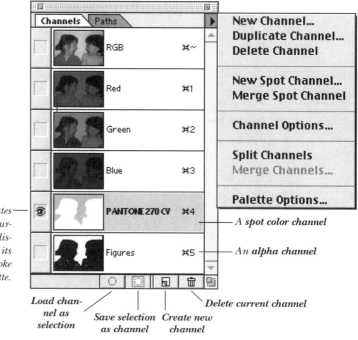

*An **eye** icon indicates that that channel is currently **displayed**. To display a channel, click its name or use the keystroke that's listed on the palette.*

*A **spot color channel***

*An **alpha channel***

Load channel as selection

Save selection as channel

Create new channel

Delete current channel

10

Brushes palette

The Brushes palette is used for choosing a preset or user-defined brush tip for a painting or editing tool. You can also load, append, and save brushes using the Brushes palette command menu.

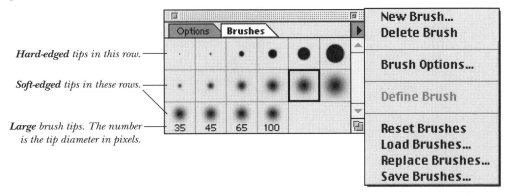

Hard-edged tips in this row.

Soft-edged tips in these rows.

Large brush tips. The number is the tip diameter in pixels.

Options palette

The Options palette is used to define attributes for a tool, such as its opacity, fade distance, or blending mode. Options are set for each tool individually, and remain in effect until they're changed. You can restore the currently selected tool or all tools to their default settings via the Options palette command menu.

If the Options palette is already open, but it's behind another palette, to bring it to the front, click the Options tab, or double-click a tool, or press Enter/Return if the tool is already selected.

Do you use a stylus?

If you're using a pressure-sensitive tablet, you can choose settings for your stylus for the Magnetic Lasso, Magnetic Pen, History Brush, Airbrush, Paintbrush, Pencil, Blur, Sharpen, Eraser, Rubber Stamp, Pattern Stamp, Smudge, Dodge, Burn, or Sponge tool. Double-click the tool, then choose one of these settings from the Options palette:

- **Size:** The heavier the pressure, the wider the stroke.
- **Color:** Light pressure applies the Background color, heavy pressure applies the Foreground color, and medium pressure applies a combination of the two.
- **Opacity/Pressure/Exposure:** The heavier the pressure, the more a tool's effect is applied.

Note: A plug-in is no longer required for a stylus.

The *blending mode* drop-down menu.

The **Options** palette when the Paintbrush tool is selected.

Opacity setting for the Gradient Fill, Pencil, Line, Paintbrush, Rubber Stamp, Pattern Stamp, Paint Bucket, and History Brush tools; **Pressure** setting for the Airbrush, Smudge, Blur, Sharpen, and Sponge tools; **Exposure** setting for the Dodge and Burn tools.

Chapter 1

Layers Palette

Layers palette

Normally, when you create a new image, it will
have an opaque Background. Using the Layers
palette, you can add, delete, hide/show, duplicate, group, link, and restack layers on top of
the Background. Each layer can be assigned
its own blending mode and opacity and can be
edited separately without changing the other
layers. You can also attach a **mask** to a layer.

TIP Click Contents: Transparent in the New
dialog box to make the bottommost tier of
a new image be a layer with transparency
instead of an opaque Background.

You'll see a special symbol on the Layers palette
for each of these editable layer features: An
adjustment layer ◐, which is a temporary layer
that is used for applying various color or tonal
adjustments to the layers below it; an **editable
type layer** T, which is created automatically
when the Type or Vertical Type tool is used;
and **layer effects** ❼ (Drop Shadow, et al.).

Only the currently highlighted layer, called
the **current** (or "active") layer, can be edited.
Click a layer name on the Layers palette to
activate that layer. The name of the current
layer (or the Background) appears on the
image window title bar.

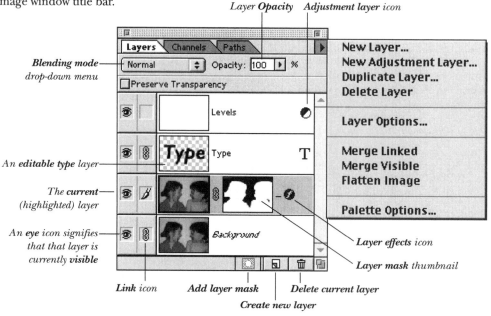

12

Paths palette

A path is a shape that is composed of curved and straight line segments connected by anchor points. A path can be drawn directly with a Pen tool or you can start with a selection and convert it into a path. A path can be filled or stroked. To create a precisely-drawn selection, you can draw a path and then convert it into a selection. The Pen tool and its relatives, the Add-anchor-point, Delete-anchor-point, and Convert-point tools, can be used to reshape a path. Paths are saved and accessed via the Paths palette.

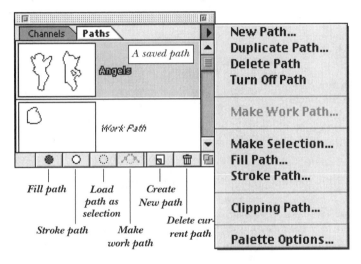

A saved path

Fill path

Stroke path

Load path as selection

Make work path

Create New path

Delete current path

New Path...
Duplicate Path...
Delete Path
Turn Off Path

Make Work Path...

Make Selection...
Fill Path...
Stroke Path...

Clipping Path...

Palette Options...

Navigator palette

The Navigator palette is used for moving an image in its window or for changing an image's view size.

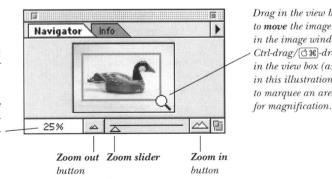

*Enter the desired **zoom percentage** (or enter a ratio, as in 1:1 or 4:1), then press **Enter/Return**. To zoom to the percentage and keep the field highlighted, press Shift-Enter/Shift-Return.*

*Drag in the view box to **move** the image in the image window. Ctrl-drag/⌘-drag in the view box (as in this illustration) to marquee an area for magnification.*

Zoom out button   Zoom slider   Zoom in button

Info palette

The Info palette displays a color breakdown of the pixel currently under the pointer. The palette will also show readouts for up to four color samplers, if they are placed on the image. If a color adjustment dialog box is open, the palette will display before and after color readouts. The Info palette also shows the *x/y* position of the pointer on the image.

Other information (such as the distance between points when a selection is moved, a line is drawn, or the Measure tool is used; the dimensions of a selection or crop marquee; or the width, height, and angle of a selection as it's transformed) may display on the palette, depending on which tool is being used.

Press an arrowhead to choose a mode for a readout: Actual Color (the current image mode); Grayscale; RGB, HSB, CMYK, or Lab Color; Total Ink; or current layer Opacity. The palette color mode can be different from the current image mode.

*During a **transform** operation, the width (W), height (H), angle (A), and horizontal skew (H) or vertical skew (V) of the transformed layer, selection, or path is shown in this area.*

*The **Width** and **Height** of an active **selection**.*

Color breakdown for the pixel currently under the pointer.

*Press on this arrowhead to choose a different **unit of measurement** for the palette (and the rulers).*

*The x/y **location** of the pointer on the image.*

*Press an arrowhead to choose a different **color mode** for that readout.*

*The #1, #2, #3, and #4 color readouts from four **color samplers** that were placed on the image.*

*Exclamation points indicate that the color currently under the pointer is outside the printable, CMYK **gamut**.*

	R :			W :	100.0%
	G :			H :	100.0%
	B :			A :	20.6°
				H :	0.0°
	X :	0.046		W :	2.625
	Y :	0.002		H :	1.931
#1	R :	0	#2	C :	22%
	G :	255		M :	0%
	B :	255		Y :	47%
				K :	0%
#3	R :	113	#4	C :	38!
	G :	108		M :	0!
	B :	23		Y :	16!
				K :	0!

Navigator   Info   Options

Info Palette

History palette

The History palette is used to selectively undo one or more previous steps in the image-editing process. Each brushstroke, filter application, or other operation is listed as a separate state on the palette, with the bottommost state being the most recent. Clicking on a prior state restores the document to that stage of the editing process. What happens to the document when you do so depends on whether the palette is in linear or non-linear mode.

In linear mode, if you click back on and then delete or resume image-editing from an earlier state, all subsequent states (dimmed, on the palette) will be deleted. In non-linear mode, you can click back on an earlier edit state or delete a state without losing subsequent states. This option is turned on or off via the Allow Non-Linear History box in the History Options dialog box (choose History Options from the palette command menu). You can switch between linear and non-linear mode at any time during editing.

The History Brush tool restores an image to a designated prior state where the brush is dragged.

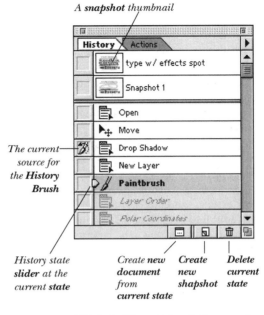

*A **snapshot** thumbnail*

*The current source for the **History Brush***

*History state **slider** at the current **state***

*Create **new document** from current **state***

*Create **new shapshot***

*Delete current **state***

*This is the **History** palette in **linear** mode. Note that some steps are grayed out.*

Actions palette

The main purpose for the Actions palette is to automate image processing. You can use it to record a series of commands and then replay those commands on one image or on a batch of images. The palette can also be used to create and access shortcuts.

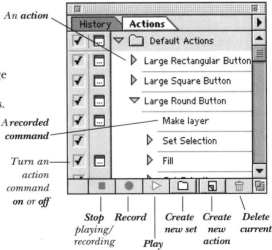

*An **action***

*A **recorded** command*

*Turn an action command **on** or **off***

Stop playing/ recording

Record

Play

Create new set

Create new action

Delete current

From the Adobe Photoshop home page on the Web, you can obtain registration info, tips, software upgrades, and other goodies. If you have a technical question, e-mail Adobe at techdocs@adobe.com.

Note: In order to access Adobe Online, your computer must have an Internet connection, which means having a modem and an Internet service provider.

To access Adobe Online using America Online as your Internet provider, you must sign on to AOL first. Click Update, then click a topic. To run an Internet application via ISP/LAN, you must restore your .TCP configuration by clicking Restore in the AOL Link panel in the AOL Preferences dialog box.

To access the Adobe Photoshop home page:

1. In Photoshop, choose File menu > Adobe Online.

   or

   Click the eye image at the top of the toolbox.

2. To update the Adobe Online screen, click Update **1**, then click OK.

3. Click a topic on the Adobe Online screen to launch your browser and connect to the Adobe home page on the Web. Once you're at the Adobe Web site, you can click on other topics to learn more about Photoshop or other Adobe products or services **2**–**3**.

TIP The Internet address for the Adobe home page is: http://www.adobe.com.

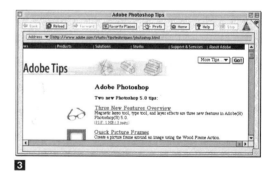

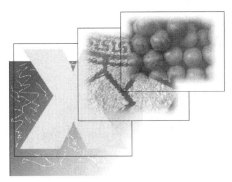

Layers are like clear acetate sheets: opaque where there is imagery and transparent where there is no imagery.

The Layers palette for a four-layer image. "Water" is the currently active layer.

Mini-glossary

Current layer and layer transparency

The currently highlighted layer on the Layers palette is the only layer that can be edited. An image can have just a Background (no layers) or you can add multiple layers to it. Layers can be restacked and moved, and they are transparent where there are no pixels, so you can see through a whole stack of them. The advantage of working with multiple layers is that you can assign image components to separate layers and edit them individually without changing the other layers.

Adjustment layer

Unlike a standard layer, modifications that are made to an adjustment layer won't alter actual pixels until it is merged with the layers below it. Adjustment layers are ideal for experimenting with color or tonal adjustments. An adjustment layer only affects the layers below it.

Pixels (picture elements)

The dots used to display a bitmapped image in a rectangular grid on a computer screen.

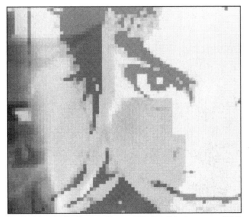

*Individual **pixels** are discernible in this image, which is shown at 500% view.*

Mini-Glossary

Selection

An area of an image that is isolated so it can be modified while the rest of the image is protected. A moving marquee marks the boundary of a selection. If you move a selection, the cutout area that's left behind is filled automatically with the current Background color if the selection is on the Background, or with transparency if the selection is on a layer.

A selection can be created using a selection tool (e.g., Lasso or Magic Wand) or a selection command (e.g., Color Range). You can also convert a path into a selection or load an alpha channel mask as a selection.

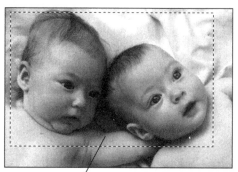

*A **selected** area of an image.*

Resolution

Image resolution is the number of pixels an image contains, and it is measured in pixels per inch. The monitor's resolution is also measured in pixels per inch. Output devices also have their own resolution, which is measured in dots per inch.

File size

The file size of an image, which is measured in bytes, kilobytes, megabytes, or gigabytes.

Dimensions

The width and height of an image.

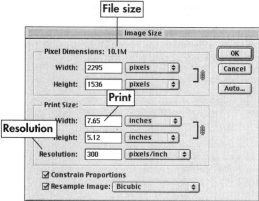

Brightness

The lightness (luminance) of a color.

Hue

The wavelength of light that gives a color its name—such as red or blue—irrespective of its brightness and saturation.

Saturation

The purity of a color. The more gray a color contains, the lower is its saturation.

(See Appendix A: Glossary for more definitions.)

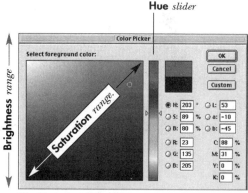

*The Photoshop **Color Picker***

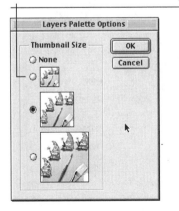

Build your image using layers

You can work on one layer at a time without affecting the other layers, and discard any layers you don't need. To conserve memory if you're working on a large image, merge two or more layers together periodically.

Using a **layer mask**, you can temporarily hide pixels on an individual layer so you can experiment with different compositions. When you're finished using a layer mask, you can discard it or permanently apply the effect to the layer.

Quick on the redraw

To speed performance, choose small **thumbnails** or no palette thumbnails for Layers, Channels, and Paths. Choose Palette Options from the palette command menu, then click Thumbnail Size: None or the smallest thumbnail option.

Production techniques

■ To undo the last modification, choose Edit menu > **Undo** (Ctrl-Z/⌘-Z) (some commands can't be undone). For multiple undos, click a prior state on the **History** palette or use the **History Brush** tool to restore selective areas.

■ Periodically click the Create new snapshot button on the History palette. Click a **snapshot** thumbnail to revert to that version of the image.

■ Save flattened versions of an image as you work on it using File menu > **Save a Copy**. When you're satisfied with one of the versions, discard the copies.

■ Use an **adjustment layer** to try out tonal and color adjustments, and then merge the adjustment layer downward to apply the effect, or discard the adjustment layer. Use the Layers palette Opacity slider to lessen the effect of an adjustment layer. Create a clipping group with the layer directly below an adjustment layer to limit the adjustment effect to that layer.

■ Use Filter menu > **Fade** (Ctrl-Shift-F/⌘-Shift-F) to lessen a filter effect or Adjust command without having to undo and redo—and choose a blending mode or opacity for the filter or color adjustment while you're at it.

■ **Interrupt screen redraw** after executing a command or applying a filter by choosing a different tool or command. (To cancel a command while a progress bar is displaying, press Esc.)

■ Choose the lowest possible **resolution** and **dimensions** for your image, factoring in your output requirements. You can create a practice image at a low resolution, saving the commands you use in an **action**, and then replay the action on a higher resolution version.

■ Display your image in **two windows** simultaneously, one in a larger view size than

(Continued on the following page)

19

the other, so you don't have to change view sizes constantly.

■ Save a complex selection to a special grayscale channel called an **alpha channel**, which can be loaded and reused on any image whenever you like. Or create a **path**, which occupies significantly less storage space than an alpha channel, and can be converted into a selection.

■ Since CMYK files process more slowly than RGB files, use the CMYK **Preview** command to preview your image as CMYK Color mode, then convert to the real CMYK Color mode when the image is completed.

■ Memorize as many **keyboard shortcuts** as you can. Start by learning the shortcuts for choosing tools (see pages 2–3). Use on-screen tool tips to refresh your memory or refer to the shortcuts list. Shortcuts are included in most of the instructions in this book.

■ Use **Quick Mask** mode to turn a selection into a mask, which will cover the protected areas of the image with transparent color and leave the unprotected area as a cutout, and then modify the mask contour using a painting tool. Turn off Quick Mask mode to convert the cutout area back into a selection.

■ Try to allot at least 60 MB of RAM to Photoshop, or four times an image's RAM document size.

■ Choose Edit > **Purge** submenu commands periodically to regain RAM that was used for the Clipboard, the Undo or Define Pattern command, the History palette, or All of the above **6**. The Purge commands can't be undone.

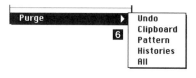

Context menus save time

To choose from an on-screen **context menu**, Right-click/Control-click on a Layers, Channels, or Paths palette thumbnail, name, or feature **2**. Or, choose a tool, then Right-click/Control-click with the pointer over the image window to choose commands or options for that tool **3**–**5**.

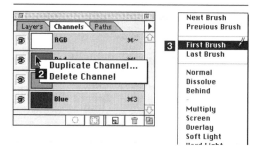

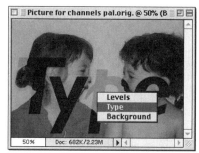

4 *Right-click/Control-click with the **Move** tool to choose from a list of **layers** that contain pixels under the pointer.*

5 *Right-click/Control-click with a **selection** tool to choose from a list of **commands**.*

Production Techniques

PHOTOSHOP COLOR 2

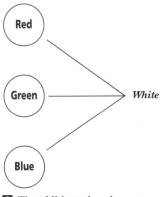

THE FOLLOWING is a brief explanation of color basics—color models, image modes, and blending modes—as well as Photoshop's color management features.

Pixels

The screen image in Photoshop is a bitmap, which is a geometric arrangement (mapping) of a layer of dots of different shades or colors on a rectangular grid. Each dot, called a pixel, represents a color or shade. By magnifying an area of an image, you can edit pixels individually **1**. Every Photoshop image is a bitmap, whether it originates from a scan, from another application, or entirely within the application using painting and editing tools. (Don't confuse Bitmap image mode with the term "bitmap.") Bitmap programs are ideal for producing painterly, photographic, or photorealistic images that contain subtle gradations of color. If you drag with a painting tool across an area of a layer, pixels under the pointer are recolored.

RGB vs. CMYK color

Red, green, and blue (RGB) light are used to display a color image on a monitor. When these additive primaries in their purest form are combined, they produce white light **2**.

The three subtractive primary inks used in four-color process printing are cyan (C), magenta (M), and yellow (Y) **3**. When they are combined, a dark, muddy color is produced. To produce a rich black, printers usually mix black (K) ink with small quantities of cyan, magenta, and/or yellow ink.

The display of color on a computer monitor is highly variable and subject to the whims of ambient lighting, monitor temperature, and room color. In addition, many colors

PHOTO: NADINE MARKOVA

1 *A close-up of an image, showing individual pixels.*

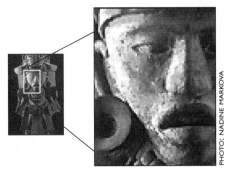

White

2 *The **additive primaries** on a computer monitor.*

3 *The **subtractive primaries**—printing inks.*

that are seen in nature cannot be printed, some colors that can be displayed on screen cannot be printed, and some printable colors can't be displayed on screen. All monitors display color using the RGB model—CMYK colors are merely simulated. You don't need to bother with a RGB-to-CMYK conversion if your image is going to be output to the Web or to a film recorder.

An exclamation point will appear on the Color palette if you choose a non-printable (out of gamut) color **1**. Exclamation points will also display on the Info palette if the color currently under the pointer is out of gamut **2**. Using Photoshop's Gamut Warning command, you can display non-printable colors in your image in gray, and then, using the Sponge tool, you can desaturate them to bring them into gamut.

You can use the grayscale, RGB (red-green-blue), HSB (hue-saturation-brightness), CMYK (cyan-magenta-yellow-black), or Lab (lightness-a axis-b axis) color model when you choose colors in Photoshop via the Color Picker or Color palette.

Channels

Every Photoshop image is a composite of one or more semi-transparent, colored-light overlays called channels. For example, an image in RGB Color mode is composed of the red, green, and blue channels. To illustrate, open a color image, then click Red, Green, or Blue on the Channels palette to display only that channel. Click RGB (Ctrl-~/⌘ ~) to restore the full channel display. (If the channels don't display in color, check the Color Channels in Color box in File menu > Preferences > Display & Cursors.)

Color adjustments can be made to an individual channel, but normally modifications are made and displayed in the multichannel, composite image (the topmost channel name on the Channels palette), and affect all of an image's channels at once. Special grayscale channels that are used for saving

Web graphics

If you're creating an image for a Web site, use the RGB color model. Bear in mind that RGB colors—or colors from any other color model, for that matter—may not match the color palette of your Web browser (see pages 317–318). For the best results, load the Web Safe Colors palette onto the Swatches palette.

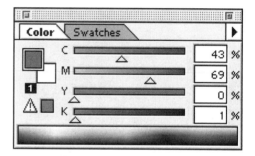

Default number of channels for each image mode

One	Three	Four
Bitmap	RGB	CMYK
Grayscale	Lab	
Duotone		
Indexed Color		

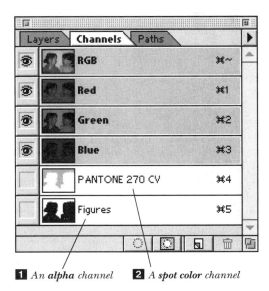

1 *An* **alpha** *channel* **2** *A* **spot color** *channel*

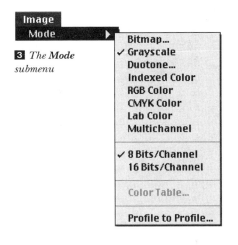

3 *The Mode submenu*

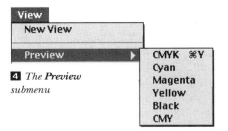

4 *The* **Preview** *submenu*

selections as masks, called alpha channels, can be added to an image **1**. You can also add spot color channels **2**. Only the currently highlighted channels can be edited.

The more channels an image contains, the larger is its file storage size. The storage size of an image in RGB Color mode, which has three channels (Red, Green, and Blue), will be three times larger than the same image in Grayscale mode, which has one channel. The same image in CMYK Color mode will have four channels (Cyan, Magenta, Yellow, and Black), and will be even larger.

Image modes

An image can be converted to, displayed in, and edited in any one of eight image modes: Bitmap, Grayscale, Duotone, Indexed Color, RGB Color, CMYK Color, Lab Color, and Multichannel. Simply choose the mode you want from the Image menu > Mode submenu **3**. To access a mode that is unavailable (whose name is dimmed), you must first convert your image to a different mode. For example, to convert an image to Indexed Color mode, it must be in RGB Color or Grayscale mode.

Some mode conversions cause noticeable color shifts; others cause subtle color shifts. Very dramatic changes may occur if an image is converted from RGB Color mode to CMYK Color mode, because printable colors will be substituted for rich, glowing RGB colors. Color accuracy may diminish if an image is converted back and forth between RGB and CMYK Color mode too many times.

Medium to low-end scanners usually produce RGB scans. If you're creating an image that's going to be printed, for faster editing and to access all the filters, edit it in RGB Color mode and then convert it to CMYK Color mode when you're ready to imageset it. You can use the CMYK Preview command (Ctrl-Y/⌘-Y) to preview an image in CMYK Color mode without actually changing its mode **4**. You can CMYK-preview your image in one window and open a second

Image Modes

window to display the same image without the CMYK preview.

Some conversions will cause layers to be flattened, such as a conversion to Indexed Color, Multichannel, or Bitmap mode. For other conversions, you'll have the option to click Don't Flatten if you want to preserve layers.

High-end scanners usually produce CMYK scans, and these images should be kept in CMYK Color mode to preserve their color data. If you find working on such large files to be cumbersome, you can work out your image-editing scheme on a low resolution version of an image, save the commands using the Actions palette, and then apply the action to the high resolution, CMYK version. You will still, however, have to perform some operations manually, like adding strokes with the Paintbrush tool.

Some output devices require that an image be saved in a particular image mode. The availability of some commands and tool options in Photoshop may also change depending on an image's current mode.

These are the image modes, in brief:

In **Bitmap** mode **1**, pixels are 100% black or 100% white only, and layers, filters, and Adjust commands are unavailable, except for the Invert command. An image must be in Grayscale mode before it can be converted to Bitmap mode.

In **Grayscale** mode **2**, pixels are black, white, or up to 255 shades of gray. If an image is converted from a color mode to Grayscale mode and then saved and closed, its luminosity (light and dark) values will remain intact, but its color information will be deleted and cannot be restored.

An image in **Indexed Color** mode has one channel and a color table containing a maximum of 256 colors or shades. To display a Photoshop image on a Web page or in certain painting or animation programs, sometimes it's better to first convert it to Indexed Color mode. You can also convert

1 *Bitmap mode, Method:* **2** *Grayscale mode*
Diffusion Dither

*The **Channels** palette for an image in various modes:*

Bitmap mode

Grayscale mode

Indexed Color mode

Duotone mode

*The **Channels** palette for an image in various modes:*

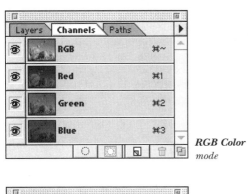

RGB Color mode

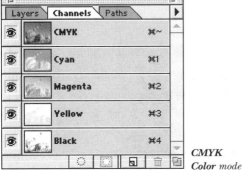

CMYK Color mode

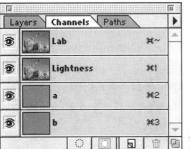

Lab Color mode

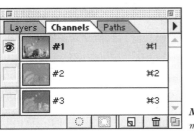

Multichannel mode

an image to Indexed Color mode to create arty color effects. The GIF89a Export command (which is one of the best options for Web graphics), is available only for an Indexed Color or RGB Color image.

RGB Color is the most versatile mode because it is the only mode in which all of Photoshop's tool options and filters are accessible. Some video and multimedia applications can import an RGB image in the Photoshop file format.

Photoshop is one of few Macintosh programs in which images can be displayed and edited in **CMYK Color** mode. You can convert an image to CMYK Color mode when you're ready to output it on a color printer or color separate it (unless the output device is a PostScript Level 2 printer, in which case you should choose Lab Color mode).

Lab Color is a three-channel mode that was developed for the purpose of achieving consistency among various devices, such as printers and monitors. The channels represent lightness, the colors green-to-red, and the colors blue-to-yellow. Photo CD images can be converted to Lab Color mode or RGB Color mode in Photoshop. Save an image in Lab Color mode to print it on a PostScript Level 2 or Level 3 printer or to export it to another operating system.

A **Duotone** is a printing method in which two or more plates are used to add richness and tonal depth to a grayscale image.

A **Multichannel** image is composed of multiple, 256-level grayscale channels. This mode is used for certain grayscale printing situations. You could use multichannel mode to assemble individual channels from several images before converting the new image to a color mode. Spot color channels are preserved if you convert an image to Multichannel mode. If you convert an image from RGB Color to Mulitchannel mode, the Red, Green, and Blue channels will be converted to Cyan, Magenta, and Yellow. The image may become lighter as a result, but otherwise it won't change significantly.

The blending modes

You can select from 18 blending modes from the Options palette, the Layers palette, or the Fill, Stroke, Fade, or Fill Path dialog box. The mode you choose for a tool or a layer affects how that tool or layer modifies underlying pixels, which in the following text is called the "base color." The "blend layer" is the layer for which a mode is chosen.

TIP To cycle through blending modes for the currently selected tool, press Shift + or Shift -.

Note: If the Preserve Transparency box is checked on the Layers palette for the target layer, only pixels—not transparent areas—can be recolored or otherwise edited.

Opacities add up

When you choose a mode and an opacity for a tool, be sure to factor in the mode and opacity of the target layer you're working on. If you choose 60% opacity for the Paintbrush tool on a layer that has a 50% opacity, for example, your resulting brush stroke will have an opacity of 30%.

NORMAL
All base colors are modified. *Note:* For an image in Bitmap or Indexed Color mode, Normal mode is called Threshold.

DISSOLVE
Creates a chalky, dry brush texture with the paint or blend layer color. The higher the pressure or opacity, the more solid the stroke.

BEHIND
(Paint color only) Only transparent areas are modified, not existing base color pixels (turn off Preserve Transparency). The effect is like painting on the reverse side of clear acetate. Good for creating shadows.

CLEAR
(Paint color only) Makes the base color transparent where strokes are applied (turn off Preserve Transparency). Available only for a multi-layer image when using the Line or Paint Bucket tool, the Fill command, or the Stroke command. Cannot be used on the Background.

MULTIPLY
A dark paint or blend layer color removes the lighter parts of the base color to produce a darker base color. A light paint or blend layer color darkens the base color less. Good for creating semi-transparent shadow effects.

SCREEN

A light paint or blend layer color removes the darker parts of the base color to produce a lighter, bleached base color. A dark paint or blend layer lightens the base color less.

OVERLAY

Multiplies (darkens) dark areas and screens (lightens) light base colors. Preserves luminosity (light and dark) values. Black and white are not changed, so detail is maintained.

SOFT LIGHT

Lightens the base color if the paint or blend layer color is light. Darkens the base color if the paint or blend layer color is dark. Preserves luminosity values in the base color. Creates a soft, subtle lighting effect.

HARD LIGHT

Screens (lightens) the base color if the paint or blend layer color is light. Multiplies (darkens) the base color if the paint or blend layer color is dark. Greater contrast is created in the base color and layer color. Good for painting glowing highlights and creating composite effects.

COLOR DODGE

Lightens the base color where the paint or blend layer color is light. A dark paint or blend layer color tints the base color slightly.

COLOR BURN

A dark paint or blend layer color darkens the base color. A light paint or blend layer color tints the base color slightly.

Blending Modes

DARKEN

Base colors that are lighter than the paint or blend layer color are modified, base colors that are darker than the paint or blend layer color are not. Use with a paint color that is darker than the base colors you want to modify.

LIGHTEN

Base colors that are darker than the paint or blend layer color are modified, base colors that are lighter than the paint or blend layer color are not. Use with a paint color that is lighter than the base colors you want to modify.

DIFFERENCE

Creates a color negative effect on the base color. When the paint or blend layer color is light, the negative (or invert) effect is more pronounced. Produces noticeable color shifts.

EXCLUSION

Grays out the base color where the paint or blend layer color is dark. Inverts the base color where the paint or blend layer color is light.

HUE

The blend color's hue is applied. Saturation and luminosity values are not modified in the base color.

SATURATION

The blend color's saturation is applied. Hue and luminosity values are not modified in the base color.

COLOR

The blend color's saturation and hue are applied. The base color's light and dark (luminosity) values aren't changed, so detail is maintained. Good for tinting.

LUMINOSITY

The base color's luminosity values are replaced by tone (luminosity) values from the paint or blend layer color. Hue and saturation are not affected in the base color.

Color Management

Why do we need it?

Myriad variables can influence color in digital images. Monitor phosphors and scanner filters vary from one vendor to the next, as do printing inks and papers.

To accurately reproduce colors, compensation must be made for the differences between the total range of colors a monitor produces based on the additive primary colors of light (Red-Green-Blue, or RGB) and the total range a printer can produce using inks based on the subtractive color model (Cyan-Magenta-Yellow-Black, or CMYK). To achieve the closest possible match between colors on your screen and those produced by your printer or other monitors, it is a good idea to spend some time on color management.

Adobe has done a great deal of work to assist you in that effort. A major new feature is support for ICC profiles. These are standard cross-platform profiles set by the International Color Consortium (www.icc.org) that describe the color spaces of images and output devices. They enable accurate colors to be maintained throughout the workflow—from input via a scanner or digital camera to output on a printer or on screen.

With the help of a Color Management Module, or CMM, Photoshop 5 can interpret the ICC profiles that are attached to images you import. In addition, you can tag files you save in Photoshop with an ICC profile, which becomes part of that file. Photoshop offers several options, including its own built-in CMM; Apple's system-level ColorSync CMM (for Mac OS) or Microsoft's ICM 2.0 (for Windows); and the Kodak Digital Science Color Management System, which is installed when you choose to install the Kodak Photo CD Acquire plug-in. (The differences between the three are small, so go with Photoshop's default CMM.)

Photoshop 5 also introduces a separate, device-independent RGB working color space for editing images—a significant benefit for color accuracy. The monitor RGB color space used by older versions of Photoshop is unreliable, because one monitor's color gamut can differ significantly from another, and using it to edit images shackles your palette-of-possible-colors to just those the monitor can display. With a separate RGB working space, colors remain consistent regardless of the device on which the image is viewed, scanned, or printed.

So here are the simple steps to better color management:

1. Calibrate your monitor.

2. Choose the RGB Setup settings that are best for you.

3. Enter CMYK Setup settings if you output CMYK images.

4. Enter Grayscale Setup information if you output grayscale images.

5. Enter information in the Profile Setup dialog box to control how Photoshop opens and saves images with ICC profiles.

Don't hesitate: calibrate

To see accurate colors on your screen, you have to define the RGB color space your monitor can display. This ten-minute process is known as calibrating your monitor, and it is accomplished using Photoshop's new Adobe Gamma control panel (which is installed in the Control Panels folder automatically with Photoshop 5.0). This utility replaces the Monitor Control dialog (Win) or the old Gamma control panel (Mac).

In the calibration process, you'll adjust the contrast, brightness, gamma, color balance, and white point of your monitor. You'll also adjust Photoshop's color-conversion settings to ensure consistent display of an image from one monitor to another. The Adobe Gamma Control Panel creates an ICC profile that defines the color space of your monitor.

On Windows 95, the calibration process is the same as listed below, but (as noted) selected steps work only with certain video cards, and Windows NT also requires a specific video card.

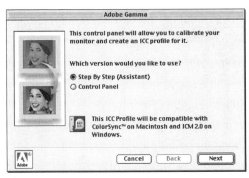

1 *This is the **Adobe Gamma** dialog box set for the **Step by Step** calibration method.*

Adobe Gamma

ICC Profile: AI Default Monitor ps5   Load...
Brightness and Contrast

Phosphors
Phosphors: Trinitron

Gamma
☐ View Single Gamma Only

Desired: Macintosh Default   1.8

White Point
Hardware: 6500°K (daylight)   Measure...
Adjusted: Same as Hardware

Assistant...

2 *This **Adobe Gamma** dialog will open if you choose the Control Panel option. With View Single Gamma Only unchecked, adjustments can be made to the individual Red, Green, and Blue components.*

To calibrate your monitor:

1. Give the monitor 30 minutes to warm up and stabilize the display, and establish a level of room lighting that will remain constant.

2. Make the desktop pattern light gray.

3. *Macintosh:* Double-click the Adobe Gamma utility alias in the Photoshop 5 > Goodies > Calibration folder.

Windows 95: Choose Start menu > Settings > Control Panels, then click the Adobe Gamma utility.

Windows NT: Run the Adobe Gamma.cpl utility from C:\Program Files\Common Files\Adobe\Calibration or double-click the utility's alias in the Photoshop 5\Goodies\Calibration folder.

4. Click Step by Step, which will walk you through the process **1**.
or
To choose settings from a single dialog box, but with no explanation, click Control Panel, click Next, then follow the remaining steps.

5. Use the default monitor ICC Profile or click Load and choose a profile that more closely matches your monitor **2**.

6. Turn up your monitor's brightness and contrast settings; leave the contrast at maximum; and adjust the brightness to make the alternating gray squares in the top bar as dark as possible, but not black, while keeping the lower bar bright white.

7. For Phosphors, select your monitor type or choose Custom and enter the Red, Green, and Blue chromaticity coordinates specified by your monitor's manufacturer.

8. Adjust Gamma via the slider under the gray box, which represents a combined grayscale reading of your monitor. Move the slider until the smaller solid-color box matches the outer box framing it. (It helps to squint.) You might find it easier to uncheck the View Single Gamma Only box and make separate adjustments based on the readings for Red, Green, and Blue.

Calibrate

9. For Desired, choose Macintosh Default gamma or Windows Default gamma. *Note:* This option is available on a Windows system with a video card that can control the monitor.

10. For Hardware, choose the white point specified by the monitor manufacturer.

11. For Adjusted, choose Same as Hardware, or, if you know the color temperature at which your image will ultimately be viewed, you can enter it here. *Note:* This option is available on a Windows system with a video card that can control the monitor.

12. Click the Adobe Gamma close box, then click Save.

If you change your monitor's brightness and contrast settings or change the room lighting, you should recalibrate your monitor. Also, keep in mind that this method is just a start. Professional-level calibration requires more precise monitor measurement using expensive hardware devices such as a colorimeter and a spectrophotometer.

Finding a space

The RGB Setup dialog box offers a number of different RGB working color spaces from which to choose, depending on how you use your files. The spaces vary in their gammas, color balance, and gamut size (range of colors). When you save a file, Photoshop can tag it with the ICC profile for the working color space you specify.

If you move your image to another computer, Photoshop can open it in the color space you specified or convert it to the space designated for the new machine. Previously, if an image was opened on a different computer, it was automatically converted to that monitor's RGB color space. The new strategy of color-space independence is especially useful for workgroups, because it allows everyone in the group to standardize to one color space.

The default RGB working space in Photoshop 5.0 is sRGB, a candidate for

```
                    RGB Setup
  RGB:  Apple RGB        ‡              OK
  Gamma: 1.80                         Cancel
  White Point:  6500°K (D65)   ‡       Load...
  Primaries:  Trinitron         ‡      Save...

  Monitor: AI Default Monitor ps5     ☑ Preview
  ☑ Display Using Monitor Compensation
```

1 *The RGB Setup dialog box.*

Bruce Fraser's **RGB**

Gamma = 2.2

White point = 6500K

Primaries = Custom

	x	y
red =	0.6400	0.3300
green =	0.2800	0.6500
blue =	0.1500	0.0600

Internet standardom. As a professional color space, however, sRGB is severely limited. Critics say sRGB's gamut is too small, especially for print, because it clips part of the CMYK gamut. You should consider changing the default from sRGB to one of the other color-space options Photoshop offers, such as ColorMatch RGB or SMPTE-240M, at least during the editing process. Then, if the final destination for your image is the Web, sRGB is a good choice for output.

To enter RGB Setup info:

1. Choose File menu > Color Settings > RGB Setup.

2. For RGB, select one of the eleven options that are described under "The preset RGB color spaces," starting on this page **1**:

You can also save and load settings for other RGB color spaces, but they must match Photoshop's RGB model.

The RGB Setup dialog box features a preview option that simulates the differences among the color spaces.

If you are implementing an ICC workflow, the option to Display Using Monitor Compensation should be left on so Photoshop can accurately compensate for the differences between the working color space and the monitor space when displaying an image. However, if you want Photoshop 5 to behave like older versions, then you can turn off this check box.

3. Click OK.

The preset RGB color spaces

The **Custom** option lets advanced users define their own RGB color space by specifying the gamma, white point, and phosphor settings. Photoshop color expert Bruce Fraser (www.pixelboyz.com) devised an ideal RGB working space that he recommends over the options Photoshop 5 offers (shown at left).

(Continued on the following page)

RGB Setup

Monitor RGB is the ICC profile for your specific monitor, so it is not device-independent. This space makes Photoshop 5 behave like previous versions, though it can still embed and read a file's profile. You can use this option if the other applications in your workflow are not ICC-aware.

While **sRGB** has been proposed by Hewlett-Packard and Microsoft as a standard for the Internet, it is also gaining support among scanner and desktop printer manufacturers. sRGB strives to reflect the average PC monitor. Photoshop defaults to this space, but critics say its gamut is too small for a general-purpose color space and recommend using something else.

Apple RGB was the default space for earlier versions of Photoshop and was used by the desktop publishing industry. Based on an Apple 13-inch Trinitron monitor, this space offers a limited gamut as well. It may be suitable for Web images that will be viewed on Macs.

CIE RGB was defined by the Commission Internationale d'Eclairage. It has a wide color gamut but does not do a good job with blue. Its gamut can handle images with 16-bit channels.

✓ The **ColorMatch RGB** space was defined by Radius for its PressView monitor, commonly used in pre-press environments. It offers an expanded RGB gamut and serves as a good general-purpose space.

NTSC (1953) is a video color space set by the National Television Standards Committee (NTSC). If your image is intended for broadcast video, this space would be a suitable choice.

PAL/SECAM is the European color television standard and is also used in parts of Asia. This is a good choice if your work is intended for European broadcast.

✓ **SMPTE 240M** is the RGB color space for high-definition television (HDTV) production. It has a large gamut, but not as wide as Wide-Gamut RGB. This is another good choice for pre-press work and general-purpose editing.

SMPTE-C is a more recent standard set forth by the NTSC. Its gamut is very limited.

Wide Gamut RGB uses pure wavelengths of the primary colors, so it includes almost all the visible colors. However, many of them cannot be reproduced on monitors or by printers. You should not use this space with 8-bit images.

CMYK setup

If you plan to edit CMYK files for print, for color separations, or for export to another application, you should enter CMYK setup information, as it is needed to convert RGB information to CMYK. (This may not be necessary if you use an ink-jet printer or some other types of low-end printers, as many are based on RGB.) See page 302 for more information about these options.

What about ICC profiles for CMYK setup? It is not yet common for print shops to provide clients with pre-made ICC profiles. This may change in the future.

Grayscale setup

If you plan to edit grayscale images, you should enter behavior information in Color Settings > Grayscale Setup. This dialog box determines whether grayscale images behave as RGB or Black Ink. If you plan to output your images to the screen (i.e., the Web), choose RGB. If your image's destination is print, choose Black Ink, since this option takes dot-gain values into consideration.

Profile setup

The Profile Setup dialog box lets you determine how Photoshop handles imported files with color spaces that are different from your working color space ◼. The default setting is to convert images to the color space you set in the RGB Setup dialog box.

According to Adobe, the conversion does not harm the integrity of a file and is essential to the color management process. Without it, your monitor could display multiple images that appear to share the same color but show different color values in the Info palette, and vice versa. Rather than keep the default settings, you should set the options to Ask When Opening so you can decide on an image-by-image basis whether or not to convert.

This dialog box also lets you specify whether the software embeds ICC profiles with your files. Embedding a profile will increase a file's storage size, but if color consistency is a high priority for you, it's worth it. This information is useful to other applications and to Photoshop when it reads the file at another time.

With images destined for the Web, file size can be more important than accurate color. You can keep profile tags with your original images, but for the Web-bound version, choose File menu > Save a Copy and click the Exclude Non-Image Data check box to avoid saving the profile. Also, don't embed profiles in an image that will have a limited color gamut—such as an indexed-color or a Web-safe color palette—or with a calibration or characterization test image.

To enter Profile Setup info:

1. Choose File menu > Color Settings > Profile Setup.

2. For Embed Profiles, check the types of image modes that you want Photoshop to tag with profiles **1**.

3. For Assumed Profiles, set RGB to Ask When Opening and CMYK and Grayscale to None, since there are no industry standards for these models.

4. For Profile Mismatch Handling, set RGB, CMYK, and Grayscale to Ask When Opening.

5. Click OK (Enter/Return).

Leaving a legacy

Photoshop 5 assumes that older, untagged RGB files use the monitor color space (Monitor RGB). You can choose Monitor RGB from the Assumed Profiles: RGB drop-

1 *The Profile Setup dialog box.*

Opening a legacy file in Photoshop 5.0

We think it's best to choose Profile Mismatch Handling: RGB to Ask When Opening in the Profile Setup dialog box.

If you open an older Photoshop file that was not saved with any RGB color space or monitor profile information, the Profile Mismatch alert box may open. The best course of action is to follow our steps at right and create a legacy monitor profile first, open the legacy files, and choose the legacy profile when any mismatch alert box opens.

Another alternative when the mismatch alert box opens is to choose Input Conversion From: sRGB (for Windows) or Apple RGB (for Mac), and then click Convert to convert legacy files—if you have **never** calibrated your monitor. (If you *have* calibrated your monitor, choose that generated profile from the From drop-down menu.)

down menu in the Profile Setup dialog box to let Photoshop 5 convert your legacy files (those that were created in earlier versions of Photoshop) to your selected working RGB space—if you have never calibrated your monitor. However, the Profile Mismatch alert dialog box may still open even if the Monitor RGB setting is used (see the sidebar for what to do if this happens).

You may want to take an added precaution to ensure color accuracy by converting your legacy files from your old Monitor Setup space to the new working space. To do so, you need to create an ICC profile of the old Photoshop Monitor Setup before using the Adobe Gamma utility to calibrate your monitor.

To create a profile for legacy files:

1. Launch Photoshop 4.0 and choose File menu > Color Settings > Monitor Setup.

2. Click Save to save the Monitor Setup data. Click Cancel.

3. Exit/Quit Photoshop 4.0.

4. Launch Photoshop 5.0.

5. Choose File menu > Color Settings > RGB Setup.

6. Click Load, and select the monitor-settings file you just saved. It will be loaded into the RGB Setup. (Win: The file extension will be ".ams".)

7. Click Save to save the old Monitor Setup data as an ICC profile, rename it "A Legacy Monitor Space" so it displays near the top of the list, and save it with the other ICC profiles (in Windows 95, in Windows > System > Color; in Windows NT, in Winnt > System32 > Color; on Macintosh, in System Folder > Preferences > Color Sync Profiles).

8. Reset the RGB working space or click Cancel to discard the changes in RGB Setup.

9. Exit/quit, and then relaunch Photoshop. When you open a legacy file and the

(Continued on the following page)

Create Profile for Legacy Files

Profile Mismatch dialog box opens, choose the legacy profile from the Input Conversion From: drop-down menu, then click Convert to convert from the Legacy Monitor Space profile **1**.

Note: The Image menu > Mode > Profile to Profile command converts an open image from one color space to another. It is intended only for advanced users, as it can destroy color data if it's not used properly.

For more information about color management, check out *Understanding Desktop Color* by Michael Kieran or *Real World Photoshop 5* by David Blatner and Bruce Fraser, both from Peachpit Press.

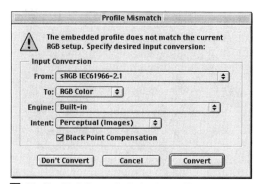

1 *The Profile Mismatch dialog box will open automatically upon opening a file if the file's embedded profile doesn't match your current RGB Setup space.*

STARTUP 3

1 *Click Adobe Photoshop 5.0.*

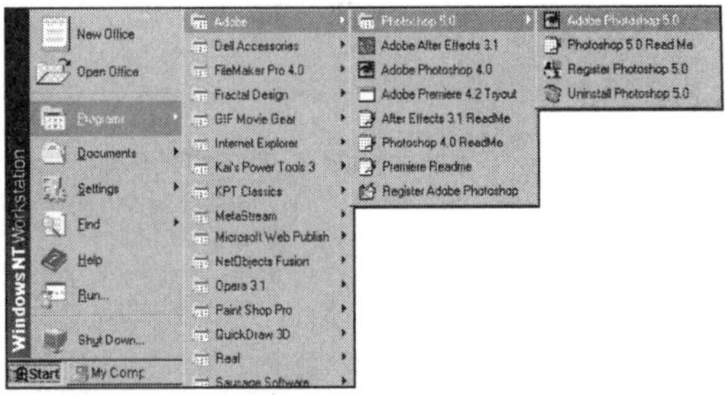

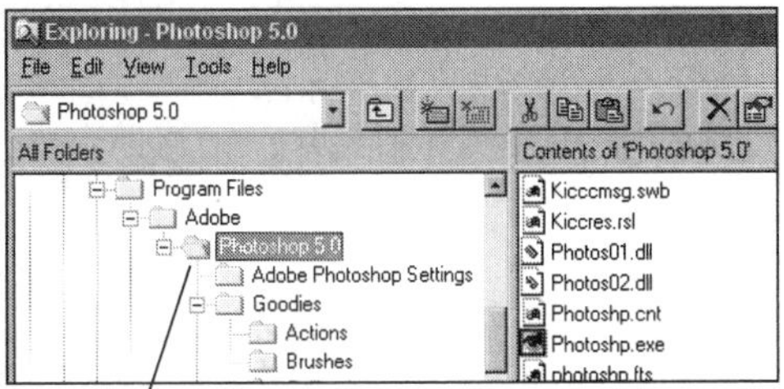

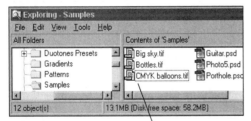

2 *Locate the **Adobe Photoshop 5.0** folder inside **My Computer**.*

3 *Double-click a **Photoshop** file icon in **Windows Explorer**.*

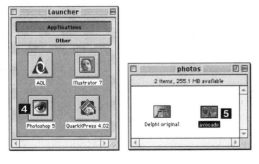

I **N THIS CHAPTER** you will learn how to get started in Photoshop: launch the application, scan an image, create a new image, open an existing image, and place an image into Photoshop. You'll also learn how to change an image's dimensions, resolution, or file storage size; apply the Unsharp Mask filter to resharpen an image after resampling; enlarge an image's canvas size; crop, flip, rotate, save, copy, and close an image; and exit/quit the application.

To launch Photoshop (Windows):

In Windows 95 or NT, click the Start button on the Taskbar, choose Programs, choose Adobe, choose Photoshop 5.0, then click Adobe Photoshop 5.0 **1**. (If you don't yet have an icon for Photoshop on your desktop, open the Adobe Photoshop folder, then drag the Photoshop application icon to the desktop.)
or
Open the Adobe Photoshop folder in My Computer, then double-click the Photoshop application icon **2**.
or
Double-click a Photoshop file icon **3**.

To launch Photoshop (Macintosh):

If you're using System 7.5 or later, click once on the Photoshop icon in the Launcher **4**. (If you don't yet have an icon for Photoshop in the Launcher, open the Adobe Photoshop folder in the Finder, then drag the Photoshop application icon into the Launcher window.)
or
Open the Adobe Photoshop folder in the Finder, then double-click the Photoshop application icon.
or
Double-click a Photoshop file icon **5**.

Launch Photoshop

39

Where images come from

An image can be created, opened, edited, and saved in 20 different file formats in Photoshop (Win) **1**/(Mac) **2**. Of these, you may use only a few, such as TIFF, PICT, EPS, and the native Photoshop file format. Because Photoshop accepts so many formats, an image can be gathered from any number of sources: scanner, drawing application, PhotoCD, still image or video capture, or another operating system. You can also create an image entirely within Photoshop. A finished image can be output to an imagesetter or a film recorder, or it can be displayed on a Web site.

Scanning

Using a scanning device and scanning software, a slide, flat artwork, or a photograph can be translated into numbers (digitized) so it can be read, displayed, edited, and printed by a computer. You can scan directly into Photoshop or you can use other scanning software and save the scan in a file format that Photoshop opens.

To produce a high-quality scan for print output, start with as high quality an original as possible. Some scanners will compress an image's dynamic range and increase its contrast, so choose a photograph with good tonal balance. If you're going to scan it yourself, set the scanning parameters carefully.

The quality of a scan will partially depend on the type of scanner you use. If you're going to dramatically transform the image in Photoshop (e.g. apply filter effects or add a lot of brushstrokes), you can use an inexpensive flat-bed scanner, which will produce an RGB scan. For more accurate color and crisper details, use a slide scanner to scan a transparency.

For professional-quality output, have your artwork scanned by a service bureau on a high-resolution CCD scanner, such as a Scitex Smart-Scanner, or on a drum scanner. A high-end scanner can capture a wide dynamic range of color and shade and can

1 CompuServe GIF (*.GIF)

Photoshop (*.PSD;*.PDD)
Amiga IFF (*.IFF)
BMP (*.BMP;*.RLE)
CompuServe GIF (*.GIF)
Photoshop EPS (*.EPS)
Photoshop DCS 1.0 (*.EPS)
Photoshop DCS 2.0 (*.EPS)
Generic EPS (*.EPS;*.AI ;*.AI5;*.AI4;*.AI3;*.PS
EPS TIFF Preview (*.EPS)
Filmstrip (*.FLM)

2 ✓ Photoshop
Photoshop 2.0
Amiga IFF
BMP
CompuServe GIF
Photoshop EPS
Photoshop DCS 1.0
Photoshop DCS 2.0
Filmstrip
FlashPix
JPEG
PCX
Photoshop PDF
PICT File
PICT Resource
Pixar
PNG
Raw
Scitex CT
Targa
TIFF

optically distinguish between subtle differences in luminosity, even in shadow areas. High-end scanners usually produce CMYK scans, which are usually large in file size.

Desktop scanning software basics

Scanning software usually offers most of the following options, although terms may vary. The quality and file storage size of a scan are partially determined by the mode, resolution, and scale you specify, and whether you crop the image.

Preview: Place the art in the scanner, then click Preview or PreScan.

Scan mode: Select Black-and-White Line Art (no grays), Grayscale, or Color (choose millions of colors, if available). An image scanned in Color will be approximately three times larger in file size than the same image scanned in Grayscale.

Resolution: Scan resolution is measured in pixels per inch (ppi). The higher the resolution of an image, the more pixels it contains, and thus the more information for detail, but the larger is its file size. Choose the minimum resolution necessary to obtain the best possible printout from your final output device. But don't choose a higher resolution than you really need—the image will be larger in storage size than necessary, it will take longer to render on screen, display on the Web, or print, and there will be no improvement in output quality. On the other hand, too low a resolution will cause a printed image to look coarse and jagged, and its details will be lost.

Before selecting a resolution for print output, ask your print shop what printer or imagesetter resolution and halftone screen frequency they plan to use. (The scan resolution is different from the resolution of the output device.)

As a general rule, for a grayscale image, you should choose a resolution that is one-and-a-half times the halftone screen frequency (lines per inch) of your final output device, or twice the halftone screen frequency for a

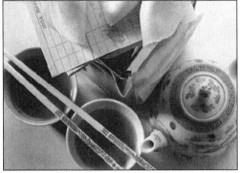

72 ppi

150 ppi

300 ppi

Scanning

color image. Use a high scanning resolution (600 ppi or higher) for line art. For example, if your print shop plans to use a 133-line screen for black-and-white printing, you should use 200 ppi as your scan resolution. If your prepress shop is going to use an imagesetter that doesn't have halftoning technology, ask them to recommend an appropriate scan resolution. To calculate the appropriate file size for a scan, see the instructions on page 44.

Cropping: If you're planning to use only part of an image, reposition the handles of the box in the preview area to reduce the scan area. Cropping can significantly reduce the storage size of a scan.

Scale: To enlarge an image's dimensions, choose a scale percentage above 100%. Enlarging an image or increasing its resolution in Photoshop or any other software program may cause it to blur, because the program uses mathematical "guesswork" (interpolation) to fill in additional information. An image's original information is only recorded at the time of scanning.

Scan: Click Scan and choose a location in which to save the file.

16-bits per channel mode

An average-quality scanner can capture 10 bits of accurate data per channel from an image. A high-end scanner can capture up to 16 bits of accurate data per channel. If the 16-bit scanner also has a wide dynamic color range and good optical density (at least 3.3), then those extra pixels of data will capture even finer detail in color and shade—even in shadow areas. Photoshop can open a CMYK file containing 16 bits per channel (a 64-bit total for four channels). All the image's original pixel information is preserved, and the image can be edited and adjusted. You must convert a 16-bit image down to 8-bit before printing (choose Image menu > Mode > 8 Bits/Channel).

There are two restrictions, however. First, the 16-bit image can only have *one* layer. And second, not all edit commands will be available for it. These commands *will* be available: Image menu > Adjust > Levels, Curves, Color Balance, Brightness/Contrast, Hue/Saturation, Channel Mixer, Invert, and Equalize, as well as Image menu > Image Size and Rotate Canvas. The Crop, Rubber Stamp, History Brush, and Pen tools can be used on a 16 bits per channel image.

Note: To scan into Photoshop, the scanner's plug-in or Twain module must be in the Import-Export folder inside the Photoshop Plug-Ins folder. The first time you choose a scanning module from the File > Import submenu, choose Twain_32 Source (Win) or Twain Select (Mac), choose a Twain device (the scanner), then choose Twain_32 (Win) or Twain Acquire (Mac). Thereafter, to access the scanning software, just choose File menu > Import > Twain_32 (Win) or Twain Acquire (Mac). (See the Photoshop documentation for information about scanning modules.)

If your scanner doesn't have a Photoshop compatible scanner driver, scan your image outside Photoshop, save it as a TIFF, then open it in Photoshop as you would any other image.

To calculate the proper resolution for a scan, follow the instructions on the next page.

To scan into Photoshop:

1. Choose a scanning module or choose File menu > Import > Twain_32 (Win) or Twain Acquire (Mac).

2. Click Prescan **1**.

3. Following the guidelines outlined on the previous two pages, choose a Scan Mode and Resolution.

4. *Optional:* Choose a different Scaling percentage and/or crop the image preview.

6. Click Scan. The scanned image will appear in a new, untitled window.

7. Save the image (see pages 65–67). If it requires color correction, see pages 302–306. If it needs to be straightened out, see the tip on page 63.

*Note how the file **Size** changes as you change the mode, resolution, and scale settings.*

The resolution of a Photoshop image, like any bitmapped image, is independent of the monitor's resolution, so it can be customized for a particular output device, with or without modifying its file storage size. An image whose resolution is greater than the monitor's resolution (96 ppi for a Windows monitor, 72 ppi for a Macintosh monitor) will appear larger than its print size when it's displayed in Photoshop at 100% view.

Note: It's always best to scan your image at the outset at the final size and resolution that are required for your final output device.

To calculate the proper resolution for a scan or for an existing image:

1. Create a new RGB document (File menu > New). Enter the final width and height dimensions, and choose 72 ppi for the image resolution. (The resolution will be readjusted in step 5).

2. Choose Image menu > Image Size.

3. Click the Auto button on the right side of the dialog box.

4. Enter the Screen resolution of your final output device (the lines per inch (lpi) setting that your print shop will be using) **1**.

5. Click Quality: Draft (1x screen frequency), Good (1½ x screen frequency), or Best (2 x screen frequency).

6. Click OK (Enter/Return).

7. Jot down the Print Size: Resolution value, which is the proper value to enter when you scan your image.

   Note: If you're going to scale the final image up or down in Photoshop, you should multiply the resolution by the scale factor to arrive at proper resolution for the scan. You don't need to multiply the resolution if you scale the original image when you scan it.

8. Click OK or press (Enter/Return). The image now has the correct resolution.

Goin' to the Web?

If the Web is the final destination for your image, create the appropriate image size by setting the resolution to 96 ppi (Win)/72 ppi (Mac) in the Image Size dialog box and entering the pixel dimensions (height and width) for the maximum desired view size of the image. For an online image, determine the most common monitor size and pixel dimensions your viewers will use. Images are normally formatted for a 13-inch monitor, which is 640 by 480 pixels. The total number of pixels in the image in turn determines the file size.

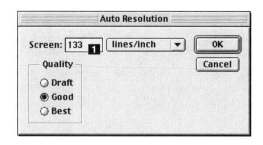

To calculate scanning parameters based on the required file size

Some scanners require that you enter the final file storage size in order to produce the necessary number of pixels for the image. To determine the final file size, choose File menu > New, enter the final Width and Height, and choose a color Mode (ask the prepress shop that will scan the image which mode to choose). Next, increase the Resolution until the Image Size figure near the top of the dialog box reaches the size recommended by your prepress shop. Change the Width and Height units to pixels, Jot down the Image Size values on a piece of paper, then click Cancel. Enter those figures when you scan the image. You can readjust the width and height of the scanned image later in Photoshop, if necessary.

Calculate Resolution

File storage sizes of scanned images

Size (In inches)	PPI (Resolution)	Black/White 1-Bit	Grayscale 8-Bit	CMYK Color 24-Bit
2 x 3	150	17 K	132 K	528 K
	300	67 K	528 K	2.06 MB
4 x 5	150	56 K	440 K	1.72 MB
	300	221 K	1.72 MB	6.87 MB
8 x 10	150	220 K	1.72 MB	6.87 MB
	300	879 K	6.87 MB	27.50 MB

Potential gray levels at various output resolutions and screen frequencies

	Output Resolution (DPI)	Screen Frequency (LPI)				
		60	85	100	133	150
Laser printers	300	26	13			
	600	101	51	37	21	
Image-setters	1270	256*	224	162	92	72
	2540		256*	256*	256*	256*

Note: Ask your print shop what screen frequency (lpi) you will need to specify when image-setting your file. Also ask your prepress shop what resolution (dpi) to use for imagesetting. Some imagesetters can achieve resolutions above 2540 dpi. Note that as the line screen frequency (lpi) goes up, the number of gray levels goes down.

*At the present time, PostScript Level 2 printers produce a maximum of 256 gray levels.

File Storage Sizes; Potential Gray Levels

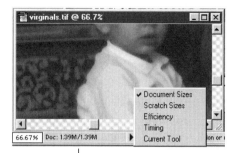

Using the Status bar

Windows: Choose Window menu > Show Status Bar to display it, or Hide Status Bar to hide it.

Windows and Macintosh:
When **Document Sizes** is chosen from the Status bar pop-up menu, the Status bar displays the file storage size when all layers are flattened and any alpha channels are removed (the first amount) and the file storage size when the layers are separate (the second amount) **1**.

1 *The Status bar with **Document Sizes** chosen. The figure on the left is the **RAM** required for the **flattened** image with no extra channels; the figure on the right is the **RAM** size for the image with **layers** and **extra channels**, if any.*

When **Scratch Sizes** is chosen, the bar displays the amount of storage space Photoshop is using for all currently open pictures and the amount of RAM currently available to Photoshop. When the first amount is greater than the second amount, Photoshop is using virtual memory on the scratch disk.

When **Efficiency** is chosen, the bar indicates the percentage of RAM being used. A percentage below 100 indicates the scratch disk is being used.

Choose **Current Tool** to display the name of the current tool.

Press and hold on the Status bar to display the page **preview**, which is a thumbnail of the image relative to the paper size, including custom printing marks, if chosen. Alt-press/Option-press on the Status bar to display the image's dimensions, number of channels, mode, and resolution.

2 *Windows: The storage size of an image is listed in the **Size** column.*

Storage size

Windows: To view the actual storage size of an image, use Windows Explorer to open the folder that contains the file you're interested in, and look in the Size column **2**. Or, for an even more accurate figure, Right-click the file icon and click on Properties.

Macintosh: To view the actual storage size of an image, look at the file information in the Finder. Or, for an even more accurate figure, click once on the file icon in the Finder, then choose File menu > Get Info ([⌘]-I) **3**.

3 *Macintosh: For the actual **storage size** of an image, use Get Info ([⌘]-I).*

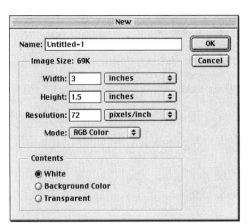

1 *In the New dialog box, enter a Name and enter Width, Height, and Resolution values. Also choose an image Mode and click a Contents type for the Background.*

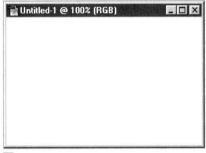

2 *A new, untitled image window (Windows).*

3 *A new, untitled image window (Macintosh).*

To create a new image:

1. Choose File menu > New (Ctrl-N/ ⌘-N).

2. Enter a name in the Name field **1**.

3. Choose a unit of measure from the drop-down menus next to the Width and Height fields.

4. Enter Width and Height values.

5. Enter the Resolution required for your final output device—whether it's an imagesetter or the Web (resolution issues are discussed on pages 41–42).

6. Choose an image mode from the Mode drop-down menu. You can convert the image to a different mode later (see "Image modes" on pages 23–25).

7. Click Contents: White or Background Color for the Background. To choose a Background color, see pages 139–142. Or choose the Transparent option if you want the background to be a layer.

Note: An image that contains one or more layers can only be saved in the Photoshop file format. If you're going to export the file to another application, though, you'll need to save a flattened copy of it in another format, since few applications can read Photoshop's layer transparency. (More about layers and transparency in Chapters 7 and 13).

8. Click OK (Enter/Return). An image window will appear (Win)**2**/(Mac)**3**.

TIP If you want the New dialog box settings to match those of another open document, with the New dialog box open, choose the name of the image that has the desired dimensions from the Window menu.

TIP If there is an image on the Clipboard from Photoshop or from Illustrator, the New dialog box will automatically display its dimensions. To prevent those dimensions from displaying, hold down Alt/Option when you choose File menu > New.

Create a New Image

Note: To open an Adobe Illustrator file, follow the instructions on page 52 or 54.

To open an image within Photoshop:

1. Choose File menu > Open (Ctrl-O/ ⌘-O).

2. *Optional (Macintosh):* For a PICT that hasn't yet been opened and saved in Photoshop, click Create on the left side of the dialog box to create a thumbnail preview of the image.

3. Locate the file you want to open (Win)**1**/(Mac)**2**. If the image was saved with a thumbnail preview, check the Show Thumbnail box to display it.

   Windows: To view files in all formats, choose All Formats from the Files of type drop-down menu.

   Macintosh: To view files in all formats, check the Show All Files box, then choose from the Format drop-down menu.

   Once it's opened, an image can be saved in any format that Photoshop reads.

   Macintosh: To search for a file, click Find, type the file name, then click Find again.

   Note: If the name of the file you want to open doesn't appear on the scroll list, it means the plug-in module for its format isn't installed in the Photoshop Plug-Ins folder. Install the plug-in.

4. Highlight the file name, then click Open.
   or
   Double-click the file name.

   Profile Mismatch? See pages 35–36.

   For some file formats, a further dialog box will open. For example, if you open an EPS, Adobe Illustrator, or PDF file that hasn't yet been rasterized (converted from object-oriented to bitmap), the Rasterize Generic Format dialog box will open. Follow steps 4–9 on pages 52–53.

TIP To open a QuarkXPress page in Photoshop, save it in QuarkXPress using the Save Page as EPS command, then follow the steps on page 52.

Pick 'n' choose

Windows: To specify a particular file format when opening a file, choose File menu > Open As, choose the necessary format from the Open as drop-down menu, then click Open.

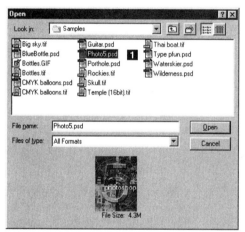

Windows: Double-click a file name.

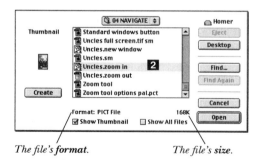

*The file's **format**.*   *The file's **size**.*

Macintosh: Double-click a file name.

Open an Image within Photoshop

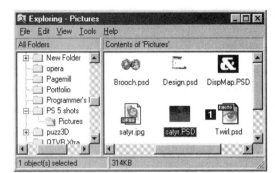

Double-click a Photoshop file icon.

Do it again

Windows: To reopen a file that was closed during the same work session, choose that file name from the File menu.

TIP To open an image in some file formats, such as Scitex CT or PICT Resource, you must use a special plug-in module. (access it via the File menu > Import submenu).

To open a Photoshop image from Windows Explorer:

Double-click a Photoshop image file icon in Windows Explorer **1**. Photoshop will launch if it hasn't already been launched.

To open a Photoshop image from the Finder:

Double-click a Photoshop image file icon in the Finder **2**. Photoshop will launch if it hasn't already been launched.

Thumbnails

Windows: To create image icons for Windows Explorer when the View menu is set to Large Icon, click the Save Thumbnail checkbox for individual files as you save them.

To create a thumbnail of all subsequently saved images for display in the Open dialog box, choose File menu > Preferences > Saving Files, then choose Image Previews: Always Save **3**. A thumbnail icon will only appear for an image that has a PSD, JPG, or TIF file extension.

Macintosh: To create image icons for the Finder, choose File menu > Preferences > Saving Files, choose Image Previews: Always Save, then check the Icon box **4**. To choose icons for individual files as you save them instead, choose Image Previews: Ask When Saving. Saving a multi-megabyte image with a preview could increase its file storage size.

To create a thumbnail icon of all subsequently saved images for display in the Open dialog box, check the Macintosh and/or Windows Thumbnail box **5**. To access this feature, the Apple QuickTime extension must be in the System Folder > Extensions folder (it's usually installed automatically).

Open File in Explorer/From Finder

To open a Kodak ICC Photo CD image, Photoshop uses the Kodak CMS Photo CD plug-in, which is accessed from the File menu. Kodak's Color Management System is designed to enhance the accuracy of the translation from the Kodak file format into Photoshop's RGB Color, CMYK Color, or Lab Color mode.

To open a Kodak Photo CD file:

1. Choose File menu > Open (Ctrl-O/ 🍎⌘-O).

2. Locate and double-click the Photo CD file name.
   or
   Highlight the Photo CD file name and click Open.

3. Choose a Resolution (Win)**1**/Image size (Mac)**2**. A size of 768 by 512 pixels will produce an image that is approximately 10.5 by 7 inches. The resolution will be 72 pixels/inch, regardless of which resolution/size you choose. The image width, followed by height, will appear on the Resolution/Image drop-down menu. They will always display in that order, regardless of the image orientation.

4. Click Image Info to read about the original film medium. Make a note of the Medium of Original and Product Type of Original info (the type of film used to create the image) **3**. Color Reversal is the term for a color slide; 52/xx is Ektachrome slide; and 116/xx is Kodachrome slide. Click OK.

5. Click Source.

6. Click on the closest available profile match to the Image Info description (Win)**4**/(Mac)**5** next page. Click Open.

7. Click Destination.

8. Choose a destination profile for the output device (a printer or a monitor) (Win)**6**/(Mac)**7**, both next page. Click Open.

9. Click OK in the Kodak ICC Photo CD dialog. The image will open in Photoshop.

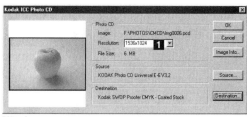

Windows

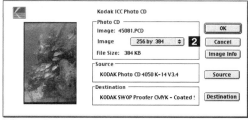

Macintosh

*Windows: Clicking Source (in the Kodak ICC Photo CD dialog box) brings up the Source Open dialog box. Click on the **source profile** that most closely matches the film medium of the original photo that was listed in the Image Info dialog box. A description of the profile displays in the lower portion of the dialog box.*

Open Kodak Photo CD

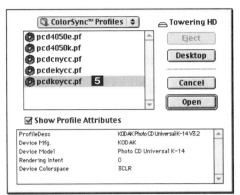

*Macintosh: Click on the **Source Profile** that most closely matches the film medium of the original photo that was listed in the Image Info dialog box. The image info dialog for this image listed Color Reversal as the Medium of Original and the Product Type as 116/-XX for an older model scanner, so we chose pcdkoycc.pf (Kodak Photo CD Kodachrome V3.2) as the profile.*

Windows: Clicking Destination in the Kodak ICC Photo CD dialog box brings up the Open dialog box. Click on a destination profile for the output device. A description of the profile displays in the lower portion of the dialog box.

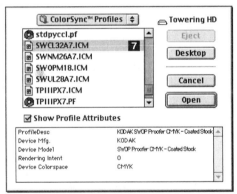

Macintosh: We're choosing a SWOP Proofer profile for coated stock as our destination profile, since we're outputting to a CMYK press.

Stop press!

Kodak has upgraded its film scanners to the 4045 and 4050 models and has also upgraded its PhotoCD transform profiles to version 3.4. The film choice and product types for the Photo CD profiles are as follows:

pcd4050e   Ektachrome scanned on 4050 model

pcd4050k   Kodachrome scanned on 4050 model

pcdekycc   Universal Ektachrome scanned on older or unspecified scanner

pcdkoycc   Universal Kodachrome scanned on older or unspecified scanner

pcdcnycc   Color negative scanned on older or unspecified scanner

Open Kodak Photo CD

When an EPS or Adobe Illustrator file is opened or placed in Photoshop, it is rasterized, which means it's converted from its native object-oriented format into Photoshop's pixel-based format. Follow these instructions to open an EPS file as a new file. Or follow the instructions on page 54 to place an EPS file into an existing Photoshop file.

Note: To open a single-page PDF file in Photoshop, you can use the Open or the Place command. To open a multi-page PDF as multiple images in Photoshop format, choose File menu > Automate > Multi-Page PDF to PSD (see page 278).

To open an EPS, PDF, or Illustrator file as a new image:

1. Choose File menu > Open (Ctrl-O/ ⌘-O).

2. If the file name isn't listed, *Windows:* Choose All Formats from the Files of type drop-down menu; *Macintosh:* Check the Show all Files box.

3. Locate and highlight an EPS image to be opened, then click Open.
or
Double-click a file name.

Note: If you're opening a PDF that contains more than one page, another dialog box will open **1**. Click the left or right arrow to locate the page that you want to open, then click OK. Or click the "1 of [ ]" button, enter a Go to page number **2**, then click OK twice.

4. *Optional:* In the Rasterize Generic EPS Format dialog box, check the Constrain Proportions box to preserve the file's height and width ratio **3**.

5. *Optional:* Choose a unit of measure from the drop-down menus next to the Height and Width fields, and enter new dimensions.

6. Enter the final resolution required for your image in the Resolution field. Entering the correct final resolution

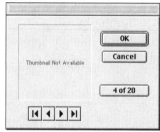

1 *For a **PDF** file, click the right or left arrow to locate the page that you want to open...*

2 *...or enter the number of the page that you want to open.*

3

before rasterizing will produce the best rendering of the image.

7. Choose an image mode from the Mode drop-down menu. (See "Image modes," beginning on page 23.)

8. Check the Anti-aliased box to reduce jaggies and soften edge transitions.

9. Click OK (Enter/Return).

TIP If you try to open a PDF or EPS file for which there is no matching profile in the current profile setups, the Missing Profile dialog box will open. See pages 35–36. If the PDF contains security settings, those settings must be disabled via Acrobat Exchange before the file can be opened.

TIP PDF and EPS files open with a transparent background. To create a white background, create a new layer, drag it below the PDF or EPS image layer on the Layers palette, then fill the new layer with white.

Pixel paste

You can copy an object in Illustrator and paste it into a Photoshop image, where the Paste dialog box will open automatically. Choose to paste the Illustrator object as pixels or as a path shape **1**.

1

When you place an object-oriented (vector) image into a Photoshop image, it becomes bitmapped and it's rendered in the resolution of the Photoshop image. The higher the resolution of the Photoshop image, the better the rendering.

Note: You can also drag a path from an Illustrator image window into a Photoshop image window—it will appear on a new layer.

To place an EPS, PDF, or Adobe Illustrator image into an existing Photoshop image:

1. Open a Photoshop image.

2. Choose File menu > Place.

3. Locate and highlight the file that you want to open 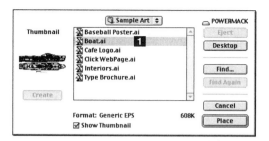. To place a PDF that contains multiple pages, choose a page, then click OK (see page 52).

4. Click Place (Enter/Return). A box will appear on top of the image. Pause to allow the image to draw inside it **2**.

5. *Perform any of these optional steps (use the Undo command to undo any of them):*

   To resize the placed image, drag a handle of the bounding box. Hold down Shift while dragging to preserve the proportions of the placed image.

   To move the placed image, drag inside the bounding box.

   To rotate the placed image, position the pointer outside the bounding box, then drag. You can move the center point.

6. To accept the placed image, press Enter/ Return or double-click inside the bounding box. The placed image will appear on a new layer.

TIP By default, the Anti-alias PostScript box is checked in the File menu > Preferences > General dialog box, and this setting produces the most optimal, but slowest, rendering of placed images.

TIP To remove the placed image, press Esc before or while it's rendering. If the image is already rendered, drag its layer into the trash on the Layers palette.

Place an EPS, PDF, or Illustrator Image

2 *The word "Delphi" was created in Adobe Illustrator and then placed into a Photoshop file.*

To produce this image, artist Wendy Grossman created the musical notes and other shapes in Illustrator and then imported them into Photoshop.

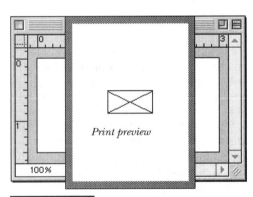

Print preview

To see the image size relative to the paper size, press and hold on the status bar at the bottom of the image window. To display the image on screen at the size it will print, choose View menu > Print Size.

P.S. At 100% view on a Macintosh monitor, the on-screen display size will match the print size only if the image resolution is the same as the monitor resolution (72 ppi). On a Windows monitor (96 ppi) at 100% view, the on-screen image will look slightly smaller than actual size. In Photoshop, 72 ppi always equals one inch, regardless of the image resolution. (Check it out yourself: Set a guide at the ruler's one-inch mark and then change the ruler units from inches to pixels. The guide will now be at the 72-pixel mark.)

Note: Changing an image's dimensions in Photoshop while preserving its current resolution (leaving the Resample Image box checked) will cause resampling, which degrades image quality. That's why it's always best to scan or create an image at the desired size. If resample you must, apply the Unsharp Mask filter afterward to resharpen (see pages 58–59).

To change an image's dimensions for print output:

1. Choose Image menu > Image Size.

2. To preserve the image's width-to-height ratio, check the Constrain Proportions box **1**. To modify the image's width independently of its height, uncheck the Constrain Proportions box.

3. *Optional:* To preserve the image's resolution, check the Resample Image box **2** and choose Nearest Neighbor, Bilinear, or Bicubic as the interpolation method. Bicubic causes the least degradation in image quality.

4. Choose a unit of measure from the drop-down menu next to the Print Size: Width and Height fields.

5. Enter new numbers in the Width and/or Height fields. The Resolution will change if the Resample Image box is unchecked.

6. Click OK (Enter/Return).

TIP To restore the original Image Size dialog box settings, hold down Alt/Option and click Reset.

TIP If you modify an image's dimensions and/or resolution with the Resample Image box checked, you will not be able to use the History Brush to restore a portion of it from an earlier history state. You will only be able to set the source of the History Brush from the current state forward.

Change Dimensions for Print Output

To change an image's pixel dimensions for on-screen output:

1. Choose Image menu > Image Size.

2. Make sure the Resample Image box is checked.

3. To preserve the image's width-to-height ratio, leave the Constrain Proportions box checked.

4. Set the Resolution to 96 ppi (Win) or 72 ppi (Mac).

5. Enter new values in the Pixel Dimensions: Width and/or Height fields.

6. Click OK (Enter/Return).

Note: If you increase an image's resolution (resample up) with the Resample Image box checked, pixels will be added and the image's file storage size will increase, but its sharpness will diminish. If you decrease an image's resolution (downsample), information will be deleted from the file, and it can only be retrieved using the History palette before the image is closed. Blurriness caused by resampling may only be evident when the image is printed; it may not be discernible on screen. That's why it's always best to scan or create an image at the proper resolution. Follow the instructions on the next page to resharpen a resampled image. (And see "Resolution" on page 41.)

To change an image's resolution:

1. Choose Image menu > Image Size.

2. To preserve the image's dimensions (Width and Height), check the Resample Image box **1**.
or
To preserve the image's total pixel count, uncheck Resample Image. The Width and Height dimensions must change to preserve the current pixel count.

3. Enter a number in the Resolution field.

4. Click OK (Enter/Return).

Cashing in on too high a resolution

An image contains a given number of pixels after scanning, and its print dimensions and its resolution are interdependent. If an image's resolution or dimensions are changed with the Resample Image box unchecked (Image Size dialog box), the file's total pixel count is preserved. Increasing an image's pixels per inch resolution will shrink its print (physical) dimensions; lowering an image's pixels per inch resolution will enlarge its print dimensions.

If your file has a higher resolution than needed (more than twice the screen frequency), you can allocate the extra resolution to the print size dimensions by unchecking the Resample Image box (the width, height, and resolution are now interdependent), and then lowering the resolution to twice the screen frequency. The width and height values will automatically increase, and the file size will remain constant—no pixels will be added or deleted from the image.

If you must further enlarge the image's dimensions, click in the Width field, check the Resample Image box, and enter a new Width value. The Height will change proportionately, and the file size will increase, but you'll be resampling, so after clicking OK, apply the Unsharp Mask filter to resharpen (see pages 58–59).

1 *Click* **Print** *or* **Online**.

2 *Enter the desired* **print size**.

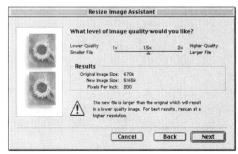

3 *Click or enter the* **lpi** *that your print shop specifies.*

5 *Click* **Finish**.

The Fit Image command has no effect on an image's resolution—it only changes its physical dimensions.

To resize an image to fit a specific width or height:

1. Chose File menu > Automate > Fit Image.

2. Enter a Width or Height value in pixels. The other field will automatically adjust after you click OK, so the width-to-height ratio will stay the same.

3. Click OK (Enter/Return).

The Resize Image command duplicates an image and resizes the duplicate auto-matically—all you have to do is respond to a sequence of dialog boxes. Photoshop will figure out the math for you.

To resize an image automatically:

1. Choose Help menu > Resize Image.

2. Click Print or Online **1**, then click Next.

3. Enter the desired output size **2**, then click Next. If you chose Online in the previous step, click Finish now. For print output, following the remaining steps.

4. Click or enter the lpi as per your print shop's instructions **3**, then click Next.

5. Move the Quality slider **4**, then note the final image size in the Results box. If there's a message below the Results box, read that as well. If you want to proceed, click Next.

6. Click Finish **5**, and then save the resized image.

Resize Image

If you change an image's dimensions or resolution with the Resample Image box checked, convert it to CMYK Color mode, or transform it, blurring may occur due to the resampling process. Despite its name, the Unsharp Mask filter has a focusing effect. It increases contrast between adjacent pixels that already have some contrast. You can specify the amount of contrast to be added (Amount), the number of surrounding pixels that will be modified around each pixel that requires more contrast (Radius), and determine which pixels the filter effects or ignores by specifying the minimum degree of existing contrast (Threshold).

Note: The Unsharp Mask effect is *more* discernible on screen than on high-resolution print output.

To apply the Unsharp Mask filter:

1. Choose Filter menu > Sharpen > Unsharp Mask.

2. Choose an Amount for the percentage increase in contrast between pixels ■. Use a low setting (below 50) for figures or natural objects; use a higher setting if the image contains sharp-edged objects. Too high a setting will produce obvious halos around high contrast areas. The larger the image, the less sharpening may be required. For a high-resolution image, use an Amount between 150 and 200%.

3. To choose an appropriate Radius value, which is a little trickier, you need to consider the final size, the resolution, and the subject matter of the image. Choose a Radius value (0.1–250) for the number of pixels surrounding high contrast edges that will be modified. Try between 1 and 2. A higher value could produce too much contrast in areas that already have high contrast.

The higher the resolution of the image, the more pixels there are on the border between high contrast areas, and thus the higher the Radius setting is required. Try a high Radius setting for

The original image, a bit blurry.

If you click on the image, that area will display here in the preview window.

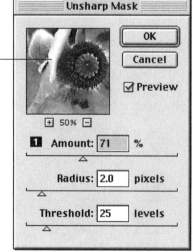

After Unsharp Masking with a high Amount (160%). Radius 1.5, Threshold 0. Notice the halos around the edges and the centers of the flowers.

After Unsharp Masking with a high Radius (6.0). Amount of 130, Threshold of 0. The soft gradations have become choppy and the image has an unnatural contrast and sharpness.

After Unsharp Masking with a high Threshold (15). Amount of 160, Radius of 1.5. Even with the same Amount setting as in the top image, the soft gradations in the petals and the background are preserved.

a low contrast image, and a lower Radius setting for an intricate, high contrast image.

Note: The higher the Radius setting, the lower the Amount setting can be, and vice versa.

4. Choose a Threshold value (0–255) for the minimum amount of contrast an area must have before it will be modified. At a Threshold of 0, the filter will be applied to the entire image. A Threshold value above 0 will cause sharpening along already high-contrast edges, less so in low contrast areas. If you raise the Threshold, you can then increase the Amount and Radius values to sharpen the edges without over-sharpening areas that don't require it. To prevent noise from distorting skin tones, specify a Threshold between 8 and 20.

5. Click OK (Enter/Return).

TIP To soften a grainy scan, apply the Gaussian Blur filter (Blur submenu) at a low setting (below 1) and then apply the Sharpen Edges filter (Sharpen submenu) once or twice afterward to resharpen.

TIP If you're unsharp masking a large image, first get close to the right settings using just the preview window to avoid waiting for the full screen preview (uncheck the Preview box), then check the Preview box to preview the results on the full screen, and finally, readjust the settings, if needed.

TIP Try applying the Unsharp Mask filter to one or two individual color channels (just the Red or Green channel, for example, in an RGB image). If you sharpen two separate channels, use the same Radius value in both. You can also convert the image to Lab Color mode then apply the filter to the L channel to sharpen luminosity without affecting color pixels.

Unsharp Mask

The Canvas Size command changes the live, editable image area.

Note: If you want enlarge the canvas area manually, right on the image, use the Crop tool (see page 62). You could also use the Crop command.

To change the canvas size:

1. If the image has a Background, choose a Background color (see pages 140–143).

2. Choose Image menu > Canvas Size.

3. *Optional:* Choose a different unit of measure from either drop-down menu. If you choose "columns," the current Column Size: Width in File menu > Preferences > Units & Rulers will be used as the increment.

4. Enter new numbers in the Width and/or Height fields **1**. Changing the Width won't change the Height, and vice versa.

5. *Optional:* To reposition the image on its new canvas, click on an unoccupied Anchor square. The dark gray square represents the existing image relative to the new canvas area.

6. Click OK (Enter/Return). Any added areas will automatically fill with the current Background color (unless the background is a layer with transparency, in which case added canvas areas will be transparent) **2**–**3**.

Note the **New** *and* **Current** *file* **Size** *as you change the canvas size.*

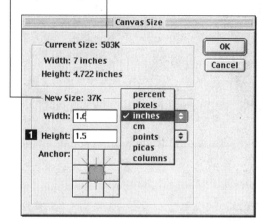

2 *The original image.*

3 *The same image with* **added canvas** *pixels.*

1 *Drag a marquee over the portion of the image that you want to keep.*

2 *The cropped image.*

To crop an image to fit exactly inside another image

Open both images, activate the destination image, choose the Crop tool, check the Fixed Target Size box and click Front Image on the Crop Options palette, activate the image you want to crop, then draw a marquee. After cropping, hold down Shift and drag-and-drop the layer or copy-and-paste the layer onto the destination image. The resolution will adjust automatically.

To crop an image:

1. Choose the Crop tool (C) ⊞ from the Marquee tool pop-out menu.

2. Drag a marquee over the portion of the image that you want to keep **1**.

3. *Do any of these optional steps:*

To resize the marquee, drag any handle (double-arrow pointer). Hold down Shift while dragging to preserve the marquee's proportions.

To reposition the marquee, drag from inside it.

To rotate the marquee, position the cursor outside it, and then drag in a circular direction. To change the axis point around which the marquee rotates, drag the circle away from the center of the marquee before rotating.

4. Press Enter/Return **2**.
or
Double-click inside the marquee. If you rotated the marquee, the rotated image will be squared off in the image window.

TIP To cancel the cropping process before accepting it, press Esc.

TIP To resharpen an image after cropping, apply the Unsharp Mask filter (see pages 58–59).

To specify dimensions and resolution as you crop an image:

1. Double-click the Crop tool. ⊞

2. Check the Fixed Target Size box on the Crop Options palette.

3. Enter values in the Width and/or Height fields.
or
Click Front Image to insert the current image's Width, Height, and Resolution values into those fields.

Note: The crop marquee will match this width-to-height ratio.

(Continued on the following page)

Crop an Image

4. *Optional:* Modify the Resolution. If, after clicking Front Image, you increase the resolution (not the width or height) and then crop the image, the print size won't change, but the image's pixel count will increase. If you enter a higher resolution, pixel resampling will occur, which may degrade the image.

   If you clear the Resolution field and then crop, the cropped image's resolution will increase or decrease to fit the Width and Height values you entered.

5. Drag a crop marquee on the image, then double-click inside the marquee or press Enter/Return.

1 *Drag any of the crop marquee handles **outside** the canvas area into the work canvas.*

Cropping with a marquee that's larger than the image will effectively increase the image's canvas size.

To enlarge an image's canvas area using the Crop tool:

1. Enlarge the image window so the work canvas (the gray area) around the image is showing.

2. Choose the Crop tool. 🔲

3. Draw a crop marquee within the image.

4. Drag any of the handles of the marquee into the work canvas **1**–**2**. If areas of the image originally extended outside the canvas border, those areas can now be included.

5. Double-click inside the marquee or press Enter/Return. If there were no hidden pixels, the added canvas area will fill with the current Background color if the Background is active, or with transparency if a layer is active.

2 *The newly **cropped** image has different proportions. In our example, the added pixels filled automatically with the current Background color (dark gray) because the Background was active on the Layers palette when the image was cropped.*

No snap?

Normally, the crop marquee will snap to the edge of the image. To override this snap function (let's say you want to crop slightly inside the edge of the image), start drawing the marquee, then hold down Ctrl/⌘ as you drag the marquee near the edge of the image.

1 *The original image.*

2 *The image flipped horizontally.*

5 *After rotating an image 180°. Compare with the flipped images, above.*

Note: The Rotate Canvas command flips all the layers in an image. To flip one layer at a time, use the Edit menu > Transform > Flip Horizontal or Flip Vertical command.

To flip an image:

To flip the image left to right, choose Image menu > Rotate Canvas > Flip Horizontal **1**–**2**.

or

To flip the image upside-down to produce a mirror image, choose Image menu > Rotate Canvas > Vertical **3**.

3 *The original image flipped vertically.*

Note: The Rotate Canvas commands rotate all the layers in an image. To rotate one layer at a time, use a rotate command from the Edit menu > Transform submenu.

To rotate an image a preset amount:

Choose Image Menu > Rotate Canvas > 180°, 90° CW (clockwise), or 90° CCW (counterclockwise).

To rotate an image by specifying a number:

1. Choose Image Menu > Rotate Canvas > Arbitrary.

2. Enter a number between -359.99° and 359.99° in the Angle field **4**.

   TIP To straighten out a crooked scan, measure the angle using the Measure tool, then enter that angle.

3. Click °CW (clockwise) or °CCW (counterclockwise)

4. Click OK (Enter/Return) **5**.

Special instructions for saving in the EPS, DCS, PICT, and TIFF file formats are on other pages. Other file formats are covered in the Photoshop User Guide.

To save a new image:

1. Choose File menu > Save (Ctrl-S/⌘-S).
or
If the image contains multiple layers, follow the Save a Copy instructions on page 67.

2. Type a name in the File name (Win) **1** / "Save this document as" (Mac) **2** field.

3. Choose a location in which to save the file.

Windows: To locate another folder or drive, click the drop-down menu at the top of the dialog box.

Macintosh: To locate a drive, click Desktop, then double-click a folder in which to save the file or create a new folder by clicking New.

4. Choose a file format from the Save As (Win)/Format (Mac) drop-down menu. If the document contains more than one layer, only the native Photoshop format will be available.

5. Click Save (Enter/Return).

TIP Choose Append File Extension: Always or Ask When Saving in File menu > Preferences > Saving Files if you want a three-character file extension to be appended automatically to your files for Windows export **3**.

And check the Include Composited Image With Layered Files box if you want a non-layered version of every image to be saved automatically with each layered version. This is useful if the Photoshop image is being exported to another application, such as Illustrator or After Effects.

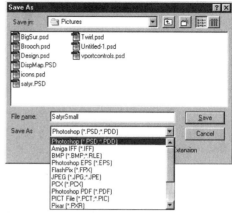

1 *Windows: Save dialog box.*

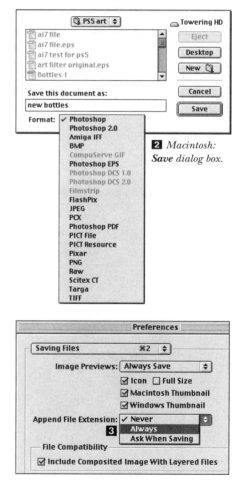

2 *Macintosh: Save dialog box.*

The Photoshop format

Photoshop is the only format in which multiple layers and layer transparency are available. You'll also need to choose the Photoshop format if you want to save an image with adjustment layers, grids, guides, or the ICC Color Management profiles; save in such image mode as Duotone or Lab Color; save editable type layers or layer effects; or save image settings created with Hue/Saturation or Channel Mixer.

Few applications can read an image in the Photoshop file format, though, so you should keep a copy of your layered, RBG image if you think there's any chance you'll want to rework it, and flatten a copy of it (see page 67).

The prior version of a file is overwritten when the Save command is chosen.

To save an existing image:

Choose File menu > Save (Ctrl-S/⌘-S).

The History palette is a full-service, multiple-undo feature. The History Brush tool is used to selectively revert a portion of an image. Both are covered in Chapter 8. The Revert command (below), which is a holdover from earlier versions of the application, should be used with caution—it clears all states from the History palette.

To revert to the last saved version:

1. Choose File menu > Revert.

2. Click Revert when the prompt appears **1**.

1 *Click Revert when this warning prompt appears.*

Using the Save As command, you can save a copy of an image in a different image mode or use the copy for a design variation. You can save a version of an image in CMYK Color mode, for example, and keep the original version in RGB Color mode.

Note: Use the Save a Copy command to copy a file and continue working on the original (instructions on the next page).

To save a new version of an image:

1. Open a file. If the image contains layers and you want to save it in a format other than Photoshop's native file format, flatten the image now.

2. Choose File menu > Save As (Ctrl-Shift-S/ ⌘-Shift-S).

3. Enter a new name or modify the existing name in the File name field (Win) **1**/ "Save this document as" (Mac) **2** field.

4. Choose a location in which to save the new version.

5. Choose a different file format from the Save As (Win)/Format (Mac) drop-down menu (available for a single-layer document only).

Macintosh: Hold down Option while choosing a format to append the format's three-character extension to the file name.

6. Click Save (Enter/Return). For an EPS file, follow the instructions on page 297. For a TIFF or PICT file, follow instructions on page 299. Consult the Photoshop manual for other formats. The new version will remain open; the original file will close automatically.

TIP If you don't change the name of the file and you click Save, a warning prompt will appear. Click Replace to save over the original file or click Cancel to return to the Save As dialog box.

TIP Your image may need to be in a particular image mode for some formats to be available.

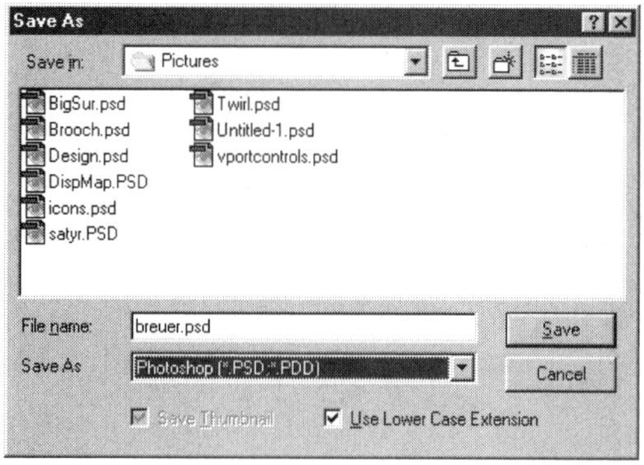

1 *Windows:* **Save As** *dialog box. Check the* **Use Lower Case Extension** *option to list the file's extension in lower case.*

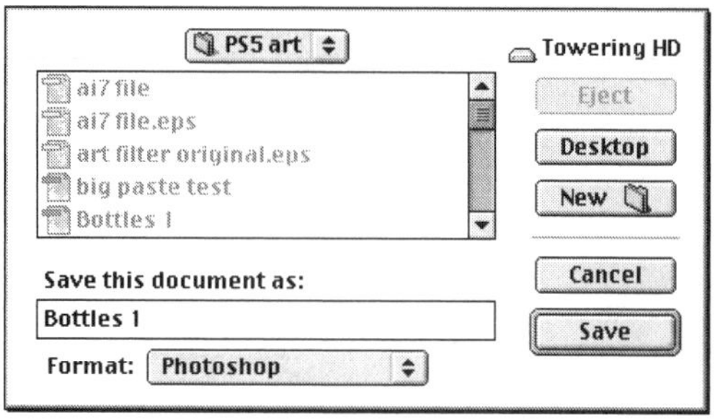

2 *Macintosh:* **Save As** *dialog box.*

What does the Duplicate command do?

The Image menu > Duplicate command copies an image and all its layers, layer masks, and channels into currently available memory. A permanent copy of the file is not saved to disk unless you then choose File > Save. An advantage of the Duplicate command is that you can use the duplicate to try out variations without altering the original file. HOWEVER, Duplicate should be used with caution, because if an application freeze or a system crash occurs, you'll lose whatever's currently in memory, including your duplicate image.

(sidebar in left margin) **Save New Version of Image**

The Save a Copy command saves a flattened copy of a multi-layer image in any file format you choose. The multi-layer version of the image will stay open so you can continue to work on it. The flattened version of an image will be smaller in file size than its multi-layer counterpart.

To copy a file and continue to work on the original:

1. With the file open, choose File menu > Save a Copy (Ctrl-Alt-S/⌘-Option-S).

2. *Optional:* Type a new name or change the name in the File name (Win) or "Save a copy in" (Mac) field. The word "copy" will automatically append to the file name.

3. Choose a location in which to save the copy (Win)**1**/(Mac)**2**.

4. *Do any of these optional steps:*

   Choose a different file **format** from the Save As drop-down menu (Win)/Format drop-down (Mac). If you choose any format other than Photoshop, the Flatten Image box will be checked automatically and layers will be flattened. For an image in the Photoshop file format, you can check the **Flatten Image** box to flatten all layers.

   Check the **Exclude Alpha Channels** box to delete alpha channels from a TIFF, Photoshop, Pixar, PNG, or Targa file.

   If you want to reduce the file size, check the **Exclude Non-Image Data** box. Such elements as grids, guides, paths, thumbnail previews, and color profiles will be removed from the file. This is a good option for an image that is going to be displayed on the Web.

5. Click Save. For an EPS file, follow the instructions on page 297. The original file will remain open.

1 *Save a Copy dialog box (Windows).*

2 *Save a Copy dialog box (Macintosh).*

Copy File, Keep Working on Original

To close an image:

Click the close box in the upper right corner of the image window (Win) /upper left corner of the image window **2** (Mac).
or
Choose File menu > Close (Ctrl-W/⌘-W).

If you attempt to close an image that was modified since it was last saved, a warning prompt will appear **3**. Click Don't Save to close the file without saving, or click Save to save the file before closing, or click Cancel to cancel the close operation.

1 *Windows: Click the close box in the upper right corner of the image window.*

2 *Macintosh: Click the close box in the upper left corner of the image window.*

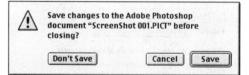

If you attempt to close an image that was modified since it was last saved, this prompt will appear.

To exit/quit Photoshop:

Windows: Choose File menu > Exit (Ctrl-Q) or click the application windows's close box.

Macintosh: Choose File menu > Quit (⌘-Q).

All open Photoshop files will close. If changes were made to an open file since it was saved, a prompt will appear **4**. Click Don't Save to close the file without saving, or click Save to save the file before quitting, or click Cancel to cancel the exit/quit operation.

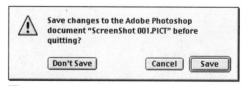

4 *If changes were made to an open file since it was saved, this prompt will appear.*

NAVIGATE 4

IN **THIS CHAPTER** you'll learn how to change the view size of an image, move an image in its window, switch screen display modes, display an image in two windows simultaneously, and recolor the work canvas.

You can display an entire image within its window, or magnify part of an image to work on a small detail. The view size is indicated as a percentage on the image window title bar, in the lower left corner of the application/image window, and in the lower left corner of the Navigator palette. The view size of an image neither reflects nor affects its printout size.

To change the view size using the Navigator palette:

*Drag in view box to **move** the image in the image window. Ctrl-drag/⌘-drag in the view box (as in this illustration) to marquee the area you want to **magnify**.*

*Enter the desired **zoom percentage** (or ratio, like 1:1 or 4:1), then press Enter/Return. To zoom to the percentage and keep the field highlighted, press Shift-Enter/Shift-Return. (You can also change the view size by double-clicking the zoom percentage box in the lower left corner of the application/image window, typing the desired zoom percentage, and then pressing Enter/Return.)*

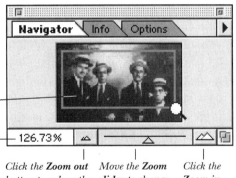

*Click the **Zoom out** button to reduce the image view size.*

*Move the **Zoom slider** to change the image view size.*

*Click the **Zoom in** button to enlarge the image display.*

TIP To change the color of the view box frame on the Navigator palette, choose Palette Options from the palette command menu, then choose a preset color from the Color drop-down menu or click the color swatch and choose a color from the Color Picker.

To change the view size using the Zoom tool:

1. Choose the Zoom tool (Z). 🔍

2. To **magnify** the image, click in the image window **1**. Or, drag a marquee across an area to magnify that area.

or

To **reduce** the view size, Alt-click/ Option-click on the image **2**.

or

To display the entire image in the largest possible size that will fit on your screen, choose View menu > Fit on Screen (Ctrl-0/⌘-0) or double-click the Hand tool.

TIP Uncheck the Resize Windows To Fit box on the Zoom Options palette if you want to prevent the image window from resizing when you change the image view size using the Zoom tool **3**.

TIP To view the image at actual pixel size, choose View menu > Actual Pixels. An image's view size equals its actual size only when the display ratio is 100% (1:1) and the image resolution and monitor resolution are the same.

TIP Ctrl-Spacebar-click/⌘-Spacebar-click to magnify the view size when another tool is selected or a dialog box with a Preview option is open. Alt-Spacebar-click/Option-Spacebar-click to reduce the view size.

TIP You can also change the view size by choosing Zoom In or Zoom Out from the View menu.

1 ***Click*** *on the image with the Zoom tool to **enlarge** the view size. Note the plus sign in the magnifying glass pointer.*

2 ***Alt-click/Option-click*** *on the image with the Zoom tool to **reduce** the view size. Note the minus sign in the magnifying glass pointer.*

Zoom Options \ Brushes

☑ Resize Windows To Fit
3

View size shortcuts

WINDOWS	
Zoom in (window doesn't resize)	Ctrl +
Zoom out (window doesn't resize)	Ctrl –
Magnify	Ctrl Alt +
Zoom Out	Ctrl Alt –
Actual pixels/100% view	Ctrl Alt 0
Fit on screen	Ctrl 0 (zero)

MACINTOSH	
Magnify	⌘ +
Zoom Out	⌘ –
Zoom in (window doesn't resize)	⌘ Option +
Zoom out (window doesn't resize)	⌘ Option –
Actual pixels/100% view	⌘ Option 0
Fit on screen	⌘ 0 (zero)

Zoom in or Out

1 *Click outside of, or drag, the view box on the* **Navigator** *palette to move an image in its window.*

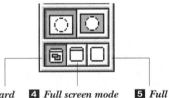

2 *Or move an image in its window using the* **Hand** *tool.*

3 *Standard screen mode*   **4** *Full screen mode with menu bar*   **5** *Full screen mode*

6 *Full screen mode with menu bar.*

Note: If the scroll bars aren't active, the entire image is displayed, and there is no need to move it.

To move a magnified image in its window:

Click outside of or drag the view box (image thumbnail) on the Navigator palette **1**.
or
Click the up or down scroll arrow on the image window. Drag a scroll box to move the image more quickly.
or
Choose the Hand tool (H) 🖑, then drag the image **2**.

TIP See other shortcuts for moving an image in its window in the shortcuts section.

To change the screen display mode:

Click the Standard screen mode button in the lower left corner of the Toolbox (F) **3** to display the image, menu bar, palettes, and scroll bars on the image window. This is the standard mode.
or
Click the Full screen mode with menu bar (middle) button (F) **4**, **6** to display the image, menu bar, and palettes, but no scroll bars. The area around the image will be gray.
or
Click the Full screen mode button in the lower right corner of the Toolbox (F) **5** to display only the image and palettes, not the menu bar or scroll bars. The area around the image will be black.

TIP Press Tab to show/hide the Toolbox and any open palettes; press Shift-Tab to show/hide the palettes, but keep the Toolbox open.

TIP Use the Hand tool (H) to move the image in its window when the scroll bars are hidden and the image is magnified, or use the Navigator palette. Hold down Spacebar to use the Hand tool while another tool is selected.

Move Image in its Window; Screen Modes

The number of images that can be open at a time depends on available RAM and scratch disk space. You can open the same image in two windows simultaneously: one in a large view size, such as 400%, to edit a detail and the other in a smaller view size, such as 100%, to view the whole image. Or, leave the image in RGB Color mode in one image window and choose View menu > Preview > CMYK (Ctrl-Y/⌘-Y) for the same image in a second window. The History palette will be identical for both windows.

To display one image in two windows:

1. Open an image.

2. Choose View menu > New View. The same image will appear in a second window .

3. *Optional:* Move either window by dragging its title bar, and/or resize either window.

1 *An image displayed in* **two windows** *simultaneously: one in a small view size for previewing, the other in a larger view size for editing.*

Note: The work canvas color will be the same for all images.

To recolor the work canvas:

1. Resize the image window, if necessary, so at least part of the work canvas is visible.

2. Choose a Foreground color (see pages 140–143).

3. Choose the Paint Bucket tool. ⬦

4. Shift-click on the work canvas **2**. You can't undo this. To restore the default gray, choose 20% gray for the Foreground color, then Shift-click the work canvas again.

2 *To* **recolor** *the* **work canvas**, *choose the Paint Bucket tool and a Foreground color, then Shift-click on the work canvas.*

WHEN A SELECTION is active on an image, only that area is editable—the rest of the image is protected. A selection border has a moving marquee.

This chapter covers the creation of selections using the Rectangular Marquee, Elliptical Marquee, Lasso, Polygon Lasso, Magic Wand, and Magnetic Lasso tools, as well as the Color Range command. You will also learn how to create a frame selection; how to deselect, reselect, inverse, or delete a selection; how to move or hide a selection marquee; how to transform, add to, or subtract from a selection; and how to create a vignette.

A selection contains pixels from whichever layer is currently active. If the Move tool is used to move a selection on the Background of an image, the current Background color will be applied automatically to the exposed area. If a selection is moved on a layer, on the other hand, the exposed area will become transparent. (Read more about layers in Chapter 7.)

A selection can be converted into a path for precise reshaping, and then converted back into a selection (see pages 212 and 222). Masks, which function like selections, but can be painted onto an image, are covered in Chapter 14.

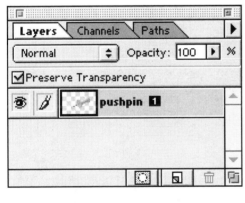

To select an entire layer:

Choose Select menu > All (Ctrl-A/⌘-A). A marquee will surround the entire layer.

To select only pixels—not the transparent areas—on a layer, Ctrl-click/⌘-click the layer name on the Layers palette **1**–**2**. Or Right-click/Control-click a layer thumbnail and choose Select Layer Transparency from the context menu.

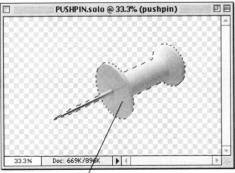

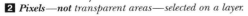

2 *Pixels—not transparent areas—selected on a layer.*

To create a rectangular or elliptical selection:

1. Choose a layer.

2. Choose the Rectangular Marquee 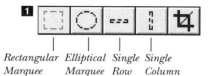 or Elliptical Marquee tool (M or Shift-M).

Rectangular   Elliptical   Single   Single
Marquee   Marquee   Row   Column

3. *Optional:* To specify the exact dimensions of the selection, with the Rectangular or Elliptical Marquee tool highlighted, press Enter/Return to open the Marquee Options palette (or double-click the tool), choose Fixed Size from the Style drop-down menu 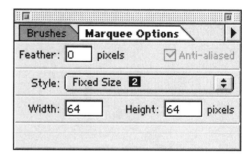, then enter Width and Height values. Remember, though, you're counting pixels based on the file's resolution, not the monitor's resolution, so the same Fixed Size marquee will appear larger in a low resolution file than in a high resolution file.

To specify the width-to-height ratio of the selection (3-to-1, for example), choose Constrained Aspect Ratio from the Style drop-down menu, then enter Width and Height values. Enter the same number in both fields to create a circle or a square.

4. *Optional:* To soften the edges of the selection before it's created, enter a Feather value above zero on the Options palette. The Anti-aliased option can be turned on or off for the Elliptical Marquee tool.

5. If you specified Fixed Size values or are using the Single Row or Single Column tool, click on the image. For any other Style, drag diagonally –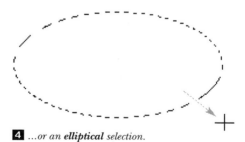. A marquee will appear. To create a square or a circular selection for the Normal style, start dragging, then finish the marquee with Shift held down.

Hold down Spacebar to move the marquee while drawing it. To move the marquee after releasing the mouse, drag inside it.

TIP As you drag the mouse, the dimensions of the selection will be indicated in the W and H area on the Info palette.

*Drag diagonally to create a **rectangular** selection...*

*...or an **elliptical** selection.*

Anti-aliasing

Check the Anti-aliased box on the Options palette before using a selection tool to create a selection with a softened edge that steps to transparency. Uncheck Anti-aliased to create a crisp, hard-edged selection.

 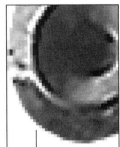

Aliased   *Anti-aliased*

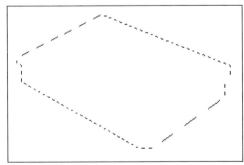

1 *A curved **Lasso** tool selection.*

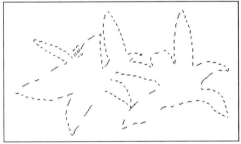

2 *A straight-edged **Polygon Lasso** tool selection.*

Erase as you go

Press Delete to erase the last-created corner. Hold down Delete to erase multiple corners.

Note: Since it's difficult to precisely reselect an area (unless you save the selection in an alpha channel or as a path), try to refine your selection before you deselect it. If the shape you want to select isn't too complex, use the Pen or Freeform Pen tool to select it instead of the Lasso—you'll get a smoother selection. You can also convert a selection into a path for precise reshaping.

To create a freeform selection:

1. Choose a layer.

2. Choose the Lasso tool (L or Shift-L).

3. *Optional:* Enter a Feather value on the Lasso Options palette to soften the edges of the selection.

4. Drag around an area of the layer **1**. When you release the mouse, the open ends of the selection will join automatically.

TIP To feather a selection after it's created, use the Select menu > Feather command (Ctrl-Alt-D/⌘-Option-D).

TIP To create a straight side using the Lasso tool, with the mouse button still down, press Alt/Option, and click to create corners. Drag, then release Alt/Option to resume drawing a freehand selection.

To create a polygonal selection:

1. Choose a layer.

2. Choose the Polygon Lasso tool (L or Shift-L).

3. To create straight sides, click to create points **2**. To join the open ends of the selection, click on the starting point (a small circle will appear next to the pointer). Or Ctrl-click/⌘-click or double-click anywhere on the image to close the selection automatically.

   Alt-drag/Option-drag to create a curved segment as you draw a polygonal selection. Release Alt/Option to resume drawing straight sides.

If you click on a layer pixel with the Magic Wand tool, a selection will be created that includes adjacent pixels of a similar shade or color. You can then add similarly colored, non-adjacent pixels to the selection using the Similar command, or add non-similar colors by Shift-clicking.

To select by color (Magic Wand):

1. Choose a layer.

2. Choose the Magic Wand tool (W). 🪄

3. On the Magic Wand Options palette, check the Use All Layers box to sample from colors in all the currently displayed layers to create the selection. Only pixels on the current layer can be edited, but you can apply changes within the same selection marquee through successive layers.

or

Uncheck the Use All Layers box to sample colors only on the current layer.

Also, check the Anti-aliased box for a smoother selection edge.

4. Click on a shade or color on the image.

5. *Do any of these optional steps:*

To enlarge the selection based on the current Tolerance setting on the Magic Wand Options palette, choose Select menu > **Grow** one or more times (use a low Tolerance).

To select other, non-contiguous areas of similar color or shade based on the current Tolerance setting on the Magic Wand Options palette, choose Select menu > **Similar**.

To change the range of shades or colors within which the Magic Wand tool selects, enter a number between 0 and 255 in the **Tolerance** field on the Magic Wand Options palette **1**, then click on the image again. At a Tolerance of 32, the Magic Wand will select within a range of 16 shades below and 16 shades above the shade on which it is clicked. Enter 0 to select only one color or shade.

To gradually expand or narrow the range of shades or colors the Magic Wand tool selects, modify the Tolerance value between clicks. The higher the Tolerance, the broader the range of colors the wand selects.

TIP Choose Edit > Undo (Ctrl-Z/⌘-Z) to deselect the last created selection area.

TIP To quickly select all the pixels on a layer (not the Background), Ctrl-click/⌘-click the layer name.

TIP If you move a selection using the Move tool and then you want to remove pixel areas from it, Alt-drag/Option-drag using another selection tool.

TIP To add to a selection with the Magic Wand tool, Shift-click outside the selection. To subtract from a selection, Alt-click/Option-click inside the selection. You can also use another selection tool with Alt/Option held down, such as the Lasso, to add to or subtract from a selection (see page 85).

TIP To Expand or Contract a selection by a specified number of pixels, choose either command from the Select menu > Modify submenu.

TIP To remove an object from a flat-color background, first select the background of the image using the Magic Wand tool, then press Backspace/Delete.

Or, to paste an object onto its own layer, select an area on the Background, then choose Layer menu > New > Layer Via Copy (Ctrl-J/⌘-J).

PHOTO: PAUL PETROFF

*A **Magic Wand** selection using a **Tolerance** of 10.*

*A **Magic Wand** selection using a **Tolerance** of 40. At a higher Tolerance, more pixels are selected.*

Select by Color (Magic Wand)

Using the Color Range command, you can select areas based on colors in the image or based on a luminosity or hue range.

To select by color (Color Range):

1. Choose a layer. The Color Range command samples colors from all the currently visible layers, but, of course, only the current layer will be available for editing. You can limit the selection range by first creating a selection.

2. Choose Select menu > Color Range.

3. Choose from the Select drop-down menu. You can limit the selection to a preset color range (e.g., Reds, Yellows), to a luminosity range (Highlights, Midtones, or Shadows), or to Sampled Colors (shades or colors you'll click on with the Color Range eyedropper). The Out of Gamut option can only be used on an image in Lab Color or RGB Color mode. If you choose a preset color range and the image contains only light saturations of that color, an alert box will warn you that the selection marquee will be present, but invisible.

4. Choose a Selection Preview option for previewing selection areas on the image.

5. To preview the selection, click the Selection button; to redisplay the whole image, click the Image button. Or, hold down Ctrl/⌘ with either option chosen to toggle between the two. If the image extends beyond the edges of image window, use the Image option—the entire image will be displayed in the preview box to facilitate sampling.

6. If you chose Sampled Colors in step 3, click or drag in the preview box or in the image window with the eyedropper cursor to sample colors in the image.

7. *Optional:* Move the Fuzziness slider to the right to expand the range of colors or shades selected, or move it to the left to narrow the range.

8. *Optional:* If you chose Sampled Colors in step 3, Shift-click in the image window or in the preview box to add more colors or shades to the selection. Alt-click/ Option-click to remove colors or shades from the selection. Or, click the "+" or "-" eyedropper icon button in the Color Range dialog box, then click on the image or in the preview box without holding down Shift or Alt/Option.

9. Click OK (Enter/Return).

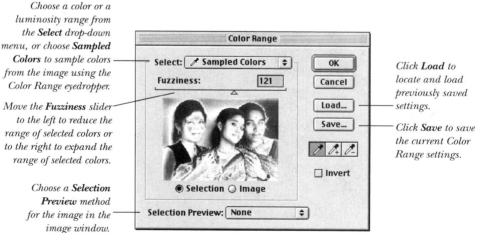

*Choose a color or a luminosity range from the **Select** drop-down menu, or choose **Sampled Colors** to sample colors from the image using the Color Range eyedropper.*

*Move the **Fuzziness** slider to the left to reduce the range of selected colors or to the right to expand the range of selected colors.*

*Choose a **Selection Preview** method for the image in the image window.*

*Click **Load** to locate and load previously saved settings.*

*Click **Save** to save the current Color Range settings.*

Select by Color (Color Range)

The "magic" Magnetic Lasso tool creates a freeform selection automatically as you move or drag the mouse. It snaps to the nearest distinct shade or color that defines the edge of a shape.

Note: This tool utilizes a lot of processor time and RAM. If you move or drag the mouse quickly, the tool may not keep pace with you.

To select using the Magnetic Lasso:

1. Choose a layer.

2. Choose the Magnetic Lasso tool (L or Shift-L). 🖐

3. *Optional:* Change any of the tool's Options palette settings. See "The Magnetic Lasso palette options" on the next page.

4. Click to establish a fastening point. Move the mouse, with or without pressing the mouse button, along the edge of the shape that you want to select **1**. As you move or drag, the selection line will snap to the edge of the shape. The temporary points that appear will disappear when you close the selection.

5. If the selection line starts to follow other adjacent shapes that you don't want to select, click on the edge of the shape that you *do* want to select to add a fastening point manually. Continue to move or drag to complete the selection.

6. To close the selection line: **2**

Double-click the mouse anywhere over the shape.
or
Click on the starting point (a small circle will appear next to the Magnetic Lasso tool pointer).
or
Press Enter/Return.
or
Ctrl-click/⌘-click.
or
Alt-double-click/Option-double-click to end with a straight segment.

(Continued on the following page)

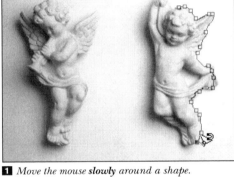

1 *Move the mouse **slowly** around a shape.*

2 *After **closing** the selection.*

Magnetic Lasso

TIP Press Esc to cancel a partial selection line (then you can start again). Press Delete to erase the last drawn fastening points in succession.

TIP Alt-click/Option-click to use the Polygon Lasso tool temporarily while the Magnetic Lasso is selected. Alt-drag/Option-drag to use the Lasso tool.

TIP To temporarily heighten contrast in an image to enhance the Magnetic Lasso tool's effectiveness, Ctrl-click/⌘-click the Create new layer button on the Layers palette, choose Type: Brightness/Contrast, click OK, and move the Contrast slider to the right. Delete the adjustment layer after using the Lasso.

The Magnetic Lasso palette options

The **Feather** amount is the softness of the edges of the selection.

The **Lasso Width** (1–40) is the size of the area in pixels under the pointer that the tool considers when it places a selection line. Use a wide Lasso Width for a high contrast image with strong edges. Use a narrow Lasso Width for an image that has subtle contrast changes or small shapes that are close together; the selection will be more precise and the line won't flip-flop back and forth across the edge.

TIP To decrease the Lasso Width setting by one pixel as you create a selection, press "[". To increase it, press "]".

Frequency (0–100) controls how often fastening points are placed as a selection is made. The lower the Frequency, the less frequently points are placed. Use a high Frequency to select an area with an irregular contour.

Edge Contrast (1–100) is the degree of contrast needed between shapes for an edge to be discerned. Use a low Edge Contrast for a low contrast image.

Tip: If you enter a low or high Lasso Width, do the same for the Edge Contrast.

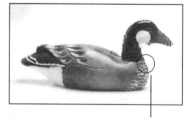

When **Other Cursors: Precise** *is chosen in File menu > Preferences > Display & Cursors, the pointer will will be a circle, and its diameter will be the current Lasso Width. Press Caps Lock to turn the Precise option on temporarily.*

Magnetic Lasso

1 *A* **frame** *selection created using the Rectangular Marquee tool.*

To create a frame selection:

1. Choose a layer.

2. Choose the Rectangular or Elliptical Marquee tool (M or Shift-M), then press and drag to create a selection, or choose Select menu > Select All (Ctrl-A/⌘-A).

3. Alt-drag/Option-drag a smaller selection inside the first selection **1**.

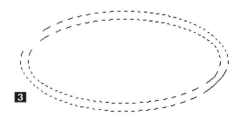

PHOTO: PAUL PETROFF

To produce this image, a frame selection was created a different way: The Marquee tool was used to select the center area, and then the Inverse command was used to reverse the selected and non-selected areas so the outer area became the selection. The Levels command was used to screen back the selected area.

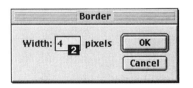

To select a narrow border around a selection:

1. Create a selection.

2. Choose Select menu > Modify > Border.

3. Enter the desired Width (1–64) of the border in pixels **2**.

4. Click OK (Enter/Return). The new selection will evenly straddle the edge of the original selection **3**.

Frame Selection; Border Selection

To deselect a selection:

With any tool selected, choose Select menu > Deselect (Ctrl-D/⌘-D).
or
Click inside the selection with any selection tool 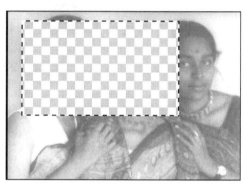.

Note: If you click *outside* the selection with the Magic Wand, Polygon Lasso, or Magnetic Lasso tool, you will create a new selection.

TIP It's difficult to reselect the same area twice, so deselect a selection only when you're sure you've finished using it. If you unintentionally deselect, choose Select menu > Reselect immediately. If you think you might want to reuse a selection, save it as a path or in an alpha channel.

1 *Click* **inside** *a selection to* **deselect** *it.*

To reselect the last selection:

Choose Select menu > Reselect (Ctrl-Shift-D/⌘-Shift-D).

TIP If you click on a prior state on the History palette that involved a selection, the Reselect command will reselect from that prior state.

2 *A selection deleted from a* **layer**.

If you delete a selection from a layer, the original selection area will become transparent **2**. If you delete a selection from the Background, the selection area will fill with the current Background color **3**.

To delete a selection:

Press Backspace/Delete.
or
Choose Edit menu > Clear.
or
Choose Edit menu > Cut (Ctrl-X/⌘-X) if you want to place the selection on the Clipboard.

3 *A selection deleted from the* **Background**.

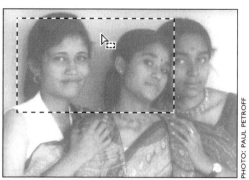

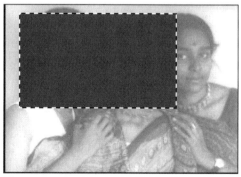

PHOTO: PAUL PETROFF

Deselect, Reselect, Delete a Selection

PHOTO: ELAINE WEINMANN

1 *Moving a marquee.*

Follow these instructions to move only the selection marquee—not its contents.

To move a selection marquee:

1. *Optional:* To aid in positioning the marquee, choose View menu > Show Grid or drag a guide or guides from the horizontal or vertical ruler, and also turn on Snap to Guides (View menu > Snap to Guides or Ctrl-Shift-;/⌘-Shift-;).

2. Choose any selection tool.

3. Drag inside the selection **1**. Hold down Shift after you start dragging to constrain movement to a multiple of 45°.
   or
   Press any arrow key to move the marquee one pixel at a time.

TIP If you drag a selection on a layer using the Move tool, the selection's pixel contents will be cut from that layer and the empty space will be replaced by layer transparency. If a selection is moved on the Background, on the other hand, the empty space will be filled with the current Background color. If you deselect it, its pixel contents will return to its original layer.

TIP You can drag a selection marquee into another image window—it will become a new layer in the destination image.

2 *The original selection—the **angels** are selected.*

3 *The selection is **inverted**—now the **background** is selected.*

To switch the selected and unselected areas:

Choose Select menu > Inverse (Ctrl-Shift-I/⌘-Shift-I) **2**–**3**.

TIP Choose Inverse again to switch back.

TIP It's easy to select a shape on a flat color background: Choose the Magic Wand tool, enter 5 or less in the Tolerance field on the Magic Wand Options palette, click on the flat color background to select it entirely, then choose Select menu > Inverse.

To hide a selection marquee:

Choose View menu > Hide Edges (Ctrl-H/
⌃⌘-H). The selection will remain active.

TIP To redisplay the selection marquee,
choose View menu > Show Edges.

TIP To verify that a selection is still active,
press on the Select menu. Most com-
mands will be available if a selection
is active.

TIP You can choose the Hide Edges command while some Image menu and
Filter menu dialog boxes are open.

To transform a selection marquee:

Choose Select menu > Transform Selection,
then follow the instructions on pages
107-109 to flip, rotate, scale, etc. **1**–**2**

Note: The Transform Selection command
affects only the selection marquee—not its
contents. To transform pixel contents, use
a command on the Edit menu > Transform
submenu.

TIP Right-click/Control-click on the image
to display a context menu from which
you can choose a transform command **3**.

1 *Scaling a selection marquee.*

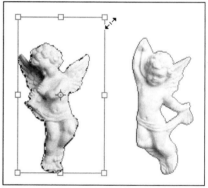

Deselect
Select Inverse
Feather...

Save Selection...
Make Work Path...

Layer Via Copy
Layer Via Cut
New Layer...
New Adjustment Layer...

Free Transform
Numeric Transform
Transform Selection

Fill...
Stroke...

Last Filter
Fade...

3

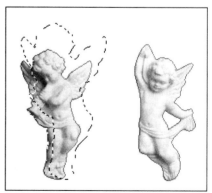

2 *The marquee is enlarged.*

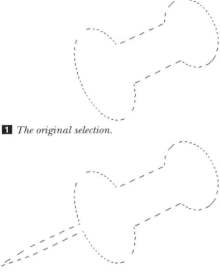

1 *The original selection.*

2 *After adding an additional selection area.*

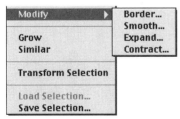

3 *A circular selection is drawn over an existing selection with* **Alt/Option** *and* **Shift** *held down.*

4 *Only the* **intersection** *of the two selections remains selected.*

5 *You can modify an existing selection via commands under the* **Select** *menu.*

To add to a selection:

Choose any selection tool other than the Magic Wand, choose Options palette settings for the tool, position the cursor over the selection, then Shift-drag to define an additional selection area **1**–**2**.

or

Click the Magic Wand tool, then Shift-click on any unselected area.

TIP If the additional selection overlaps the original selection, it will become part of the new, larger selection. If the addition does not overlap the original selection, a second, separate selection will be created.

To subtract from a selection:

Choose any selection tool other than the Magic Wand, choose Options palette settings for the tool, then Alt-drag/Option-drag around the area to be subtracted.

or

Choose the Magic Wand tool, then Alt-click/Option-click on the area of shade or color in the selection to be subtracted.

TIP Alt-Shift-drag/Option-Shift-drag to select the intersection of an existing selection and a new selection **3**–**4**.

To modify a selection via a menu command:

Choose Select menu > Modify > Smooth (see page 102) **5** or Select menu > Modify > Expand or Contract, enter a value, then click OK.

or

Choose Select menu > Grow or Similar. These two commands use the current Magic Wand Tolerance setting (see page 76). You can repeat either command to further extend the selection.

To vignette an image:

1. For a multi-layer image, choose a layer, and uncheck the Preserve Transparency box. The vignette you create is going to appear to fade into the layer or layers below it.

For an image with a Background only, choose a Background color (see pages 140–143) for the area around the vignette.

2. Choose the Rectangular Marquee , Elliptical Marquee ○, or Lasso tool ♀.

3. On the Options palette, enter 15 or 20 in the Feather field. Alternatively, you can feather the selection after it's created (step 4) using Select menu > Feather.

4. Create a selection **1**.

5. Choose Select menu > Inverse (Ctrl-Shift-I/⌘-Shift-I).

6. Press Backspace/Delete.

7. Deselect (Ctrl-D/⌘-D) **2**.

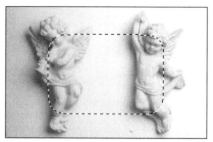

1 *First create a **feathered**-edge selection.*

2 *The **vignette**.*

The original image.

*The **vignette**.*

For this illustration, we applied the Glass filter for step 6.

Vignette an Image

COMPOSITING 6

THIS **CHAPTER** covers methods for composing image elements: the Clipboard (Cut, Copy, Paste, and Paste Into), drag-and-drop, cloning, and pattern stamping. Also covered are techniques for precisely positioning and aligning image elements and smoothing the seams between them.

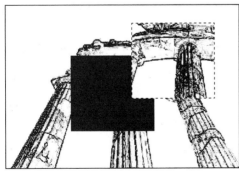

1 *Moving a selection on a* ***layer...***

2 *...a* ***transparent*** *hole is left behind.*

3 *Moving a selection on the* ***Background:*** *the exposed area fills with the current* ***Background color.***

In these instructions and in the "drag-copy" instructions on the next page, you'll be moving actual image pixels. (To move just a selection marquee without moving its contents, see page 83.)

To move a selection's contents:

1. *Optional:* To help you position the selection, choose View menu > Show Grid (Ctrl-"/⌘-"), or drag a guide or guides from either ruler, and also turn on Snap to Guides (View menu > Snap to Guides, or Ctrl-Shift-;/⌘-Shift-;).

2. If the selection is on the Background, choose a Background color. The area the moved selection exposes will fill with this color automatically. If the selection is on a layer, the exposed area will fill with transparency.

3. Choose the Move tool (V). ✛ Or hold down Ctrl/⌘ to access the Move tool while any tool other than a Pen tool or the Hand tool is chosen.

4. Position the pointer over the selection, then drag. The selection marquee and its contents will move together **1**–**3**.

Note: When you deselect the selection, its pixel contents will drop back into its original layer, in its new location, regardless of which layer is currently active.

TIP Press an arrow key to move a selection marquee in 1-pixel increments.

To drag-copy a selection:

1. Choose the Move tool. ✛ (You can use the Ctrl/⌘ key to access the Move tool while almost any other tool is selected.)

2. Hold down Alt/Option before and as you drag the selection you want to copy. Release the mouse before you release Alt/Option. The copied pixels will remain selected **1**–**2**.

TIP Press Alt-arrow/Option-arrow to offset a copy of a selection one pixel from the original. Press Alt-Shift-arrow/Option-Shift-arrow to offset a copy by ten pixels.

1 *Alt/Option-dragging a selection.*

2 *A copy of the selected pixels is moved.*

The Align to Selection command aligns layer pixels to a currently active selection marquee. To align objects on multiple layers, you can align each one individually to the same marquee or you can link them first and then align them all at once.

To align a layer or layers to a selection marquee:

1. Create a selection.

2. Choose a layer or one layer in a group of linked layers.

3. Choose Layer menu > Align To Selection > Top, Vertical Center, Bottom, Left, Horizontal Center, or Right **3**. The layer pixels will align to the edges or center of the selection marquee, depending on which alignment option you chose.

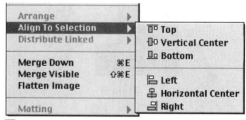

3 *Choose an option from the **Align To Selection** submenu to align layer pixels to a selection marquee.*

Clipboard facts

You can use the Cut or Copy command to save a selection to a temporary storage area called the Clipboard, and then use the Paste or Paste Into command to paste the Clipboard imagery onto another layer in the same image or in another image. The Cut, Copy, and Paste Into commands are available only when a selection is active.

If you create a selection and choose the Cut command, the selection will be placed on the Clipboard. (The Clear command doesn't use the Clipboard.) If you Cut or Clear a selection from the Background, the exposed area will be filled with the current Background color. If you remove a selection from a layer, the area left behind will be transparent. For the most seamless transition, check the Anti-aliased box on the Options palette for your selection tool before using it to create a selection.

The Paste command pastes the Clipboard contents into a new layer and preserves any areas that extend beyond the image window. You can move the entire layer to reveal the extended areas. If you then save your document, the extended areas will save with it. If you crop the image, however, the extended areas will be discarded.

The Clipboard can contain only one selection at a time, and it is replaced each time Cut or Copy is chosen. The same Clipboard contents can be pasted an unlimited number of times, and will be retained even if you exit/quit Photoshop. They will also be retained if you switch to another application if the Export Clipboard box is checked in File menu > Preferences > General.

The dimensions in the New dialog box automatically match the dimensions of imagery on the Clipboard.

TIP If the Clipboard imagery is large, the remaining available memory for processing is reduced. To empty the Clipboard and reclaim memory, choose Edit menu > Purge > Clipboard. This can't be undone.

Before copying between images

Before using the Clipboard commands or the drag-and-drop method, compare the **dimensions** of the source image with the dimensions of the destination image. If the imagery being copied is larger than the destination image, some of the copied pixels will extend beyond the image window when they're pasted or dropped, and they will be hidden from view. Move the layer using the Move tool if you want to reveal the out-of-view pixels.

The size of a selection may also change when it's pasted or dropped for another reason: it is rendered in the **resolution** of the destination image. If the resolution of the destination image is higher than that of the source imagery, the copied image will appear smaller when it's pasted or dropped. Conversely, if the resolution of the destination image is lower than that of the source image, the source imagery will appear to be enlarged when it's pasted or dropped. You can use the Image Size command to choose the same resolution (and dimensions, if desired) for both images. Follow the instructions on page 93 to paste into a smaller image.

To copy and paste a selection:

1. Select an area on a layer or on the Background. To feather the selection, choose Select menu > Feather, and enter a value.

2. Choose Edit menu > Copy **1** (Ctrl-C/⌘-C) (or choose Edit menu > Cut to cut the selection).

3. Choose the layer above which you want the paste layer to appear.

4. Choose Edit menu > Paste (Ctrl-V/⌘-V) **2**.

5. *Optional:* Restack, move, or defringe the new layer.

TIP To turn a selection into a new layer, choose Layer menu > New > Layer Via Copy or Layer Via Cut (see page 105).

1 *An area of the Background is placed on the Clipboard via Edit menu > **Copy**.*

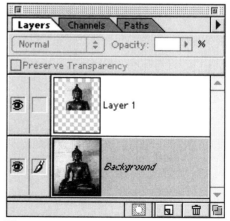

2 *The **pasted** imagery appears on a new layer.*

Copy and Paste a Selection

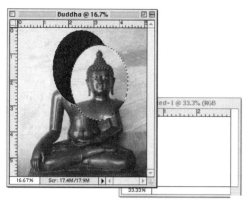

1 *A selection is dragged from the Background. The exposed area **temporarily** fills with the Background color.*

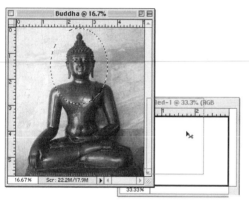

2 *A **dark border** appears in the destination image window.*

3 *The mouse is released, and the copied pixels appear in the **destination** image window. The source image is unchanged.*

If you drag selected pixels from one image to another, presto, those selected pixels will be copied onto a new layer in the destination image. This drag-and-drop method bypasses the Clipboard, so it saves memory and preserves the current Clipboard contents. If your monitor is too small to display two image windows simultaneously, use the copy-and-paste method instead.

To drag-and-drop a selection between images:

1. Open the source and destination images, and make sure the two image windows don't completely overlap.

2. Select an area on a layer or on the Background.

3. Choose the Move tool. ⤧
   or
   Hold down Ctrl/⌘.

4. Drag the selection into the destination image window, and release the mouse where you want the pixels to be dropped **1**–**3**. You can move the new layer around using the Move tool.

TIP Hold down Shift before and as you drag to automatically drop the selection in the exact center of the destination image. You can release the mouse when the pointer is anywhere inside the destination image window.

TIP To drag-and-drop a whole layer to another image, see pages 115–116.

Drag-Drop Selection Between Images

If you use the Paste Into command to paste the Clipboard contents into the boundary of a selection, a new layer will be created automatically and the active marquee will become a layer mask. The pasted image can be repositioned within the boundary of the visible part of the layer mask, and the mask itself can also be edited.

To paste into a selection:

1. Select an area of a layer. If you want to feather the selection, choose Select menu > Feather and enter a value.

2. Choose Edit menu > Copy to copy pixels only from the active layer, or choose Edit menu > Copy Merged (Ctrl-Shift-C/ ⌘-Shift-C) to copy pixels within the selection area from all the currently visible layers.

3. Leave the same layer active, or activate a different layer, or activate a layer in another image.

4. Select an area (or areas) into which the Clipboard image will be pasted.

5. Choose Edit menu > Paste Into (Ctrl-Shift-V/⌘-Shift-V). A new layer and layer mask will be created **1**–**3**.

6. *Optional:* The entire Clipboard contents were pasted onto the layer, but the layer mask may be hiding some of them. To reposition the imagery within the area the layer mask reveals, choose the Move tool, click on the layer thumbnail, then drag in the image window.

To select the layer mask, click on the layer mask thumbnail. Drag the layer mask to reposition the area the layer mask reveals. Paint on the layer mask in the image window with white to reveal parts of the image, or with black to hide parts of the image.

To move the layer and layer mask in unison, first, on the Layers palette, click in the space between the layer and layer mask thumbnails to link the two layer components together (click the link icon to unlink them).

1 *The music layer was selected in another image, and then pasted into a Type Mask tool selection.*

2 *The layer contents can be repositioned within the layer mask, since the two aren't linked together. For this image, the music layer thumbnail was activated and then the layer contents were moved upward using the* **Move** *tool.*

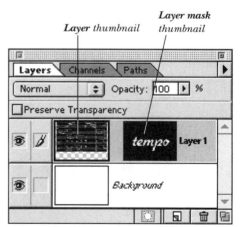

3 *The pasted image appears on a new layer via* **Paste Into***, and a layer mask is created automatically. The pasted image (the music) is only visible within the white areas in the* **layer mask** *(the letter shapes).*

Off the edge?

■ To **remove** pixels that extend beyond the edge of a layer, make sure the layer is active, choose Edit menu > Select All, then choose Image menu > Crop. Trimming off the extra pixels will reduce the file's storage size.

■ If you apply an image editing command, such as a filter, to a whole layer, any pixels beyond the edge of the layer will also be modified. To **include** these pixels by making them visible in the image window, increase the Canvas Size.

Normally, in Photoshop, if you move a large selection or layer or paste into another image, all the pixels on a layer are preserved, even those that may extend beyond the visible edge of the layer. If you want to trim the pasted imagery as it's pasted, follow these instructions, but read "Before copying between images" on page 90 before you proceed.

To paste into a smaller image:

1. Click on the destination image, then Alt-press/Option-press and hold on the Status bar at the bottom of the image window. Jot down the image's width, height, and resolution on a piece of paper.

2. Click on the source image, choose Image menu > Duplicate, and click OK.

3. With the duplicate image window active, choose Image menu > Image Size.

4. Check the Resample Image box, and change the resolution to the same value as that of the destination image **1**. In the Print Size: Width or Height field, enter a smaller number than the dimensions that you jotted down for step 1 **2**, then click OK (Enter/Return).

5. Choose the layer you want to copy.

6. Choose Select menu > All to select the layer, choose Edit menu > Copy, click in the destination image, then choose Edit menu > Paste.
or
Shift-drag the source layer name into the destination image window.

7. Close the duplicate image. Save the original image, if desired.

TIP In lieu of steps 3 and 4 above, you can choose File menu > Automate > Fit Image and enter the desired pixel dimensions for the width or the height (from step 1). This command won't change the image resolution, so use it only if you don't need to change resolution.

Image Size

Pixel Dimensions: 1.49M (was 563K)

Width:	1200	pixels
Height:	1300	pixels

OK
Cancel
Auto...

Print Size:

2

Width:	5.333	inches
Height:	5.78	inches
Resolution:	225	pixels/inch

☑ Constrain Proportions
1 ☑ Resample Image: Bicubic

The Blur tool decreases contrast between pixels. Use it to soften edges between shapes. The Sharpen tool increases contrast between pixels. Use it to delineate edges between shapes. Neither tool can be used on a image in Bitmap or Indexed Color mode.

To sharpen or blur edges:

1. Choose the Blur tool ◊ or the Sharpen tool △ (R or Shift-R). Each tool keeps its own Options palette settings.

2. On the Sharpen or Blur Options palette, choose a Pressure percentage **1**. Try a setting of around 30% at first.
and
Choose a blending mode **2**. Choose Normal to sharpen or blur pixels of any shade or color. Choose Darken to sharpen or blur only pixels that are darker than the Foreground color. Choose Lighten to sharpen or blur only pixels that are lighter than the Foreground color. Hue or Color mode will cause a slight buildup of complementary colors. Saturation mode will cause a buildup of existing colors. Luminosity mode will intensify luminosity. (The blending modes are described on pages 26–28.) You'll see a greater difference between modes using the Sharpen tool than with the Blur tool.

   TIP Right-click/Control-click on the image to choose a blending mode.

3. *Optional:* Check the Use All Layers box on the Options palette to pick up pixels from other visible layers under the pointer to place on the active layer.

4. Click the Brushes tab on the Options palette group, then click a hard-edged or soft-edged tip.

5. Drag across the area of the image that you want to sharpen or blur **3**–**4**. To intensify the effect, stroke again.

TIP To avoid creating an overly grainy texture, use the Sharpen tool with a medium Pressure setting and stroke only once on the same area.

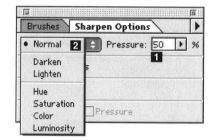

3 *The original image.*

4 *After using the **Sharpen** tool on the strawberry in the center, and the **Blur** tool on the rest of the image.*

Sharpen or Blur

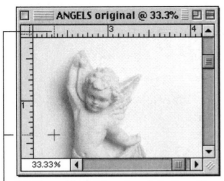

1 *The position of the pointer is indicated by a marker on each ruler.*

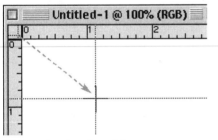

2 *Dragging the **ruler origin**.*

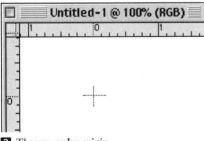

3 *The **new ruler origin**.*

Grids, rulers, and guides can help you position objects precisely.

To hide or show rulers:

Choose View menu > Show Rulers (Ctrl-R/ ⌘-R). Rulers will appear on the top and left sides of the image window, and the current position of the pointer will be indicated by a dotted marker on each ruler **1**. To hide the rulers, choose View menu > Hide Rulers.

TIP To quickly access the Units & Rulers Preferences dialog box to change the ruler units, double-click on either ruler.

The ruler origin is the point from which an object's location is measured.

To change the rulers' zero origin:

1. *Optional:* To make the new ruler origin snap to gridlines, first display the grid by choosing View menu > Show Grid (Ctrl-"/⌘-"). Then choose View menu > Snap To Grid (Ctrl-Shift-"/ ⌘-Shift-").

To make the ruler origin snap to a guide, choose View menu > Snap To Guides (Ctrl-Shift-;/⌘-Shift-;), and drag in a guide, if you haven't already done so.

2. Drag from the intersection of the rulers in the upper left corner of the image window diagonally into the image **2–3**. Note where the zeros are now located on the rulers.

TIP To reset the ruler origin, double-click where the rulers intersect in the upper left corner of the image window.

Rulers

The grid is a non-printing framework that can be used to align image elements. Guides are individual guidelines that you drag into the image window yourself. With View > Snap To Guides turned on, a selection or tool pointer will snap to a guide if it's moved within 8 screen pixels of the guide. Ditto for View menu > Snap to Grid.

To hide or show the grid:

Choose View menu > Show Grid (Ctrl-"/ ⌘-"). 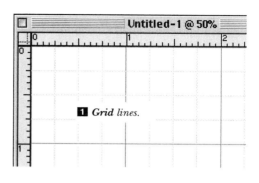 To hide the grid, choose View menu > Hide Grid.

1 *Grid* lines.

To create a guide:

Make sure the rulers are displayed, then drag from the horizontal or vertical ruler into the image window **2**. Hold down Shift as you drag to snap the guide to a ruler increment. If the grid is displayed and View menu > Snap to Grid is turned on, the guide can be snapped to a grid line. A guide can also be snapped to a selection marquee.

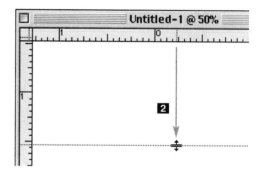

TIP To **lock** all guides, choose View menu > Lock Guides (Ctrl-Alt-;/⌘-Option-;).

TIP To **switch** a guide from vertical to horizontal (or vice versa) as you create it, drag with Alt/Option held down.

TIP To **move** an existing guide, drag it using the Move tool (make sure guides aren't locked). Guides will keep their relative positions if you resize the image.

TIP You can choose a new guide color or style in File menu > Preferences > Guides & Grid (double-click a guide with the Move tool to quickly open that dialog box).

To remove guides:

To remove one guide, drag it out of the image window using the Move tool.
or
To remove all guides, choose View menu > Clear Guides.

1 *Drag on the image using the **Measure** tool.*

2 *Angle (A) and **distance (D)** readouts appear on the **Info** palette.*

| Navigator | Info | ▶ |

R :
G :   ∠ A : 3.5°
B :   D : 4.130

+, X : 3.518   ⌐ W : 4.122
  Y : 2.979   H : -0.250

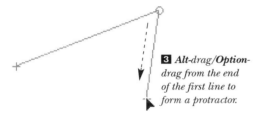

3 *Alt-drag/**Option**-drag from the end of the first line to form a protractor.*

4 *If you create a **protractor**, its **angle (A)**, as well as the distance of each line from its starting point (**D1** and **D2**) will be displayed on the **Info** palette.*

| Navigator | Info | ▶ |

K :   ∠ A : 59.6°
           D1 : 0.365
           D2 : 0.273

+, X : 0.724   ⌐ W :
  Y : 0.902   H :

To use the Measure tool:

1. Choose the Measure tool (U).

2. Drag on the image **1**. The angle (A) and distance (D) of the measure line will be displayed on the Info palette **2**. Hold down Shift while dragging to constrain the angle to a multiple of 45°.

3. *Optional:* After dragging with the Measure tool, Alt-drag/Option-drag from either end of the line to create a protractor **3**. The angle formed by the two lines will display on the Info palette **4**. You can readjust the angle at any time by dragging either end of the line.

4. Choose another tool when you're finished using the Measure tool. If you reselect it, the measure line will redisplay. To remove a measure line, drag it off the image using the Measure tool.

TIP You can drag a measure line or protractor to another area of the image using the Measure tool. Drag any part of the line except an endpoint.

Measure Tool

The Rubber Stamp tool is used to clone imagery from one layer to another within the same image or to clone imagery from one image to another.

To clone areas in the same image:

1. Choose the Rubber Stamp tool (S or Shift S). 🖋️

2. On the Rubber Stamp Options palette:

    Choose a blending mode.
    and
    Choose an Opacity percentage.

    Then:
    Check the Aligned box if you want to create a single, uninterrupted clone from the same source point. You can release the mouse and drag in another area, or even switch modes or brushes between strokes **1**–**2**.
    or
    Uncheck the Aligned box if you want to create repetitive clones from the same source point. The crosshair pointer will return to the same source point each time you release the mouse **3**.

3. Check the Use All Layers box on the Options palette to sample pixels from all currently visible layers that you Alt-click/ Option-click over. Uncheck Use All Layers to sample pixels from only the current layer.

4. Click a small tip on the Brushes palette to clone a small detail or a medium- to large-size brush to clone larger areas.

5. Activate the layer from which you want to clone.

6. In the image window, Alt-click/Option-click on the area of the layer you want to clone from to establish a source point. Don't click on a transparent part of a layer—nothing will be cloned.

7. On the same layer, drag the mouse back and forth where you want the clone to appear.
    or
    Choose or create another layer, then drag the mouse. Two pointers will

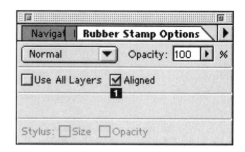

2 *Drag the mouse where you want the clone to appear. To produce this illustration, the **Aligned** option was turned on for the Rubber Stamp tool.*

3 *Uncheck the **Aligned** option for the Rubber Stamp tool to create multiple clones from the same source point.*

1 *An* **opacity** *of 50% was chosen for the Rubber Stamp tool to create this double exposure effect.*

2 *Select an area of an image, then choose Edit menu > **Define Pattern**.*

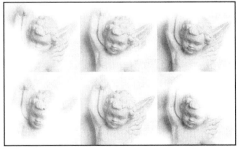

3 *The pattern is then applied in another image using various opacities for the **Pattern Stamp** tool.*

appear on the screen: A crosshair pointer over the source point and a Rubber Stamp pointer (or Brush Size pointer) where you drag the mouse. Imagery from the source point will appear where the mouse is dragged, and it will replace any underlying pixels.

Note: If the Preserve Transparency box is checked on the Layers palette, the cloned imagery will only appear where existing pixels are on that layer.

8. *Optional:* To establish a new source point from which to clone, Alt-click/ Option-click on a different area of the source image.

TIP You can change the Option palette settings for the Rubber Stamp tool between strokes. To create a "double exposure" effect, choose a low Opacity percentage so the underlying pixels will partially show through the cloned pixels **1**.

TIP To paint areas from earlier stages of a current editing session, use the History Brush tool. (This replaces the Rubber Stamp tool's From Saved option.)

To use the Pattern Stamp tool:

1. Choose the Rectangular Marquee tool, then select an area of an image that you want to become the pattern tile **2**.

2. Choose Edit menu > Define Pattern.

3. Deselect (Ctrl-D/⌘-D).

4. Choose the Pattern Stamp tool.

5. On the Pattern Stamp Options palette, check the Aligned box to stamp pattern tiles in a perfect grid, regardless of how many separate strokes you use. Uncheck this option if you don't want the tiles to align.

6. Drag on a layer in the same image or another image to stamp the pattern **3**. No source point is required for this tool.

TIP Right-click/Control-click on the image to choose a blending mode for the Pattern Stamp.

To clone from image to image:

1. Open two images, and position the two windows side by side.

2. If both images are color, choose the same image mode for both. You can also clone between a color image and a grayscale image. *Note:* Choose the Don't Flatten option to preserve layers.

3. Choose the Rubber Stamp tool (S or Shift S). ♨

4. On the Rubber Stamp Options palette, check the Aligned box to reproduce a continuous area from the source point or uncheck the Aligned box to produce multiple clones from the source point **1**. *and*
Choose an Opacity. *and*
Choose a blending mode.

5. Click a tip on the Brushes palette.

6. Click on the image where the clone is to appear, and choose a layer for the clone.

7. Alt-click/Option-click on the area of the source (non-active) image from which you want to clone **2**.

8. Drag back and forth on the destination (active) image to make the clone appear.

TIP To create a brushstroke version of an image, clone to a new document with a white or solid-colored background **3**.

TIP Use the image-to-image clone method to brush one image onto another. You could also duplicate an image, add brushstrokes or apply filters, and then clone the changed areas back onto the original image.

(Rubber Stamp Options palette)

Navigat | **Rubber Stamp Options** ▶

Normal ▼ Opacity: 100 ▶ %

☐ Use All Layers ☑ Aligned
1

Stylus: ☐ Size ☐ Opacity

Source image.

rock horse.gr drk clone @ 100%

Destination image.

100% (Black)

2 *Alt-click/Option-click on the **non-active** image to establish a **source** point, then drag back and forth in short strokes on the **active** (destination) image to make the **clone** appear.*

3 *To create this effect, an image was cloned to a new document with a white background.*

Physique Medley, David Humphrey. *To produce this image, Humphrey composited scanned embroidery and his own charcoal drawings and photographs, among other things. He adjusted luminosity levels of the various components on individual layers using blending modes (Darken, Multiply) and the Eraser and Burn tools.*

1 *The original image, with a **feathered** selection.*

2 *After inversing the selection and pressing Delete.*

Apply the Feather command to fade the edge of a selection a specified number of pixels inward and outward from the marquee. A feather radius of 5, for example, would create a feather area 10 pixels wide.

Note: The feather won't be visible until the selection is modified with a painting tool, copied/pasted, moved, or filled, or a filter or Image menu command is applied to it.

To feather a selection:

1. Choose Select menu > Feather (Ctrl-Alt-D/⌘-Option-D).

2. Enter a number up to 250 in the Feather Radius field. The width of the feather is affected by the image resolution. A high resolution image will require a wider feather radius.

3. Click OK (Enter/Return) **1**–**2**. *Note:* If the feather radius is too wide, the message "No pixels are more than 50% selected" will appear.

TIP To specify a feather radius for a selection before it's created, choose a Marquee or Lasso tool and enter a number in the

To eliminate a noticeable seam after pasting or moving layer pixels, use the Defringe command. It recolors pixels on the edge of the selection with pixel colors from just inside the edge within a specified radius.

Note: If the moved selection or pasted imagery was originally on a black background and was anti-aliased, you can choose Select menu > Matting > Remove Black Matte command to remove unwanted remnants from the black background. Choose Select menu > Matting > Remove White Matte command if the imagery was originally on a white background.

To defringe a layer:

1. With the paste layer chosen, choose Layer menu > Matting > Defringe.
2. Enter a Width for the Defringe area **1**. Try a low number first (1, 2, or 3) so your edges don't lose definition. Some non-edge areas may also be affected.
3. Click OK (Enter/Return).

The Smooth command adds unselected pixels to, or removes unselected pixels from, a selection from within a specified radius.

To smooth a selection edge:

1. Choose Select menu > Modify > Smooth.
2. Enter a Sample Radius value between 1 and 16 **2**. The larger the Sample Radius, the more unselected pixels will be added to or removed from the selection.
3. Click OK (Enter/Return) **3**–**4**.

3 *The original Magic Wand tool selection.*

4 *After applying the Smooth command, Sample Radius of 3.*

LAYERS 7

Chapter topics

Create a new layer
Turn a selection into a layer
Hide or show a layer
Duplicate a layer
Flip a layer
Transform a layer
Convert the Background into a layer
Create a Background for an image
Preserve Transparency
Restack a layer
Move a layer
Save a copy of a layer in a separate file
Delete a layer
Drag-and-drop/copy a layer to another image
Merge layers
Flatten layers

For additional layer topics, see Chapter 13

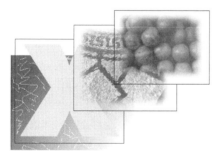

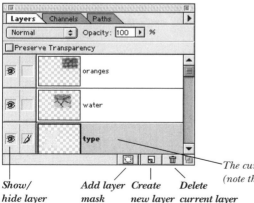

Show/ hide layer *Add layer mask* *Create new layer* *Delete current layer*

*The currently **active** layer (note the brush icon).*

LAYERS ARE LIKE clear acetate sheets: opaque where there is imagery and transparent where there is no imagery. To each layer, you can assign a different opacity and mode to control how that layer blends with the layers below it. You can change the stacking order of layers, and you can also assign a layer mask to any layer.

If you choose Contents: White or Background Color for a new image, the bottommost area of the image will be the Background, which is not a layer. If you choose Contents: Transparent, the bottommost component of the image will be a layer. Other layers can be added to an image at any time. Only one layer can be edited at a time, which means you can easily modify one part of an image without disturbing the other layers.

Layers are listed on the Layers palette from topmost to bottommost, with the Background, of course, at the bottom of the list. The layer that is currently highlighted on the palette is the only layer that can be edited. Click on a layer name to make it the active layer. The active layer name (or the Background) is listed on the image window title bar.

If you've already learned how to paste a selection or create type, you know that both operations create a new layer automatically. And in Chapter 9, you'll learn about a special variety of layers called adjustment layers, which are used to preview color adjustment effects on underlying layers. Meanwhile, if you want to learn the layer basics, such as how to deliberately add layers to an image, start with the instructions on the next page.

Layers

Important notes: Only the Photoshop file format supports multiple layers and the option to create a transparent bottommost layer. If you save your image in any other file format via the Save a Copy command, all the layers will be flattened, and any transparency in the bottommost layer will become opaque white. If you change image modes (e.g., from RGB to CMYK), click Don't Flatten if you want to preserve layers.

An image can contain as many layers as available memory and storage allow, but since the pixel (non-transparent) areas on a layer occupy storage space, when your image is finished, you can merge two or more layers together or flatten all the layers into one to reduce the file's storage size **1**.

To create a new layer:

1. To create a layer with 100% opacity and Normal mode, click the Create new layer button at the bottom of the Layers palette **2** and skip the remaining steps.
or
To choose options for the new layer when it's created, choose New Layer from the Layers palette command menu or Alt-click/Option-click the Create new layer button at the bottom of the palette **2**, then follow the remaining steps.

2. *Do any of the following optional steps:*

Enter a new name for the layer in the Name field **3**.

Choose a different opacity or blending mode (either one can be changed later).

Click the Group With Previous Layer box to make the new layer a part of a clipping group (see page 197).

3. Click OK (Enter/Return). The new layer will appear directly above the previously active layer.

TIP To improve Photoshop's performance, choose Palette Options from the Layers palette command menu, then click the smallest thumbnail size **4**.

1 *Before adding a new layer to your image, choose* **Document Sizes** *from the Status bar drop-down menu and note the current image size.*

The second figure is the amount of **RAM** *the layered, unflattened file is using. Note how much the file's storage size increases when you add pixels to a new layer. The image in this illustration contains three layers.*

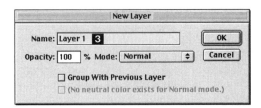

2 Create new layer

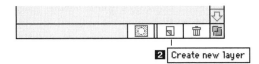

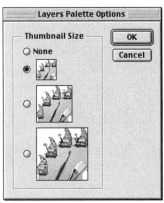

4 *Click a different* **Thumbnail Size** *or turn off thumbnail display altogether (None) in the* **Layers Palette Options** *dialog box.*

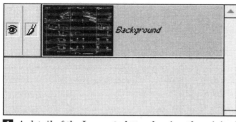

1 *A detail of the Layers palette, showing the original Background.*

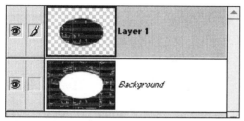

2 *After choosing the **Layer Via Cut**, a selection is cut from the Background and placed on its **own layer**.*

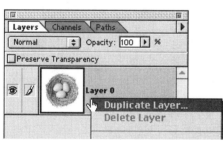

3 *Right-click/Control-click, then choose **Duplicate Layer** from the context menu.*

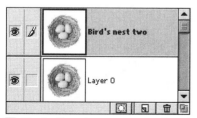

4 *The **duplicate** layer appears on the palette.*

To turn a selection into a layer:

1. Create a selection.

2. To place a copy of the selected pixels on a new layer and leave the original layer untouched, choose Layer menu > New > Layer Via Copy (Ctrl-J/⌘-J).

or

To place the selected pixels on a new layer and remove them from the original layer, choose Layer menu > New > Layer Via Cut (Ctrl-Shift-J/⌘-Shift-J) **1**–**2**.

3. *Optional:* Click the eye icon for the original layer to temporarily hide it from view.

To duplicate a layer in the same image:

To create a new layer without naming it, drag the name of the layer that you want to duplicate over the Create new layer button at the bottom of the Layers palette. The duplicate layer will appear above the original layer, and it will be the active layer.

or

To name the duplicate as you create it, Right-click/Control-click the name of the layer that you want to duplicate or Alt-drag/Option-drag the layer over the Create new layer button. Type a name for the duplicate layer, then click OK (Enter/Return) **3**–**4**.

You can hide layers you're not currently working on if you find them distracting, or to improve performance.

Note: A hidden layer, if made active, *can* be edited, but only currently visible layers can be merged or printed. When layers are flattened, hidden layers are discarded.

To hide or show layers:

Click the eye icon on the Layers palette for any individual layer you want to hide **1**–**3**. Click in the eye column again to redisplay the layer.

or

Drag in the eye column to hide or show multiple layers.

or

Alt-click/Option-click an eye icon to hide all other layers except the one you click on. Alt-click/Option-click again to redisplay all the layers.

or

Right-click/Control-click in the eye column and choose "Show/Hide all other layers" from the context menu **4**.

To flip a layer:

1. On the Layers palette, activate the layer that you want to flip. Any layers that are linked to the active layer will also flip. Only pixels will flip—not transparent areas.

2. Choose Edit menu > Transform > Flip Horizontal **5** or Flip Vertical.

*Click the eye icon to **hide** a layer. Click again to **redisplay** it.*

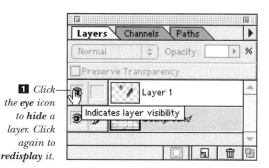

2 *Layer 1 **hidden**.*

3 *Layer 1 redisplayed.*

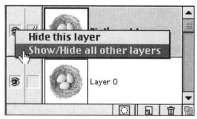

4 *Choose a command from a **context** menu.*

5 *Layer 1 **flipped** horizontally.*

Scale

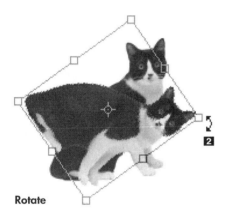

Rotate

Distort

To transform (scale, rotate, skew, distort, or apply perspective to) a layer by dragging:

1. On the Layers palette, activate the layer you want to transform. Any layers that are linked to the active layer will also transform. *Note:* You can also limit the transformation to only selected pixels on a layer. You can't transform a 16-bits/channel image.

2. Choose Edit menu > Transform > Scale, Rotate, Skew, Distort, or Perspective. A bounding border will appear.
or
Right-click/Control-click on the image and choose a command from the context menu.

Note: If you want to perform multiple transformations, to save time and preserve image quality, after performing step 3 for the first command, choose and then perform additional transform commands, and then accept them all at once (step 4).

3. To **scale** the layer horizontally and vertically, drag a corner handle **1**. To scale only the horizontal or vertical dimension, drag a side handle. Hold down Shift while dragging to scale proportionately. Hold down Alt/Option to scale from the center of the layer.

To **rotate** the layer, position the pointer outside the bounding border (the pointer will become a double-headed arrow), then drag in a circular direction **2**. Hold down Shift while dragging to constrain the rotation to a multiple of 15°.

To **skew** the layer, drag a corner handle to reposition just that handle or drag a side handle to skew along the current horizontal or vertical axis. Hold down Alt/Option while dragging to skew symmetrically from the center of the layer.

To **distort** the layer **3**, drag a corner handle to freely reposition just that

(Continued on the following page)

Transform a Layer

107

handle or drag a side handle to distort the side of the bounding border along the horizontal and/or vertical axis. Alt-drag/Option-drag to distort symmetrically from the center of the layer. Distort can be more drastic than Skew.

To apply **perspective** to the layer, drag a corner handle along the horizontal or vertical axis to create one-point perspective along that axis **4**–**5**. The adjacent corner will move in unison. Or drag a side handle to skew along the current horizontal or vertical axis.

4. To accept the transformation(s), double-click inside the bounding border.
or
Press Enter/Return.

TIP To cancel the entire transformation, press Esc. To undo the last handle modification, choose Edit menu > Undo.

TIP Position the cursor inside the bounding border to move the layer image.

Once you're acquainted with the individual Transform commands, you'll probably want to start using the Free Transform command, especially if you want to perform a series of transformations. With Free Transform, the various commands are accessed using keyboard shortcuts—you don't have to choose each command individually from a menu. And image data is resampled only once: when you accept the changes.

To free transform:

Follow the instructions starting on the previous page, but for step 2, choose Edit menu > Free Transform (Ctrl-T/⌘-T), and for step 3, the instructions are the same, with these exceptions:

To **Skew**, Ctrl-Shift-drag/⌘-Shift-drag.

To **Distort**, Ctrl-drag/⌘-drag. To distort from the center, Alt-drag/Option-drag.

To apply **Perspective**, Ctrl-Alt-Shift-drag/ ⌘-Option-Shift-drag a corner handle.

4 *The original image.*

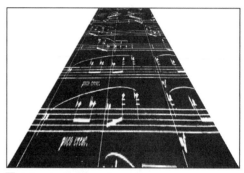

5 *A **perspective** transformation.*

General information

Choose an **interpolation method** for the transform commands in File menu > Preferences > General (Ctrl-K/⌘-K). Bicubic (Better)—the slowest method—causes the least degradation to the image.

To **repeat** the last transformation, choose Edit menu > Transform > Again (Ctrl-Shift-T/⌘-Shift-T).

To transform a **duplicate** of a selection, hold down Alt/Option as you choose the command or use this shortcut: Ctrl-Alt-T/⌘-Option-T.

You can move the **center point** from which transformations are calculated—even outside the area you're transforming.

You can transform an **alpha channel**, a **selection** (see also page 84), a **path** (see also page 217), a **layer**, or an unlinked, active **layer mask**.

What's left?

If you transform a layer (or a selection on a layer), any empty space remaining after the transformation will be replaced by layer transparency. If you transform a selection on the Background, any empty space will be filled with the current Background color.

The transformation will automatically occur from the center of the layer image.

TIP When you transform, the Info palette shows the change in width (W), height (H), angle of rotation (A), and horizontal skew (H) or vertical skew (V).

Use Numeric Transform if you'd rather transform a layer by entering exact numeric values than by dragging the mouse.

To transform a layer by entering numeric values:

1. On the Layers palette, activate the layer that you want to transform. Any layers that are linked to it will also transform.

2. Choose Edit menu > Transform > Numeric or Right-click/Control-click on the image and choose Numeric Transform.

3. Do any of the following:

   Uncheck the check box for any transformation that you don't want to perform.

   To **move** the layer, enter *x* and *y* Position values **1**. Choose units for those values from the drop-down menu. Leave the Relative box checked to move the layer relative its former location. Uncheck the Relative box to position the layer relative to the upper-left corner of the image.

   To **scale** the layer, enter Width and/or Height values **2**. Choose units for those values from the drop-down menu. Check the Constrain Proportions box to maintain the current width-to-height ratio.

   To **skew** the layer, enter degree values (the amount of slant) in the Horizontal and/or Vertical Skew fields **3**.

   To **rotate** the layer, enter an Angle or move the dial in the circle **4**.

4. Click OK (Enter/Return).

TIP If you use the Measure tool to define an angle, that angle will appear in the Angle field in the Numeric Transform dialog box and the Rotate Canvas dialog box.

Transform using Numeric Values

The standard things that you can do to a layer—move it upward or downward in the layer stack, choose a blending mode or opacity for it, or create a layer mask for it—can't be done to the Background—unless you first convert it into a layer.

To convert the Background into a layer:

1. Double-click Background on the Layers palette **1**.

2. Type a new name **2**, and choose a blending mode and opacity for the layer.

3. Click OK (Enter/Return) **3**.

TIP If you move the Background using the Move tool, it will turn into a layer automatically.

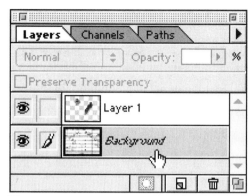

1 *Double-click the Background.*

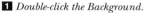

2

3 *The former Background is now a **layer**.*

Let's say you've converted the Background into a layer so you could move it upward in the layer stack or for some other purpose, but now you want a flat-color Background. In other words, your image doesn't have a Background and you'd like to create one.

To create a Background for an image:

1. Choose a Background color.

2. Choose Layer menu > New > Background. The Background will, of course, appear at the bottom of the layer stack.

Back we go

After turning the Background into a layer, you change your mind and you want to make it the Background again. Create a new Background for the image, and make sure the former Background is just above the new Background. Then choose Merge Down from the Layers palette command menu.

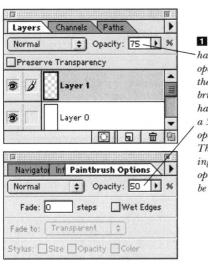

1 *Layer 1 has a 75% opacity and the Paintbrush **tool** has a 50% opacity: The resulting stroke opacity will be 37%.*

2 *Recoloring a rendered type layer with **Preserve Transparency** on.*

Tools and layers

You can use any painting or editing tool to edit pixels on the currently active layer, but keep in mind that in addition to the Options palette blending mode and opacity settings for each **tool**, a tool's effect will also be controlled by the blending mode and opacity of the currently active **layer 1**. For example, if a layer has a 60% opacity, a painting or editing tool with an opacity of 100% will work at a maximum opacity of 60% on that layer, and even less if the tool's opacity is below 100%.

Preserve transparency

With the **Preserve Transparency** box checked on the Layers palette, only **existing** pixels on a layer can be edited or recolored **2**; blank areas will remain transparent. Turn this option off if you want to **add** new pixels. Preserve Transparency can be turned on or off for individual layers.

Note: Preserve Transparency is in a fixed "on" position for a non-rendered type layer. It can be turned on or off for a rendered type layer.

TIP Press / to toggle Preserve Transparency on or off.

You can change the size or color of the checkerboard pattern that is used to indicate transparent areas on a layer or turn off the checkerboard pattern altogether in File menu > Preferences > Transparency & Gamut (Ctrl-K/⌘-K, then Ctrl-4/⌘-4).

Use all layers

With the **Use All Layers** box checked on its Options palette, the Rubber Stamp, Blur, Sharpen, Smudge, Paint Bucket, and Magic Wand tool will sample pixels from all the currently visible layers, though pixels will only be altered on the currently active layer.

Image mode changes

Click **Don't Flatten** to preserve layers in a multi-layered image as you change its color mode.

To restack a layer:

1. On the Layers palette, click the name of the layer that you want to restack.

2. Drag the layer name up or down on the palette, and release the mouse when a dark horizontal line appears where you want the layer to end up **1**–**2**.

TIP You can also restack an active layer by choosing Layer menu > Arrange > Bring to Front, Bring Forward, Send Backward, or Send to Back. A layer cannot be placed below the Background.

TIP To move the Background upward on the list, it must first be converted into a layer. See page 110.

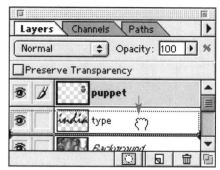

1 *Dragging the "Puppet" layer downward.*

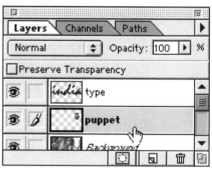

2 *The "Puppet" layer is in a new position in the stack.*

Restacking shortcuts

WINDOWS

Bring Forward Ctrl]

Bring to Front Ctrl Shift]

Send Backward Ctrl [

Send to Back Ctrl Shift [

MACINTOSH

Bring Forward ⌘]

Bring to Front ⌘ Shift]

Send Backward ⌘ [

Send to Back ⌘ Shift [

Restack a Layer

1 *The original image.*

2 *After **moving** the "cow toy" layer with the **Move** tool.*

3 ***Right-click/Control-click*** *in the image window with the **Move** tool to choose a different layer name from a context menu.*

To move multiple layers at one time, see page 198.

To move a layer:

1. On the Layers palette, click the name of the layer that you want to move.

2. Choose the Move tool (V) ⊹ or hold down Ctrl/⌘.

3. Drag in the image window. The entire layer will move **1**–**2**. *Note:* If you move the Background, it will become Layer 0, and the exposed area will become transparent.

TIP Press an arrow key to move an active layer one pixel at a time. Press Shift-arrow to move a layer 10 screen pixels at a time.

TIP If pixels are moved beyond the edge of the image, don't worry—they'll be saved with the image.

Using the Move tool

■ With the Move tool selected, you can also Right-click/Control-click in the image window and choose a different layer name from a context menu **3**. Or Ctrl-right-click/⌘-Control-click with any other tool selected. Only layers that contain pixels under the pointer will be listed.

■ *Macintosh:* With the Move tool selected, you can ⌘-click on an object in the image window to quickly activate that object's layer. ⌘-Option-Control-click with any other tool selected.

■ For faster previewing when using the Move tool, check the **Pixel Doubling** box on the Move Options palette. Pixels will temporarily double in size while you drag (they'll be half their normal resolution).

■ Check the **Auto Select Layer** box to move pixels on the uppermost layer under the pointer that contains pixels—which is not necessarily the currently active layer.

Move Layer; Using the Move Tool

Use the following technique to save an individual layer in a new document or in an existing, open document. You might want to do this before you perform an operation that requires flattening, such as converting to Indexed Color mode (which does not support multiple layers) or saving your document in a file format other than Photoshop if you need to preserve only one or two individual layers.

To save a copy of a layer in a separate file:

1. Activate the layer that you want to save a copy of.

2. Right-click/Control-click that layer, and choose Duplicate Layer from the context menu.

3. Choose Destination Document: New 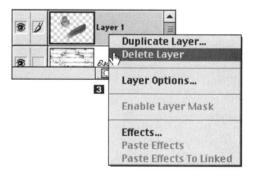.

4. Enter a name for the new document in the As field.

5. Click OK (Enter/Return), and save the new document.

To delete a layer:

On the Layers palette, click the name of the layer you want to delete. Then click the trash button and click Yes or Alt-click/Option-click the trash button **2**–**4**.
or
Right-click/Control-click the name of the layer you want to delete, then choose Delete Layer from the context menu.

TIP Change your mind? No problem. Choose Edit menu > Undo or click a prior state on the History palette.

2 *The original image.*

4 *After **deleting** Layer 1.*

1 *Choose a layer, then drag the layer name into the destination image window.*

2 *The destination image after dragging the "baby" layer name onto the image.*

PHOTOS: ELAINE WEINMANN

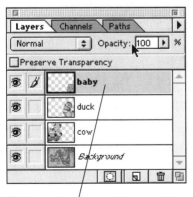

3 *The new layer name appears on the Layers palette for the destination image.*

The method you use to copy a layer (or linked layers) to another image depends on how much of the layer(s) you want to copy. The quickest way to copy a layer to another image is by dragging its name from the Layers palette to the destination image window. With this method, any areas that extend beyond the edge of the image boundary will also move. Use the method on the next page if you want to trim the layer as you copy it. To copy linked layers, you can't use the method on this page; use the method described on the next page instead.

To drag-and-drop a layer to another image (Layers palette):

1. Open the image that contains the layer that you want to move and the image the layer is to be placed into (the "destination image"), and make sure the two windows don't completely overlap.

2. Click in the source image window.

3. Click on the name of the layer you want to move on the Layers palette **1**. Any tool can be selected.

4. Drag the layer name from the Layers palette into the destination image window. Hold down Shift to place the layer in the center of the destination image. Release the mouse when the darkened border is where you want the layer to appear. It will be stacked above the previously active layer in the destination image **2**–**3**.

TIP If the dimensions of the layer being moved are larger than those of the destination image, the moved layer will extend beyond the edges of the destination image window. Use the Move tool to move the layer in the image window. The hidden parts will save with the image.

Drag-and-Drop a Layer

This is one of several methods that can be used to copy a single layer to another image. It is the only method that will work for copying linked layers to another image.

To drag-and-drop a layer to another image (Move tool):

1. Open the image that contains the layer that you want to move (the "source" image) and the image to which the layer is to be moved (the "destination" image).

2. On the Layers palette, click the name of the layer that you want to copy. (To move multiple layers, link them first. See page 198.)

3. *Optional:* Click in the destination image window, then click on the name of the layer on the Layers palette above which you want the added layer to appear.

4. Choose the Move tool (V). ⤴

5. Click in the source image window. Drag the active layer(s) from the current image window into the destination image window **1**. The new layer(s) will be positioned where you release the mouse, above the currently active layer **2**.

6. *Optional:* Use the Move tool ⤴ to move the layer in the destination image window.

7. *Optional:* Restack the new layer or layers (drag them upward or downward).

TIP To copy a layer into the center of another image, start dragging the layer, hold down Shift, then continue to drag. If the two images have the same pixel count, the moved layer will be positioned in the exact *x/y* location as it was in the source image.

Getting to a layer

Choose the Move tool, position the pointer over a layer in the image window, Right-click/Control-click to view a menu of layers that are directly below the cursor, then choose a layer from the menu. With any other tool selected, Ctrl-right-click/⌃⌘-Control-click.

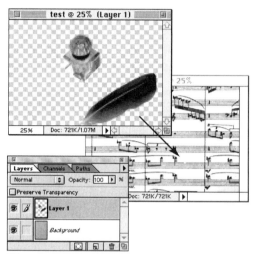

1 *Drag the current layer from the **source image window** into the **destination image window**.*

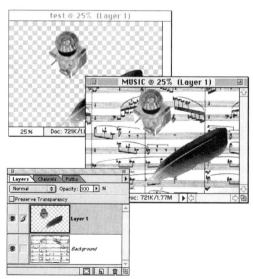

2 *The new layer appears in the **destination** image.*

Not so simple

Bear in mind, when you copy-and-paste or drag-and-drop between images, that the size of the layer imagery may look different in its new location, because it is rendered in the resolution of the destination image. If the resolution of the destination image is higher than that of the source image, the layer will become smaller when it's pasted or dropped. Conversely, if the resolution of the destination image is lower than that of source image, the layer will become larger when it's pasted or dropped. You can use Image menu > Image Size to choose the same resolution (and dimensions, if desired) for both images.

Use this copy and paste method if you want to copy only the visible portion of a layer (when displayed at 100% view) and *not* copy any pixels that may extend beyond the layer's edge.

To copy and paste only the visible part of a layer to another image:

1. On the Layers palette, activate the layer that you want to copy.

2. Choose Select menu > All (Ctrl-A/⌘-A). Any areas that extend beyond the edge of the image won't be selected.

3. Choose Edit menu > Copy (Ctrl-C/⌘-C).

4. Click in the destination image window.

5. Choose Edit menu > Paste (Ctrl-V/⌘-V). A new layer will be created for the pasted pixels, and it can be restacked, like any other layer, using the Layers palette.

6. Click back in the original image window, then choose Select menu > Deselect (Ctrl-D/⌘-D) to deactivate the selection.

Merge or flatten

Layers increase an image's file size, so when you've completely finished editing your image, consider merging or flattening it to conserve storage space. Learn the difference between the merge and flatten commands before you choose which one to use.

Note: Only the Photoshop file format supports multiple layers. To save your image in any other file format, multiple layers must be flattened down to one. To reserve the layered version for future editing, flatten a copy of it using File menu > Save a Copy. The layered version will remain open.

To merge two layers:

1. Activate the topmost layer of the two layers that you want to merge.

2. Choose Merge Down (Ctrl-E/⌘-E) from the Layers palette command menu. The active layer will merge into the layer directly below it.

The Merge Visible command merges all the currently visible layers into the bottommost displayed layer and **preserves** hidden layers.

To merge multiple layers:

1. Display only the layers that you want to merge (all should have eye icons on the Layers palette) and hide the layers that you *don't* want to merge. They don't have to be consecutive. Hide the Background if you don't want to merge layers into it.

2. Click on one of the layers to be merged (not on an editable type layer or an adjustment layer).

3. Choose Merge Visible (Ctrl-Shift-E/⌘-Shift-E) from the Layers palette menu.

The Flatten Image command merges currently displayed layers into the bottommost displayed layer and **discards** hidden layers.

To flatten layers:

1. Make sure all the layers you want to flatten are visible (have eye icons).

2. Choose Flatten Image from the Layers palette command menu **1**–**2**, then click OK (Enter/Return). Any transparent areas in the bottommost layer will turn white.

Other merge commands

■ To merge a **copy** of all the currently visible layers into the bottommost visible layer (it can be a new layer), hold down Alt/Option and choose **Merge Visible** from the Layer menu or the Layers palette command menu.

■ To merge linked layers, choose **Merge Linked** from the Layers palette command menu or the Layer menu. The Merge Linked command **discards** hidden, linked layers.

■ To merge layers in a clipping group, activate the underlined layer, then choose **Merge Group** from the Layers palette command menu or the Layer menu. The Merge Group command **discards** hidden grouped layers.

Merge Layers; Flatten Layers

2 *The Layers palette for the* **merged** *or* **flattened** *image.*

HISTORY 8

IN THIS CHAPTER you'll learn how to use the History palette to selectively undo up to 99 previous stages of an image-editing session, called states. You'll also learn how to restore selective areas to a prior state using the History Brush tool, by filling a selection with a history state, or by erasing to a history state.

The History palette displays a list of the most recent states that were applied to an image, with the bottommost being the most recent. Clicking on a prior state restores the image to that stage of the editing process. What happens to the image when you do this depends on whether the palette is in linear or non-linear mode, so it's essential to learn the difference between the two.

Linear versus non-linear mode

There are two ways in which the History palette can be used: Linear mode or Non-Linear mode. This option is turned on/off via the Allow Non-Linear History box in the History Options dialog box (choose History Options from the palette command menu). You can switch between these two modes at any time during an editing session.

In **linear** mode, if you click back on an earlier state and resume image-editing from that state or delete it, all subsequent (dimmed) states will be deleted **1**.

In the History palette's **non-linear** mode, if you click back on or delete an earlier state, subsequent states won't be deleted (or dimmed). If you then resume image-editing while that earlier state is selected, the new edits will show up as the latest states on the palette and earlier states will be preserved. If you delete an earlier state and then click on the latest state, the deleted edits will still appear in the actual image. So non-linear is the more flexible mode.

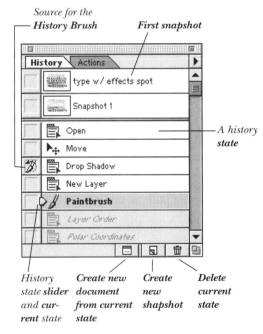

Source for the
History Brush   First snapshot

                                                    A history
                                                    state

History   Create new   Create   Delete
state **slider**   document   new   current
and **cur-**   from current snapshot   state
rent state   state

1 *The History palette in linear mode. Note that some steps are grayed out. The illustration on the following page shows the palette in non-linear mode.*

Linear versus Non-Linear Mode

When would you want to work in non-linear mode? 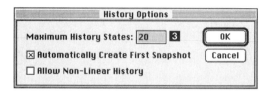 When you need flexibility. Let's say you apply paint strokes to a layer, try out different blending modes for that layer, and then settle on a mode that you like. If you want to reduce the number of states on the palette, you can then delete any of the other blending mode states, whether they're before or after the one you settled on. You can pick and choose.

When would you want to work in linear mode? If you find non-linear mode confusing or disorganized or if you want the option to revert back to an earlier state with a nice, clean break.

Other history options

To specify the number of states that can be listed on the palette for an editing session, choose History Options from the palette command menu, then enter a number (1–100) in the **Maximum History States** field **3**. If you exceed that maximum during an editing session, earlier steps will automatically be **removed** to make room for the new ones. *Note:* The maximum number of states may be limited by various factors, including the image size, the kind of edits that are made to the image, and currently available memory. Each open image keeps its own list of states.

To have a snapshot be created at the beginning of every new editing session, check the **Automatically Create First Snapshot** box.

Clearing the palette

If you close an image or choose File menu > Revert, all the history states for that image will be removed from the palette. To preserve history states as you restore an image, instead of using Revert, put the History palette into non-linear mode, then click on the First Snapshot thumbnail at the top of the palette.

To deliberately clear the History palette for all currently open images to free up memory, choose Edit menu > Purge > Histories. To clear the History palette for the current

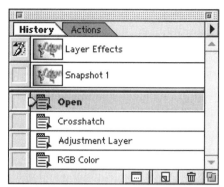

2 *The* **History** *palette in* **non-linear** *mode.*

(History Options dialog box with: Maximum History States: 20, Automatically Create First Snapshot checked, Allow Non-Linear History unchecked, OK and Cancel buttons)

History Options: Clearing the Palette

History shortcuts

Step Forward   Ctrl-Shift-Z/⌘-Shift-Z

Step Backward   Ctrl-Alt-Z/⌘-Option-Z

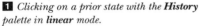

1 *Clicking on a prior state with the History palette in linear mode.*

2 *Clicking on a prior state with the History palette in non-linear mode.*

document only, choose Clear History from the palette command menu. The Purge *can't* be undone; Clear History *can* be undone.

To revert to a prior history state:

1. Choose Window > Show menu History.

2. Click on a prior state **1**–**2**.
or
Drag the slider on the left side of the palette to the desired state.
or
Choose Step Forward or Step Backward from the palette command menu (see the shortcuts at left).

Note: If the palette is in linear mode (Allow Non-Linear History is turned off), the states below the one you clicked on will be dimmed. If you delete the state you clicked on or edit the image at that state, all the dimmed states will be deleted. If you change your mind, choose Undo immediately to restore them. If the palette is in non-linear mode, you can restore the document to the latest stage of editing by clicking on the bottommost state.

To duplicate a state:

1. Turn on Allow Non-Linear History.

2. Alt-click/Option-click a state. The duplicate will become the latest state.

Note: If the Allow Non-Linear History option is on and you delete a state, **only** that state will be deleted. If this option is off and you delete a state, **all** subsequent states will be deleted along with it. You can choose Edit menu > Undo to restore them.

To delete a state:

Drag the name of the state that you want to delete over the trash button on the History palette.

TIP Keep Alt-clicking/Option-clicking the trash button to delete a series of states from the current state backward.

A snapshot is like a copy of a history state, with one major difference: unlike a state, a snapshot will stay on the palette even if the state from which it was created is deleted because the maximum number of history states is reached or the palette is cleared or purged. It's a good idea to create a snapshot before performing a long series of editing steps or running an action on an image.

Note: All snapshots are deleted when an image is closed.

To create a snapshot of a history state:

1. With the History palette in non-linear mode, click on the state that you want to create a snapshot of **1**.

2. To create a snapshot without naming it or choosing options for it, click the Create new snapshot button **2** and skip the remaining steps.
or
To choose options for the snapshot as you create it, choose New Snapshot from the palette command menu; or Alt-click/Option-click the Create new snapshot button; or Right-click/Control-click the state and choose Create New Snapshot from the context menu.

3. Type a Name for the snapshot **3**.

4. Choose From: Full Document to make a snapshot of all the layers in the image at that state; or choose Merged Layers to create a snapshot that merges all layers in the image at that state; or choose Current Layer to make a snapshot of only the currently active layer at that state.

5. Click OK (Enter/Return). A thumbnail for the new snapshot will appear in the top portion of the palette **4**.

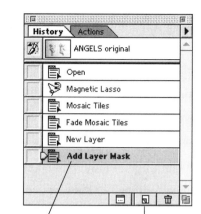

1 *First click a state on the History palette.*   **2** *Then click or Alt-click/ Option-click the* **Create new snapshot** *button.*

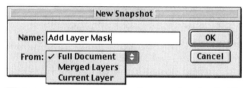

3 *Enter a* **name** *and choose* **layer** *options in the* **New Snapshot** *dialog box.*

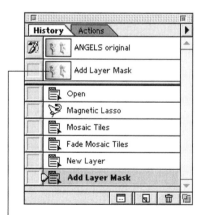

4 *A* **thumbnail** *for the new snapshot appears on the History palette.*

Create Snapshot

Power tip

To replace the contents of one image with a history state from another image, drag the state from the source document's history palette into the destination image window.

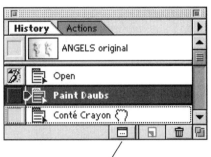

1 *Drag a snapshot or state over the* **Create new document from current state** *button.*

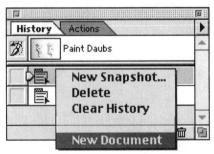

2 *Or* **Right-click/Control-click** *on the state that you want to duplicate and choose* **New Document** *from the context menu.*

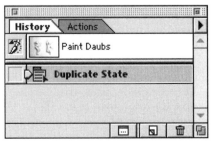

3 *A* **duplicate** *of the state is in a new document.*

To make a snapshot become the latest state:

Click a snapshot thumbnail. If the Allow Non-Linear History option is turned off and edits were made to the image since that snapshot was taken, the document will revert to that stage of editing and all the states will be grayed out. If you then resume editing, all dimmed states will be deleted. If Allow Non-Linear History is turned on, subsequent states will remain on the palette.
or
Alt-click/Option-click a snapshot thumbnail. The other states will remain available and that snapshot will become the latest state.

To delete a snapshot:

Click on the snapshot thumbnail, choose Delete from the palette command menu or click the Trash button, then click Yes.
or
Drag the snapshot to the Trash button.

If you turn a history snapshot or state into a new document, you'll have a sort of freeze insurance—something to fall back on in the event of a system or power failure. *Note:* Only one of a document's history states can be copied—not an entire list.

To create a new document from a history state or snapshot:

Drag a snapshot or a state over the Create new document from current state button **1**.
or
Click a snapshot or a state, then click on the Create new document from current state button.
or
Right-click/Control-click a snapshot or a state, then choose New Document from the context menu **2**.

A new image window will appear, bearing the title of the state from which it was created, and "Duplicate State" will be the name of the starting state for the new image **3**. Now save the new image!

You can select any snapshot or state on the History palette to use as a source of earlier pixel data for the History Brush. Dragging with the brush restores pixels from that prior state of editing. This replaces the Rubber Stamp's From Saved option.

Note: The History Brush can't be used on an image whose pixel count was changed since it was opened (it was resampled or cropped, its image mode or canvas size was changed, or layers were added to or deleted from it).

To use the History Brush:

1. Choose the History Brush tool. 🖌

2. Choose an opacity and a blending mode from the History Brush Options palette. *Optional:* Check the Impressionist box to restore pixels in "Impressionist" strokes.

3. Click a brush tip on the Brushes palette.

4. On the History palette, click in the box next to the state or snapshot that you want to use as a source for the History Brush.

5. Choose the layer on which you want to paint the restored pixels.

6. Draw strokes on the image. Pixel data from the prior state of that layer will replace the current pixel data where you draw strokes **1**–**2**.

   Note: If you add a new layer and you want to use the History Brush on that layer, you can only choose that "New Layer" state or a subsequent state as a source for the History Brush; you can't work from a state prior to New Layer.

TIP Here's an example of how the History brush could be used to restore an earlier stage of an image. You add brushstrokes to a layer and then decide several editing steps later that you want to remove them. Clicking on the state prior to brushstrokes state could cause other edits to be deleted. Instead, click in the box next to any state prior to the state in which the strokes were added to set the source for the History Brush, click on

1 *The original image.*

2 *After applying the Graphic Pen filter, positioning the **History Source** icon at a prior state, and then painting across parts of the image using the **History Brush** at 95% opacity.*

Snapshot as History Brush source

Modify a layer (apply an Adjust command, a filter, or paint strokes), take a snapshot of the current state, and then delete that state or choose Undo. Set the History Source icon to the snapshot, then stroke with the History Brush on the layer that you modified to selectively restore it.

the layer in the Layers palette to which the brush strokes were added, choose the History Brush tool, then paint out the added strokes.

TIP To paint pixel data from a later state onto an earlier state, click on an earlier state, and then choose a later state as the source for the History Brush. The new data will become the latest state.

2 *The original image.*

3 *We applied the Glass filter to a layer, selected the area around the tree, and then filled the selection with an earlier history state (Use: History). Try doing the same thing using the Distort > Wave or Ripple filter or an Artistic or Sketch filter.*

Note: The Fill with History command won't work if you have changed the image's pixel count (resampled or cropped the image, changed its image mode, or added or deleted a layer from it) since it was opened.

To fill a selection or a layer with a history state:

1. Choose a layer.

2. *Optional:* Create a selection.

3. On the History palette, choose the state that you want to use as a fill.

4. Choose Edit menu > Fill.

5. Choose Use: History **1**.

6. Choose an Opacity and a blending Mode.

7. Click OK (Enter/Return) **2**–**3**.

Fill with History

You can use the Eraser tool with its Erase to History option to restore pixels to the currently active state on the History palette. An advantage of using the Eraser is that in addition to choosing an opacity and mode for the tool, you can also choose a tool type (Paintbrush, Airbrush, Pencil, or Block).

Note: The Erase to History feature won't be available if you have changed the image's pixel count (resampled or cropped the image, changed its image mode, or added or deleted a layer from it) since it was opened.

To erase to history:

1. Choose the Eraser tool (E) ✐.

2. On the Eraser Options palette:

Choose a tool type from the drop-down menu.
and
Check the Erase to History box.
and
Choose an Opacity percentage.

3. *Optional:* Check the Wet Edges box to make the erasure stronger at the edges of the stroke. You can also enter a number of Fade steps to make the eraser stroke fade gradually.

4. Establish the History source by clicking the box next to a state or a snapshot on the History palette.

5. Choose a layer.

6. Drag in the image window.

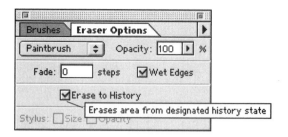

*A **snapshot** is made of the original image, and then the Rough Pastels filter is applied.*

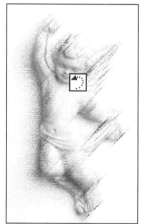

*Then the **Eraser** tool is used with its **Erase to History** option to restore the angel's face, belly, and toes from the snapshot.*

LIGHTS & DARKS 9

THIS **CHAPTER** covers many methods for adjusting an image's light and dark values. You can make simple adjustments, like invert a layer to make it look like a film negative, posterize it to restrict its luminosity levels to a specified number, or change all its pixels to black and white to make it high contrast. Or you can make more precise lightness or contrast adjustments to a layer's highlights, midtones, or shadows using such features as Levels or Curves. And you can darken smaller areas by hand using the Burn tool or lighten areas using the Dodge tool.

Note: All the commands discussed in this chapter can be applied to a color image, but we suggest you try applying them to a grayscale image first to learn how they work.

Adjustment basics

To apply any of the commands that are discussed in this chapter to a selected area of a layer rather than to an entire layer, create a **selection** before you choose the command.

In Windows, changes do not preview at all with the **Preview** box unchecked in an adjust dialog box; in Macintosh, changes preview on the entire screen with Preview unchecked. On both Windows and Mac, changes preview only in the image or in a selection with the Preview box checked. CMYK color displays more acccurately with Preview on.

To **reset** the settings in a dialog box, hold down Alt/Option and click the Reset button.

To reopen a dialog box with its **last used** settings, hold down Alt/Option while choosing the command or include Alt/Option in the keyboard shortcut for that command.

And finally, you can progressively reduce an adjust command's effect in increments using Filter menu > **Fade** (Ctrl-Shift-F/ ⌘-Shift-F)—it's not just for filters.

Adjustment Basics

Adjustment layer basics

Normally, the Adjust commands affect only the current layer or a selection on the current layer. You can also apply most Adjust submenu commands using a different method: via an adjustment layer. Unlike normal layers, the adjustment layer affects all the currently visible layers below it—not just the current layer. But the beauty of an adjustment layer is that it doesn't actually change pixels until it's merged with the layer below it (Ctrl-E/⌘-E), so you can use it to try out various effects.

To change settings for an adjustment layer, just double-click the adjustment layer name. If you're not happy with an adjustment layer effect, you can just trash it.

To create an adjustment layer:

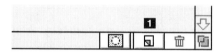

1. Activate the layer above which you want the adjustment layer to appear.

2. Ctrl-click/⌘-click the Create new layer button on the Layers palette **1**.
   or
   Choose New Adjustment Layer from the Layers palette command menu.

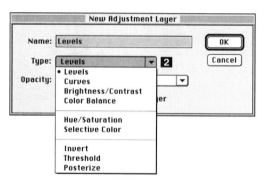

3. Choose an adjustment type from the Type drop down menu **2**.

4. *Optional:* Choose other layer options (opacity or mode) or rename the layer. You can change these options later on.

5. *Optional:* To limit the adjustment layer effect to just the layer directly below it, check the Group with Previous Layer box. (To do this to an existing adjustment layer, Alt-click/Option-click the line between them on the Layers palette.)

6. Click OK (Enter/Return).

7. Make the desired adjustments, then click OK **3**. To modify an existing adjustment layer, double-click the layer name.

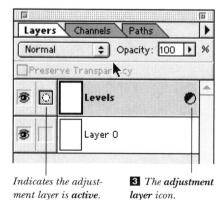

Indicates the adjust-
ment layer is **active**.

3 *The **adjustment layer** icon.*

Create Adjustment Layer

An adjustment layer is a special type of layer mask that is used to alter color and tonal characteristics in the layers below it, but those alterations don't permanently affect pixels in underlying layers until the adjustment layer is merged down. The adjustment layer is really a method for previewing color and tonal adjustments, and it's a great way to experiment with effects before committing to them.

To edit an adjustment layer:

1. Double-click the adjustment layer name on the Layers palette.

2. Change the dialog box settings.

3. Click OK (Enter/Return).

TIP Want to use an adjustment layer in another image? Drag-and-drop it from the source image's Layers palette into the destination image window.

When you merge down an adjustment layer, the adjustments become permanent for the image layer below it, so be certain you want the effect to become permanent before you perform another operation. If you change your mind, choose Edit menu > Undo or click the prior state on the History palette.

To merge an adjustment layer:

1. Activate the adjustment layer.

2. Choose Merge Down from the Layers palette command menu (Ctrl-E/⌃⌘-E).

TIP If you have more than one adjustment layer or you want to merge one adjustment layer with more than one other image layer, use either the Merge Visible or the Flatten Image command (see pages 117–118).

TIP An adjustment layer cannot be merged with another adjustment layer; since they don't contain pixels, there's nothing to merge.

Edit, Merge Adjustment Layer

Ways to use adjustment layers

Normally, an adjustment layer will affect all the currently visible layers below it, but you can use a **clipping group** to limit an adjustment layer's effect to only the layer or layers it's grouped with (see step 5 on page 128).

Hide an adjustment layer to temporarily remove its effect.

Change an adjustment layer's **blending mode** to produce a variety of visual effects in relationship to its underlying layers. Overlay mode will heighten contrast, Multiply mode will darken the image, Screen mode wlll lighten the image.

To prevent an underlying layer from being affected by an adjustment layer, **restack** it above the adjustment layer.

To limit the area an adjustment layer affects, create a **selection** before you create it. Or paint or fill with black on the adjustment layer to remove the adjustment effect or white to reveal the adjustment effect (instructions on page 137).

To **compare** different settings for the same adjustment command, create multiples of the same adjustment layer, like Levels or Color Balance, hide all the adjustment layers, and then show them one at a time. You can restack adjustment layers among themselves or place them at different locations within the overall layer stack.

The Equalize command redistributes the active layer's brightness values. It may improve an image that lacks contrast or is too dark.

To equalize a layer:

Choose Image menu > Adjust > Equalize **1**–**2**.

Note: To limit the Equalize effect to part of a layer, select that area before choosing the command, then click "Equalize selected area only" in the Equalize dialog box. To equalize an entire layer based on the values within the selected area, click "Equalize entire image based on selected area." **3**

1 *The original image.*

PHOTO: PAUL PETROFF

2 *After applying the **Equalize** command.*

Equalize

Options
○ Equalize selected area only
3 ⦿ Equalize entire image based on selected area

OK
Cancel

PHOTO: NADINE MARKOVA

1 *The original image.*   **2** *The image inverted.*

Choose the Invert command to make a layer or the Background look like a film negative, or a negative look like a positive. Each pixel will be replaced with its opposite brightness and/or color value.

To invert lights and darks:

Choose a layer, then choose Image menu > Adjust > Invert (Ctrl-I/⌘-I) **1**–**2**.
or
To use an adjustment layer to invert the layers below it, Ctrl-click/⌘-click the Create new layer button at the bottom of the Layers palette, choose Type: Invert, then click OK.

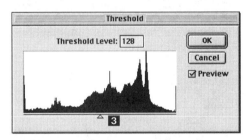

3

PHOTO: PAUL PETROFF

4 *The original image.*

5 *After using the **Threshold** command.*

The Threshold dialog box makes the current layer or the Background high contrast by converting color or gray pixels into black and white pixels.

To make a layer (or the Background) high contrast:

1. Choose a layer, then choose Image menu > Adjust > Threshold.
or
To use an adjustment layer, Ctrl-click/⌘-click the Create new layer button at the bottom of the Layers palette, choose Type: Threshold, then click OK.

2. Move the slider to the right to increase the number of black pixels **3**.
or
Move the slider to the left to increase the number of white pixels.
or
Enter a value (1–255) in the Threshold Level field. Pixels lighter than this number will become white, pixels darker than this number will become black.

3. Click OK (Enter/Return) **4**–**5**.

Use the Posterize command to reduce the number of color or value levels in the current layer or the Background to a specified number.

To posterize:

1. Choose a layer, then choose Image menu > Adjust > Posterize.

or

To use an adjustment layer, Ctrl-click/⌘-click the Create new layer button at the bottom of the Layers palette, choose Type: Posterize, then click OK (Enter/Return).

2. Make sure the Preview box is checked, then enter the desired number of Levels (2–255) 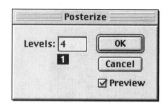. To produce a dramatic effect, enter a number between 4 and 8.

3. Click OK (Enter/Return) **2**–**4**.

TIP If the number of shades in an image is reduced using the Posterize command (or any other tonal adjustments are made, for that matter, without using an adjustment layer), and the image is saved and closed, the original levels information will be permanently lost.

2 *The original image.*

3 *Post posterization.*

4 *Another posterized image.*

Posterize

Brightness/Contrast

Brightness: [-14]   [OK]
        △ **1**   [Cancel]
Contrast: [+23]
        △   ☑ Preview

PHOTO: PAUL PETROFF

2 *The original image.*

3 *The **Brightness** slider moved to the right.*

4 ***Brightness** and **contrast** adjusted.*

If you use the Levels dialog box to make tonal adjustments, you'll be able to adjust the shadows, midtones, and highlights individually, but the Brightness/Contrast command, discussed here, is simpler to use.

To adjust brightness and contrast (Brightness/Contrast):

1. Choose a layer, then choose Image menu > Adjust > Brightness/Contrast.
   or
   To use an adjustment layer, Ctrl-click/ ⌘-click the Create new layer button at the bottom of the Layers palette, choose Type: Brightness/Contrast, then click OK.

2. To lighten the layer, move the brightness slider to the right **1**.
   or
   To darken the layer, move the Brightness slider to the left.
   or
   Enter a value (-100–100) in the Brightness field.

3. To intensify the contrast, move the Contrast slider to the right.
   or
   To lessen the contrast, move the Contrast slider to the left.
   or
   Enter a value (-100–100) in the Contrast field.

4. Click OK (Enter/Return) **2**–**4**.

TIP If you move a slider in an Adjust submenu dialog box, note its position relative to the other sliders and how the layer or Background changes.

Adjust Brightness and Contrast

Use the Levels dialog box to make fine adjustments to a layer or image's highlights, midtones, or shadows.

To adjust brightness and contrast using Levels:

1. Choose a layer, then choose Image menu > Adjust > Levels (Ctrl-L/⌘-L).
or
To use an adjustment layer, Ctrl-click/⌘-click the Create new layer button at the bottom of the Layers palette, choose Type: Levels, then click OK.

2. Do any of the following:

To brighten the highlights and intensify contrast, move the Input highlights slider to the left **1**. The midtones slider will move along with it. Readjust the midtones slider, if necessary.

To darken the shadows, move the Input shadows slider to the right. The midtones slider will move along with it. Readjust the midtones slider, if necessary.

To adjust the midtones independently, move the Input midtones slider.

To decrease contrast and lighten the image, move the Output shadows slider to the right.

To decrease contrast and darken the image, move the Output highlights slider to the left.

Note: You can enter values in the Input Levels or Output Levels fields instead of moving the sliders.

3. Click OK (Enter/Return) **2**–**4**.

TIP To make a layer high contrast, move the Input shadows and highlights sliders very close together. Position them left of center to lighten the image or right of center to darken the image.

TIP To adjust levels automatically, choose Image menu > Adjust > Auto Levels (Ctrl-Shift-L/⌘-Shift-L) or click Auto in the Levels dialog box.

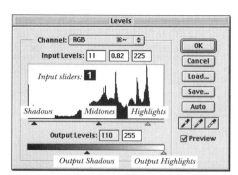

2 *The original image.*

3 *After **Levels** adjustments.*

PHOTO: PAUL PETROFF

4 *To produce this image, an area of the image was selected before the adjustment layer was created (Type: Levels). The type was added in QuarkXPress.*

Adjust Brightness and Contrast (Levels)

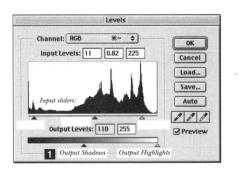

1 *Output Shadows — Output Highlights*

2 *The original image.*

3 *The music layer **screened back**.*

4 *The Output slider positions reversed.*

To screen back a layer (or the Background):

1. Choose a layer, then choose Image menu > Adjust > Levels (Ctrl-L/⌘-L).
or
To use an adjustment layer, Ctrl-click/⌘-click the Create new layer button at the bottom of the Layers palette, choose Type: Levels, then click OK.

2. To reduce contrast, move the Output highlights slider slightly to the left.
and
Move the Output shadows slider to the right **1**.

3. To lighten the midtones, move the Input midtones slider to the left.

4. Click OK (Enter/Return) **2**–**3**.

TIP To make a layer look like a film negative, reverse the position of the two Output sliders **4**. The farther apart the sliders are, the more each pixel's brightness and contrast attributes will be reversed. The Invert command produces a similar effect.

PHOTO: PAUL PETROFF

The original image.

*The **screened back** version.*

Screen Back a Layer

135

To lighten pixels by hand in small areas, use the Dodge tool. To darken pixels, use the Burn tool. You can choose different Brushes palette settings for each tool. The Dodge and Burn tools can't be used on a image in Bitmap or Indexed Color mode.

To lighten using the Dodge tool or darken using the Burn tool:

1. Choose a layer.

2. Choose the Dodge ✎ or Burn ✋ tool (O or Shift-O).

3. On the tool's Options palette **1**:

Choose an Exposure setting between 1% (low intensity) and 100% (high intensity). Try a low exposure first (20%-30%) so the tool won't bleach or darken areas too quickly.

and

Choose Shadows, Midtones, or Highlights from the drop-down menu to Dodge or Burn only pixels in that value range.

4. Click the Brushes tab, then click a hard-edged or soft-edged tip. A large, soft tip will produce the smoothest result.

5. Stroke on any area of the layer. Pause between strokes to allow the screen to redraw **2**–**3**.

TIP If you Dodge or Burn an area too much, choose Edit menu > Undo or use the History palette to remove those states. Don't use the opposite tool to fix it—you'll get uneven results.

TIP To create a smooth, even highlight or shadow line, dodge or burn a path using the Stroke Path command with the Dodge or Burn tool chosen (see page 223). To dodge or burn in a straight line, click on the image, move the pointer, then Shift-click again on the image.

2 *The **Dodge** tool with **Shadows** chosen from the Dodge Options palette was used to eliminate dark spots in the background of this image.*

3 *After **dodging**.*

1 *In this image, the adjustment layer contains a mask on the left side that is hiding a Threshold effect.*

2 *In this image, the adjustment layer's opacity was lowered to 60%, which causes the Threshold effect to blend with the overall underlying image.*

Adjustment layer mask shortcuts

- **Alt**-click/**Option**-click the adjustment layer thumbnail to **view** the mask in the image window.

- **Alt-Shift**-click/**Option-Shift**-click the adjustment layer thumbnail to view the mask in a rubylith color.

- **Shift**-click the adjustment layer thumbnail to **temporarily turn off** a mask for an adjustment layer.

- **Ctrl**-click/⌘-click the adjustment layer thumbnail to convert the non-masked area into a **selection**.

Because an adjustment layer is a type of mask, when you activate an adjustment layer, the Color palette automatically resets to Grayscale and the Foreground and Background colors revert to black and white, or vice versa.

To restrict the area a new adjustment layer affects:

1. Create a selection on the layer above which the new adjustment layer will appear **1**.

2. Create an adjustment layer. The adjustment layer thumbnail will be black, with an area of white to indicate where the selection was.

To restrict the area an existing adjustment layer affects:

1. Activate the adjustment layer.

2. Choose black as the Foreground color. (Press "X" to swap the Foreground and Background colors, if necessary.)

3. To lessen the adjustment layer effect:

   Create a selection (or selections) and fill them with black.
   or
   Choose the Paintbrush tool, Normal mode, 100% opacity, then paint with black on the image. Choose a lower opacity to partially remove the adjustment layer effect.

4. *Optional:* To restore the adjustment layer effect, paint or fill with white.

TIP To reveal just a small area of the adjustment effect, fill the entire layer with black and then paint with white over specific areas. Fill the whole adjustment layer with white to make the adjustment effect visible on the entire image. To diminish the adjustment layer's effect over the entire layer by a percentage, lower its opacity via the Layers palette **2**.

To make a layer (or the Background) grayscale using Channel Mixer:

1. Choose a layer, then choose Image menu > Adjust > Channel Mixer.

or

To use an adjustment layer, Ctrl-click/⌘-click the Create new layer button at the bottom of the Layers palette, choose Type: Channel Mixer, then click OK.

2. Check the Monochrome box. The layer or image will become grayscale and Black will be the only choice on the Output Channel drop-down menu.

3. Move any Source Channels slider to modify how much that color channel is used as a source for the luminosity levels in the grayscale image.

4. Move the Constant slider to the left to add black or to the right to add white.

5. Click OK (Enter/Return).

Note: The image is still in its original color mode. You can now convert it to Grayscale mode.

TIP If you used the Channel Mixer on a layer, you can now choose a different layer opacity or blending mode.

TIP To add a color tint to a layer, first check the Monochrome box, and then uncheck it to restore the color Output Channels. Choose an Output Channel and move the Source Channel sliders to produce a different color tint. Repeat for any other Output Channels.

Try one of theirs

To use a preset Channel Mixer effect (e.g., RGB Rotate Channels, CMYK Swap Cyan & Magenta), first make sure the Presets folder has been copied from the Photoshop 5.0 CD-ROM into the Photoshop 5.0 application folder. To load an effect, click Load in the Channel Mixer dialog box, open the Presets folder inside the application folder, open any one of the four folders there, then double-click a mixer. *Windows:* The abbreviated names represent Channel Swap, Grayscale, Special Effects, and YCC Color.

CHOOSE COLORS 10

N THIS CHAPTER you will learn how to choose colors. Colors are applied using various painting and editing tools, as well as some commands.

What are the Foreground and Background colors?

When you use a painting tool, create type, or use the Stroke command, the current Foreground color is applied.

When you use the Eraser tool, increase an image's canvas size, or move a selection on the Background using the Move tool, the hole that's left behind is automatically filled with the current Background color. The Gradient tool can produce blends using the Foreground and/or Background colors.

The Foreground and Background colors are displayed in the Foreground and Background color squares on the Toolbox **1** and on the Color palette **2**. (When written with an uppercase "F" or "B," these terms refer to colors, not the overall foreground or background areas of a picture.)

There are several ways to choose a Foreground or Background color, and they are described on the following pages:

■ Enter values in fields or click on the big color square in the **Color Picker**.

■ Choose premixed matching system colors using the **Custom Colors** dialog box.

■ Pluck a color from an image using the **Eyedropper** tool.

■ Enter values in fields or move sliders on the **Color** palette.

■ Click a swatch on the **Swatches** palette.

(To add a spot color channel to an image, see page 165.)

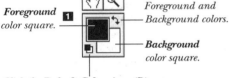

Foreground color square.

Click the **Switch Colors** icon (X) to swap the Foreground and Background colors.

1

Background color square.

Click the **Default Colors** icon (D) to make the Foreground color black and the Background color white.

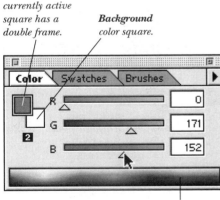

Foreground color square. The currently active square has a double frame.

Background color square.

2

Color bar.

To choose a color using the Color Picker:

1. Click the Foreground or Background color square on the Toolbox.

or

Click the Foreground or Background color square on the Color palette if it is already active (has a double frame).

or

Double-click the Foreground or Background color square on the Color palette if it is not active.

Note: If the color square you click on is a Custom color, the Custom Colors dialog box will open. Click Picker to open the Color Picker dialog box.

2. To choose from the Photoshop Color Picker:

Click a color on the vertical color bar to choose a hue **1**, then click a variation of that hue in the large square **2**.

or

To choose a specific process color for print output, enter percentages from a matching guide in the C, M, Y, and K fields. For an on-screen image, you can specify specific percentages in the R, G, and B fields. RGB colors range from 0 (black) to 255 (pure R, G,or B). You can also enter numbers in the HSB or Lab fields.

3. Click OK (Enter/Return).

TIP To use the Photoshop Color Picker, choose Color Picker: Photoshop in File menu > Preferences > General (Ctrl-K/⌘-K). Alternatively, you can choose the System color picker from the same drop-down menu (Windows Color Picker/Apple Color Picker). Only one color picker is accessible at a time.

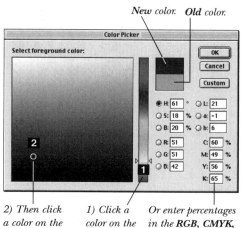

New color. Old color.

2) Then click a color on the large square.   *1) Click a color on the color bar.*   *Or enter percentages in the RGB, CMYK, HSB, or Lab fields.*

Out of gamut?

An exclamation point in the Color Picker or on the Color palette indicates there is no ink equivalent for the color you chose—it is out of printable gamut. If you're planning to print your image, choose an in-gamut color or click the exclamation point to have Photoshop substitute the closest printable color (shown in the swatch below the exclamation point). When you convert your image to CMYK Color mode, the entire image will be brought into printable gamut. The out-of-gamut range is defined by the current settings in the CMYK Setup dialog box.

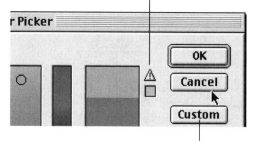

*Click **Custom** to choose a predefined color.*

Color-separate from somewhere else

To color separate a Photoshop image that contains spot color channels using QuarkXPress, Illustrator, or FreeHand, first convert the file to CMYK Color mode and save it in the Photoshop DCS 2.0 format (see page 298). If you use a Pantone color in a spot channel, check the Short PANTONE Names box in File menu > Preferences > General (Ctrl-K/⌘-K) so other applications will recognize the Pantone name.

1 *Choose a matching system from the* **Book** *pop-up menu, then type a* **number**.

The number you type will appear here.

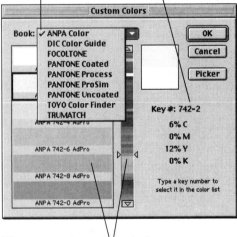

2 *Or click a color on the vertical color bar, then click a* **swatch**.

Normally, Photoshop separates all colors in an image into the four process colors, regardless of whether they are process or spot colors. In order to separate a spot color to a separate plate from Photoshop, you must create a spot color channel for it (see page 165).

Note: Don't rely on your monitor to represent matching system colors accurately—you must choose them from a printed Pantone, Trumatch, Toyo, DIC, Focoltone, or Anpa-Color swatch book. But before you do so, find out which brand of ink your printer is planning to use.

To choose a custom color:

1. Click the Foreground or Background color square on the Toolbox.
   or
   Click the Foreground or Background color square on the Color palette if it is already active.
   or
   Double-click the Foreground or Background color square on the Color palette if it is not active.
   Note: If the color square you click on is not a Custom color, the Color Picker dialog box will open. Click Custom to open the Custom Colors dialog box.

2. Choose a matching guide system from the Book drop-down menu **1**.

3. Type a number (it will appear on the "Key #" line).
   or
   Click a color on the vertical color bar, then click a swatch **2**.

4. *Optional:* Click Picker to return to the Color Picker.

5. Click OK (Enter/Return).

TIP To load a matching system palette onto the Swatches palette, see page 144.

TIP For the addresses of the various companies that publish matching system guides (e.g., Pantone, Trumatch), see the Photoshop User Guide.

Custom Colors

To choose a color from an image using the Eyedropper:

1. On the Color palette, click the Foreground or Background color square if it is *not* already active.

2. Click on a color in any open image window ■. Or drag to capture a mixture of colors. A breakdown of that color will appear on the Info palette.

TIP To change the area within which the Eyedropper tool samples, choose Point Sample (the exact pixel that's clicked on) or 3 by 3 or 5 by 5 Average (an average within a 3- or 5-pixel range) from the Eyedropper Options palette ②. If you Right-click/Control-click on the image with the Eyedropper, you can choose any of those settings from a context menu.

TIP Alt-click/Option-click or drag in the image window with the Eyedropper tool to choose a Background color when the Foreground color square is active or a Foreground color when the Background color square is active.

To choose a color using the Color palette:

1. Click the Foreground or Background color square if it isn't already active ③.

2. Choose a color model for the sliders from the Color palette command menu ④.

3. Move any of the sliders ⑤.
   or
   Click or drag on the color bar.
   or
   Enter values in the fields.

TIP In the RGB model, white (the presence of all colors) is produced when all the sliders are in their rightmost positions, black (the absence of all colors) is produced when all the sliders are in their leftmost positions, and gray is produced when all the sliders are vertically aligned in any other position.

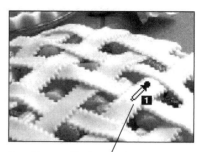

Sampling a color from an image using the Eyedropper tool.

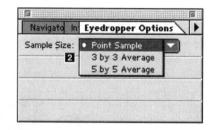

Color palette tips

Choose Color Bar from the command menu to choose a different spectrum **style**. Or Right-click/Control-click the color bar and choose from a context menu.

Alt-click/Option-click the color bar to choose a color for the **non-selected** color square.

The colors on the slider bars will **update** as you drag. To turn this feature off, uncheck the Dynamic Color Sliders box in File menu > Preferences > General.

The **model** you choose for the Color palette doesn't have to match the current **image mode**. For example, you can choose the CMYK color model from the Color palette for an RGB picture.

③ *Click the Foreground or Background color square.*   ④ *Choose a model for the sliders.*

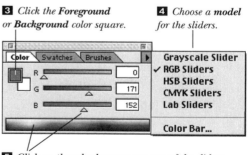

⑤ *Click on the color bar or move any of the sliders.*

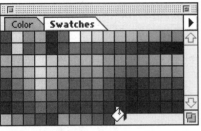

1 *Click in the white area below the swatches.*

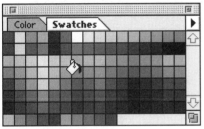

2 *Or Option-Shift-click between two swatches to insert a color between them.*

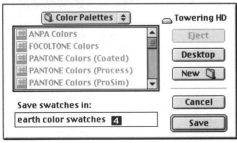

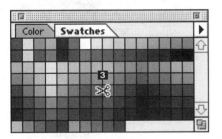

To choose a color from the Swatches palette:

To choose a Foreground color, just click on a color swatch.

To choose a Background color, Alt-click/ Option-click a color swatch.

To add a color to the Swatches palette:

1. Choose a Foreground color.

2. Click the Swatches tab to display the Swatches palette.

3. Position the cursor in the blank area below the swatches on the palette, and click (paint bucket pointer) **1**. The new color will appear next to the last swatch.

TIP To replace an existing swatch with the new color, Shift-click on the color to be replaced.

TIP To insert the new color between two swatches, Alt-Shift-click/Option-Shift-click on either swatch **2**.

To delete a color from the Swatches palette:

Ctrl-click/⌘⌘-click on a swatch (scissors cursor) **3**.

TIP To restore the default Swatches palette, choose Reset Swatches from the Swatches palette command menu, then click OK.

Note: If you edit the Swatches palette and then exit/quit and re-launch Photoshop, your edited palette will reopen.

To save an edited swatches set:

1. Choose Save Swatches from the Swatches palette command menu.

2. Enter a name for the edited palette in the "Save swatches in" field **4**.

3. Choose a location in which to save the palette.

4. Click Save.

Nine preset color swatch palettes are supplied with Photoshop, and they can be
loaded onto the Swatches palette: ANPA,
Focoltone, Pantone (Coated, Process,
ProSim, and Uncoated), Toyo, Trumatch,
and Web Safe Colors.

To replace a swatches set:

1. Choose Replace Swatches from the
Swatches palette command menu.

2. Open the Color Palettes folder in the
Goodies folder inside the Photoshop 5
application folder.

3. Double-click a palette █. The loaded
swatches will appear on the Swatches
palette.
or
Highlight a palette, then click
Load (Win)/Open (Mac).

TIP Choose Reset Swatches from the
Swatches palette command menu to
restore the default palette.

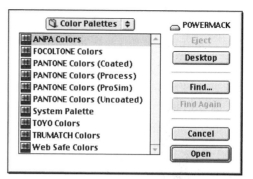

█ *Double-click a palette in the Color Palettes folder.*

You can append to an existing swatches set
any swatches set that you've edited and
saved or any of the palettes that are supplied
with Photoshop.

To load a swatches set:

1. Choose Load Swatches from the
Swatches palette command menu █.

2. Open the Color Palettes or another
palettes folder in the Goodies folder
inside the Photoshop 5 application folder.

3. Double-click a palette (swatches set) █.
or
Highlight a palette and click Load (Win)/
Open (Mac).

4. The appended swatches will appear
below the existing swatches.

TIP To enlarge the palette to display the
loaded swatches, drag the palette resize
box or click the palette zoom box.

Gate, ©Jeff Brice

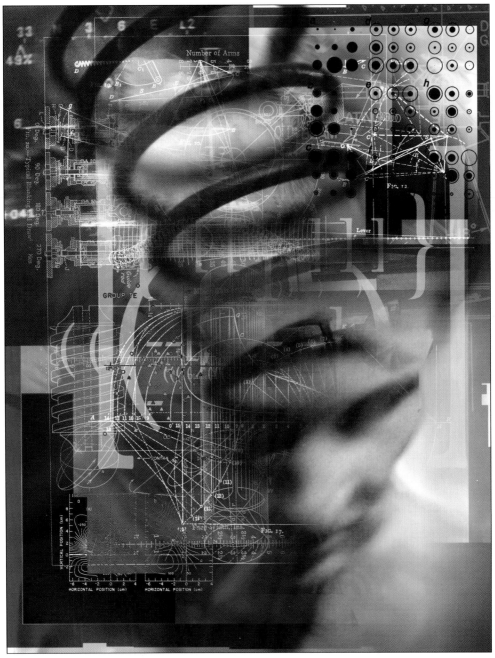

Springhead, ©Jeff Brice

Mapping Poem, ©Jeff Brice

Trustfear, ©Alicia Buelow

Comfort, ©Alicia Buelow

Taste, ©Alicia Buelow

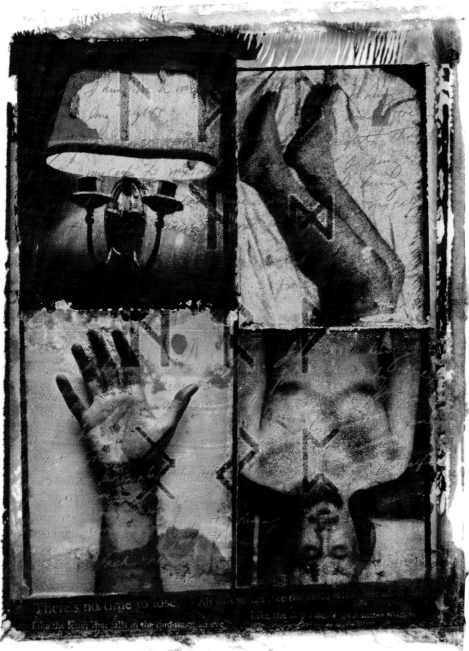

Canto nine, ©1996 Diane Fenster

Labyrinth of Lights, ©1996 Annette Weintraub

Universal Language, ©1996 Annette Weintraub

Partitions, ©1996 Annette Weintraub

Underpinnings, ©1996 Annette Weintraub

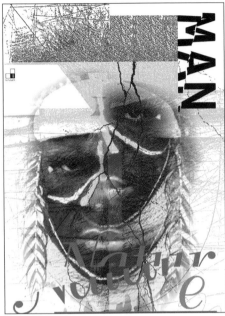

Man and nature, ©Min Wang

Transformation, ©1996 Diane Fenster

Arch, ©Jeff Brice

Sight, ©Alicia Buelow

Koolhaas, ©John Hersey

Webhouserino, ©John Hersey

Video conferencing, ©Wendy Grossman

Seasonal Specialties (tree catalog) ©1996 All Rights Reserved

Seasonal Specialties ©1996 All Rights Reserved

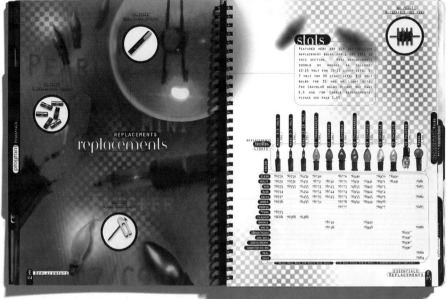

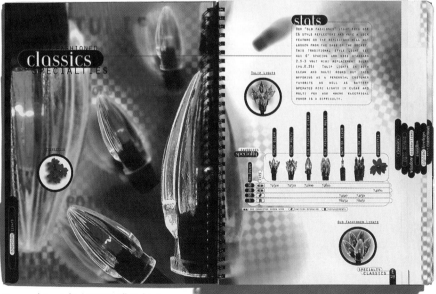

Radiowaver, ©John Hersey

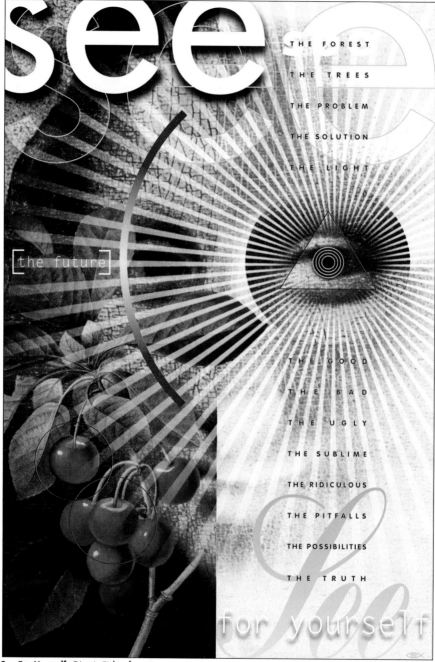

See For Yourself, ©Louis Fishauf

SHORTCUTS

	Windows 95/NT	Mac OS
GENERAL SHORTCUTS		
Show/hide all palettes, including Toolbox	Tab	Tab
Show/hide all but Toolbox	Shift + Tab	Shift + Tab
Undo	Ctrl + Z	⌘ + Z
Accept crop, transform, or any dialog	Enter	Return or Enter
Toggle Cancel to Reset in dialog	Alt	Opt
Cancel crop, transform, or any dialog	Esc or Ctrl + . (period)	Esc or ⌘ + . (period)
Exit type dialog from keyboard	Enter (on numeric keypad)	Enter
Activate button in alert dialog	First letter of button (e.g., N = No)	First letter of button (e.g., N = No)
Increase value in highlighted field by 1 (or .1)	Up Arrow	Up Arrow
Increase value in highlighted field by 10 (or 1)	Shift + Up Arrow	Shift + Up Arrow
Decrease value in highlighted field by 1 (or .1)	Down Arrow	Down Arrow
Decrease value in highlighted field by 10 (or 1)	Shift + Down Arrow	Shift + Down Arrow
Adjust angle in 15° increments	Shift + drag in angle wheel	Shift + drag in angle wheel
Cancel out of pop-up slider (mouse button up)	Esc	Esc
Commits edit in pop-up slider (mouse button up)	Enter	Return or Enter
Reset pop-up slider to prev (mouse button down)	Hold Alt and move cursor outside slider rectangle	Hold Opt and move cursor outside slider rectangle
Help	F1	Help
Access Adobe Online	Click on identifier icon on Toolbox	Click on identifier icon on Toolbox
PALETTES		
Show/hide Brushes	F5	F5
Show/hide Color	F6	F6
Show/hide Layers	F7	F7

	Windows 95/NT	Mac OS
Show/hide Info	F8	F8
Show/hide Actions	F9	F9
Show Options palette	Double-click tool, or press Enter if tool is selected	Double-click tool, or press Return if tool is selected

TOOLS

Choose a tool

Rectangular Marquee	M	M
Move	V	V
Lasso	L	L
Crop	C	C
Magic Wand	W	W
Airbrush	J	J
Paintbrush	B	B
Rubber Stamp	S	S
History Brush	Y	Y
Eraser	E	E
Pencil	N	N
Blur	R	R
Dodge	O	O
Pen	P	P
Add-anchor-point	+ (plus)	+ (plus)
Delete-anchor-point	- (minus)	- (minus)
Direct-selection	A	A
Type	T	T
Measure	U	U
Gradient	G	G
Paint Bucket	K	K
Eyedropper	I	I
Hand	H	H
Zoom	Z	Z

Cycle through tools

Marquee tools	Shift + M	Shift + M
Lasso tools	Shift + L	Shift + L

	Windows 95/NT	**Mac OS**
Rubber Stamp tools	Shift + S	Shift + S
Blur, Sharpen, and Smudge tools	Shift + R	Shift + R
Toning tools	Shift + O	Shift + O
Pen tools	Shift + P	Shift + P
Type tools	Shift + T	Shift + T
Eyedropper tools	Shift + I	Shift + I
Cycle through above tools	Alt + click in tool slot	Option + click in tool slot

Toggle tools

Move tool	Ctrl	⌃⌘
Precise cursors	Caps Lock	Caps Lock
Pencil to Eyedropper	Alt	Option
Line to Eyedropper	Alt	Option
Paint Bucket to Eyedropper	Alt	Option
Blur to Sharpen; Sharpen to Blur	Alt	Option
Dodge/Burn tool	Alt	Option

TOOL BEHAVIOR

Change brush opacity in 10% increments	Number keys (2 = 20%, 3 = 30%)	Number keys (2 = 20%, 3 = 30%)

Constrain tools

Constrain to horizontal or vertical axis (Eraser, Paintbrush, Pencil, Blur, Sharpen, Smudge, Dodge, or Burn tool)	Shift + drag	Shift+ drag
Draw, erase, etc. in straight lines (Eraser, Paintbrush, Pencil, Blur, Sharpen, Smudge, Dodge, or Burn tool)	Shift + click	Shift + click
Constrain to 45° axis (Line, Gradients, (or Convert-point tool)	Shift + drag	Shift + drag

Crop tool

Rotate crop marquee	Drag outside crop marquee	Drag outside crop marquee
Move crop marquee	Drag inside crop marquee	Drag inside crop marquee
Resize crop marquee	Drag crop handles	Drag crop handles
Maintain aspect ratio of crop box	Shift + drag handles	Shift + drag handles
Resize crop from center	Alt + drag handles	Option + drag handles
Constrain crop from center	Alt + Shift + drag handles	Option + Shift + drag handles
Apply crop	Enter	Enter/Return

	Windows 95/NT	**Mac OS**
Move tool		
Move constrained to 45°	Shift + drag	Shift + drag
Copy selection or layer	Alt + drag	Option + drag
Select layer by name	Right-click	Control + click
Select topmost visible layer	Right-mouse + Alt + click	Control + Option + click
Link with topmost visible layer	Right mouse + Shift + click	Control + Shift + click
Nudge layer/selection 1 pixel	Ctrl + arrow key	⌘ + arrow key
Nudge layer/selection 10 pixels	Ctrl + Shift + arrow key	⌘ + Shift + arrow key
Lasso tool		
Add to selection	Shift + click, then draw	Shift + click, then draw
Delete from selection	Alt + click, then draw	Option + click, then draw
Intersect with selection	Alt + Shift + click, then draw	Option + Shift + click, then draw
Draw using Polygonal Lasso	Click, then Alt-drag	Click, then Option-drag
Polygonal Lasso tool		
Add to selection	Shift + click, then draw	Shift + click, then draw
Delete from selection	Alt + click, then draw	Option + click, then draw
Intersect with selection	Alt + Shift + click, then draw	Option + Shift + click, then draw
Draw using Lasso	Alt + drag	Option + drag
Constrain to 45° while drawing	Shift + drag	Shift + drag
Magnetic Lasso tool		
Add to selection	Shift + click, then draw	Shift + click, then draw
Delete from selection	Alt + click, then draw	Option + click, then draw
Intersect with selection	Alt + Shift + click, then draw	Option + Shift + click, then draw
Add point	Single click	Single click
Remove last point	Backspace or Delete	Delete key
Close path	Double-click or Enter	Double-click or Enter or Return
Close path over start point	Click on start point	Click on start point
Close path using straight line segment	Alt + double-click	Option + double-click
Cancel operation	Esc/Ctrl + . (Period)	Esc/⌘ + . (Period)
Switch to Lasso	Alt + drag	Option + drag
Switch to Polygonal Lasso	Alt + click	Option + click

SHORTCUTS

	Windows 95/NT	Mac OS
Eraser tool		
Erase to History	Alt + drag	Option + drag
Smudge tool		
Smudge using Foreground color	Alt	Option
Burn and Dodge tools		
Set Burn or Dodge to Shadows	Alt + Shift + W	Option + Shift + W
Set Burn or Dodge to Midtones	Alt + Shift + V	Option + Shift + V
Set Burn or Dodge to Highlights	Alt + Shift + Z	Option + Shift + Z
Sponge tool		
Desaturate setting	Alt + Shift + J	Option + Shift + J
Saturate setting	Alt + Shift + A	Option + Shift + A
Magnetic Pen tool		
Add point	Single click	Single click
Remove last point	Backspace or Delete	Delete
Close path	Double-click/Enter	Double-click/Enter
Close path over start point	Click on start point	Click on start point
Close path using straight line segment	Alt + double-click	Option + double-click
Cancel operation	Esc/Ctrl + . (Period)	Esc/⌘ + . (Period)
Switch to Freeform Pen	Alt + drag	Option + drag
Switch to Pen	Alt + click	Option + click
Increase magnetic width	[(open bracket)	[(open bracket)
Decrease magnetic width	] (close bracket)	] (close bracket)
Measure tool		
Measure constrained to 45° axis	Shift + drag	Shift + drag
Create protractor	Alt + click + drag on end point	Option + click + drag on end point
Paint Bucket tool		
Change color of area around canvas	Shift + click outside canvas	Shift + click outside canvas
Eyedropper tool		
Choose Background color	Alt + click	Option + click
Toggle to Color Sampler tool	Shift	Shift
Delete sampler	Alt + Shift + click on sampler	Option + Shift + click on sampler
Color Sampler tool		
Delete sampler	Alt + click on sampler	Option + click on sampler

	Windows 95/NT	**Mac OS**

DISPLAY

Change view size

Zoom in	Ctrl + Spacebar + click or drag or Ctrl + Alt + + (plus)	⌘ + Spacebar + click or drag or ⌘ + + (plus)
Zoom out	Ctrl + Alt + Spacebar + click or Ctrl + Alt + - (minus)	⌘ + Option + Spacebar + click or ⌘ + - (minus)
Zoom to 100%	Double-click Zoom tool	Double-click Zoom tool
Zoom to fit in window	Double-click Hand tool	Double-click Hand tool
Fit on screen	Ctrl + 0	⌘ + 0
Actual pixels	Ctrl + Alt + 0	⌘ + Option + 0
Zoom in without changing window size	Ctrl + + (plus)	⌘ + Option + + (plus)
Zoom out without changing window size	Ctrl + - (minus)	⌘ + Option + - (minus)
Change zoom %, keep zoom field highlighted	Shift + Enter	Shift + Return

Hand tool

Toggle to zoom in	Ctrl	Z
Toggle to zoom out	Alt	Option
Fit image on screen	Double-click tool slot	Double-click tool slot

Zoom tool

Zoom out	Alt + click	Option + click
Actual size	Double-click tool slot	Double-click tool slot

Show/hide

Show/hide Edges	Ctrl + H	⌘ + H
Show/hide Path	Ctrl + Shift + H	⌘ + Shift + H
Show/hide Rulers	Ctrl + R	⌘ + R
Show/hide Guides	Ctrl + ; (semicolon)	⌘ + ; (semicolon)
Show/hide Grid	Ctrl + " (quote)	⌘ + " (quote)

Grid and guides

Snap to Guides	Shift + Ctrl + ; (semicolon)	Shift + ⌘ + ; (semicolon)
Lock Guides	Alt + Ctrl + ; (semicolon)	Option + ⌘ + ; (semicolon)
Snap to Grid	Shift + Ctrl + " (quote)	Shift + ⌘ + " (quote)
Snap guide to ruler	Shift + drag guide	Shift + drag guide
Toggle guide orientation (H/V)	Alt + drag guide	Option + drag guide

	Windows 95/NT	**Mac OS**

Move image in window

Scroll up one screen	Page up	Page up
Scroll up 10 units	Shift + page up	Shift + page up
Scroll down one screen	Page down	Page down
Scroll down 10 units	Shift + page down	Shift + page down
Scroll left one screen	Ctrl + page up	⌘ + page up
Scroll left 10 units	Ctrl + Shift + page up	⌘ + Shift + page up
Scroll right one screen	Ctrl + page down	⌘ + page down
Scroll right 10 units	Ctrl + Shift + page down	⌘ + Shift + page down
Move view to upper left corner	Home key	Home key
Move view to lower right corner	End key	End key

Navigator palette

Scroll viewable area of image	Drag view proxy	Drag view proxy
Move view to new portion of image	Click in preview area	Click in preview area
View new portion of image	Ctrl + drag in preview area	⌘ + drag in preview area
Change zoom %, keep zoom field highlighted	Shift-Enter	Shift-Return

Screen modes

Toggle Standard/Full Screen with Menu/Full Screen modes	F	F
Toggle menu when in Full Screen with Menu mode	Shift + F	Shift + F

View

Preview > CMYK	Ctrl + Y	⌘ + Y
Gamut Warning	Ctrl + Shift + Y	⌘ + Shift + Y

FILE MENU

New	Ctrl + N	⌘ + N
Open	Ctrl + O	⌘ + O
Open As	Ctrl + Alt + O	⌘ + Option + O
Close	Ctrl + W	⌘ + W
Save	Ctrl + S	⌘ + S
Save As	Ctrl + Shift + S	⌘ + Shift + S
Save A Copy	Ctrl + Alt + S	⌘ + Option + S
Revert	F12	F12
Page Setup	Ctrl + Shift + P	⌘ + Shift + P

	Windows 95/NT	Mac OS
Print	Ctrl + P	⌘ + P
Preferences > General	Ctrl + K	⌘ + K
Saving Files	Ctrl + 2	⌘ + 2
Display & Cursors	Ctrl + 3	⌘ + 3
Transparency & Gamut	Ctrl + 4	⌘ + 4
Units & Ruler	Ctrl + 5	⌘ + 5
Guides & Grid	Ctrl + 6	⌘ + 6
Plug-Ins & Scratch Disks	Ctrl + 7	⌘ + 7
Memory & Image Cache	Ctrl + 8	⌘ + 8
Exit/Quit	Ctrl + Q	⌘ + Q
New with default settings	Ctrl + Alt + N	⌘ + Option + N
Preferences with last settings	Ctrl + Alt + K	⌘ + Option + K

CLIPBOARD

	Windows 95/NT	Mac OS
Cut	Ctrl + X	⌘ + X
Copy	Ctrl + C	⌘ + C
Copy Merged	Ctrl + Shift + C	⌘ + Shift + C
Paste	Ctrl + V	⌘ + V
Paste Into	Ctrl + Shift + V	⌘ + Shift + V

BLENDING MODES

Layer blending modes

	Windows 95/NT	Mac OS
Set layer to next blend mode	Shift + + (plus)	Shift + + (plus)
Set layer to previous blend mode	Shift + - (minus)	Shift + - (minus)

Blending mode for brush or layer

	Windows 95/NT	Mac OS
Normal	Alt + Shift + N	Option + Shift + N
Dissolve	Alt + Shift + I	Option + Shift + I
Multiply	Alt + Shift + M	Option + Shift + M
Screen	Alt + Shift + S	Option + Shift + S
Overlay	Alt + Shift + O	Option + Shift + O
Soft Light	Alt + Shift + F	Option + Shift + F
Hard Light	Alt + Shift + H	Option + Shift + H
Color Dodge	Alt + Shift + D	Option + Shift + D
Color Burn	Alt + Shift + B	Option + Shift + B
Darken	Alt + Shift + K	Option + Shift + K

	Windows 95/NT	**Mac OS**
Lighten	Alt + Shift + G	Option + Shift + G
Difference	Alt + Shift + E	Option + Shift + E
Exclusion	Alt + Shift + X	Option + Shift + X
Hue	Alt + Shift + U	Option + Shift + U
Saturation	Alt + Shift + T	Option + Shift + T
Color	Alt + Shift + C	Option + Shift + C
Luminosity	Alt + Shift + Y	Option + Shift + Y
Threshold (Bitmap mode)	Alt + Shift + L	Option + Shift + L
Dissolve	Alt + Shift + I	Option + Shift + I
Behind	Alt + Shift + Q	Option + Shift + Q

COLOR

Colors

Swap Foreground/Background colors	X	X
Reset to default colors	D	D

Fill

Open Fill dialog	Shift + Backspace	Shift + Delete
Fill with Foreground color	Alt + Delete/Backspace	Option + Delete
Fill with Foreground color, Preserve Transparency on	Shift + Alt + Delete/Backspace	Shift + Option + Delete
Fill with Background color	Ctrl + Delete/Backspace	⌘ + Delete
Fill with Background color, Preserve Transparency on	Shift + Ctrl + Delete/Backspace	Shift + ⌘ + Delete
Fill from History	Ctrl + Alt + Backspace	⌘ + Option + Delete

Color palette

Cycle through color bars	Shift + click on color bar	Shift + click on color bar
Open Color Bar dialog	Ctrl + click on color bar	⌘ + click on color bar
Choose specific color bar	Right-click on color bar	Control + click on color bar

Swatches palette

Add Foreground color as a new swatch	Click in empty slot	Click in empty slot
Insert new swatch color	Shift + Alt + click in palette	Shift + Option + click in palette
Replace swatch color with Foreground color	Shift + click	Shift + click
Delete swatch	Ctrl + click on swatch	⌘ + click on swatch
Choose swatch as Foreground color	Click on swatch	Click on swatch
Choose swatch as Background color	Alt + click on swatch	Option + click on swatch

	Windows 95/NT	Mac OS
BRUSHES		
Brushes palette		
Select first brush	Shift + [	Shift + [
Select previous brush	[	[
Select next brush	]	]
Select last brush	Shift +]	Shift +]
Create new brush	Click in empty slot	Click in empty slot
Delete brush	Ctrl + click	⌘ + click
Edit brush	Double-click on brush	Double-click on brush
SELECTIONS		
All	Ctrl + A	⌘ + A
Deselect	Ctrl + D	⌘ + D
Reselect	Ctrl + Shift + D	⌘ + Shift + D
Inverse	Ctrl + Shift + I	⌘ + Shift + I
Feather	Ctrl + Alt + D	⌘ + Option + D
Nudge selection marquee 1 pixel	Arrow key	Arrow key
Nudge selection marquee 10 pixels	Shift + arrow key	Shift + arrow key
FILTERS		
Reapply last filter	Ctrl + F	⌘ + F
Fade last filter	Ctrl + Shift + F	⌘ + Shift + F
Reapply filter with the last settings	Ctrl + Alt + F	⌘ + Option + F
Lighting Effects dialog		
Clone light in preview area	Alt + drag light	Option + drag light
Delete light in preview area	Delete key	Delete key
Adjust light footprint without affecting angle	Shift + drag handle	Shift + drag handle
Adjust light angle without changing footprint	Ctrl + drag handle	⌘ + drag handle
LAYERS		
Layer menu		
New > Layer	Ctrl + Shift + N	⌘ + Shift + N
New Layer without dialog	Ctrl + Alt + Shift + N	⌘ + Option + Shift + N

	Windows 95/NT	**Mac OS**
Layer via Copy	Ctrl + J	⌘ + J
Layer via Cut	Ctrl + Shift + J	⌘ + Shift + J
Group with previous	Ctrl + G	⌘ + G
Ungroup	Ctrl + Shift + G	⌘ + Shift + G
Merge Down/Linked/Group	Ctrl + E	⌘ + E
Merge Visible	Shift + Ctrl + E	Shift + ⌘ + E

Layers palette

Show/hide layer	Click in eye icon area	Click in eye icon area
Toggle show all layers/show just this layer	Alt + click on eye icon area	Option + click on eye icon area
Show/hide multiple layers	Click + drag thru eye icon area	Click + drag thru eye icon area
Link layer to current target layer	Click in link icon area	Click in link icon area
Turn on/off linking for multiple layers	Click + drag thru link icon area	Click + drag thru link icon area
Create new, empty layer	Click Create new layer button	Click Create new layer button
Create new, empty layers with Layer Options dialog	Alt + click Create new layer button	Option + click Create new layer button
Duplicate layer	Drag layer to Create new layer button	Drag layer to Create new layer button
Delete layer using warning alert	Click Delete current layer button	Click Delete current layer button
Delete layer, bypass warning alert	Alt + click Delete current layer button	Option + click Delete current layer button
Change layer opacity in 10% increments	Number keys (2 = 20%, 3 = 30%)	Number keys (2 = 20%, 3 = 30%)
Toggle preserve transparency for target layer	/ (forward slash)	/ (forward slash)
Load layer pixels as selection	Ctrl + click layer thumbnail	⌘ + click layer thumbnail
Add layer pixels to selection	Ctrl + Shift + click layer thumbnail	⌘ + Shift + click layer thumbnail
Subtract layer pixels from selection	Ctrl + Alt + click layer thumbnail	⌘ + Option + click layer thumbnail
Intersect layer pixels with selection	Ctrl + Alt + Shift + click layer thumbnail	⌘ + Option + Shift + click layer thumbnail
Activate top layer	Shift + Alt +]	Shift + Option +]
Activate next layer (up)	Alt +]	Option+]
Activate previous layer (down)	Alt + [	Option + [
Activate bottom layer	Shift + Alt + [	Shift + Option + [
Edit Layer Options	Double-click layer name	Double-click layer name

	Windows 95/NT	Mac OS

Layer Effects

	Windows 95/NT	Mac OS
Toggle effects without dialog on or off	Alt + menu item	Option + menu item
Edit Layer Effect Options (last edited)	Double-click layer effect icon	Double-click layer effect icon
Clear each effect on layer one at a time	Alt + double-click effect icon	Option + double-click effect icon
Move effect	Drag in image	Drag in image
Move effect constrained to 45° axis	Shift + drag in image	Shift + drag in image

In Layer Effects dialog

	Windows 95/NT	Mac OS
Drop shadow	Ctrl + 1	⌘ + 1
Inner shadow	Ctrl + 2	⌘ + 2
Outer glow	Ctrl + 3	⌘ + 3
Inner glow	Ctrl + 4	⌘ + 4
Bevel and emboss	Ctrl + 5	⌘ + 5

Adjustment layers

	Windows 95/NT	Mac OS
New adjustment layer	Ctrl + click Create new layer button	⌘ + click Create new layer button
Edit adjustment layer	Double-click adjustment icon	Double-click adjustment icon

Layer masks

	Windows 95/NT	Mac OS
Create layer mask with Reveal All/ Reveal Selection	Click on mask button	Click on mask button
Create layer mask with Hide All/ Hide Selection	Alt + click on mask button	Option + click on mask button
Link/unlink layer and layer mask	Click Lock layer mask icon	Click Lock layer mask icon
Open Layer Mask Options dialog	Double-click layer mask thumbnail	Double-click layer mask thumbnail
Toggle layer mask on/off	Shift + click layer mask thumbnail	Shift + click layer mask thumbnail
Toggle rubylith mode on/off	\	\
Toggle viewing layer mask/composite	Alt + click layer mask thumbnail	Option + click layer mask thumbnail
Toggle Group/Ungroup with previous	Alt + click line between layers	Option + click line between layers

Merge layers

	Windows 95/NT	Mac OS
Merge down a copy of current layer into layer below	Alt + Merge Down	Option + Merge Down
Merge a copy of all visible layers into current layer	Alt + Merge Visible	Option + Merge Visible
Merge a copy of linked layers into layer below	Alt + Merge Linked	Option + Merge Linked

	Windows 95/NT	Mac OS
Arrange layers		
Bring to Front	Ctrl + Shift +]	⌘ + Shift +]
Bring Forward	Ctrl +]	⌘ +]
Send to Back	Ctrl + Shift + [	⌘ + Shift + [
Send Backward	Ctrl + [	⌘ + [

CHANNELS PALETTE

	Windows 95/NT	Mac OS
Target individual channels	Ctrl + [1–9]	⌘ + [1–9]
Target composite channel	Ctrl + ~ (tilde)	⌘ + ~ (tilde)
Show or hide channel	Click in eye icon area	Click in eye icon area
Add/remove channel to targeted channels	Shift + click on channel	Shift + click on channel
Create new channel	Click on New Channel button	Click on New Channel button
Create new channel with Channel Options dialog	Alt + click New Channel button	Option + click New Channel button
Duplicate channel	Drag channel to New Channel button	Drag channel to New Channel button
Delete channel using warning alert	Click Delete Channel button	Click Delete Channel button
Delete channel bypassing warning alert	Alt + click Delete Channel button	Option + click Delete Channel button
Create new spot color channel	Ctrl + click New Channel button	⌘ + click New Channel button
Create new channel from selection	Click on Save Selection button	Click on Save Selection button
Create new channel from selection with Channel Options	Alt + click Save Selection button	Option + click Save Selection button
Load channel as selection	Click Load Selection button or Ctrl + click channel thumbnail	Click Load Selection button or ⌘ + click channel thumbnail
Add channel to selection	Shift + click Load Selection button or Ctrl + Shift + click channel thumbnail	Shift + click Load Selection button or ⌘ + Shift + click channel thumbnail
Subtract channel from selection	Alt + click Load Selection button or Ctrl + Alt + click channel thumbnail	Option + click Load Selection button or ⌘ + Option + click channel thumbnail
Intersect channel with selection	Alt + Shift + click Load Selection button or Ctrl + Alt + Shift + click thumbnail	Option + Shift + click Load Selection button or ⌘ + Option + Shift + click thumbnail
Edit Channel Options	Double-click channel name	Double-click channel name

QUICK MASK

	Windows 95/NT	Mac OS
Toggle Quick Mask on/off	Q	Q
Invert Quick Mask mode	Alt + click Quick Mask button	Option + click Quick Mask button

	Windows 95/NT	**Mac OS**
Open Quick Mask Options dialog	Double-click Quick Mask button	Double-click Quick Mask button

PATHS

Paths palette

Create new path	Click New Path button	Click New Path button
Create new path with New Path dialog	Alt + click New Path button	Option + click New Path button
Duplicate path	Drag path to New Path button	Drag path to New Path button
Delete path using warning alert	Click Delete Path button	Click Delete Path button
Delete path, bypass warning alert	Alt + click Delete Path button	Option + click Delete Path button
Save work path into path item	Drag Work Path onto New Path button	Drag Work Path onto New Path button
Convert selection into work path	Click Make Work Path button	Click Make Work Path button
Convert selection into work path with Work Path dialog	Alt + click Make Work Path button	Option + click Make Work Path button
Convert path into selection	Click Load Selection button	Click Load Selection button
Convert path into selection with Make Selection dialog	Alt + click Load Selection button	Option + click Load Selection button

Stroke/fill path

Stroke path with Foreground color	Click Stroke Path button	Click Stroke Path button
Stroke path using Stroke Path dialog	Alt + click Stroke Path button	Option + click Stroke Path button
Fill path with Foreground color	Click Fill Path button	Click Fill Path button
Fill path using Fill Path dialog	Alt + click Fill Path button	Option + click Fill Path button

Paths and selections

Load path as selection	Ctrl + click path thumbnail	⌘ + click path thumbnail
Add path to selection	Ctrl + Shift + click path thumbnail	⌘ + Shift + click path thumbnail
Subtract path from selection	Ctrl + Alt + click path thumbnail	⌘ + Option + click path thumbnail
Intersect path with selection	Ctrl + Alt + Shift + click thumbnail	⌘ + Option + Shift + click thumbnail

HISTORY

History palette

Toggle back/forward one step	Ctrl + Z	⌘ + Z
Step forward	Shift + Ctrl + Z	⌘ + Shift + Z
Step backward	Alt + Ctrl + Z	⌘ + Option + Z
Duplicate history state (other than current)	Alt + click state	Option + click state

	Windows 95/NT	**Mac OS**
Create new snapshot	Click Create new snapshot button	Click Create new snapshot button
Create new document from state/snapshot	Click Create new document button	Click Create new document button

History brush tool

Constrain to horizontal or vertical axis	Shift + drag	Shift + drag
Paint straight lines	Shift + click	Shift + click

TRANSFORM

Free Transform	Ctrl + T	⌘ + T
Transform > Again	Ctrl + Shift + T	⌘ + Shift + T
Free Transform with duplication	Ctrl + Alt + T	⌘ + Option + T
Transform Again with duplication	Ctrl + Alt + Shift + T	⌘ + Option + Shift + T
Scale using center point (free transform)	Alt + drag corner handles	Option + drag corner handles
Skew using center point (free transform)	Ctrl + Alt + Shift + drag side handles	⌘ + Option + Shift + drag side handles

ADJUST DIALOGS

Levels	Ctrl + L	⌘ + L
Auto Levels	Ctrl + Shift + L	⌘ + Shift + L
Curves	Ctrl + M	⌘ + M
Color Balance	Ctrl + B	⌘ + B
Hue/Saturation	Ctrl + U	⌘ + U
Desaturate	Ctrl + Shift + U	⌘ + Shift + U
Invert	Ctrl + I	⌘ + I

Reopen dialog

Levels with last settings	Ctrl + Alt + L	⌘ + Option + L
Curves with last settings	Ctrl + Alt + M	⌘ + Option + M
Color Balance with last settings	Ctrl + Alt + B	⌘ + Option + B
Hue/Saturation with last settings	Ctrl + Alt + U	⌘ + Option + U

TYPE

Type tool

Designate type origin	Click or click + drag	Click or click + drag
Designate type origin while over existing type	Shift + click or click + drag	Shift + click or click + drag
Re-edit existing type	Click on type in image	Click on type in image

	Windows 95/NT	Mac OS
Edit Type Options	Double-click type icon	Double-click type icon
Toggle to Eyedropper tool	Alt	Option

Vertical Type tool

Designate type origin	Click + drag	Click + drag
Toggle to Eyedropper tool	Alt	Option

Type Tool dialog

Reposition type	Drag type in image	Drag type in image
Zoom in on image	Ctrl + + (plus)	⌘ + + (plus)
Zoom out of image	Ctrl + - (minus)	⌘ + - (minus)

Alignment

Left/Top	Ctrl + Shift + L	⌘ + Shift + L
Center	Ctrl + Shift + C	⌘ + Shift + C
Right/Bottom	Ctrl + Shift + R	⌘ + Shift + R

Size

Increase point size by 2 pts.	Ctrl + Shift + >	⌘ + Shift + >
Increase point size by 10 pts.	Ctrl + Alt + Shift + >	⌘ + Option + Shift + >
Decrease point size by 2 pts.	Ctrl + Shift + <	⌘ + Shift + <
Decrease point size by 10 pts.	Ctrl + Alt + Shift + <	⌘ + Option + Shift + <

Leading

Increase leading by 2 pts.	Alt + Down Arrow	Option + Down Arrow
Increase leading by 10 pts.	Ctrl + Alt + Down Arrow	⌘ + Option + Down Arrow
Decrease leading by 2 pts.	Alt + Up Arrow	Option + Up Arrow
Decrease leading by 10 pts.	Ctrl + Alt + Up Arrow	⌘ + Option + Up Arrow

Kerning/tracking

Increase kern/track $^{20}/_{1000}$ em space	Alt + Right Arrow	Option + Right Arrow
Increase kern/track $^{100}/_{1000}$ em space	Ctrl + Alt + Right Arrow	⌘ + Option + Right Arrow
Decrease kern/track $^{20}/_{1000}$ em space	Alt + Left Arrow	Option + Left Arrow
Decrease kern/track $^{100}/_{1000}$ em space	Ctrl + Alt + Left Arrow	⌘ + Option + Left Arrow

Baseline shift

Increase baseline shift by 2 pts.	Alt + Shift + Up + Arrow	Option + Shift + Up + Arrow
Increase baseline shift by 10 pts.	Ctrl + Alt + Shift + Up Arrow	⌘ + Option + Shift + Up Arrow
Decrease baseline shift by 2 pts.	Alt + Shift + Down + Arrow	Option + Shift + Down + Arrow
Decrease baseline shift by 10 pts.	Ctrl + Alt + Shift + Down Arrow	⌘ + Option + Shift + Down Arrow

	Windows 95/NT	**Mac OS**
Move insertion point		
Move to the right one character	Right arrow	Right arrow
Move to the left one character	Left arrow	Left arrow
Move up one line	Up arrow	Up arrow
Move down one line	Down arrow	Down arrow
Move to the right one word	Ctrl + Right Arrow	⌘ + Right Arrow
Move to the left one word	Ctrl + Left Arrow	⌘ + Left Arrow
Select		
Select word	Double-click	Double-click
Select one character to the right	Shift + Right Arrow	Shift + Right Arrow
Select one character to the left	Shift + Left Arrow	Shift + Left Arrow
Select one word to the right	Ctrl + Shift + Right Arrow	⌘ + Shift + Right Arrow
Select one word to the left	Ctrl + Shift + Left Arrow	⌘ + Shift + Left Arrow
Select one line above	Shift + Up Arrow	Shift + Up Arrow
Select one line below	Shift + Down Arrow	Shift + Down Arrow
Select all characters	Ctrl + A	⌘ + A
Select characters from insertion point	Shift + click	Shift + click

Type Mask and Vertical Type Mask tools

Add to selection	Shift + click, then draw	Shift + click, then draw
Delete from selection	Alt + click, then draw	Option + click, then draw
Intersect with selection	Alt + Shift + click, then draw	Option + Shift + click, then draw
Designate type origin	Click + drag	Click + drag

CURVES DIALOG

Add color as new point on curve	Ctrl + click in image	⌘ + click in image
Add color as individual points for each curve	Ctrl + Shift + click	⌘ + Shift + click
Move points	Arrow keys	Arrow keys
Move points in multiples of 10	Shift + arrow keys	Shift + arrow keys
Add point	Click in grid	Click in grid
Delete point	Ctrl + click on point	⌘ + click on point
Deselect all points	Ctrl + D	⌘ + D
Toggle grid between fine/coarse	Alt + click in grid	Option + click in grid
Select next control point	Ctrl + Tab	⌘ + Tab

	Windows 95/NT	**Mac OS**
Select previous control point	Ctrl + Shift + Tab	⌘ + Shift + Tab
Select multiple control points	Shift + click	Shift + click

HUE/SATURATION DIALOG

Move range to new location	Click in image	Click in image
Add to range	Shift + click/drag in image	Shift + click/drag in image
Subtract from range	Alt + click/drag in image	Option + click/drag in image
Edit master	Ctrl + tilde	⌘ + tilde
Edit individual colors	Ctrl + 1–6	⌘ + 1–6
Slide color spectrum	Ctrl + drag on ramp	⌘ + drag on ramp

GRADIENT EDITOR

New gradient	Ctrl + N	⌘ + N
Save gradient as map settings	Ctrl + Alt + click Save button	⌘ + Option + click Save button
Discontiguous selection of gradients in list	Ctrl + click gradient name	⌘ + click gradient name
Contiguous selection of gradients in list	Shift + click gradient name	Shift + click gradient name

3D TRANSFORM DIALOG

Select tool	V	V
Direct-selection tool	A	A
Cube tool	M	M
Sphere tool	N	N
Cylinder tool	C	C
Add-anchor-point tool	+ (plus)	+ (plus)
Delete-anchor-point tool	- (minus)	- (minus)
Pan Camera tool	E	E
Trackball tool	R	R
Hand tool	H	H
Zoom tool	Z	Z
Toggle Select/Direct-selection tools	Ctrl + Tab	⌘ + Tab
Pan image	Spacebar + drag	Spacebar + drag
Zoom in	Ctrl + Spacebar + drag/click	⌘ + Spacebar + drag/click
Zoom out	Ctrl + Alt + Spacebar + click	⌘ + Option + Spacebar + click

RECOLOR 11

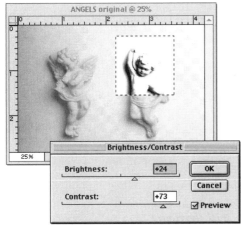

N THIS CHAPTER you will learn to fill a selection with color, a pattern, or imagery; apply a stroke to a selection or a layer; adjust a color image using the Hue/Saturation, Color Balance, Variations, Curves, and Levels commands; use the Color Sampler tool to get multiple color readouts; change colors using the Replace Color command; strip color from a layer; saturate or desaturate colors using the Sponge tool; blend channels using the Channel Mixer; use a neutral color layer to heighten color; tint a grayscale image; and create and print spot color channels.

Adjust command basics

Every Image menu > Adjust submenu dialog box has a **Preview** box. Changes preview in the image or selection when the Preview box is checked **1**. CMYK color displays more acccurately with Preview on. (Macintosh: If you're working on a normal layer—not an adjustment layer—changes affect the entire screen when the Preview box is unchecked.)

Note: Make sure your monitor is calibrated before performing color adjustments.

Macintosh: To display the **unmodified** image in the image window while an adjust dialog box is open, uncheck the Preview box, then press and hold on the title bar of the dialog box. *Windows:* Just uncheck Preview.

While a dialog box is open, you can Ctrl-Spacebar-click/⌘-Spacebar-click to **zoom in** or Alt-Spacebar-click/Option-Spacebar-click to **zoom out**, or press Spacebar to **move** the image in the image window.

In addition to the standard method for applying an Adjust command, many Adjust commands can be applied via an **adjustment layer 2**. Unlike the standard method,

1 *Changes preview only in the image window or selection when the **Preview** box is checked.*

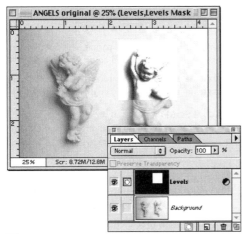

2 *For more flexibility, try out adjustments via an* **adjustment layer**.

(Continued on the following page)

which affects only the currently active layer, the adjustment layer affects all the currently visible layers below it. The adjustment layer, however, doesn't actually change pixels until it's merged with the layer below it. Adjustment layers are used in this chapter, but to learn how to create and use them, follow the instructions on pages 128–130.

You can use the **Save** command in the Levels, Curves, Replace Color, Selective Color, Hue/Saturation, Channel Mixer, or Variations dialog box to save color adjustment settings. You can then apply them to another layer or to another image via the **Load** button for the same command.

Any Adjust command can be recorded and applied via an **action**.

Some of the color adjustment commands or techniques, such as Variations, Color Balance, and Brightness/Contrast, produce broad, overall changes. Other commands, such as Levels, Curves, Hue/Saturation, Replace Color, Selective Color, and Channel Mixer, offer a greater degree of control, but are more complicated to use. Which command you decide to use will depend on the kind of imagery you're working with and whether it will be color separated or output online. A color cast (i.e. too blue or too magenta) will be most noticeable in figurative photography. This kind of imagery demands the most precise color adjustment.

To fill a selection or a layer with a color, a pattern, or imagery:

1. To fill with a flat Foreground or Background **color**, choose that color now from the Color or Swatches palette.
 or
 To create a tiling **pattern**, select an area on a layer using the Rectangular Marquee tool, choose Edit menu > Define Pattern, then Deselect (Ctrl-D/⌘-D).
 or
 To fill with **history**, click in the box next to a state on the History palette to establish a source for the History Brush.

Fill shortcuts

WINDOWS

Fill with Foreground color, 100% opacity	Alt-Backspace
Fill with Background color, 100% opacity	Ctrl-Backspace
Fill existing pixels (not transparent areas) with the Foreground color	Alt-Shift - Backspace
Fill existing pixels (not transparent areas) with the Background color	Ctrl-Shift- Backspace

MACINTOSH

Fill with Foreground color, 100% opacity	Option-Delete
Fill with Background color, 100% opacity	⌘-Delete
Fill existing pixels (not transparent areas) with the Foreground color	Option-Shift- Delete
Fill existing pixels (not transparent areas) with the Background color	⌘-Shift- Delete

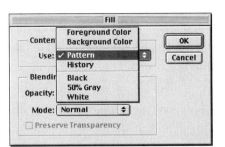

1 *In the* **Fill** *dialog box, choose a Fill option from the* **Use** *drop-down menu, enter an* **Opacity**, *and choose a* **Mode**.

Select an area to use as a **tile** *for a pattern.*

The tile used as a **fill pattern** *in another image.*

To produce this image, the pattern layer was duplicated, the opacity of the duplicate was lowered to 43%, and its blending mode was changed to Multiply.

2. Choose a layer. To fill the entire layer, uncheck the **Preserve Transparency** box on the Layers palette; to fill only non-transparent areas on the layer, check the Preserve Transparency box.

To limit the fill area, create a **selection** using any method described in Chapter 5.

3. Choose Edit menu > Fill (Shift-Backspace/ Shift-Delete).

4. Choose one of the following from the **Use** drop-down menu: **1**

Foreground Color, Background Color, Black, 50% Gray, or White.

Pattern to fill with the pattern you defined for step 1.

History to fill with imagery from the active layer at the state that you chose as a source.

5. Enter a Blending Opacity percentage and choose a Mode.

6. *Optional:* If you forgot to check the Preserve Transparency box on the Layers palette, you can check it here.

7. Click OK (Enter/Return).

TIP If you dislike the new fill color, choose Edit menu > Undo now so it won't blend with your next color or mode choice.

More about pattern-making

When you create a new pattern using the Define Pattern command, it replaces the last one. You can, of course, save any image that contains a pattern and use the Define Pattern command any time you want to redefine it as a fill pattern.

You can define a pattern in one image and use it as a fill in another image. If the resolution of the pattern is higher than that of the image in which it is used as a fill, the pattern will enlarge. If the resolution of the pattern is lower than that of the destination image, the pattern will shrink.

You can also apply a pattern using the Pattern Stamp tool (see page 99) or the Paint Bucket tool.

Patterns

Apply a stroke to a selection or a layer:

1. Choose a layer. If you don't want the stroke to extend into transparent areas on the layer, check the Preserve Transparency box and don't choose the Location: Outside option for step 6.

2. *Optional:* Select an area on the layer.

3. Choose a Foreground color.

4. Choose Edit menu > Stroke.

5. Enter a Width (1–16).

6. Click Location: Inside, Center, or Outside (the position of the stroke on the edge of the selection or layer imagery).

7. Enter a number in the Opacity field.

8. Choose a Blending Mode.

9. Click OK (Enter/Return).

TIP To stroke a path, see page 223.

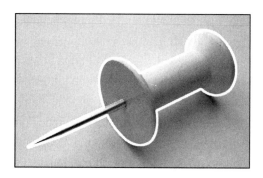

Apply a Stroke

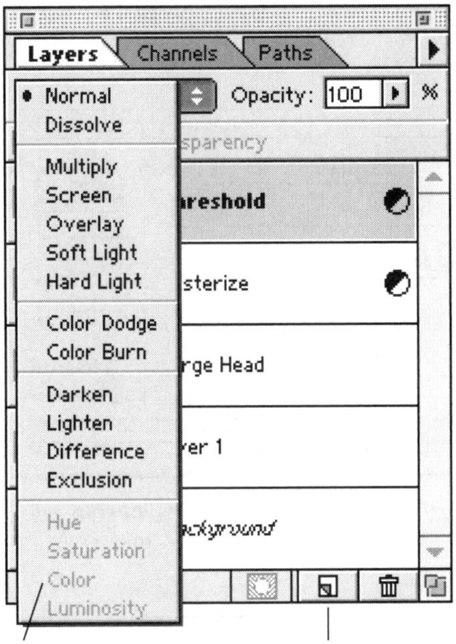

2 *Blending modes*

1 *Create new layer*

To preview fill modes and opacities on a selection or a layer:

1. Activate the layer on which you want to preview the fill.

2. Select the area that you want to fill.
or
Ctrl-click/⌘-click the layer name or thumbnail to select all the pixels on that layer.

3. Click the Create new layer button at the bottom of the Layers palette **1**. You will be filling on the new layer.

4. Uncheck the Preserve Transparency box on the Layers palette.

5. Choose a Foreground color.

6. Press Alt-Backspace/Option-Delete to fill the selection or layer with the Foreground color, 100% opacity.

7. To experiment with various color effects, choose an opacity and a blending mode from the Layers palette **2**.

8. If you created a selection, choose Select menu > Deselect (Ctrl-D/⌘-D) or click inside the selection with a Marquee or Lasso tool.

9. *Optional:* To merge the new layer with the layer below it, choose Merge Down from the Layers palette command menu (Ctrl-E/⌘-E).

TIP To remove parts of the color fill, use the Eraser tool, or create a layer mask before you merge the layer downward, or delete the layer altogether.

TIP To use further options for blending the new layer with the layer below it, choose Layer Options from the Layers palette command menu (see page 191). You can also paint on the new layer with any painting tool.

Preview Fill Modes and Opacities

Adjust Color using Hue/Saturation

To adjust a color image using Hue/Saturation:

1. Choose a layer. *Optional:* Select an area of the layer to recolor only that area.

2. Choose Image menu > Adjust > Hue/Saturation (Ctrl-U/⌘-U).
   or
   Create an adjustment layer: Ctrl-click/⌘-click the Create new layer button at the bottom of the Layers palette, choose Type: Hue/Saturation, then click OK.

3. From the Edit drop-down menu, choose Master to adjust all the image colors at once or choose a preset range to adjust only colors within that range **1**.

4. Make sure the Preview box is checked.

5. Do any of the following:
   Move the **Hue** slider to the left or the right **2** to shift colors to another part of the color bar.

   Move the **Saturation** slider to the left to decrease saturation or to the right to increase saturation.

   To lighten the image or layer, move the **Lightness** slider to the right. To darken the image or layer, move it to the left.

   TIP To add Color Sampler points while the Hue/Saturation dialog is open, choose Edit: Master, then Shift-click on the image.

6. If a preset color range was chosen from the Edit drop-down menu, the adjustment slider and color selection droppers will become available **3**. You can use the adjustment slider to narrow or widen the range that the Hue, Saturation, and Lightness sliders will affect.
   Do any of the following to the adjustment slider:

   Drag the dark gray area in the center to reposition the whole slider, as is, to a new spot on the color bar, and thus choose another color range (**4**, next page). The Edit drop-down menu will update to reflect the new color range choice.

1 *From the **Edit** drop-down menu, choose **Master** or choose a preset **color** range.*

2 *Then move the **Hue, Saturation,** or **Lightness** sliders.*

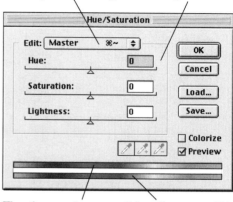

*The **reference** color bar won't change.*

*Color **adjustments** will be displayed in this color bar.*

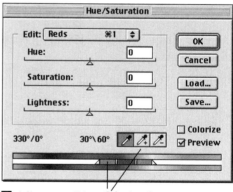

3 *Adjustment slider.   Selection droppers.*

To colorize a color or grayscale image

Check the Colorize box to tint the current layer. Move the Hue slider to apply a different tint; move the Saturation slider to reduce/increase tint color intensity; move the Lightness slider to lighten or darken the tint (and the image). The Edit drop-down menu defaults to Master when the Colorize option is on. To produce a duotone, see page 300.

To tint a grayscale image using this method, convert it to RGB Color or CMYK Color mode first.

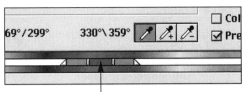

4 *The adjusment slider repositioned into a new range.*

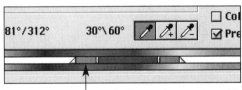

5 *The vertical white bar moved inward to* **narrow** *the* **color range**.

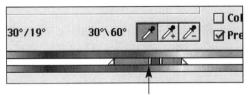

6 *The gray area (the fall-off) moved outward to* **widen** *the* **color range**. *The fall-off is unchanged.*

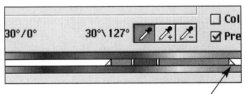

7 *The triangle moved outward to* **widen** *the* **fall-off**. *The color range is unchanged.*

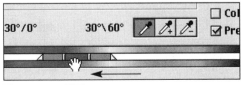

8 *Ctrl-drag/⌘⌘-drag to reposition the display position of the slider and the colors on the color bars.*

Drag either or both of the vertical white bars on the slider to narrow or expand the range. Decreasing the range increases the fall-off area, and vice versa **5**.

Drag either or both of the gray areas to widen or narrow the range without altering the fall-off area **6**.

Drag the triangles on the slider to alter how much of the current range falls off into adjacent colors **7**. Drag outward to increase fall-off or inward to decrease it. *Note:* A very short fall-off may produce dithering in the image.

Ctrl-drag/⌘⌘-drag either color bar to adjust where colors are displayed on the bar **8**. Colors wrap from one edge to the other. This won't affect the actual image.

If you alter the slider for any of the six preset color ranges, then that current color adjustment will become a new listing on the Edit drop-down menu. If, for example, you move the preset Reds range slider so it enters the Yellows range, then the menu will list Yellows and Yellows 2, and will no longer list Reds, since the Yellows range now includes Reds.

Click on a color in the image window—related colors will be adjusted. Or use the + or - dropper to add to or subtract from any current color range by clicking on the image. Hold down Shift while the regular dropper is selected to make it function temporarily like an add dropper; hold down Alt/Option to make the regular dropper function temporarily like a subtract dropper.

7. Click OK (Enter/Return).

TIP To restore the original dialog box settings, Alt-click/Option-click Reset.

TIP By default, the adjustment slider covers 90° of the color bar, the gray areas to the left and right (the fall-off) occupy 30° each, and the dark gray area (the color range) occupies 30°.

Instead of using the Eyedropper tool to get a color readout from one spot, you can use the Color Sampler tool to place up to four color readout markers, called color samplers, on an image. As you perform color and shade adjustments, before and after color breakdown readouts will display on the Info palette. You can also place color samplers while a color adjustment dialog box is open (Shift-click on the image). Color samplers save with the file in which they are placed.

1 *Clicking on an image with the **Color Sampler** tool to create four sampler locations.*

To place color samplers on an image:

1. Choose the Color Sampler tool 🖋 from the Eyedropper tool pop-out menu.

2. Click on up to four locations on the image to position color samplers **1**.

Note: If you choose a tool other than the Color Sampler, Eyedropper, or a painting or editing tool, the samplers will disappear from view. To redisplay them, choose one of the above-mentioned tools or open an Adjust submenu dialog box. To deliberately hide them, choose Hide Color Samplers from the Info palette command menu.

TIP Color samplers gather data from the topmost visible layer that contains pixels in the spot where the sampler is located. If you hide a layer from which a sampler is reading, the sampler will then read from the next layer down that contains pixels in that spot. The Info palette will update if you hide a layer from which it was reading sampler data.

TIP The samplers are located on the canvas. They won't move if a layer is transformed or flipped, but they *will* move if the canvas is rotated.

To move a color sampler:

Choose the Color Sampler tool, then drag a color sampler.
or
Choose the Eyedropper tool, then Ctrl-drag/⌘-drag a color sampler.

TIP Use Shift-I to toggle between the Color Sampler and Eyedropper tools.

Color Samplers

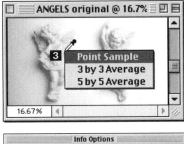

1 *The four **color sampler** readouts appear at the bottom of the **Info** palette.*

Before   After

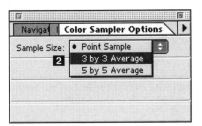

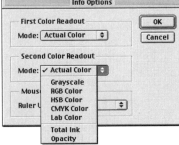

4 *Choose a **color space** for the Info palette from the Info Options dialog box.*

Using the Info palette with the Color Sampler tool

The Info palette displays before-adjustment and after-adjustment color breakdowns of the pixel or pixel area under each color sampler **1**. The size of the sample area depends on which **Sample Size** setting is chosen on the Color Sampler Options palette **2**. Choose Point Sample to sample only the pixel under the pointer; choose 3 by 3 Average or 5 by 5 Average to sample an average color from a 3- or 5-pixel area. You can also choose a Sample Size from a context menu by Right-clicking/Control-clicking on the image with the Color Sampler tool **3**. If you change the Sample Size for the Color Sampler tool, that setting will also change for the Eyedropper, and vice versa.

To choose a **color model** (Grayscale, RGB Color, etc.) for a section of the Info palette, press the tiny arrowhead next to the dropper icon on the palette, then choose from the pop-up menu that opens **4**. Actual Color is the image's current color mode; Total Ink is the total percentage of CMYK under the pointer based on the current CMYK Setup settings. The model you choose for the Info palette doesn't have to match the current image mode.

To remove a color sampler:

Choose the Color Sampler tool, then Alt-click/Option-click on a sampler or drag the sampler out of the image window. That sampler's readout area will be removed from the Info palette, and the remaining samplers will be renumbered automatically.

or

Choose the Eyedropper tool, then Alt-Shift-click/Option-Shift-click a sampler.

Info Palette; Remove Sampler

Use the Replace Color command to change colors in an image without having to first select them.

To replace colors:

1. *Optional:* For an RGB image, choose View menu > Preview > CMYK (Ctrl-Y/⌘-Y) to see a preview of the actual image and modifications to it in CMYK color. (The Sample swatch in the Replace Color dialog box will continue to display in RGB.) You can choose this command even while the dialog box is open.

2. Choose a layer.

3. *Optional:* Create a selection to restrict color replacement to that area.

4. Choose any tool other than the Eyedropper or Color Sampler.

5. Choose Image menu > Adjust > Replace Color.

6. Click on the color you want to replace in the preview window in the Replace Color dialog box or in the image window **1**.

7. *Optional:*
Move the Fuzziness slider to the right to add related colors to the selection **2**.
or
Shift-click in the preview window or on the image to add other color areas to the selection. Or choose the **+** eyedropper and click without holding down Shift.
or
Alt-click/Option-click in the preview window or on the image to subtract color areas from the selection. Or choose the **–** eyedropper icon and click without holding down Shift.

8. Move the Hue, Saturation, or Lightness sliders to change the selected colors (only the Lightness slider will be available for a Grayscale image). The Sample swatch will change as you move the sliders **3**.

The Transform sliders will stay in their current position even if you click on a different area of the image.

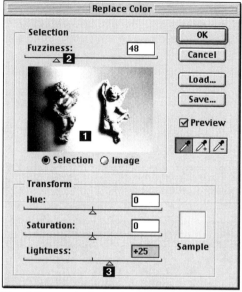

*The **white** areas in the preview window are the areas that will be modified.*

4 *The original image.*

5 *After a **Lightness** adjustment to the background.*

9. Click OK (Enter/Return) **4**–**5**.

TIP To restore the original dialog box settings, Alt-click/Option-click Reset.

TIP Choose Edit menu > Undo to restore the previous selection in the preview window.

TIP The Sample swatch color from the Replace Color dialog box will also display in the currently active square on the Color palette, and the Color palette sliders will reflect its individual components. If the gamut alarm displays, you have produced a non-printable color using the Transform sliders. The Transform sliders won't change the amount of Black (K) in a color for an image in CMYK Color mode. That component is set by Photoshop's Black Generation function.

TIP Click the Selection button to preview the selection in the preview window or click the Image button to display the entire image (Macintosh: press Control to toggle between the two display modes). If your image extends beyond the edges of your monitor, turn the Image preview option on so you'll be able to sample from the entire image with the eyedropper.

Use the Desaturate command to strip color from a layer without actually changing image modes.

To strip color from a layer or the Background:

1. Choose a layer or the Background.

2. Choose Image menu > Adjust > Desaturate (Ctrl-Shift-U/⌘-Shift-U).

Use the Color Balance dialog box to apply or correct a warm or cool cast in a layer's highlights, midtones, or shadows. Color adjustments will be easiest to see in an image that has a wide tonal range.

To colorize or color correct using Color Balance:

1. Make sure the composite color image is displayed (the first channel on the Channels palette). To colorize a Grayscale image, first convert it to a color image mode.

2. Choose a layer.

3. Choose Image menu > Adjust > Color Balance (Ctrl-B/⌘-B).
   or
   Create an adjustment layer: Ctrl-click/⌘-click the Create new layer button at the bottom of the Layers palette, choose Type: Color Balance, then click OK.

4. Click the tonal range that you want to adjust: Shadows, Midtones, or Highlights **1**.

5. *Optional:* Check the Preserve Luminosity box to preserve brightness values.

6. Move any slider toward a color you want to add more of. Cool and warm colors are paired opposite each other.

   Move sliders toward related colors to make an image warmer or cooler. For example, move sliders toward Cyan and Blue to produce a cool cast. Pause to preview.

7. *Optional:* Repeat step 6 with any other button selected for step 4.

8. Click OK (Enter/Return).

TIP Use a Paintbrush with a light opacity to tint small areas manually.

1 *Click **Shadows**, **Midtones**, or **Highlights**, then move any of the sliders.*

Thumbnail previews in the Variations dialog box represent how an image will look with various color adjustments. To make more precise adjustments and preview changes in the image window, use the Color Balance or Levels dialog box.

Notes: The Variations command can't be used on an Indexed Color image.

To adjust color using thumbnail Variations:

1. Choose a layer.

2. Choose Image menu > Adjust > Variations.

3. Click Shadows, Midtones, or Highlights to modify only those areas **1**.
or
Click Saturation to adjust only saturation.

4. Position the Fine/Coarse slider to the right of center to make major adjustments or to the left of center to make minor adjustments **2**. Each notch to the right doubles the adjustment per click. Each notch to the left halves the adjustment per click.

5. Click any "More..." thumbnail to add more of that color to the layer **3**. Pause to preview. To lessen the amount of a color, click its diagonally opposite color.

Note: Compare the Current Pick thumbnail, which represents the modified layer, with the Original thumbnail. Click the Original thumbnail to undo the Variations adjustment.

6. *Optional:* Click Lighter or Darker to change the luminosity without changing the hue **4**.

7. *Optional:* If you chose to adjust Shadows, Highlights, or Saturation, you can check the Show Clipping box to display neon highlights in areas that will be converted to black or white.

8. *Optional:* Repeat steps 3–6.

9. Click OK (Enter/Return).

*Click the **Original** thumbnail to restore the unmodified layer.*

1 *First click **Shadows**, **Midtones**, **Highlights**, or **Saturation**.*

*The **Current Pick** thumbnail represents the modified layer.*

2 *Move the **Fine/Coarse** slider to control the degree of adjustment.*

3 *Click any **More [...]** thumbnail to add more of that color to the layer. Click the diagonally opposite thumbnail to undo the modification.*

4 *Click **Lighter** or **Darker** to modify the luminosity without modifying the hue.*

Use the Sponge tool to make color areas on the current layer more or less saturated. (The Sponge tool is also discussed on page 305, where it's used to bring colors into printable gamut.) This tool can't be used on a Bitmap or Indexed Color image.

To saturate or desaturate colors using the Sponge tool:

1. Double-click the Sponge tool (Shift-O cycles through the Dodge, Burn, and Sponge tools).

2. On the Sponge Options palette, choose a Pressure setting between 1% (low intensity) and 100% (high intensity) **1**. Try a low Pressure percentage first (20%-30%) so the tool won't saturate or desaturate areas too quickly. You can press a number on the keyboard to change the Pressure.

and

Choose Desaturate or Saturate from the drop-down menu **2**.

3. On the Brushes palette, click a hard-edged or soft-edged tip. A soft tip will produce the smoothest result.

4. Choose a layer.

5. Stroke on any area of the layer, pausing to allow the screen to redraw **3**. Stroke again to intensify the effect.

TIP If you Saturate or Desaturate an area too much, choose Edit menu > Undo or click an earlier state or snapshot on the History palette. Don't try to use the tool with its opposite setting to fix it—you'll get uneven results.

TIP You can also adjust saturation in an image using the Image menu > Adjust > Hue/Saturation or Replace Color command.

3 *Using the Sponge tool to desaturate colors in an image.*

The Channel Mixer produces unique mixtures of RGB or CMYK channels—mixtures that may be too difficult to achieve using other commands. To use the Channel Mixer to perform a color-to-grayscale conversion or tint a grayscale image, see page 138.

To use the Channel Mixer:

1. Choose a layer, and make sure the composite color channel is displayed (Channels palette).

2. Choose Image menu > Adjust > Channel Mixer.

3. Choose a channel from the Output Channel drop-down menu.

4. Do any of the following:

Move whichever slider is set at 100% (the chosen Output channel) below 100 to reduce the amount of that color in the channel or above 100 to increase the amount of that color.

Move any of the other sliders to the left to add more of that color to the Output channel (a negative value) or to the right to subtract more of that color (a positive value). *Note:* for a Black source channel, move it to the left to reduce or to the right to increase the amount of black.

Bear in mind the mixing relationship between the six color components that are used in Photoshop: Cyan to Red, Magenta to Green, and Yellow to Blue. Decreasing Cyan, for example, will result in more Red in the channel, and vice versa. If you forget these relationships, open up the Color Balance dialog box.

Move the Constant slider to the right to add the current output channel color as a wash over the entire image. Move it to the left to subtract that color and add its related colors to the entire image.

5. Click OK (Enter/Return).

TIP Click Save in the Channel Mixer dialog box to save the current settings to a file. Click Load to load in those settings at a later time.

Channel Mixer

Curves and Levels

If you use the Curves or Levels command to make color or tonal adjustments, you should adjust the overall tone of the image first (the composite channel), and then adjust the individual color channels, if necessary (a bit more cyan, a bit less magenta, etc.).

If you adjust an individual color channel, keep in mind that color opposites (cyan and red, magenta and green, yellow and blue) work in tandem. Lowering cyan, for example, adds more red; lowering red adds more cyan. The moral of the story is, you'll probably have to adjust more than one channel to remove an undesirable color cast. If you overzealously adjust only one channel, you'll throw off the color balance of the whole image.

Using the Curves command, you can correct a picture's highlights, quarter tones, mid-tones, three-quarter tones, or shadows separately. You can even use multiple adjustment layers to do this. Use one adjustment layer for the composite channel first and then use another one for each individual channel to tweak the color. And you can experiment with the layer opacity or layer mask to remove or lessen the effect in specific areas.

To adjust color or values using the Curves command:

1. *Optional:* To adjust a combination of two or more channels at the same time, Shift-click those channel names on the Channels palette now. *Note:* You can't do this for a Curves adjustment layer.

2. Choose Image menu > Adjust > Curves (Ctrl-M/⌘-M).
or
Create an adjustment layer: Ctrl-click/⌘-click the Create new layer button at the bottom of the Layers palette, choose Type: Curves, then click OK.

3. With the pointer over the grid, the default Input and Output readouts are the brightness values for RGB Color mode or percentage values for CMYK

Curves

Highlights.

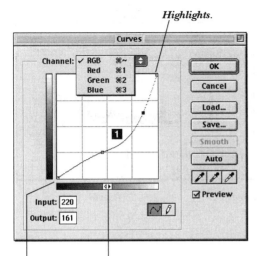

Shadows.   *Click on the **gradient bar** to **reverse** the curve.*

2 *The original image.*

3 *After a **Curves** adjustment.*

Color mode. Click on the gradient bar to switch between the two readouts.

4. *Optional:* Choose a channel name to adjust it separately (this won't work if you're working on an adjustment layer). If you chose more than one channel in step 1, you can select that combo now (i.e. "RB" for the red and blue channels).

5. If the gradient on the gradient bar is white on the left side, drag the part of the curve you want to adjust upward to darken or downward to lighten **1**.
and/or
For more precise adjusting, click on the curve to create up to 14 points to force the curve to remain fixed, then drag between points to make subtle adjustments. (To remove a point, drag it off the graph; click on it and press Backspace/ Delete; or Ctrl-click/⌘⌘-click on it.)
and/or
Move the extreme end of the curve to reduce absolute black to below 100%, or absolute white to above 0%.

Note: Once you've added a point, you can then enter numbers in the Input and/or Output fields.

6. Click OK (Enter/Return) **2**–**3**.

TIP We don't recommend using the Curves pencil tool to draw a curve—it tends to produce a bumpy curve, which in turn produces sharp color transition jumps.

TIP For an image in RGB Color mode, click on the image to see that pixel value placement on the curve. Ctrl-click/ ⌘⌘-click to place that point on the curve. The pixel value will show on the individual C, M, Y, and K channels, but not on the composite CMYK channel.

TIP Alt-click/Option-click on the grid in the Curves dialog box to narrow the grid spacing; Alt-click/Option-click again to widen the grid spacing.

TIP Shift-click on the image to place Color Sampler points while the Curves dialog box is open.

Curves

To adjust individual color channels using Levels:

1. Display the Info palette.

2. Choose Image menu > Adjust > Levels
(Ctrl-L/⌘-L).
or
Create an adjustment layer: Ctrl-click/
⌘-click the Create new layer button at
the bottom of the Layers palette, choose
Type: Levels, then click OK.

3. Check the Preview box.

4. If there's an obvious predominance of
one color in the image (like too much
red or green), choose that channel name
from the Channel drop-down menu **1**.

Follow any of these steps for a **CMYK**
Color image (the sliders will have the
opposite effect in an **RGB** image):

To increase the amount of that particular
color, move the black or gray Input
Levels slider to the right. The black
triangle affects the shadows in the image,
the gray triangle affects the midtones.
or
To decrease the amount of that color,
move the gray or white Input Levels
slider to the left. The white slider affects
the highlights.
or
To tint the image with the chosen channel color, move the white Output Levels
slider to the left. To lessen the chosen
channel color, move the black Output
Levels slider to the right. The Output
sliders are particularly effective for
adjusting skin tones in a photograph.

Repeat these steps for any other channels that need adjusting, bearing in
mind that one channel adjustment may
affect another.

5. Click OK (Enter/Return).

TIP Alt-click/Option-click Reset to restore
the original dialog box settings.

TIP Shift-click on the image to place Color
Sampler points while the Levels dialog
box is open.

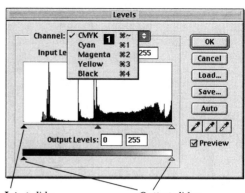

Input *slider*   **Output** *sliders*

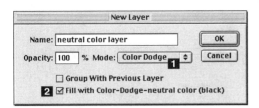

In this exercise, you'll be painting shades of gray on a neutral black or white layer with the Color Dodge or Color Burn mode setting to heighten or lessen color in the underlying layer. Though this exercise uses the Color Dodge and Color Burn modes, you can use the neutral color layer option with other layer modes.

To heighten color or silhouette color areas on black:

1. Convert the image to RGB image mode, and activate the layer to which you want to make color changes.

2. Choose Layer menu > New > Layer.
   or
   Alt-click/Option-click the Create new layer button on the Layers palette.

3. Type a name for the layer.

4. We chose Color Dodge mode for our illustration **1**, but you can choose any mode other than Normal, Dissolve, Hue, Saturation, Color, or Luminosity.

5. Check the "Fill with [mode name]-neutral color" box **2**, then click OK. Our layer was filled with black.

6. Choose the Paintbrush tool. ✏

7. Choose Grayscale Slider from the Color palette command menu.

8. Paint with 60-88% gray. You'll actually be changing the neutral black on the layer. Areas you stroke over will become much lighter.

   If you're displeased with the results, paint over areas or fill the entire layer again with black to remove all the changes, and start over. Repainting or refilling with black will remove any existing editing effects while preserving pixels in the underlying layers.

9. To heighten the color effect, you can choose another mode from the Layers palette. We chose Color Burn mode. Your image strokes will be silhouetted against black **3**–**6**. Paint with a medium gray to restore more original color.

3 *The original image.*

4 *After painting on the Color Dodge mode layer, choosing Color Burn as the layer mode, and painting medium gray strokes on the Color Burn mode layer.*

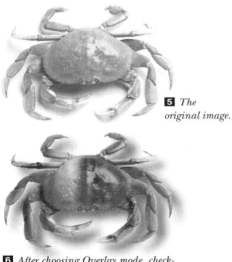

5 *The original image.*

6 *After choosing Overlay mode, checking the "Fill with…" option for the neutral layer, and applying Dodge and Burn strokes to the neutral layer to heighten the highlights and shadows.*

To convert a color layer to grayscale and selectively restore its color:

1. Choose a layer in a color image. Layers below this layer will be affected by the adjustment layer you're about to create.

2. Ctrl-click/⌘-click the Create new layer button on the Layers palette to create an adjustment layer, choose Type: Hue/Saturation, then click OK.

3. Move the Saturation slider all the way to the left (to -100) **1**.

4. Click OK (Enter/Return).

5. Set the Foreground color to black.

6. On the adjustment layer, paint across the image where you want to restore the original colors from the underlying layers **2**. (Paint with white to reset areas to grayscale.)

7. *Optional:* You can also restack a layer above the adjustment layer to fully restore that layer's color.

TIP Choose any of the following mode and opacity combinations for the adjustment layer:

Dissolve with a 40%–50% Opacity to restore color with a chalky texture.

Multiply with a 100% Opacity to restore subtle color in the darker areas of the image.

Color Dodge to lighten and intensify color or Color Burn to darken and intensify color.

TIP To limit the adjustment layer effect to just the layer directly below it, Alt-click/ Option-click the line between them on the Layers palette to create a clipping group.

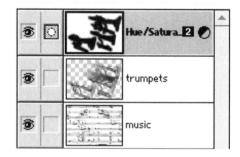

1 *In the **Hue/Saturation** dialog box, move the Saturation slider all the way to the left to remove color from the layer.*

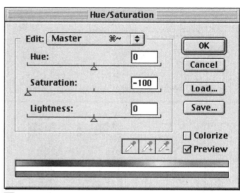

Use a mask

Duplicate a color layer, choose Image menu > Adjust > Desaturate (Ctrl-Shift-U/⌘-Shift-U), choose Layer menu > Add Layer Mask > Hide All to create a layer mask for that layer, and then paint with white to reveal parts of the grayscale layer above the color layer. You can gradually reshape the mask this way, alternately painting with black to add to the mask or white to remove the mask.

Copy to a spot color channel

To copy an image shape to a spot color channel, first make a selection on a layer. Then, with the selection active, create a new spot color channel. Or choose an existing spot color channel and fill the selection with black.

To copy an image's light and dark values to a spot color channel, first create a selection and copy it to the Clipboard. Then create or choose a spot color channel, and paste onto that channel.

1 *Click the* **Color** *swatch in the* **New Spot Channel** *dialog box.*

2 *The new spot channel.*

A spot color can be placed in its own separate channel. When the image is color separated, this spot color channel will appear on its own plate.

To create a spot color channel:

1. Display the Channels palette, and drag it away from the Layers palette so you can see both palettes at once.

2. Choose New Spot Channel from the Channels palette command menu.

3. Click the Color swatch, **1** and if necessary, click Custom to open the Custom Colors dialog box.

4. Choose a Pantone or other spot color matching system name from the Book drop-down menu, choose a color, then click OK.

5. *Optional:* To change the way color in the spot channel displays on screen, enter a new Ink Characteristics: Solidity percentage. At 100%, it will display as a solid color; at a lower percentage, it will appear more transparent.

6. Click OK. The new spot channel will automatically display the name of the color you chose **2**. Any stroke that is applied or image element that is created while the spot color channel is active will appear in that color.

   Note: To **change** the spot color in a channel, double-click the channel name, then follow steps 3–6, above. The channel will automatically be renamed for the new color and all the pixels on the channel will display in that new color.

Create a Spot Color Channel

Paint on a Spot Color Channel

To paint on a spot color channel:

1. Create a spot color channel (instructions on the previous page).

2. Double-click the spot color channel name, enter 100% in the Solidity field, then click OK (Enter/Return).

3. Choose the Paintbrush tool. (The Color palette will display in grayscale mode while a spot color channel is active.)

4. On the Paintbrush Options palette, choose Normal for the painting mode and choose an Opacity percentage to set the tint percentage for the spot color ink on the spot color plate.

5. Make sure the spot color channel is still active, then paint on the image.

Spot color channel basics

If the **eye** icon is present for both the spot color channel and the topmost (composite) channel on the Channels palette, then the spot channel will be displayed along with the other image layers. To display the spot channel by itself, hide (click) the eye icon for the composite channel.

If you want to know the **opacity** of a spot color area, choose the spot color channel, choose Actual Color mode for the readout on the Info palette, move the pointer over the image, and then note the K (grayscale percentage) on the palette.

When a spot color channel is active, the most recently active **layer** will have a gray highlight and edits will affect only the spot channel. If you click the topmost (composite) channel on the Channels palette, edits will now affect the most recently active layer—not the the spot channel.

To add **type** to a spot color channel, see page 239.

If a continuous-tone grayscale image is converted to Duotone mode (with a spot color set to print with black to generate the image), and then the image is converted to Multichannel mode, any spot colors in the duotone will be placed in separate spot

Lighten or darken a spot channel tint

Choose the channel, then choose Image menu > Adjust > Levels. To darken the tint, move the black Input slider to the right; to lighten the tint, move the black Output slider to the right. Position the pointer over the image so you can get an opacity readout on the Info palette (choose Actual Color mode for the readout). Readjust either slider, if desired.

channels. Preexisting spot channels, if any, will remain after the conversion. To **tint** an entire image with a spot color, convert the image to Duotone mode and specify the desired spot color as the monotone color (see page 301).

To **export** a file that contains spot channels, save it in the DCS 2.0 format. Each spot channel will be preserved as a separate file, along with the composite DCS file. Also, let Photoshop assign the spot channel name for you. If you do this, other applications will recognize it as a spot color.

Printing spot color channels

Spot channel colors **overprint** all other image colors. The stacking order of a spot channel on the Channels palette controls the order in which that color overprints. To prevent a spot color from overprinting, you must manually knock out (delete) any areas from other channels that fall beneath the spot color shapes (read more about this in the *Adobe Photoshop 5.0 User Guide*). And talk with your print shop to see if this step is necessary.

Choosing **Merge Spot Channel** (Channels palette command menu) merges the spot color into the existing color channels, so you can then print a composite (single-page) proof on a color printer. Otherwise, non-merged spot channels will print as separate pages. Merging a spot color channel into the other color channels will change the actual spot color, because CMYK inks can't exactly replicate spot color inks. When a spot color channel is merged into other color channels, its Solidity value will determine the merged spot color's tint percentage. The lower the Solidity, the more transparent will be the newly merged color. All image layers are flattened when spot channels are merged.

TIP Use the Solidity option to produce an on-screen simulation of the actual ink opacity for the spot plate. For an opaque ink, such as a metallic ink, use 100% Solidity. For a transparent, clear varnish, use 0% Solidity.

Print Spot Color Channels

To convert an alpha channel into a spot color channel:

1. Double-click an alpha channel on the Channels palette.

2. Choose Color Indicates: Spot Color **1**.

3. Click the color swatch **2**, click Custom, if necessary, to open the Custom Colors dialog box, choose a spot color (see page 141), then click OK (Enter/Return).

4. Click OK (Enter/Return). Former non-white (black or gray) areas on the channel will now be displayed in the spot color.

TIP To reverse the spot color and white areas, choose the channel, then choose Image menu > Adjust > Invert (Ctrl-I/ ⌘-I).

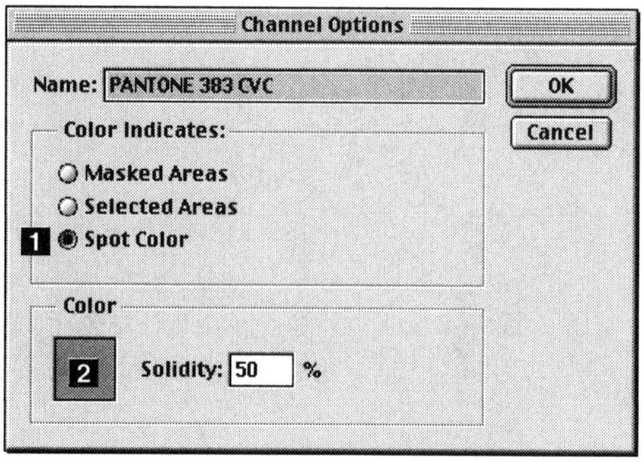

Channel Options

Name: PANTONE 383 CVC   OK   Cancel

Color Indicates:
○ Masked Areas
○ Selected Areas
1 ● Spot Color

Color
2 Solidity: 50 %

Convert Alpha Channel to Spot Channel

PAINT 12

Painting tool shortcuts

Cycle through the brush tips on the Brushes palette	[or]
Cycle through the blending modes on the Options palette	Shift + or Shift -
Choose an opacity level	0 through 9 (e.g., 2 = 20 %) or quickly type a percentage (e.g. "38")

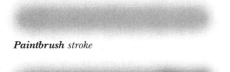

Paintbrush stroke

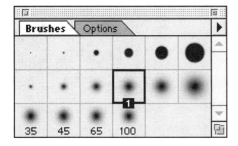

Airbrush stroke

IN THIS CHAPTER you will learn how to use Photoshop's Line, Airbrush, Pencil Paintbrush, Paint Bucket, Eraser, Smudge, and Gradient tools. You can paint on a scanned image or you can paint a picture from scratch. You will also learn how to create custom brush tips for the painting tools using the Brushes palette; how to save and load brush sets; and how to choose options for individual tools, like a blending mode and an opacity percentage.

To use the Paintbrush or Airbrush tool:

1. Choose a layer. Create a selection on the current layer if you want to paint in a restricted area.

2. Click the Paintbrush (B) 🖊 or Airbrush (J) tool. ✍

3. Choose a Foreground color (see pages 140–143).

4. Click a hard-edged tip in the first row of the Brushes palette or a soft-edged tip in the second or third row **1**. If a tip is too large to be displayed at its actual size, its width in pixels will be indicated by a number instead.

5. On the tool's Options palette, choose an Opacity (or Pressure) percentage **2**. At 100%, the stroke will completely cover underlying pixels.
and
Choose a blending mode (see "Blending modes" on pages 26–28).

6. *Optional:* To create a stroke that fades as it finishes, enter a number of steps (1–9999) in the Fade field. The higher the Fade value, the longer the stroke will be before it fades. Choose Transparent from the "Fade to" drop-down menu to

(Continued on the following page)

Use the Paintbrush or Airbrush Tool

Use the Paintbrush or Airbrush Tool

fade from the Foreground color to no color, or choose Background to fade from the Foreground color to the Background color.

7. *Optional:* Check the Wet Edges box for the Paintbrush tool to produce a stroke with a higher concentration of color at the edges, like the pooling effect in traditional watercoloring –❸.

8. Drag across any area of the picture. If you press and hold on an area with the Airbrush tool without dragging, the paintdrop will gradually widen and become more saturated.

TIP If you have a stylus hooked up but you're not using it, uncheck the Stylus Pressure box on the Options palette so the Paintbrush tool will work properly with a mouse.

TIP To draw a straight stroke, click once to begin the stroke, then hold down Shift and click in a different location to complete the stroke.

TIP Alt-click/Option-click on any open image to sample a color while a painting tool is chosen.

TIP With the Preserve Transparency box checked on the Layers palette, paint strokes will recolor only existing pixels—not transparent areas.

TIP Each tool keeps its own Options palette settings.

❶ *Strokes created with the Paintbrush tool with the **Wet Edges** box checked on the Paintbrush Options palette.*

❷ *More Wet Edges.*

❸ *The stroke on top was created with the Wet Edges box unchecked for the Paintbrush tool. The stroke on the bottom was created with the Wet Edges box checked.*

1 *Choose settings for the **Line** tool from its **Options** palette.*

2 *Straight lines added to an image using the **Line** tool.*

To draw straight lines:

1. Choose the Line tool ╲ (N or Shift N).
2. From the Line Options palette **1**:
   Choose a Weight (1–1000).
   and
   Choose a blending mode from the drop-down menu.
   and
   Choose an Opacity.
3. *Optional:* Check the Anti-aliased box to produce soft-edged lines.
4. Choose a Foreground color.
5. Draw a line by dragging the mouse. The line will fill with the Foreground color when the mouse is released **2**–**3**.

TIP Hold down Shift while dragging to constrain the line to a multiple of 45°.

TIP To create an arrow, first click the Start and/or End box on the Line Options palette. Click Shape, enter numbers in the Width, Length, and Concavity fields in the Arrowhead Shape dialog box **4**, click OK, then draw a line (hold down Shift to constrain the angle).

3 *A border was created with the Line tool (Dissolve mode at 85% opacity), and then Filter menu > Stylize > Diffuse was applied to it.*

4 *After clicking the **Start** or **End** box on the Line Options palette, you can then shape the arrowhead by choosing settings in the **Arrowhead Shape** dialog box.*

15% Concavity

-35% Concavity

Draw Straight Lines

To modify a brush tip:

1. Double-click a brush tip on the Brushes palette **1**.
or
Click a tip, then choose Brush Options from the palette command menu.

2. Move the Diameter slider **2**.
or
Enter a value for the Diameter (width) of the stroke (1–999).

3. Move the Hardness slider.
or
Enter a Hardness value for the percentage of the diameter of the stroke that's opaque (0–100).

4. Move the Spacing slider.
or
Enter a Spacing value (0–999). The higher the Spacing, the farther apart each paintdrop will be.
or
Uncheck the Spacing box to have the brush respond to mouse or stylus speed. The faster the mouse or stylus is dragged, the more paintdrops will skip (see page 11).

5. Enter an Angle (-180–180).
or
Move the gray arrow in a circular direction in the left preview box.

6. Enter a Roundness value (0–100). The higher the value, the rounder the tip.
or
Reshape the tip by dragging either black dot inward or outward in the left preview box.

7. Click OK (Return/Enter) **3**.

TIP Only the Spacing percentage can be changed for the Assorted brushes and most of the Drop Shadow brushes.

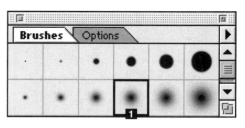

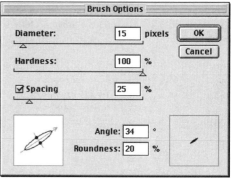

2 *Choose* **Diameter, Hardness, Spacing, Angle,** *and* **Roundness** *values in the* **Brush Options** *dialog box.*

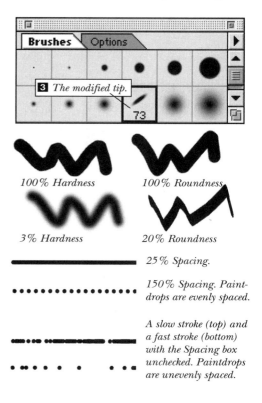

3 *The modified tip.*

100% Hardness

100% Roundness

3% Hardness

20% Roundness

25% Spacing.

150% Spacing. Paint-drops are evenly spaced.

A slow stroke (top) and a fast stroke (bottom) with the Spacing box unchecked. Paintdrops are unevenly spaced.

Modify a Brush Tip

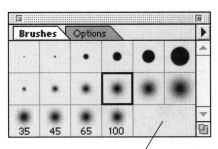

1 *Click here to create a **new** brush tip.*

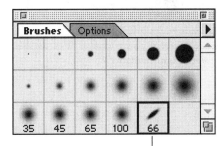

2 *The new tip appears after the last tip.*

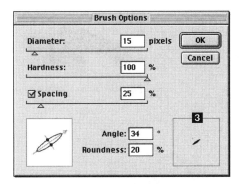

4 *A **calligraphic** line added to an image.*

To create a new brush tip:

1. Click on the blank area at the bottom of the Brushes palette **1**.
or
Choose New Brush from the palette command menu.

2. Follow steps 2–7 on the previous page to customize the tip. The new tip will appear after the last tip on the palette **2**.

To delete a brush tip:

Ctrl-click/⌘-click the brush tip that you want to delete.
or
Right-click/Control-click the brush tip that you want to delete, then choose Delete Brush from the context menu.

You can use the Pencil, Airbrush, or Paintbrush tool to create a linear element, such as a squiggly or a calligraphic line. Use different Angle and Roundness values to create your own line shapes.

To create a calligraphic brush tip:

1. Click the Pencil (N or Shift-N), Airbrush (J) ✎, or Paintbrush (B) ∥ tool.

2. Choose a Foreground color.

3. On the Brushes palette, double-click a hard-edged brush tip or click on the blank area at the bottom of the palette to create a new tip.

4. The brush will preview in the dialog box as you choose these settings: **3**

Choose a Diameter that will produce a wide enough brushstroke at your image resolution.

Position the Hardness slider at 100%.

Choose a Spacing value between 1 and 25.

Enter 34 in the Angle field.

Enter 20 in the Roundness field.

5. Click OK (Enter/Return). To draw a line, move the Pressure/Opacity slider on the Options palette, if desired, then draw shapes or letters **4**.

By drawing colored strokes on a separate layer to apply tints to a grayscale image, you'll have a lot of flexibility: You can change the blending mode or opacity for the Paintbrush or Airbrush tool or for the color layer, or erase or dodge here or there without affecting the underlying gray image.

To apply tints to a grayscale image:

1. Open a Grayscale mode image, and convert it to RGB Color mode (Image menu > Mode > RGB Color).

2. Alt-click/Option-click the Create new layer button on the Layers palette to create a new layer above the grayscale image, and choose Color blending mode for the new layer.

3. Choose the Paintbrush or Airbrush tool.

4. Choose a Foreground color and a brush.

5. Choose an Opacity/Pressure percentage below 100% from the Options palette. Choose a low-ish opacity for a subtle tint. You can change opacities between strokes. You can also lower the opacity of the whole layer via the Layers palette.

6. Paint strokes on the new layer 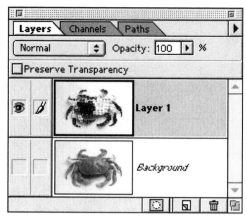.

7. *Optional:* Use the Eraser tool to remove areas of unwanted color (uncheck the Preserve Transparency box for this), then repaint, if desired. Or use the Dodge tool at a low Exposure percentage to gently lighten the tints.

8. *Optional:* Choose a different blending mode for the color layer. Try Soft Light, Color Burn, or Multiply. You can also use the Channel Mixer to apply colors.

To create a brush tip from an image:

1. Choose the Rectangular Marquee tool.

2. Marquee an area of a picture (maximum 1,000 by 1,000 pixels). Try using a distinct shape on a white background 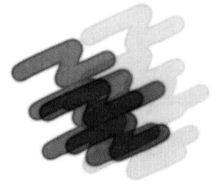.

3. Choose Define Brush from the Brushes palette command menu. The new tip will appear after the last tip on the palette. Use it with the Paintbrush  or

1 *The **color tints** are on Layer 1.*

2 *Select an area of an image.*

3 *The **custom brush tip** used with the Paintbrush tool at various opacities, and with the Wet Edges option turned on (Paintbrush Options palette).*

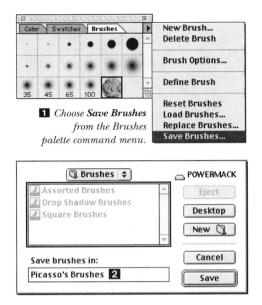

1 *Choose Save Brushes from the Brushes palette command menu.*

Airbrush tool. Specify a Spacing value for the gap between paintdrops (1–999) in the Brush Options dialog box.

4. Deselect (Ctrl-D/⌘-D).

To save a brush set:

1. Choose Save Brushes from the palette command menu **1**.

2. Enter a name in the "Save brushes in" field **2**. *Windows:* The extension for a brush set is ".abr".

3. Choose a location in which to save the set.

4. Click Save (Enter/Return).

Three Brushes palettes are supplied with Photoshop in addition to the Default Brushes: Assorted Brushes, which are special shapes and symbols; Drop Shadow Brushes, which are brush tips with soft edges that you can use to make drop shadows; and hard-edged Square Brushes.

To load a brush set:

1. To append a brush set to the existing set, choose Load Brushes from the palette command menu **3**.
or
To replace the currently displayed set with the new brush set, choose Replace Brushes from the palette command menu.

2. Open the Brushes folder, which is in the Goodies folder inside the Photoshop application folder.

3. Double-click a palette name (or click a palette name, then click Load (Win)/ Open (Mac)) **4**. The brushes will be added to the existing set.

TIP The brushes that were on the Brushes palette when you last exit/quit Photoshop will still be there next time you launch Photoshop. To restore the default Brushes palette, choose Reset Brushes from the palette command menu, then click OK.

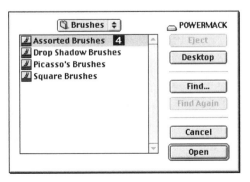

3 *Choose Load Brushes from the Brushes palette command menu.*

Save Brush Set; Load Brush Set

The Paint Bucket tool replaces pixels with the Foreground color or a pattern, and fills areas of similar shade or color within a specified Tolerance range. You can use the Paint Bucket without creating a selection.

Note: The Paint Bucket tool won't work on an image in Bitmap color mode.

To fill an area using the Paint Bucket tool:

1. Choose a layer. If you don't want to fill transparent areas on the layer, check the Preserve Transparency box.

2. Choose the Paint Bucket tool (K). ✍

3. On the Paint Bucket Options palette **1**:

Enter a number up to 255 in the Tolerance field. The higher the Tolerance value, the wider the range of colors the Paint Bucket will fill. Try a low number first.
and
Choose Contents: Foreground.
and
Choose a blending mode from the drop-down menu (Shift + or Shift - to cycle through the modes). (Try Soft Light, Multiply, or Color Burn.)
and
Choose an Opacity.
and
Check the Anti-aliased box to smooth the edges of the filled area.
and
Check the Use All Layers box if you want the Paint Bucket to fill areas on the active layer based on colors the tool detects on all the currently visible layers.

4. Choose a Foreground color.

5. Click on the image **2**–**3**.

TIP To fill with a pattern, before choosing the Paint Bucket, select an area of an image, choose Edit menu > Define Pattern, and deselect. Choose Contents: Pattern from the Paint Bucket Options palette.

1 *Choose settings for the **Paint Bucket** tool on its **Options** palette.*

2 *The original image.*

3 *After clicking with the **Paint Bucket** tool.*

PHOTO: PAUL PETROFF

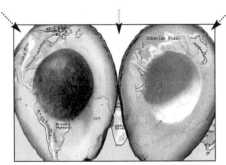

2 *The original image.*

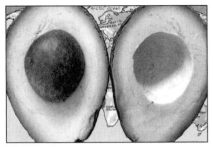

3 *After erasing part of the avocados layer to reveal the map underneath it (Airbrush option, 55% opacity), and erasing part of the map layer to white (Paintbrush option, 100% opacity).*

4 *A detail of the partially **erased** map layer.*

Note: If you use the Eraser tool on a layer with the Preserve Transparency box checked or on the Background of an image, the erased area will be replaced with the current Background color. If you erase on a layer with Preserve Transparency unchecked, the erased area will be replaced with transparency.

To erase part of a layer:

1. Choose a layer.

2. Choose the Eraser tool (E). ⌀

3. Choose Paintbrush, Airbrush, Pencil, or Block from the drop-down menu on the Eraser Options palette (Shift-E to cycle through the tool options) **1**.

4. Choose an Opacity/Pressure percentage.

5. Click a tip on the Brushes palette. (Don't bother to choose a tip for the Block option; its size won't change.)

6. If you're going to erase the Background of the image or if Preserve Transparency is checked on the Layers palette, choose a Background color.

7. Click on or drag across the layer **2**–**4**.

TIP To restore areas on the current layer from a history state, move the History source icon to the desired state on the History palette, then use the Eraser tool with the Erase to History box checked on the Options palette (or Alt-drag/Option-drag to turn on Erase to History temporarily).

TIP To produce a wet-edged eraser effect, choose Paintbrush from the drop-down menu and check the Wet Edges box.

The auto eraser paints the Background color if you begin dragging over the Foreground color; it paints the Foreground color if you begin dragging over any other color.

To auto erase:

1. Choose a Foreground color and a Background color.

2. Double-click the Pencil tool.

3. Check the Auto Erase box on the Pencil Options palette.

4. Draw strokes on the image.

Erase Part of a Layer; Auto Erase

The Smudge tool can't be used on an image in Bitmap or Indexed Color mode.

To smudge colors:

1. Choose the Smudge tool (R or Shift-R). 🖉

2. On the Smudge Options palette **1**, move the Pressure slider below 100%. *and*
Choose a blending mode (see pages 26–28), such as Normal to smudge all shades or colors, or Darken to push dark colors into lighter colors, or Lighten to push light colors into darker colors.

3. *Optional:* To start the Smudge with the Foreground color, check the Finger Painting box on the Smudge Options palette. With Finger Painting turned off, the smudge will start with the color under the pointer where the stroke begins. The higher the Pressure percentage, the more Foreground color is applied.

Hold down Alt/Option to temporarily turn on the Finger Painting option if the Finger Painting box is unchecked.

4. *Optional:* Check the Use All Layers box on the Options palette to start the smudge with colors from all the currently visible layers in the image (uncheck Finger Painting if you use this option). Uncheck Use All Layers to smudge only with colors from the active layer. In either case, of course, pixels will only smudge on the currently active layer.

5. Click a hard-edged or soft-edged tip on the Brushes palette.

6. Drag across an area of the image **2**–**5**. Pause to allow the screen to redraw.

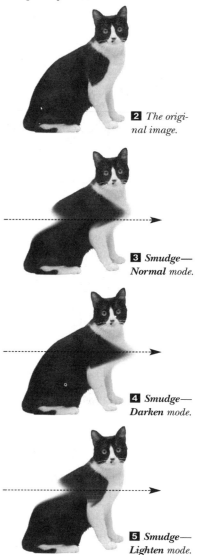

1 *Choose settings for the **Smudge** tool on its **Options** palette.*

2 *The original image.*

3 *Smudge— Normal mode.*

4 *Smudge— Darken mode.*

5 *Smudge— Lighten mode.*

Smudge Colors

1 *Choose settings for any of the five gradient tools on the* **Options** *palette.*

2 *The Gradient tool dragged from the middle to the right. This is a* **Linear** *gradient.*

3 *The Gradient tool dragged a short distance in the middle using the same colors.*

4 *Angular gradient.*

5 *Diamond gradient.*

6 *Reflected gradient.*

7 *The original image.*

8 *A* **Radial** *gradient in the background. The arrow shows where the mouse was dragged.*

A gradient is a gradual blend between two or more colors. According to Adobe, Inc., Photoshop version 5 gradients are improved and will produce fewer banding problems.

Note: The Gradient tool can't be used on an image in Bitmap or Indexed Color mode.

To apply a gradient:

1. Choose a layer.

2. *Optional:* Select an area of a layer. Otherwise, the gradient will fill the entire layer.

3. Choose the Linear ▥, Radial ▢, Angular ▨, Reflected ▭, or Diamond ▢ Gradient tool (G or Shift-G).

4. On the Gradient Options palette **1**:
Choose an Opacity.
and
Choose an existing gradient from the Gradient drop-down menu.
and
Choose a blending mode.

5. *Do any of the following optional steps:*
Check the Dither box to minimize banding (stripes) in the gradient.

Check the Transparency box to enable any transparency that was edited into the gradient.

Check the Reverse box to reverse the order of colors in the gradient.

6. Choose Foreground and/or Background colors if the gradient Style you chose uses them.

7. For a linear gradient, drag from one side of the image or selection to the other. Drag a long distance to produce a subtle transition area **2** or drag a short distance to produce an abrupt transition **3**. Hold down Shift while dragging to constrain the gradient to a multiple of 45°. To produce a diagonal gradient, drag from corner to corner.

For a non-linear gradient, press to establish a center point, then drag outward **4**–**8**.

(Continued on the following page)

Apply a Gradient

TIP To delete a gradient fill, remove that state from the History palette.

TIP To produce more of the Foreground color than the Background color in a gradient, click Edit on the Gradient tool Options palette, then move the little Midpoint diamond, or click the diamond and enter a percentage above 50 in the Location field 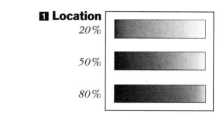.

❶ Location
20%
50%
80%

To create or edit a gradient:

1. Choose a Gradient tool (G or Shift-G). ▣▣▣▣▣ Open the Swatches palette if you're going to use it to choose colors for the gradient.

2. Click Edit on the Gradient Options palette.

3. Click New **❷**, enter a name for the gradient, then click OK (or Ctrl-N/⌘-N to create a new gradient without naming it).
or
Highlight a gradient that you want to duplicate, click Duplicate, enter a name for the duplicate, then click OK.
or
Highlight the name of gradient on the scroll list that you want to edit.

4. Click the starting color stop under the gradient bar to set the starting color **❸**.

5. Click the Adjust: Color button, then click a color on the Swatches palette, on the Color palette color bar, or in any open image window.
or
To create a gradient that will use the current Foreground color, click the Foreground selection box **❹**.
or
To create a gradient that will use the current Background color, click the Background selection box **❺**.
or
Click the color swatch in the Gradient Editor **❻**, then choose a color from the Color Picker.

Saving gradient

Click Save in the Gradient Editor dialog box to save all the gradients that are currently highlighted on the list to a separate file. This is a good way to organize a bunch of gradients so you can access them easily. Click Load to load in previously saved gradients. They'll append to the current list.

Ctrl-click/⌘-click Save to save the currently highlighted gradient as a Curves map. In the Curves dialog box, load in the gradient file to have the gradient colors replace colors in the image according to their respective luminosity levels.

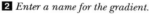

❷ *Enter a name for the gradient.*

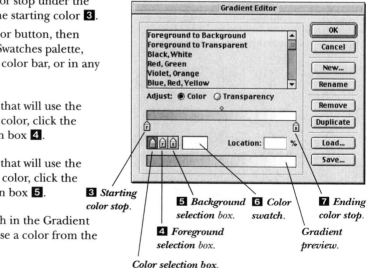

❸ *Starting color stop.*

❺ *Background selection box.*

❻ *Color swatch.*

❼ *Ending color stop.*

❹ *Foreground selection box.*

Gradient preview.

Color selection box.

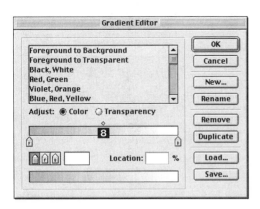

6. Click the ending color stop under the gradient bar to set the ending color (**7**, previous page), then repeat the previous step.

7. *Do any of these optional steps:*

   To **add** an intermediate color to the gradient, click below the gradient bar to create a new square, then click a swatch on the Swatches palette. Or double-click the new square to choose a color from the Color Picker. Relocate it by dragging.

   To reposition a **midpoint** diamond , which controls where the colors to the left and right of the diamond are 50% each, drag it to a new position **8**. Or click on it, then enter a percentage in the Location field.

   Move the **starting** or **ending** square, or enter a new value in the Location field for either square. 0% is at the left, 100% is at the right.

   To **remove** a color, drag its square downward off the bar. A gradient must always contain a minimum of two colors.

   Ctrl-Z/⌘-Z to undo the previous operation.

8. Click OK (Enter/Return).

*Wendy Grossman, in her image, **Guitar with Wine**, used Photoshop gradients and Illustrator patterns.*

To remove a gradient:

1. Choose a Gradient tool (G or Shift-G).
2. Click Edit on the Options palette.
3. On the scroll list, highlight the name of gradient you want to remove.
4. Click Remove.

TIP To restore the default gradients, choose Reset Tool from the Gradient Options palette command menu.

Remove a Gradient

To change the opacity of gradient colors:

1. Choose a Gradient tool (G or Shift-G).

2. Click Edit on the Options palette.

3. Highlight the name of the gradient you want to edit.

4. Click Adjust: Transparency **1**.

5. Click the leftmost or rightmost square under the transparency bar.

6. Enter an Opacity percentage. Note how transparent that color is in the color bar at the bottom of the dialog box **2**.

7. To add other opacity levels, click just below the transparency bar to produce a new square, then enter an opacity percentage. To delete a square, drag it downward off the bar. To move a square, drag it or change its Location percentage.

8. To adjust the location of the midpoint opacity, drag or click on the diamond above the transparency bar, then enter a Location percentage.

9. Click OK (Enter/Return).

To create a multicolor wash:

1. Choose a layer (not the Background).

2. *Optional:* Select an area of a layer.

3. Choose a Gradient tool (G or Shift-G).

4. On the Gradient tool's Options palette, choose an Opacity.
   and
   Choose Foreground to Transparent from the Gradient drop-down menu, or choose a gradient that you've created that finishes with transparency.

5. Drag from left to right on the image.

6. Choose another layer or create a new layer, then repeat step 4.

7. Drag from right to left on the image **3**.

8. *Optional:* Using the Layers palette, change the opacity or blending mode for, or restack, the gradient layers.

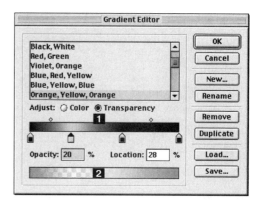

Two gradients, on separate layers, were applied to this image. The middle of the gradients have a 20% opacity to allow the balloons to peek through.

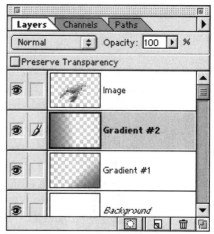

3 *Create a subtle painterly effect by placing translucent gradient washes on separate **layers**.*

Gradient Opacity; Multicolor Wash

MORE LAYERS **13**

IN THIS CHAPTER you will learn about Photoshop's intermediate and advanced layers features. You should read Chapter 7, Layers, to learn about basic layer operations first. (Adjustment layers are discussed on pages 127–130 and 137.)

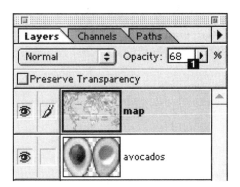

To change the opacity of a layer:

Choose an opacity from the Layers palette **1**. The lower the opacity, the more pixels from the layer below will show through the active layer **2**–**3**. The opacity of the Background cannot be changed.
or
Choose a tool other than a painting tool, then press 1 on the keyboard to change the opacity of an active layer to 10%, 2 to change the opacity to 20%, and so on. Or type both digits quickly (i.e. 15, for 15%).

TIP You can also choose an opacity for a layer using the Layer Options dialog box (see page 191).

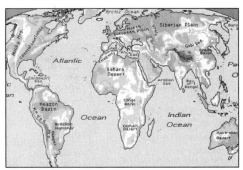

2 *The map layer, 100% Opacity, on top of the avocados layer.*

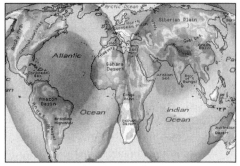

3 *The map layer opacity reduced to 68%.*

Change a Layer's Opacity

Layer effects basics

Layer effects create special effects—Drop Shadow, Inner Shadow, Outer Glow, Inner Glow, Bevel, and Emboss—from one central dialog box. A layer effect can be applied to any layer, even an editable type layer, and it can be turned on or off at any time. Layer effects automatically affect a whole layer, and will update if pixels are added, modified, or deleted from the layer. A layer effect can't be applied to the Background of an image.

■ To **apply** an effect, choose a layer, then choose an effect from the Layer menu > Effects submenu or Right-click/Control-click the layer name and choose Effects from the context menu. Check the Apply box to turn on an effect. More than one effect can be applied to the same layer.

■ Click **Next** to cycle to the next effect, click **Prev** to cycle backwards, or choose a different effect from the topmost drop-down menu **1**. Check the **Preview** box to preview the effect in the image window.

■ A check mark will appear next to any effect on the Layer menu > Effects submenu that is currently applied to the current layer **2**. On the Layers palette, any layer to which a layer effect is currently applied will have an 🔵 icon **3**.

■ To **edit** an existing layer effect (or add another one), double-click the 🔵 icon, or Right-click/Control-click the 🔵 icon and choose an effect from the context menu.

■ To **turn off** an individual layer effect, Alt-choose/Option-choose the same command again from the Layer menu. Or open the dialog box for the layer effect that you want to turn off, and uncheck the Apply box.

■ To **clear** all effects from the currently active layer, choose Layer menu > Effects > Clear Effects.

■ To temporarily **hide** all effects from all layers and speed performance, choose Layer menu > Effects > Hide All Effects. Choose Show All Effects to redisplay.

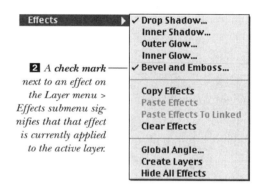

1 *The* **Drop Shadow Effects** *dialog box.*

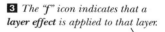

2 *A* check mark *next to an effect on the Layer menu > Effects submenu signifies that that effect is currently applied to the active layer.*

3 *The "f" icon indicates that a* **layer effect** *is applied to that layer.*

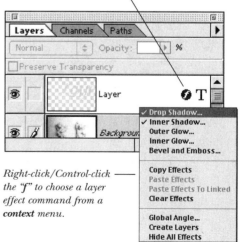

Right-click/Control-click the "f" to choose a layer effect command from a **context** *menu.*

Effects

Inner Shadow   ⌘2 ⬍ ☑ Apply   OK

Mode: Multiply ⬍ ■   Cancel

Opacity: 81 ▸ %   Prev

Angle: 118 ▸ ° ☑ Use Global Angle   Next

Distance: 5 ▸ pixels   ☑ Preview

Blur: 2 ▸ pixels

Intensity: 15 ▸ %

Drop Shadow.

Inner Shadow (with a Drop Shadow).

To create a Drop Shadow or Inner Shadow:

1. Choose a layer.

2. Choose Layer menu > Effects > Drop Shadow or Inner Shadow.

3. Check the Apply box.

4. Change any of the following settings:

Choose a blending **Mode** from the drop-down menu. These modes work exactly like the blending modes on the Layers palette.

Click the color swatch to choose a different **shadow color** from the Color Picker (the new color will preview immediately), then click OK.

Choose an **Opacity** for the transparency for the shadow.

Choose an **Angle** for the angle of the shadow relative to the original layer shapes. Check the Use Global Angle box to use the angle that was entered in the Layer menu > Effects > Global Angle dialog box. Uncheck this option if you want to use a unique angle setting for this particular effect. *Note:* If you readjust the Angle for an individual effect while Use Global Angle is checked, all effects that utilize the Global Angle option will also be modified. This option helps to make the lighting on multiple layer effects look more uniform.

Choose a **Distance** for the distance (in pixels) of a drop shadow from the original layer shapes or the width of an inner shadow.

TIP You can drag the actual shadow in the image while the dialog box is open.

Choose a **Blur** amount for the bluriness (softness) of the shadow.

Choose an **Intensity** (width) for the shadow.

5. Click OK (Enter/Return).

To transform a Drop Shadow (method 1):

1. Apply a Drop Shadow effect (instructions on the previous page) **1**.

2. Choose Layer menu > Effects > Create Layer to transfer the shadow effect to its own layer.

3. Choose the new shadow layer **2**.

4. Choose Edit menu > Transform > Distort, then drag the handles of the bounding box to achieve the desired shape **3**–**4**.

5. *Optional:* Change the luminosity of the shadow via an adjustment layer or choose a different blending mode or opacity for the shadow layer.

1 *The original type layer with a Drop Shadow.*

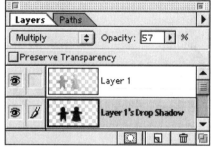

2 *Choosing the new Drop Shadow layer.*

Note: To use a type mask selection for these steps, save the active selection to a channel and then load the channel as a selection.

To transform a Drop Shadow (method 2):

1. Create a selection for the shadow shape. You can Ctrl-click/⌘-click a silhouetted object's layer to select that object.

2. Feather the selection (Ctrl-Alt-D/ ⌘-Option-D).

3. Choose Select menu > Transform Selection (if a selection tool is active, you can Right-click/Control-click on the selection and choose the command from a context menu), then transform the selection marquee.

4. Click the Create new layer button on the Layers palette, then restack the new layer directly below the layer that contains the silhouetted object.

5. Choose Edit menu > Fill, choose Fill: Black, Mode: Normal, and Opacity: 75%, click OK, then deselect.

3 *Distorting the Drop Shadow.*

4 *The final image.*

Effects

Outer Glow ⌘3 ⬍	☑ Apply	OK
Mode: Screen ⬍	☐	Cancel
Opacity: 75 ▸ %		Prev
Blur: 5 ▸ pixels		Next
Intensity: 0 ▸ %		☑ Preview

Effects

Inner Glow ⌘4 ⬍	☑ Apply	OK
Mode: Screen ⬍	☐	Cancel
Opacity: 75 ▸ %		Prev
Blur: 7 ▸ pixels		Next
Intensity: 0 ▸ %		☑ Preview
○ Center ⦿ Edge		

Outer Glow.

Inner Glow (Center) (with a Drop Shadow).

To create an Outer or Inner Glow:

1. Choose a layer.

2. Open the Swatches palette.

3. Choose Layer menu > Effects > Outer Glow or Inner Glow.

4. Check the Apply box.

5. Do any of the following:

Choose a blending **Mode** (see "Blending modes" on pages 26–28).

To change the glow **color**, click the color swatch, choose a color from the Color Picker or from the Swatches palette (the new color will preview on the image), then click OK. Choose a color that contrasts with the background color. It might be hard to see a light Outer Glow color against a light background color.

Choose an **Opacity** for the degree of transparency of the glow.

Choose a **Blur** amount for the amount that the glow spreads.

Choose an **Intensity** for the overall amount of the effect.

For an Inner Glow, click **Center** to create a glow that spreads from the center of the layer pixels. (Choose this option to create a soft color wash effect across type.) Click **Edge** to create a glow that spreads from the inside edges of the layer pixels.

6. Click OK (Enter/Return).

TIP To apply a layer effect to type, make the type large and don't track it tightly.

Outer or Inner Glow

The Bevel and Emboss command creates an illusion of depth by adding a highlight and a shadow to layer shapes.

To create a Bevel or Emboss effect:

1. Open the Swatches palette.

2. Choose a layer. It can be a type layer.

3. Choose Layer menu > Effects > Bevel and Emboss.

4. Check the Apply box.

5. *Do any of the following:*

Choose a blending **Mode** and an **Opacity** for the Highlight and Shadow areas (see "Blending modes" on pages 26-28).

To change the highlight or shadow **color**, click either color swatch, then choose a color from the Color Picker or from the Swatches palette (the color will preview on the image), then click OK.

6. Choose a **Style**: Outer Bevel **1**, Inner Bevel **2**, Emboss **3** or Pillow Emboss **4**.

7. *Do any of the following:*

Choose an **Angle** to change the location of the highlight and shadow. Check the Use Global Angle box to use the Angle setting entered in the Layer menu > Effects > Global Angle dialog box. Uncheck this option if you want to use a unique setting for this particular effect.

Note: If you readjust an individual effect's Angle while the Use Global Angle box is checked, all other effects that utilize the Global Angle option will also update.

Choose a **Depth** for the amount the highlight and shadow are offset from the layer shapes.

Click the **Up** or **Down** button to switch the highlight and shadow positions.

Choose a **Blur** amount for the softness of the highlight and shadow. If you raise the Blur amount, try also raising the Depth, and vice versa. Move this slider in small increments.

8. Click OK (Enter/Return).

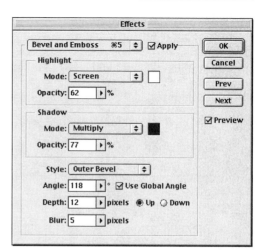

1 *Outer Bevel.*

2 *Inner Bevel (with a Drop Shadow).*

3 *Emboss (with a Drop Shadow).*

4 *Pillow Emboss.*

Bevel or Emboss

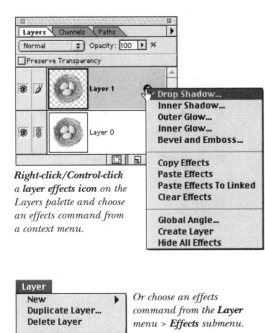

Right-click/Control-click
a layer effects icon on the
Layers palette and choose
an effects command from
a context menu.

Or choose an effects
command from the **Layer**
*menu > **Effects** submenu.*

Other Effects commands

Copy Effects copies all effects from a selected layer for pasting into another layer.

Paste Effects pastes effects onto the current layer in the same document or in a different document; **Paste Effects To Linked** (layers) pastes effects onto any layers that are linked to the currently selected layer. In either case, a pasted effect will override an already applied effect if they are both in the same category (e.g., pasted Drop Shadow replaces existing Drop Shadow).

Global Angle establishes a common Angle for all current and future effects for which the Use Global Angle option is turned on. And conversely, if you change any individual layer effect's Angle with the Use Global Angle option on, all the other effects that have a Global Angle option will update, along with the Angle in the Global Angle dialog box. Using a Global Angle helps to unify lighting across multiple effects.

If more than one effect has been applied to a layer and you choose **Create Layer(s),** each effect will be placed on its own layer. The image won't look different after this command is chosen, but the effects will no longer be editable via the Effects dialog box and they will no longer be associated with the layer to which they were originally applied.

After applying the Create Layer(s) command, any layer effect that is inside a shape (an inner glow, or a highlight or a shadow for a bevel or an inner emboss) will be placed on a new, separate layer, but it will be joined with the original shape layer in a clipping group, with the original layer being the base layer of the group. Any effect that is outside a shape (a drop shadow, an outer glow, or a shadow for a bevel or an outer emboss) will convert into separate layers below the original shape layer. Use Create Layer(s) to export a file to a multimedia program, such as Adobe After Effects or Macromedia Director. The Create Layer(s) command cannot be applied to the Background of an image.

The layer blending modes

The layer blending mode you choose for a layer affects how that layer's pixels blend with pixels in the layer directly below it. Some modes produce subtle effects (e.g., Soft Light), while others produce dramatic color shifts (e.g., Difference). Normal is the default mode.

You can choose a blending mode for a layer from the mode drop-down menu on the Layers palette **1**–**4**. Or use the Shift + or Shift - shortcut to cycle through the modes for the currently active layer (make sure a painting tool isn't selected when you do this). The blending modes are discussed in detail on pages 26–28. You can also choose a mode for a layer in the Layer Options dialog box (double-click a layer name to open it). Shortcuts for choosing individual blending modes are on the shortcuts list.

You can choose Behind mode for the Paintbrush, Airbrush, Paint Bucket, Pencil, Line, History Brush, or Rubber Stamp tool (Options palette), but not for a layer. In Behind mode, it will appear as if you're painting on the back of the current layer. And for the Line or Paint Bucket tool, you can choose yet another mode, Clear, which works like an eraser. You must uncheck the Preserve Transparency box on the Layers palette to access Behind and Clear modes.

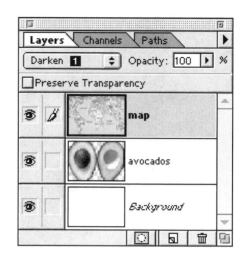

2 *The layer blending modes.*

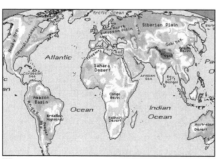

3 *The map layer is above the avocados layer.*

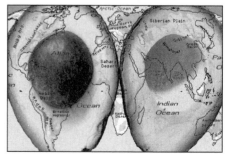

4 *After **Darken** mode is chosen for the map layer.*

Layer Blending Modes

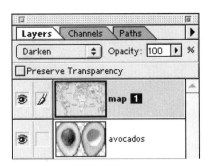

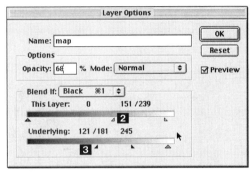

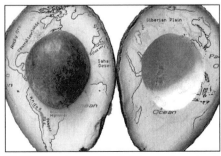

You can control which pixels in a pair of layers will be visible using the Underlying sliders in the Layer Options dialog box.

To blend pixels between two layers:

1. Double click a layer name on the Layers palette **1**.
or
Choose a layer, then choose Layer Options from the Layers palette command menu.

2. *Optional:* To remove or restore colors from one channel at a time, choose from the Blend If drop-down menu.

3. Make sure the Preview box is checked, then move the leftmost Blend If: This Layer slider to the right to remove shadow areas from the active layer **2**.
and/or
Move the rightmost This Layer slider to the left to remove highlights from the active layer.
and/or
Move the leftmost Underlying slider to the right to restore shadow areas from the layer directly below the active layer **3**.
and/or
Move the rightmost Underlying slider to the left to restore highlights from the layer directly below the active layer.

4. Click OK (Enter/Return) **4**–**5**.

TIP To adjust the midtones independently of the shadows, Alt-drag/Option-drag the right part of the leftmost slider (it will divide in two). To adjust the midtones independently of the highlights, Alt-drag/Option-drag the left part of the rightmost slider.

4 *The map layer is above the avocados layer.*

5 *The same image after dividing and moving the white **This Layer** slider and the black **Underlying** slider in the **Layer Options** dialog box.*

Blend Layers

In these instructions, a filter is applied to a duplicate layer and then the original and duplicate layers are blended using Layers palette opacity and mode controls. Use this technique to soften the effect of an image editing command, like a filter, or to experiment with various blending modes or adjust commands. You can also use a layer mask to limit the area of the effect. If you don't like an effect, you can just delete the new layer and start over.

To blend a modified layer with the original layer:

1. Choose a layer ■.

2. Drag that layer over the Create new layer button on the Layers palette.
   or
   Choose Duplicate Layer from the Layers palette command menu, then click OK.

3. Modify the duplicate layer. (Apply a filter or other image editing command.)

4. On the Layers palette, move the Opacity slider to achieve the desired degree of transparency between the original layer and the modified, duplicate layer ■.
   and/or
   Choose a different mode.

5. *Optional:* Create a layer mask to partially hide pixels on the top layer. Try adding a gradient to the layer mask (see page 179).

TIP To create a beautiful textural effect, duplicate the Background in a color image (preferably a Background that isn't solid white), highlight the new layer, and choose Image menu > Adjust > Desaturate (Ctrl-Shift-U/⌘-Shift-U) to make it grayscale. Next, apply the Add Noise or Pointillize filter ■. And finally, lower the opacity of, and try out different blending modes for, the new layer via the Layers palette.

■ *The original image.*

■ *After applying the Mezzotint filter to the duplicate layer, then lowering the opacity of the duplicate layer.*

■ *A blended layer effect using the Pointillize filter.*

Active layer mask.   Mask **link** icon.   Layer mask **thumbnail**.

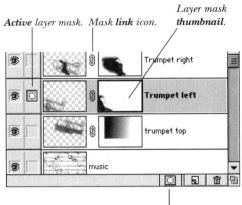

1 *Add layer mask* button.

*The Layers palette showing the three trumpet layers, each with its own **layer mask**.*

*The trumpets **without layer masks**.*

*The trumpets **with layer masks**. The topmost trumpet fades out due to a gradient in its layer mask and portions of the middle and bottom trumpets are hidden via a black-and-white layer mask.*

What is a layer mask?

A layer mask is simply an 8-bit grayscale channel that has white or black as its background color. By default, white areas on a layer mask permit pixels to be seen, black areas hide pixels, and gray areas partially mask pixels. You can use a mask to temporarily hide pixels on a layer so you can view the rest of the composite picture without them. Later, you can modify the mask, apply the mask effect to make it permanent, or discard the mask altogether.

An advantage of using a layer mask is that you can access it from both the Layers and Channels palettes. You'll see a thumbnail for the layer mask on the Layers palette and on the Channels palette when a layer that contains a mask is highlighted. Unlike an alpha channel selection, however, which can be loaded onto any layer, a layer mask can only be turned on or off for the layer or clipping group (group of layers) with which it's associated.

To create a layer mask:

1. On the Layers palette, click on the name of the layer to which you want to add a mask.

2. *Optional:* Create a selection if you want to create a mask in that shape.

3. To create a white mask in which all the layer pixels are visible, choose Layer menu > Add Layer Mask > Reveal All **1**.
or
To create a black mask in which all the layer pixels are hidden, choose Layer menu > Add Layer Mask > Hide All.
or
To reveal only layer pixels within an active selection, choose Layer menu > Add Layer Mask > Reveal Selection or Ctrl-click/⌘-click the Add layer mask button at the bottom of the Layers palette.
or

(Continued on the following page)

Create a Layer Mask

To hide layer pixels within the selection, choose Layer menu > Add Layer Mask > Hide Selection or Alt-click/Option-click the Add layer mask button at the bottom of the Layers palette.

To reshape a layer mask:

1. Choose the Paintbrush tool (B). ✐

2. On the Options palette, choose 100% Opacity and Normal mode. (Or choose an opacity below 100% to partially hide layer pixels.)

3. Click a brush tip on the Brushes palette.

4. To reshape the layer mask while viewing the layer pixels, click the layer mask thumbnail (not the layer name) on the Layers palette **1**. The thumbnail will have a dark border and a mask icon will appear for that layer.
or
To display the mask by itself in the image window, Alt-click/Option-click the layer mask thumbnail. (Alt-click/Option-click the layer mask thumbnail to redisplay the mask on the image.)
or
Alt-Shift-click/Option-Shift-click the layer mask thumbnail to display the mask in red, like a rubylith. (Alt-Shift-click/Option-Shift-click the thumbnail again to restore the normal display.)

5. Paint on the picture with black as the Foreground color to enlarge the mask and hide pixels on the layer.
and/or
Paint with white as the Foreground color to reduce the mask and restore pixels on the layer.
and/or
Paint with gray as the Foreground color to partially hide pixels on the layer.

6. When you're finished modifying the layer mask, click the layer thumbnail **2**–**3**.

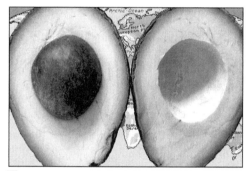

Mask icon.   **1** *Layer mask thumbnail.*

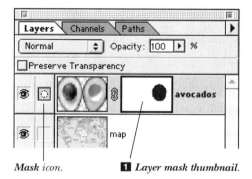

2 *The original image.*

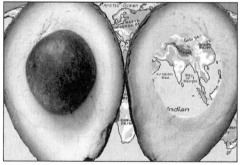

3 *The center of the avocado on the right is blocked by a layer mask.*

Reshape a Layer Mask

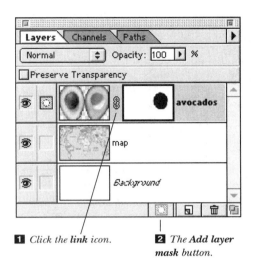

1 *Click the* **link** *icon.*

2 *The* **Add layer mask** *button.*

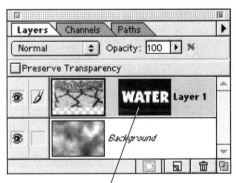

3 *The* **layer mask thumbnail.** *Layer 1 pixels are revealed through the* **white** *areas in the layer mask.*

4 *In this image, the water layer is visible only through the letter shapes of the* **layer mask.**

By default, a layer and its layer mask move together. Follow these steps to move layer pixels or a layer mask independently.

To move a mask without moving its layer:

1. On the Layers palette, click the link icon 🔗 between the layer and the layer mask thumbnails **1**.

2. Click on the layer mask icon.

3. Choose the Move tool (V). ✛

4. Drag the layer mask in the image window.

5. Click again between the layer and layer mask thumbnails to re-link them.

To duplicate a layer mask:

1. Activate the layer on which you want the duplicate to appear.

2. Drag the thumbnail of the layer mask that you want to duplicate over the Add layer mask button **2**. Or Alt-drag/ Option-drag to switch the hidden and revealed areas in the duplicate.

To fill type with imagery using a layer mask:

1. Activate a layer that contains pixels (not the Background).

2. Choose the Type Mask tool ⊤ or the Vertical Type Mask tool (T or Shift-T).

3. Click on the image, type the letters you want to appear on the image, choose a font and other type specifications, then click OK.

4. Reposition the type selection, if desired, by placing the pointer inside the selection and dragging.

5. Choose Layer menu > Add Layer Mask > Reveal Selection to restrict pixels to the selection.
or
Choose Layer menu > Add Layer Mask > Hide Selection to hide pixels within the selection.

6. Reselect the layer thumbnail **3**–**4**.

To temporarily remove the effects of a layer mask:

Shift-click the layer mask thumbnail on the Layers palette. A red "X" will appear over the thumbnail and the entire layer will be displayed **1** (this doesn't select the layer mask thumbnail). (Shift-click the layer mask thumbnail again to remove the "X" and restore the mask effect.)

TIP To invert the effect of a layer mask, click the layer mask thumbnail, then choose Image menu > Adjust > Invert (Ctrl-I/⌘-I). Hidden areas will be revealed, formerly visible areas will be hidden.

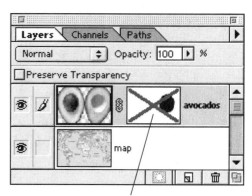

1 *Shift-click the layer mask thumbnail.*

Layer masks that are no longer needed should be discarded, because they occupy storage space.

To apply or discard the effects of a layer mask:

1. On the Layers palette, click on the thumbnail of the mask that you want to remove **2**.

2. Click the trash button.
or
Choose Layer menu > Remove Layer Mask.

3. To make the mask effect permanent, click Apply **3**.
or
To remove the mask without applying its effect, click Discard.

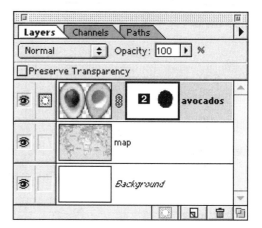

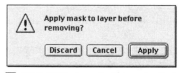

3 *Click **Apply** to make the mask effect permanent.*

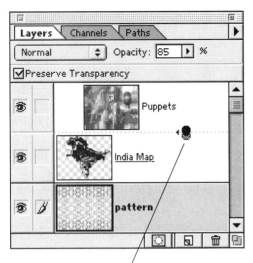

1 *Option-click between two layers to join them in a* ***clipping group***. *A dotted line will appear, and the* ***base*** *layer will be underlined.*

2 *The map of India is clipping (limiting) the view of the puppets.*

The bottommost layer of a clipping group of layers (the base layer) clips (limits) the display of pixels, and also controls the mode and opacity of the layers above it. Only pixels that overlap pixels on the base layer are visible.

To create a clipping group of layers:

1. Click on a layer name.

2. Alt-click/Option-click the line between that layer name and the name just above it (the pointer will be two overlapping circles) **1**–**2**. (The layers you choose for a clipping group must be listed **consecutively** on the palette.)

3. *Optional:* Repeat step 2 to add more layers to the clipping group.

A dotted line will appear between each pair of layers in the group, the base layer name will be underlined, and the thumbnail for the other layers in the group will be indented.

TIP To create a clipping group from linked layers, choose Layer menu > Group Linked (Ctrl-G/⌘-G).

TIP To fill type with imagery using a clipping group, see the instructions on page 235.

Note: An indented layer's blending mode affects only those layers in the clipping group. The base layer's blending mode controls how the entire clipping group blends with the layers below it.

To remove a layer from a clipping group:

Alt-click/Option-click on the dotted line underneath the layer that you want to remove. The solid line will reappear.
or
Click on the name of the layer you want to remove, then choose Layer menu > Ungroup.

To ungroup an entire clipping group:

1. Click on the base layer in the group.

2. Choose Layer menu > Ungroup (Ctrl-Shift-G/⌘-Shift-G).

Use linking when you want to secure the position of multiple layers in relationship to one another. Once layers are linked together, they can be moved as a unit in the image window or drag-copied to another image, and they can be distributed or aligned.

Note: You can transform linked layers. In fact, you'll minimize image distortion due to resampling by transforming multiple layers all at once instead of one by one.

To link layers (and move them as a unit):

1. On the Layers palette, click on one of the layers that you want to link.

2. Click in the second column for any other layer you want to link to the layer you chose in the previous step. The layers you link **don't** have be consecutive. The link icon will appear next to any non-active, linked layers **1**.

3. *Optional:* Choose the Move tool (V) ✛, then press and drag the linked layers in the image window.

TIP To unlink a layer, click the link icon.

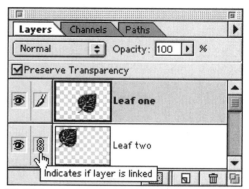

1 *Click to display the* **link** *icon in the second column on the Layers palette for any layers you want to link to the active layer. In this illustration, the two layers are linked.*

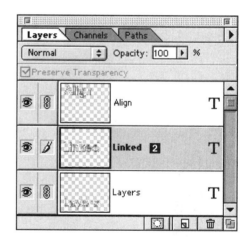

Note: The Align Linked command only affects pixels that are at least 50% opaque.

To align two or more linked layers:

1. Choose a layer to which one or more other layers are linked **2**. The layer you choose will be the reference position to which the other linked layers will align.

2. *Optional:* Create a selection for the other layers to align to.

3. Choose Layer menu > Align Linked (or Align To Selection, if a selection is active) > Top, Vertical Center, Bottom, Left, Horizontal Center, or Right **3** (and **4**–**5**, next page).

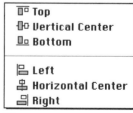

3 *Choose one of these options from the Layer menu >* **Align Linked** *or* **Distribute Linked** *submenu.*

4 *The original image.*

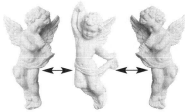

5 *The layers **aligned**: Bottom.*

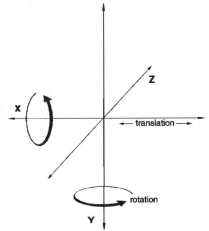

6 *The layers **distributed**: Horizontal Center.*

1 *In a **3D application**, objects are manipulated in **three** dimensions.*

Note: The Distribute Linked command only affects pixels that are at least 50% opaque.

To distribute three or more linked layers:

1. Choose a layer to which two or more other layers are linked.

2. *Optional:* Create a selection on that layer for the other layers to align to.

3. Choose Layer menu > Distribute Linked > Top, Vertical Center, Bottom, Left, Horizontal Center, or Right. The layers will be distributed evenly between the two layers that are furthest apart **5**–**6**.

TIP If you're not happy with the align or distribute option and you want to try a different one, Undo the last option first.

3D Transform

Using the 3D Transform filter, you can perform typical 3D manipulations (rotation, translation, scaling, and adjusting point-of-view) to objects within a two-dimensional image. Photoshop uses a two-dimensional coordinate system in which a location in a picture is measured by horizontal *(x)* and vertical *(y)* values. This kind of space could be thought of as a flat canvas. Shapes like squares, circles, and triangles can be described using this system.

In 3D applications, a z-axis is added to define recession (depth) into and out of the canvas **1**. The addition of a third dimension makes for an accurate description of 3D forms, such as cubes, spheres, and cylinders.

Since Photoshop's 3D Transform filter can rotate and translate only on the horizontal *(x)* and vertical *(y)* axes, it is really more like a 2.5D Transform. It places the selected area of an image on an object primitive (cube, sphere, or cylinder), but only on the currently visible side of the 3D object. It cannot add information to the hidden sides of an object. This becomes evident if you rotate a sphere about 45 degrees on the *y*-axis. In

(Continued on the following page)

this illustration, the transformed sphere **3** reveals that the image is only mapped to the part of the sphere that was visible in the original image **2**.

Photoshop's 3D Transform filter works with three types of 3D forms: a sphere, a cube, or a cylinder. The cylinder transform is the most complex and sophisticated aspect of the filter. If you understand it, you will understand all the features of the filter.

To apply the 3D Transform filter:

1. Make sure the image is in Grayscale, Duotone, RGB Color, or Multichannel image mode.

2. Select the area of the image that you want to transform **4**, choose Layer menu > New > Layer Via Copy (Ctrl-J/⌘-J) to copy the selection to a new layer, then choose the new layer.
or
Choose a layer that already has a shape, surrounded by transparency, that can easily be translated into a cube, a sphere, or for these instructions, a cylinder.

3. Choose Filter menu > Render > 3D Transform.

4. Choose the Cylinder tool (C). Beginning at the upper left corner of the shape, drag downward and to the right in the preview window to surround the object with the cylinder wireframe. *Note:* It's better for the wireframe to be a little too large than too small. Cropping an object with the wireframe could cause ghosting and distortion.

5. To reposition the entire wireframe, choose the Selection tool (V), then drag the wireframe.

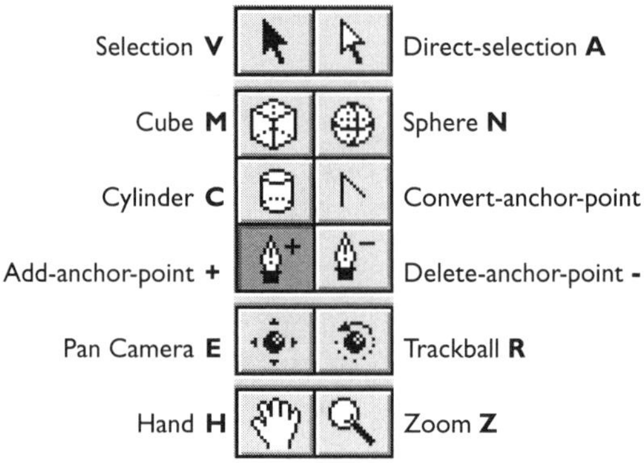

To reshape the wireframe:

1. To zoom in on an anchor point, choose the Zoom tool (Z), then click in the preview window.
or
To zoom in without choosing the Zoom tool, Ctrl-Spacebar-click/⌘-Spacebar-click in the preview window.

2 *The original image.*

3 *The sphere transformed in Photoshop—the pattern doesn't cover the back of the sphere.*

3D Transform tools
in the 3D Transform dialog box

Selection **V**	Direct-selection **A**
Cube **M**	Sphere **N**
Cylinder **C**	Convert-anchor-point
Add-anchor-point **+**	Delete-anchor-point **-**
Pan Camera **E**	Trackball **R**
Hand **H**	Zoom **Z**

4 *An area of an image is selected.*

3D Transform (side tab)

5 *Adding a point using the Add-anchor-point tool.*

6 *Dragging a point with the Direct-selection tool.*

7 *A rotation along the y-axis.*

8 *A rotation along the x-axis.*

(To zoom out, Alt-Spacebar-click/ Option-Spacebar-click.)

Use the Hand tool (H) to move the image in the preview window. (Spacebar-drag to do this without choosing the Hand tool).

2. Drag the anchor points to fit the object.

3. Do any of the following until you're satisfied with the way the wireframe fits on the cylinder imagery:

For a cylinder transformation, you can **add** anchor points to the wireframe to more accurately fit your object (not so with a cube or sphere). Click the Add-anchor-point tool (+), then, while zoomed out to a 1:1 preview ratio, add anchor points to the section where the edge of the object changes direction, on the right side of the wireframe **5**.

Choose the Direct-selection tool (A), then **drag** points so they all fit snugly around the the object's contour **6**. The left side of the wireframe will reshape automatically to match to any changes that are made to the right side.

Use the Delete-anchor-point tool (-) to **remove** anchor points, where necessary.

Use the Convert-anchor-point tool to **convert** a smooth point into a corner point, or vice versa.

4. To rotate the cylinder on the y-axis, choose the Trackball tool (R). Place the pointer about halfway up the left side of the cylinder, and drag to the right. Note that, as in figure **3** on page 200, a rotation along the y-axis will reveal the empty, hidden side of the object **7**. Drag back to the left if you want to restore the cylinder to its former position. *and/or*

To rotate along the x-axis, place the cursor at the top of the cylinder, centered horizontally, and drag downward **8**. Since the object already has a top, you

(Continued on the following page)

3D Transform

can rotate it more on this axis before revealing the back of the cylinder.

5. Choose the Pan Camera tool (E), then drag the 3D preview to move it.

TIP To delete a wireframe altogether, choose the Selection tool (V), select the wireframe, then press Delete (and start again). This can't be undone.

To render the object:

1. Click Options.

2. Choose a Render Resolution and the desired degree of Anti-aliasing **1**. A High resolution and High anti-Aliasing will usually produce the best results, but at a cost. With each increase in resolution, there will be an approximate 50% increase in rendering time, and with each increase in Anti-aliasing there will be an approximate 100% increase in rendering time. This can prove tedious if you're working on a large, high resolution image. Try to match the rendering and anti-alaising quality to the quality of the initial image and to its final function (pre-press, Web, or presentation).

Uncheck the Display Background box if you want to separate the rendered object from its original background.

3. Click OK (Return/Enter).

4. Accept the default values for Field of View and Dolly, then click OK **2**–**3**.

Note: To dolly a camera means to move it closer to or further from the subject. The higher the Dolly value in the 3D Transform dialog box (0–99), the farther the distance between subject and camera, and thus the smaller the shape will appear.

TIP To toggle between the before and after 3D Transform results, choose Edit menu > Undo (Ctrl-Z/⌘-Z), then Edit menu > Redo.

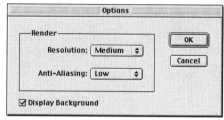

1 *Choose **rendering** options.*

2 *The original object.*

3 *The object rendered on the x-axis.*

The active (selected) area is clear, the **Quick Mask** *is partially opaque.*

THIS CHAPTER COVERS two special methods for saving and reshaping a selection: alpha channels and Quick Mask mode.

If you save a selection to a specially created grayscale channel, called an **alpha channel**, you can load the selection onto the image at any time. A selection that has an irregular shape that would be difficult to reselect would be a logical candidate for this operation. A file can contain up to 24 channels, though from a practical standpoint, since each channel increases a picture's storage size, (depending on the size of the selection area), you should be judicious when adding alpha channels. Alpha channels are accessed via the Channels palette **1**, and are saved or loaded onto an image via Select menu commands or the Channels palette. (See our "Tip" on page 212 for converting an alpha channel to a path to conserve file storage space.)

Using Photoshop's **Quick Mask** mode, the selected or unselected areas of an image can be covered with a semi-transparent colored mask, which can then be reshaped using any editing or painting tool. Masked areas are protected from editing. Unlike an alpha channel, a Quick Mask cannot be saved, but when you return to Standard (non-Quick Mask) mode, the mask will turn into a selection, which can be saved.

Note: If you're unfamiliar with Photoshop's basic selection tools, read Chapter 5 before reading this chapter.

Layer masks are covered in Chapter 13.

The **composite color channel**

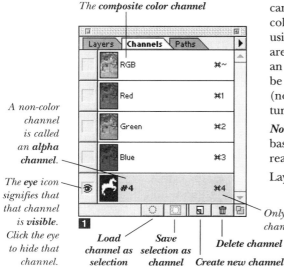

A non-color channel is called an **alpha channel**.

The **eye** *icon signifies that that channel is* **visible**. *Click the eye to hide that channel.*

1

Load channel as selection

Save selection as channel

Delete channel

Create new channel

Only the currently highlighted channel or channels can be edited.

A selection that is saved in an alpha channel can be loaded onto any image whenever it's needed.

Note: To convert an alpha channel into a spot color channel, see page 168.

To save a selection to a channel using the current options settings:

1. Create a selection ■.

2. Click the Save selection as channel (second) button ▣ at the bottom of the Channels palette **2**.

To save a selection to a channel and choose options:

1. Create a selection ■. *Optional:* Also choose a layer if you want to create a layer mask for it.

2. Choose Select menu > Save Selection. Enter a new Name for the selection, if desired.

3. *Do any of these optional steps:*

Leave the Document setting as the current file or choose **Document**: New to save the selection to an alpha channel in a new, separate document **3**.

Choose **Channel**: "[   ] Mask" to turn the selection into a layer mask for the current layer. Layer pixels will only be visible where the selection was.

Choose an **Operation** option to combine a current selection with an existing alpha channel that you choose from the Channel drop-down menu. (The Operation options are illustrated on page 206.)

Note: You can save an alpha channel with an image only in the Photoshop, TIFF, PICT, Photoshop DCS 2.0, Pixar, PNG, or Targa format. To save a copy of a file without alpha channels, check the Exclude Alpha Channels box in the save dialog, if it's available.

TIP If you save a selection to a channel, the selection will remain active.

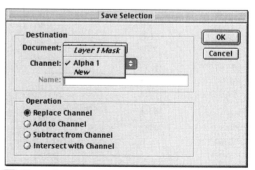

1 *Select an area on a layer.*

2 Save selection as channel

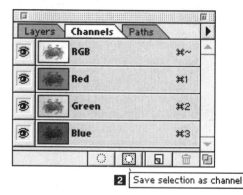

3 *Choose **Document**, **Channel**, and **Operation** options in the **Save Selection** dialog box.*

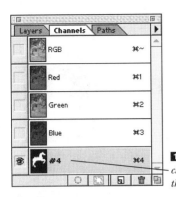

1 *Click an alpha channel name on the Channels palette.*

2 *An **alpha channel** displayed in the image window. The **selected** area is **white**, the **protected** area is **black**.*

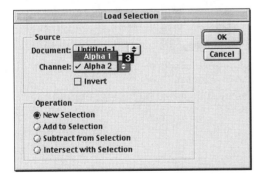

Load channel selection to another image

Make sure the source and destination images have the same dimensions and resolution, activate the destination image, then follow steps 2–6 at right, choosing the source document in the Load Selection dialog box. To load a layer mask selection, activate that layer first in the source image.

An alpha channel can be displayed without loading it onto the image as a selection.

To display a channel selection:

1. Click an alpha channel name on the Channels palette **1**. The selected area will be white, the protected area black **2**.

2. To restore the normal image display, click the top (composite) channel name on the palette (Ctrl-~/⌘-~).

TIP If the selection has a Feather radius, the faded area will be gray and will only be partially affected by editing.

TIP Reshape the mask with any painting tool using black, gray, or white "paint."

To load a channel selection onto an image using the current options:

On the Channels palette, Ctrl-click/⌘-click the name of the alpha channel that you want to load.

To load a channel selection onto an image and choose options:

1. If the composite image isn't displayed, click the top channel name on the Channels palette. You can combine the channel selection with an existing selection in the image (see the next page).

2. Choose Select menu > Load Selection.

3. Choose the channel name from the Channel drop-down menu **3**.

4. To combine the channel with an existing selection in the image, choose an Operation option (see the next page).

5. *Optional:* Check the Invert box to switch the selected and unselected areas in the loaded selection.

6. Click OK (Enter/Return).

TIP To select only pixels on an active layer—not transparent areas—choose Channel: "[ ] Transparency" or Ctrl-click/⌘-click the layer name.

Save Selection Operations

When saving a selection, you can choose from these Operation options in the **Save Selection** dialog box:

Channel and selection to be saved

Resulting channel

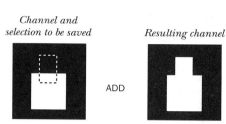

ADD

New Channel saves the current selection in a new channel.

Shortcut: Click the Save selection as channel button on the Channels palette. ▣

Add to Channel adds the new selection to the channel.

Channel and selection to be saved

Resulting channel

SUBTRACT

INTERSECT

Subtract from Channel removes white or gray areas that overlap the new selection.

Intersect with Channel preserves only white or gray areas that overlap the new selection.

Load Selection Operations

If a channel is loaded while an area of a layer is selected, you can choose from these Operation options in the **Load Selection** dialog box:

Selection and channel to be loaded

Resulting selection

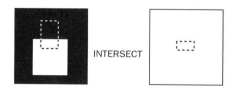

ADD

New Selection—the channel becomes the current selection.

Shortcut: Ctrl-click/⌘-click the channel name or drag the channel name over the Load channel as selection button. ⬚

Add to Selection adds the channel selection to the current selection.

Shortcut: Ctrl-Shift-click/⌘-Shift-click the channel name.

Selection and channel to be loaded

Resulting selection

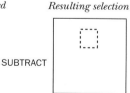

SUBTRACT

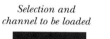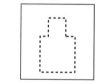

INTERSECT

Subtract from Selection removes areas of the current selection that overlap the channel selection.

Shortcut: Ctrl-Alt-click/⌘-Option-click the channel name.

Intersect with Selection preserves only areas of the current selection that overlap the channel selection.

Shortcut: Ctrl-Alt-Shift-click/⌘-Option-Shift-click click the channel name.

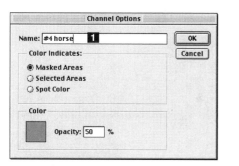

2 *The horse is the selected area.*

3 *The horse is still the selected area, but it is now black instead of white.*

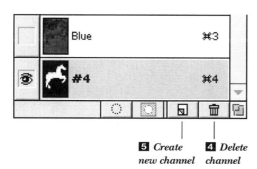

5 *Create new channel* **4** *Delete channel*

To rename a channel:

1. Double-click a channel name on the Channels palette.
or
Click a channel name, then choose Channel Options from the palette command menu.

2. Type a new name in the Name field **1**.

3. Click OK (Enter/Return).

TIP Normally, the selected areas of an alpha channel are white and the protected areas are black or colored. To reverse these colors without changing which area is actually selected, double-click an alpha channel name on the Channels palette, then click Color Indicates: Selected Areas **2**–**3**.

TIP To change the size of the channel thumbnails, choose Palette Options from the Channels palette command menu, then click a different thumbnail size.

To delete a channel:

Drag the channel over the trash button.
or
Click the name of the channel that you want to delete on the Channels palette, click the trash button at the bottom of the palette **4**, then click Yes. Alt-click/Option-click the trash button to bypass the prompt.
or
Right-click/Control-click the Channel name, then choose Delete Channel from the context menu.

To duplicate a channel:

Drag the name of the channel that you want to duplicate over the Create new channel button or into another image window **5**.
or
Right-click/Control-click the Channel name, choose Duplicate Channel from the context menu, then click OK **6**.

You can superimpose an alpha channel selection as a colored mask over an image, and then reshape the mask.

To reshape an alpha channel mask:

1. Make sure there is no selection on the image.

2. Click an alpha channel name on the Channels palette. An eye icon will appear next to it **1**.

3. Click in the left column at the top of the palette. An eye icon will appear. The alpha channel should be the only highlighted channel **2**.

4. Choose the Pencil 🖉 or Paintbrush tool. 🖉

5. On the Options palette, choose Normal mode.
   and
   Choose 100% Opacity to create a full mask or a lower opacity to create a partial mask.

6. Click a tip on the Brushes palette.

7. To enlarge the masked (protected) area, stroke on the cutout with black as the Foreground color **3**. (Click the Switch colors icon on the Toolbox or press "X" to switch the Foreground color between black and white **4**.)
   or
   To enlarge the unmasked area, stroke on the mask with white as the Foreground color **5**.

8. To hide the mask, click the alpha channel's eye icon.
   or
   Choose a layer on the Layers palette.

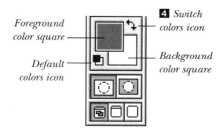

Foreground color square

4 *Switch colors icon*

Default colors icon

Background color square

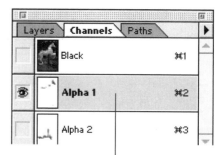

1 *Click the alpha channel name on the Channels palette.*

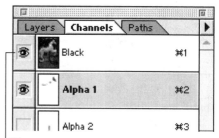

2 *Click in the left column at the top of the palette. Make sure the alpha channel name stays highlighted.*

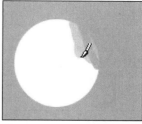

3 *Enlarge the **masked** area by stroking on the cutout with **black** as the Foreground color.*

5 *Enlarge the **unmasked** area by stroking on the mask with **white** as the Foreground color.*

1 *Select an area on a layer.*

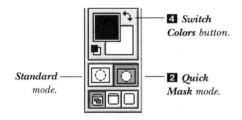

4 *Switch Colors button.*

Standard mode.

2 *Quick Mask mode.*

3 *The unselected area is covered with a* ***mask.***

If you choose Quick Mask mode when an area of a layer is selected, a semi-transparent tinted mask will cover the unselected areas, and the selected areas will be revealed in a cutout. You'll still be able to see the image through the mask. The cutout (mask) can be reshaped using the Pencil, Airbrush, or Paintbrush tool.

Note: You can't save a Quick Mask via Save Selection while your image is in Quick Mask mode, but you can save your selection to a channel once you restore the standard screen display mode.

To reshape a selection using Quick Mask mode:

1. Select an area of a layer **1**.

2. Click the Quick Mask mode button on the Toolbox (Q) **2**. A mask will cover part of the picture **3**.

3. Choose the Pencil ✏ or Paintbrush tool. 🖌

4. On the Options palette, move the Opacity slider to 100%.
and
Choose Normal from the mode drop-down menu.
and
Make sure all the check boxes on the palette are unchecked.

5. Click a tip on the Brushes palette.

6. Stroke on the cutout with black as the Foreground color to enlarge the masked (protected) area.
or
Stroke on the mask with white as the Foreground color to enlarge the cutout (unmasked area). (Click the Switch Colors icon on the Toolbox or press "X" to swap the Foreground and Background colors **4**.)
or
Stroke with gray or a brush with an opacity below 100% (Options palette) to create a partial mask. When you edit

(Continued on the following page)

the layer, that area will be partially affected by modifications.

"Quick Mask" will be listed on the Channels palette and on the image window title bar while the image is in Quick Mask mode.

7. Click the Standard mode icon on the Toolbox (Q) to turn off Quick Mask mode. The non-masked areas will turn into a selection.

8. Modify the layer. Only the unmasked (selected) area will be affected.

In these instructions, you'll create a mask without first creating a selection.

To create a Quick Mask:

1. Choose the Pencil or Paintbrush tool, and choose options for the tool as per steps 4 and 5 on the previous page.

2. Double-click the Quick Mask button on the Toolbox.

3. Click Selected Areas, then click OK.

4. Stroke with black on the layer . The selected areas (not the protected areas) will be covered with a mask so you'll be creating what will be the selected area.

The Quick Mask options affect the Quick Mask's appearance on screen—not its function.

To choose Quick Mask display options:

1. Double-click "Quick Mask" on the Channels palette.
  or
  Double-click the Quick Mask mode button on the Toolbox.

2. Do any of the following:

  Choose whether Color Indicates: Masked Areas or Selected Areas.

  Click the Color square, then choose a new Quick Mask color.

  Change the Opacity of the mask color.

3. Click OK (Enter/Return).

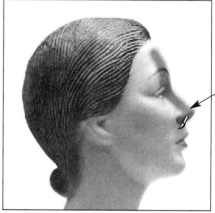

1 *Painting a mask on an image in* **Quick Mask** *mode.*

Quick switch

To switch the mask color between the selected and masked areas without opening the Quick Mask Options dialog box, Alt-click/Option-click the Quick Mask mode button on the Toolbox.

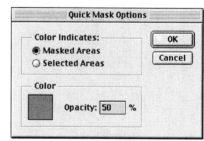

2 *In the Mask Options dialog box, choose whether Color Indicates:* **Masked Areas** *or* **Selected Areas***. Click the Color square to choose a different mask* **color***.*

The **Quick Mask** *buttons on the Toolbox.*

Color Indicates: **Masked areas**	*Color Indicates:* **Selected Areas**

PATHS 15

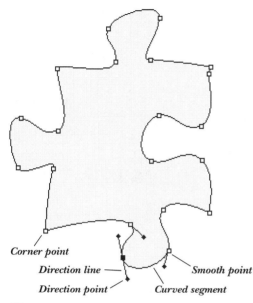

Corner point

Direction line — **Smooth point**

Direction point — **Curved segment**

1 *A Bézier path.*

PHOTOSHOP'S Pen, Magnetic Pen, and Freeform Pen tools create precise outlines, called paths, that consist of anchor points connected by curved or straight line segments **1**. To reshape a path, you can drag, add, or delete an anchor point or move a segment. A curved line segment can also be reshaped by adjusting its Bézier direction lines. A path can be used on any layer. If you stroke or fill a path, the color pixels will appear on the currently active layer.

You can convert a selection into a path, reshape it, and then convert it back into a selection. This is a good method for creating a selection with a very exacting fit. For certain kinds of shapes, this will work better than using the Lasso tool or a Quick Mask. And there's an added bonus: paths occupy much less storage space than channels.

Paths are displayed, activated, restacked, saved, and deleted using the Paths palette **2**. The Toolbox contains seven path-making and reshaping tools **3**.

You can also export a Photoshop path to Illustrator, where it can also be used as a path, and you can silhouette part of an image using a clipping path in the EPS format to place in an illustration or page layout program.

A saved path. *A work path.*

2 *The Paths palette.*

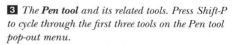

Fill path **Stroke path** **Make work path** **Delete current path**

Load path as selection **Create new path**

3 *The Pen tool and its related tools. Press Shift-P to cycle through the first three tools on the Pen tool pop-out menu.*

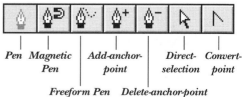

Pen **Magnetic Pen** **Add-anchor-point** **Direct-selection** **Convert-point**

Freeform Pen **Delete-anchor-point**

Paths

If you convert a selection into a path, you can precisely reshape it and then use it as a path or convert it back into a selection.

Note: When you convert a selection into a path, any feathering on the selection is removed.

To convert a selection into a path:

1. Select an area of an image 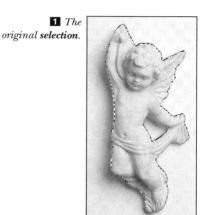.

2. Alt-click/Option-click the Make work path button at the bottom of the Paths palette **2**.
or
Choose Make work path from the Paths palette command menu.

3. Enter a Tolerance value (0.5–10) **3**. At a low Tolerance value, many anchor points will be created and the path will conform precisely to the selection marquee, but a low Tolerance can cause a printing error. At a high Tolerance value, fewer anchor points will be created and the path will be smoother, but it will conform less precisely to the selection. Try 4 or 5.

4. Click OK (Enter/Return) **4–5**. The new work path name will appear on the Paths palette. Don't leave it as a work path, though. Save it by following the steps on page 218.

TIP To quickly convert a selection into a path using the current Make Work Path Tolerance setting, click the Make work path button at the bottom of the Paths palette.

TIP To reclaim storage space occupied by an alpha channel, load the alpha channel as a selection (click the Load channel as selection button on the Channels palette), convert the selection into a path (instructions on this page), save the path, drag the original alpha channel into the Channels palette trash, and then save the image. Later on, if you want to save the path to an alpha channel again (maybe after you've reshaped it), convert the path back into a selection (see page 222) and then save the selection.

1 *The original **selection**.*

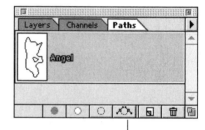

2 *Click the **Make work path** button on the Paths palette.*

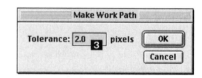

4 *The **selection** converted into a **path**: Tolerance 2.*   **5** *The **selection** converted into a **path**: Tolerance 6.*

1 *Click to create **straight** sides.*

2 *Press and drag to create a **curved** segment.*

3 *Drag in the direction in which you want the curve to follow. Place anchor points at the **ends** of a curve, not at the height of a curve. The fewer the anchor points, the more graceful the curves.*

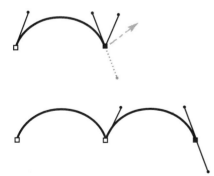

4 *To draw **non-continuous** curves, **Alt**-drag/**Option**-drag from the last anchor point in the direction you want the next curve to follow. Both direction lines will be on the same side of the curve segment.*

To create a path using the Pen tool:

1. Choose the Pen tool (P or Shift-P). 🖋
Note: If a path name is currently active, the new path will save under that name.

2. *Optional:* To list the path on the Paths palette before you draw it, click the Create new path button at the bottom of the Paths palette. 🖫 To name the path before you draw it, Alt-click/Option-click the New Path button.

3. Check the Rubber Band box on the Pen Options palette to preview the line segments as you draw.

4. Click, move the mouse, then click again to create a straight segment **1**. Hold down Shift while clicking to draw the line at a multiple of 45°.
or
Press and drag to create a curved segment, then release the mouse. Direction lines will appear **2**–**3**.
or
To create a non-continuous curve, starting from on top of the last anchor point, Alt-drag/Option-drag in the direction in which you want the next curve to follow, release Alt/Option and the mouse, then drag in the direction of the new curve **4**.

5. Repeat the previous step as many times as necessary to complete the shape.

6. To end the path but leave it open, Ctrl-click/⌘-click outside the path or click on the blank area of the Paths palette. *Note:* If you don't deselect the path name or end the path—closed or open—any additional paths you draw will be saved under the same name.
or
To close the path, click on the starting point (a small circle icon will appear next to the pointer).

7. The path will be a work path. To save it, follow the instructions on page 218. To reshape it, see pages 220–221.

TIP As you're drawing, you can press Delete once to erase the last created anchor point, or twice to delete an entire path.

Like the Magnetic Lasso tool, the Magnetic Pen tool creates a path automatically as you move or drag along areas of high contrast. The path will snap to the nearest distinct shade or color edge that defines a shape.

To create a selection using the Magnetic Pen tool:

1. *Optional:* Hide any layers that you don't want to trace.

2. Choose the Magnetic Pen tool (P or Shift P). ✒

3. *Optional:* Change the palette options. See "The Magnetic Pen palette options" on the next page.

4. Click to start the path, then move the mouse—with or without pressing the mouse button—along the edge of the shape that you want the path to describe **1**. As you move or drag, the path will snap to the edge of the shape. *Note:* If you move or drag the mouse quickly, the tool may not keep pace with you.

5. If the path snaps to neighboring shapes that you *don't* want to select, click on the edge of the shape that you *do* want to select to manually create an anchor point, and then continue to move or drag to finish the path.

6. To **close** the path **2**:

   Double-click anywhere over the shape to close with magnetic segments or Alt-double-click/Option-double-click to close with a straight segment.
   or
   Click on the starting point (a small circle will appear next to the Magnetic Pen tool pointer).
   or
   Ctrl-click/⌘-click anywhere over the shape.

   To end the path but leave it **open**, press Enter/Return. You can then reposition the Pen tool and click to start another path under the same Work Path name.

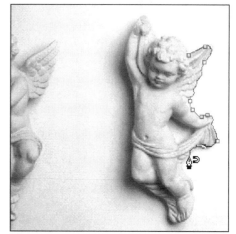

1 *Click to start the path, then move the mouse around the object you want to select.*

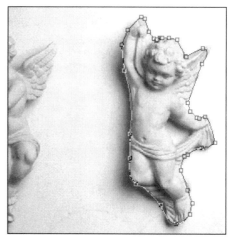

2 *The completed **Magnetic Pen** path.*

TIP Alt-drag/Option-drag to temporarily use the Freeform Pen tool. Or Alt-click/Option-click and continue clicking to draw straight segments with a temporary Pen tool. Release Alt/Option, then click, to bring back the Magnetic Pen.

TIP Press Esc to cancel a partial path.

The Magnetic Pen palette options

The **Curve Fit** (.5–10) controls the exactness with which the path fits around the shape. The higher the curve fit, the fewer the points, and thus the smoother the shape.

The **Pen Width** (1–40) is the width in pixels under the pointer that the tool considers when placing points. You can use a wide Pen Width for a high-contrast image with strong edges. For an image that has subtle contrast changes or closely-spaced shapes, you'll need the more exact line placement that a narrow Pen Width produces.

TIP To display the Magnetic Pen pointer as a circle in the current Pen Width **2**, choose File menu > Preferences > Display & Cursors, then click Other Cursors: Precise. Or press Caps Lock to turn this option on temporarily.

TIP To decrease the Pen Width while creating a path, press [. To increase the Pen Width, press].

Frequency (5–40) controls how quickly fastening points are placed as you draw a path. The lower the Frequency, the faster fastening points will be placed and the more anchor points will result.

Edge Contrast (1–100) is the degree of contrast needed between shapes for the tool to discern an edge. At a low Edge Contrast setting, even edges between low contrast areas will be discerned.

1 *Choose settings for the **Magentic Pen** from its* **Options** *palette.*

The Freeform Pen tool creates a path by dragging. Anchor points will appear automatically when you release the mouse.

To create a path using the Freeform Pen:

1. Choose the Freeform Pen tool (P or Shift-P).

2. Drag in the image window. (To draw a straight segment, keep the mouse button down and Alt-click/Option-click.)

3. To **close** the path:

   Drag back over the starting point **1**–**2**. A small circle will display next to the Freeform Pen tool pointer.
   or
   Hold down Ctrl/⌘ and release the mouse to close the path with a final curved segment.
   or
   Hold down Ctrl-Alt/⌘-Option and release the mouse to close the path with a final straight segment.

   To end the path but leave it **open**, just release the mouse.

   Note: If you leave the path open and then draw another path, the new path will be saved under the same Work Path name. To stop creating paths for the current Work Path, click on the blank area of the Paths palette. To save the path so the next work path won't delete it, see page 218.

TIP The Curve Fit setting (0.5–10) on the Freeform Pen Options palette controls the number of anchor points that the Freeform Pen tool produces **3**. The higher the curve fit, the fewer the anchor points and the smoother the shape.

To move a path:

1. On the Paths palette, activate the name of the path you want to move.

2. Choose the Direct-selection tool (A).

3. Alt-click/Option-click the path in the image window to select all its points.

4. Drag the path in the image window.

1 *To **close** the path, you can drag back over the **starting point**.*

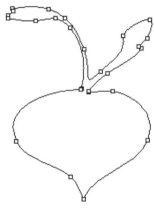

2 *The completed **Freeform Pen** path.*

Brushes	Freeform Pen Options	▶
Curve Fit:	2	pixels

3 *Choose a **Curve Fit** setting on the **Freeform Pen Options** palette.*

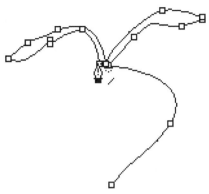

1 *To **add** to a path, drag from an **endpoint** using the Pen, Freeform Pen, or Magentic Pen tool.*

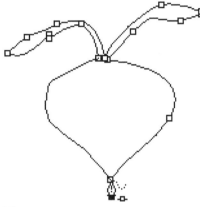

2 *Completing the addition.*

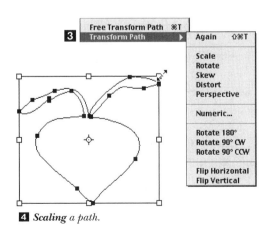

4 *Scaling a path.*

To add to an existing, open path:

1. Choose the Freeform Pen tool, Magnetic Pen, or Pen tool.

2. Click on the open path or work path name on the Paths palette.

3. Drag from either endpoint of the path **1**–**2**. To end the path, follow step 3 in the first set of instructions on the previous page.

To transform an entire path:

1. Choose the Direct-selection tool (A).

2. Activate the path name on the Paths palette, then click on the path in the image window. Make sure no points on the path are selected (see page 222).

3. Choose Edit menu > Transform Path > Scale, Rotate, Skew, Distort, or Perspective; or choose Edit menu > Transform Path > Numeric; or choose Edit menu > Free Transform Path (Ctrl-T/⌘-T).

4. Follow the instructions on pages 107–109 to perform the transformation.

TIP To repeat the transformation, choose Edit menu > Transform Points > Again or Edit menu > Transform Path > Again (Ctrl-Shift-T/⌘-Shift-T).

To transform points on a path:

1. Choose the Direct-selection tool (A), then select one or more individual points on a path (see page 219).

2. Choose Edit menu > Transform Points > Scale, Rotate, or Skew **3** (the Distort and Perspective commands won't be available); or choose Edit > Transform Points > Numeric; or choose Edit menu > Free Transform Points (Ctrl-T/⌘-T).

3. Follow the instructions on pages 107–109 to perform the transformation **4**.

To copy a path in the same image:

To make the copy a separate path name, on the Paths palette, Alt-drag/Option-drag the path name over the Create new path button at the bottom of the palette **1**, enter a name **2**, then click OK. (To copy the path without naming it, drag the path name without holding down Alt/Option.)

or

To add the copy to an existing path name, click the path name, choose the Direct-selection tool (A) ▸, click on the path in the image window, then Alt-drag/Option-drag it.

To drag-and-drop a path to another image:

1. Open the source and destination images, and click in the source image window.

2. Drag the path name from the Paths palette into the destination image window.

   or

   Choose the Direct-selection tool (A), ▸ Alt-click/Option-click the path, then drag it from the source image window into the destination image window.

   or

   Click the path name on the Paths palette, choose Edit menu > Copy (Ctrl-C/⌘-C), click in the destination image window, then choose Edit menu > Paste (Ctrl-V/⌘-V).

   Note: If there is already an active path in the destination image, the path you drag-and-drop will be added to its name.

A new path created with the Pen tool will be labeled "Work Path" automatically and it will save with the file. The next path you create, however, will replace the existing one. Follow these instructions to save a path so it won't be deleted by a new path. Once a path is saved, it's resaved automatically each time it's modified.

To save a work path:

Double-click the path name, enter a name **3**, then click OK (Enter/Return).

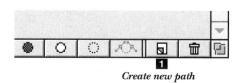

Create new path

Duplicate Path

Name: Path 1 copy **2**   OK   Cancel

Save Path

Name: Path 1   OK   Cancel

3 *Type a Name in the* **Save Path** *dialog box.*

To quickly save a work path under the default name

Drag the path name over the New Path button 🔲 at the bottom of the Paths palette. To rename it, double-click the path name, then type a new name.

Copy Path; Drag-and-Drop Path; Save Path

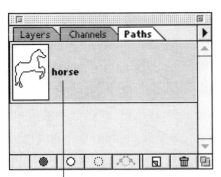

1 *To display a path, click its name on the Paths palette.*

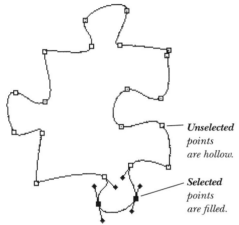

Unselected points are hollow.

Selected points are filled.

2 *Click with the Direct-selection tool to select individual points on a path.*

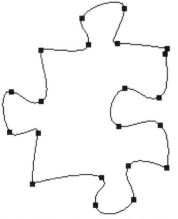

3 *Alt-click/Option-click with the Direct-selection tool to select all the points on a path.*

To display a path:

Click the path name or thumbnail on the Paths palette **1**.

TIP To change the size of or turn off palette thumbnails, choose Palette Options from the Paths palette command menu, and choose a Thumbnail Size.

To hide a path:

Shift-click the path name on the Paths palette.
or
Click below the path names on the Paths palette.
or
Activate the name of the path you want to hide on the Paths palette, then choose View menu > Hide Path (Ctrl-Shift-H/⌘-Shift-H). If you choose this option, you'll have to choose View menu > Show Path to redisplay all the paths.

To select anchor points on a path:

1. Click a path name on the Paths palette.

2. Choose the Direct-selection tool (A). ⬉

3. Click on the path or subpath, then click on an anchor point **2**. Shift-click to select additional anchor points.
or
Alt-click/Option-click the path or subpath to select all its anchor points **3**. An entire path can be moved when all its points are selected.

TIP To change the stacking position of a path, simply drag the path name up or down on the Paths palette.

TIP Hold down Ctrl/⌘ to use the Direct-selection tool while any Pen tool is currently chosen.

Display/Hide Path; Select Anchor Points

To reshape a path, you can move, add, or delete an anchor point or move a segment. To modify the shape of a curved line segment, move a direction line toward or away from its anchor point or rotate it around its anchor point.

To reshape a path:

1. On the Paths palette, click on the name of the path you want to reshape.

2. Choose the Direct-selection tool (A). ↳ To access the Direct-selection tool when another pen tool is chosen, press Ctrl/⌘.

3. Click on the path in the image window.

4. Do any of the following:

Drag an anchor **point** or a **segment 1**. To select a segment, drag a marquee that includes both of the segment's endpoints. Shift-drag to marquee additional segments (or subpaths).

Drag or **rotate** a **direction line 2**. If you move a direction line on a smooth point, the two segments that are connected to that point will also move. If you move a direction line on a corner point, on the other hand, only one curve segment will move.

To **add** an anchor **point**, choose the Add-anchor-point tool (+) ✒⁺, then click on a line segment (the pointer will be a pen icon with a plus sign when it's over a segment) **3**–**4**.

(Continued on the following page)

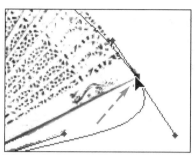

2 *Pulling a direction line.*

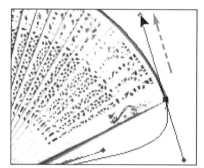

1 *Dragging an anchor point.*

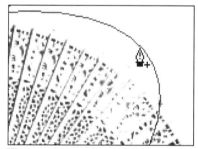

4 *The new anchor point.*

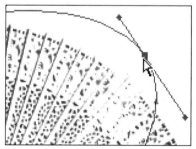

3 *Adding an anchor point.*

Reshape a Path

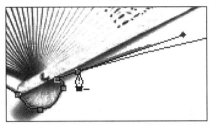

1 *Deleting an anchor pont.*

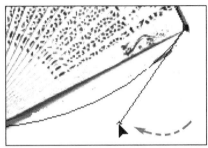

2 *Converting a direction line.*

To **delete** an anchor **point**, choose the Delete-anchor-point tool (-) 🖋, then click on the anchor point (the pointer will be a pen icon with a minus sign when it's over a point) **1**.

To **convert** a **smooth point** into a **corner point**, choose the Convert-point tool ⌐ (or hold down Ctrl-Alt/⌃⌘-Option if the Direct-selection tool is chosen or Alt/Option if a Pen tool is chosen), then click the anchor point (deselect the Convert-point tool by choosing another tool). To **convert** a **corner point** into a **smooth point**, click the Convert-point tool, then drag away from the anchor point.

Use the Convert-point tool ⌐ to rotate one direction line independently of the other direction line in the pair **2**. Once the Convert-point tool has been used on part of a direction line, you can use the Direct-selection tool (A) to move its partner.

5. Click outside the path to deselect it.

Note: If the path you want to delete is a Work Path, simply drawing a new work path with the Pen tool will cause the original Work Path to be replaced.

To delete a path:

1. On the Paths palette, activate the name of the path that you want to delete.

2. Right-click/Control-click the path name, then choose Delete Path from the context menu **3**.
or
Alt-click/Option-click the trash button on the Paths palette.
or
Click the trash button, then click Yes.
or
Drag the path name over the trash button.

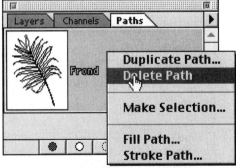

3 *To delete a path, **Right-click/Control-click** the path name, then choose **Delete Path** from the context menu.*

Delete a Path

To deselect a path:

1. Choose the Direct-selection tool (A). ⟨cursor⟩

2. Click outside the path in the image window. The path will still be visible in the image window, but its anchor points and direction lines will be hidden.

To convert a closed path into a selection:

1. *Optional:* Create a selection if you want to add, delete, or intersect the new path selection with it.

2. Ctrl-click/⌘-click the name of the path you want to convert into a selection.
or
On the Paths palette, activate the name of the path that you want to convert into a selection, then click the Load path as selection button at the bottom of the palette **1**. The last used settings will apply.

To choose options as you load the path as a selection, Right-click/Control-click the path name and choose Make Selection from the context menu. You can apply a Feather Radius to the selection (enter a low number to soften the edge slightly) **2** or add, subtract, or intersect the path with an existing selection on the image (click an Operation option). The Operation shortcuts are listed in the sidebars on this page. Click OK. *Note:* If you turn on the Anti-aliased option, make the Feather Radius 0.

3. On the Layers palette, activate the name of the layer on which you want to use the selection.

Path-into-selection shortcuts

WINDOWS

Make path current selection	Ctrl-click path name
Add path to current selection	Ctrl-Shift-click path name
Subtract path from current selection	Ctrl-Alt-click path name
Intersect path with current selection	Ctrl-Alt-Shift-click path name

MACINTOSH

Make path current selection	⌘-click path name
Add path to current selection	⌘-Shift-click path name
Subtract path from current selection	⌘-Option-click path name
Intersect path with current selection	⌘-Option-Shift-path name

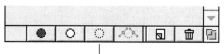

1 *Load path as selection button*

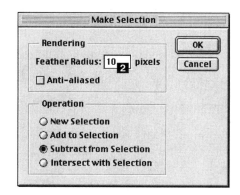

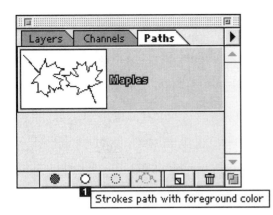

Strokes path with foreground color

When you apply color to (stroke) the edge of a path, the current tool (e.g., Paintbrush or Pencil) and its current Options palette attributes (e.g., opacity and mode) are used to produce the stroke.

To stroke a path:

1. On the Paths palette, activate the path to which you want to apply the stroke. The path can be closed or open.

2. Using the Layers palette, activate the layer on which you want the stroke pixels to appear.

3. Choose the Pencil, Paintbrush, Airbrush, Rubber Stamp, Pattern Stamp, Eraser, Smudge, Blur, Sharpen, Dodge, Burn, or Sponge tool.

4. On that tool's Options palette, choose a mode.
and
Choose an Opacity (or Pressure).

5. Click a brush tip on the Brushes palette. The stroke thickness will be the same as the diameter of the brush tip.

6. Choose a Foreground color.

2 *The original image. (The path is shown in the thumbnail in figure* **1**.)

7. Click the Stroke path (second) button at the bottom of the Paths palette **1**. (If you want to switch tools, Alt-click/ Option-click the Stroke path button, choose from the Tool drop-down menu, then click OK. That tool will be used with its current Options palette settings.)
or
Choose Stroke Path (or Stroke Subpath, for a Work Path) from the Paths palette command menu, then click OK **2**–**3**.

8. *Optional:* Click the Stroke Path button again to widen the stroke.

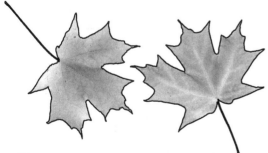

3 *A* **Pencil** *tool* **Stroke** *is applied to the* **path**.

Stroke a Path

Use the Fill Path command to fill a path with a color, a pattern, or imagery.

To fill a path:

1. On the Paths palette, activate an open or closed path.

2. Using the Layers palette, activate the layer on which you want the fill pixels to appear.

3. To fill with a solid color other than white or black, choose a Foreground color.
or
To fill with a pattern, select an area of an image using the Rectangular Marquee tool, then choose Edit menu > Define Pattern.
or
To fill with imagery from a history state, move the History Brush icon to the state that you want to use as a fill.

4. Alt-click/Option-click the Fill path (first) button at the bottom of the Paths palette **1**.
or
Right-click/Control-click the path name and choose Fill Path from the context menu.

5. Choose from the Contents: Use drop-down menu **2**.

6. Enter an Opacity percentage.
and
Choose a Mode. Choose Clear mode to fill the path on a layer with transparency.

7. *Optional:* If a layer (not the Background) is active, check the Preserve Transparency box to recolor only existing pixels on that layer, not transparent areas.

8. *Optional:* Choose Rendering options (feathering and anti-aliasing).

9. Click OK (Enter/Return) **3**–**4**.

TIP To fill a path using the current Fill Path dialog box settings, highlight the path name, then click the Fill path button at the bottom of the Paths palette.

TIP To change a path's stacking order, drag its name upward or downward.

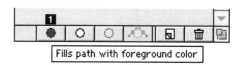

Fills path with foreground color

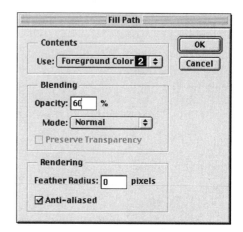

3 *The original path.*

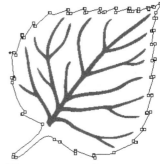

4 *The path filled with a pattern, 50% opacity.*

Fill a Path

Clipping Path

Path: [Crabby   ‡] **1**   [OK]

Flatness: [   ] device pixels   [Cancel]

You can silhouette an image in Photoshop for use in another application, such as Adobe Illustrator or QuarkXPress. The area outside the image will be transparent, so it can be layered over other page elements.

Note: In QuarkXPress 4 or later, you can create an editable clipping path or create a clipping path based on an embedded Photoshop path.

To clip the background from an image for use in another application:

1. Create a path around the portion of the image that you want to keep.

2. Save the path, and keep it active.

3. Choose Clipping Path from the Paths palette command menu.

4. Choose the path name from the Path drop-down menu **1**.

5. Enter a number in the Flatness field or leave this field blank to use the printer's default setting. Enter 8, 9, or 10 for high-resolution printing; enter 1, 2, or 3 for low resolution printing (300–600 dpi).

6. Click OK (Enter/Return).

7. Save the document in the Photoshop EPS file format (see page 297). When you open or import it into another application, only the area inside the clipping path will display and print **2**–**4**.

TIP If you transform the silhouetted image in Adobe Illustrator, the area outside it will remain transparent.

2 *Type wrapping* **around** *a* **Photoshop clipping path** *in QuarkXPress.*

3 *A Photoshop clipping path layered* **over** *type in QuarkXPress.*

4 *If the image were to be imported without a clipping path, it would have an opaque white background.*

You can create a path in Photoshop, export it to Adobe Illustrator or Macromedia FreeHand, and then use it as a path in that program. If you like, you can then place it back into Photoshop (see page 54).

Note: You could also use the Direct-selection tool and the Clipboard to copy and paste an active path to another application (or another image).

To export a path to Illustrator or FreeHand:

1. Create and save a path.

2. Choose File menu > Export > Paths to Illustrator.

3. *Optional:* Change the name in the File Name (Win) field **1**/Export paths to file (Mac) field **2**.

4. From the Paths (Win)/Write (Mac) drop-down menu, choose an individual path name, or choose All Paths to export all the paths in the image as one file.

5. Choose a location in which to save the path file.

6. Click OK (Win)/Save (Mac). The path can be opened as an Adobe Illustrator document.

TIP To ensure that the path fits when you reimport it into Photoshop, don't alter its crop marks in Illustrator.

TIP You may have to choose Artwork view in Illustrator to see the exported path, because it won't have a stroke.

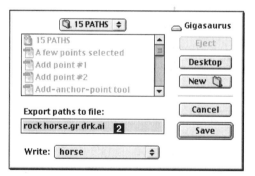

A bitmap is a bitmap is a bitmap

Rendered into pixels or not, all type in Photoshop is bitmapped—not outline. The resolution of Photoshop type always matches the resolution of the image, so the higher the image resolution, the smoother the type (for print output, choose 200 ppi or higher).

If you're going to superimpose standard type over a Photoshop image and the type design doesn't require any special Photoshop features, import the finished Photoshop image into a page layout or illustration program and layer PostScript type over it there—it will look crisper.

*The side of a character with the **Anti-aliased** box **unchecked** in the Type Tool dialog box.*

***Check** the **Anti-aliased** box in the Type Tool dialog box for smooth rendering.*

WHEN TYPE IS created in Photoshop using the **Type** or **Vertical Type** tool, it automatically appears on its own layer. Its attributes—font, style, point size, kerning, tracking, leading, alignment, and baseline shift—can be changed *after* it's created. What's more, different attributes can be applied to different characters on the same **editable type layer**. You can also transform it, apply layer effects to it, or change its blending mode or opacity.

What can't you do to a type layer? You can't apply filters or paintstrokes to it or fill it with a gradient or a pattern. You *can* perform such operations on type, however, if you **render** the type layer into pixels (Layer menu > Type > Render Layer). But you can't have your cake and eat it. Once type is rendered, however, its type attributes (font, style, etc.) can't be changed. Text, if placed from Adobe Illustrator into Photoshop, is rendered into pixels automatically.

In addition to the standard type tools, there are also two masking tools—**Type Mask** and **Vertical Type Mask**—both of which create a type selection above the current layer.

In this chapter you'll learn how to create, rotate, transform, edit, and move an editable type layer; render a type layer into pixels; screen back type or screen back an image behind type; fill type with imagery using Paste Into or a clipping group of layers; create fading type; create and use a type mask selection; add type to a spot color channel; and create a type mask for an adjustment layer.

Type that is created using the Type or Vertical Type tool automatically appears on its own layer, and it can be edited, moved, transformed, restacked, or otherwise modified without affecting any other layer.

Note: Type that is created in a Bitmap, Indexed Color, or Multichannel image will appear on the Background—not on a layer, and it can't be edited or previewed on the image.

To create an editable type layer:

1. Choose a Foreground color. The type color can be changed easily later on.

2. Choose the Type **T** or Vertical Type tool **IT** (T or Shift-T).

3. Click on the image where you want the type to appear. (Don't sweat it—you can move it easily later on.)

4. Check the Preview box to make the type preview in the image window.

5. Enter characters in the text field in the Type Tool dialog box **1**. Press (←Enter)/ Return when you want to start a new line. If you don't press (←Enter)/Return, all the type will appear in one line on the image. Use the zoom options described in the illustration at right to adjust the size of the text area.

6. Select the type (see the sidebar), then:

Choose a typeface from the **Font** drop-down menu and choose a **style** for that font from the adjacent drop-down menu. *and*

Choose points or pixels from the **Size** drop-down menu next to the Size field, then enter a size (.1–1296) in the field. *and*

If you entered more than one line of type, enter a **Leading** value (.1–1296) for the vertical space between the lines. *and*

Click an **Alignment** icon to align horizontal type to the left, center, or right relative to the insertion point, or align vertical type to the top, center, or bottom. *and*

Zoom, zoom

You can Ctrl-Spacebar-click/⌘-Spacebar-click to zoom in on the image window while the Type Tool dialog box is open. Ctrl-Alt-Spacebar-click/ ⌘-Option-Spacebar-click to zoom out. But don't press the Spacebar to temporarily bring up the Hand tool—the highlighted text will be replaced with a space, or spaces will be added to the text!

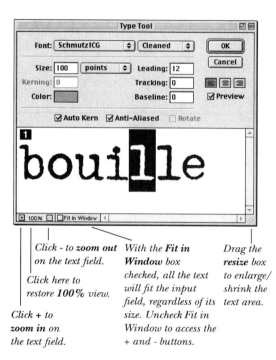

*Click - to **zoom out** on the text field.*

*Click here to restore **100%** view.*

*Click + to **zoom in** on the text field.*

*With the **Fit in Window** box checked, all the text will fit the input field, regardless of its size. Uncheck Fit in Window to access the + and - buttons.*

*Drag the **resize** box to enlarge/ shrink the text area.*

Selecting type in the input field

Select text string	Press and drag. Or click at beginning of the text string, then Shift-click at the end.
Select word	Double-click
Select all	Ctrl-A/⌘-A

Create an Editable Type Layer

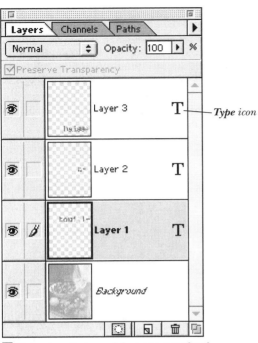

Type icon

1 *To produce the image below, type was placed on three separate layers so they could be moved around easily. This method provides even more flexibility in placement than does using leading in a single block of type.*

To kern manually, uncheck the Auto Kern box, click between two characters, then enter a **Kerning** value (-1000–1000) to adjust the space between them.
and
Select two or more characters and enter a **Tracking** value (-1000–1000) to adjust the space between those characters uniformly.
and
Select one or more characters and enter a **Baseline** value (-1296–1296) to shift those characters above or below their baseline.
and
Leave the **Anti-aliased** box checked to smooth the type edges (don't turn this option on for small type). Uncheck the Anti-aliased box only if you're planning to output the image to a multimedia program that might display an unwanted halo around smooth-edged shapes.
and
Click the **color** swatch, choose a color from the Color Picker, check out the preview in the image window, then click OK.

7. *Optional:* If the Preview option is on, you can drag the type in the image window.

8. *Optional:* To rotate vertical type 90°, select some or all of the type in the dialog box, then check the Rotate box (**3**, next page).

9. Click OK or press Enter on the numeric keypad (don't press Return). The type will appear on a new layer **1**. Preserve Transparency will be in a fixed "on" position for that layer. You *can* change the type layer's opacity or mode.

Note: To change the type color, activate the type layer, choose a Foreground color, then Alt-Backspace/Option-Delete.

Use the Layer menu > Type > Horizontal or Vertical command to change the orientation of horizontal or vertical type.

To rotate type:

1. On the Layers palette, highlight the name of the horizontal or vertical type layer that you want to rotate **1**.

2. Choose Layer menu > Type > Horizontal or Vertical **2**. You will probably need to reposition the type after applying either command.

TIP To rotate vertical type another way, double-click its layer, highlight the characters that you want to rotate, then check or uncheck the Rotate box **3**. This option is unavailable for horizontal type.

Spaced out?

To adjust the vertical spacing between lines of horizontal type, highlight the type, then change the Leading value. To adjust the spacing between characters in vertical type, in the Type Tool dialog box, highlight the characters you want to adjust, then change the Tracking value; to remove space, enter a negative tracking value.

1 *The original vertical type.*

2 *The vertical type after choosing Layer menu > Type > Horizontal.*

3 *The original vertical type (**1**) after highlighting some characters and then checking the **Rotate** box in the Type Tool dialog box.*

To transform type:

Follow the instructions on pages 107–109. All the Edit menu > Transform commands are available for rendered type. All the Transform commands except Distort and Perspective are available for editable (non-rendered) type. To transform part of a type layer, it has to be rendered first.

TIP To scale editable type, use Edit menu > Transform > Scale or double-click the type layer and change the type Size.

Somethin' missing?

If a font is missing (not installed) when you open a file that contains editable type, and you then edit the type layer, font substitution will occur.

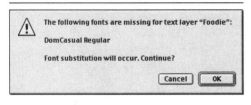

Line 'em up

To align or distribute multiple type layers, link them together, then choose from the Layer menu > Align Linked submenu or the Layer menu > Distribute Linked submenu.

Type filled with a pattern, Difference mode.

Type filled with a pattern and the Fresco filter applied.

Type filled with a pattern and a gradient.

Type filled with a pattern and the Palette Knife filter applied.

To edit a type layer:

To change type characters or attributes, double-click the layer name on the Layers palette. The Type Tool dialog box will reopen.
or
Choose either Type tool (T or Shift-T), then click on the type in the image window.

TIP To choose Layer Options, double-click the Layer thumbnail (not the name).

To move a type layer:

1. Choose the Move tool (V). ✛

2. Right-click/Control-click on the type in the image window and selects its layer name.
   or
   On the Layers palette, click the name of the layer that you want to move.

3. Drag in the image window.
   or
   Press an arrow key.

In order to rework type shapes using a filter, using a tool such as the Paintbrush, Blur, Gradient, or Smudge, using an Image menu > Adjust command, or using the Transform > Distort or Perspective command, the type must first be converted into pixels, a process that's called rendering. You can't have it both ways, though. Once type is converted to pixels, even though it remains on its own layer, its typographic attributes can't be changed.

To render type into pixels:

1. On the Layers palette, choose the layer that contains the type that you want to render. If you want to preserve the original, editable layer for later use, duplicate it and then render the duplicate.

2. Choose Layer menu > Type > Render Layer. The ways in which rendered type can be dressed up are almost limitless—just use your imagination! Here are a

(Continued on the following page)

few suggestions: Fill it with a pattern (see page 146) or a gradient (see pages 179–182). (Turn on Preserve Transparency for both fill techniques.) Or apply a filter to it.

To paint on rendered type, choose the Paintbrush tool and a Foreground color, turn on Preserve Transparency for the type layer, then draw brushstrokes in the image window ■. To paint behind the type, do it on the layer directly below the type layer ■.

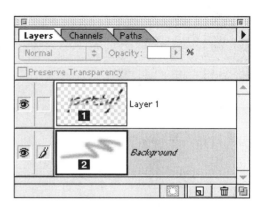

Render without rendering

To make an editable type layer look painterly without rendering it into pixels, make the editable type layer the base layer in a clipping group (see page 197), and then draw brushstrokes on the layer directly above the type layer. An advantage of using this method is that you can repaint the strokes or reposition them without affecting the type layer.

To screen back an image behind type:

1. Activate the background image on the Layers palette. You can use these instructions to lighten the background behind a Drop Shadow layer effect.

2. Choose Layer menu > New > Adjustment Layer.
   or
   Ctrl-click/⌘-click the Create new layer icon on the Layers palette.

3. Choose Type: Levels, then click OK.

4. Check the Preview box.

5. Move the gray Input slider a little to the left.
   and
   Move the black Output slider a little to the right.

6. Click OK (Enter/Return) ■–■.

TIP To further adjust levels, try a different blending mode (try Screen or Overlay) or opacity for the Levels adjustment layer.

■ *After applying the **Levels** command to an adjustment layer over an image Background (Input Levels 0, .95, and 255, and Output Levels 92 and 255).*

■ *After filling the adjustment layer with a black-to-white **gradient** (upper right to lower left corner) to mask out the Levels effect in the upper right corner.*

Screen Image Behind Type

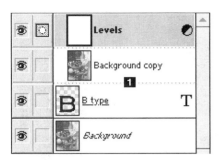

2 *Screened back type.*

To screen back type:

1. Follow the steps on page 228 to create a type layer. It can be editable or rendered to pixels. Use a chunky typeface in a substantial size.

2. Click the name of the layer that is to be the backdrop image behind the type, and then drag it over the Create new layer icon. ▣

3. On the Layers palette, drag the duplicate layer name above the type layer.

4. Alt-click/Option-click on the line between the two layer names to create a clipping group. A dotted line will appear and the name of the base (bottom) layer of the group will be underlined **1**. The clipping effect won't be visible until you change the duplicate layer.

5. Click on the duplicate layer name.

6. Choose New Adjustment Layer from the palette command menu.

7. Choose Type: Levels, check the Group with Previous Layer box, then click OK.

8. Move the Input midtones slider to the left to lighten the midtones in the type, and pause to preview.
   and
   Move the Output shadows slider to the right to reduce the contrast in the type, and pause to preview.

9. Click OK (Enter/Return) **2**.

TIP Change the blending mode for the adjustment layer or the base layer to restore some of the background color (try Overlay, Color Burn, or Hard Light mode). Lower the layer's opacity to soften the Levels effect.

TIP: *To screen back an image with type, follow the same steps, but this time lighten the background image using another adjustment layer and use the topmost Levels adjustment layer to darken the type.*

Screen Back Type

233

To fill type with imagery from another document using Paste Into:

1. Create a type layer. It can be editable or rendered to pixels.

2. Activate the layer in another document that contains the imagery with which you want to fill the type.

3. Choose All from the Select menu or create a selection.

4. Choose Edit menu > Copy (Ctrl-C/ ⌘-C).

5. Activate the image that contains the type layer, then Ctrl-click/⌘-click the type layer name.

6. Choose Edit menu > Paste Into (Ctrl-Shift-V/⌘-Shift-V) **1**–**2**. A new layer with a layer mask will be created automatically, and the pasted image will be revealed through the mask character shapes.

7. *Optional:* With the layer thumbnail selected on the Layers palette, choose the Move tool (V) ✛ and drag to move the pasted image within the type shapes. Click in the space between the layer thumbnail and the layer mask thumbnail to link the mask to the layer image. The position of the image inside the mask can't be changed while they remain linked. (Dragging with the Move tool now would move both the mask shape and the image inside it and expose the type layer underneath.)

TIP To fill type with imagery using a layer mask, see page 195.

1 *Type filled with an image using the **Paste Into** command.*

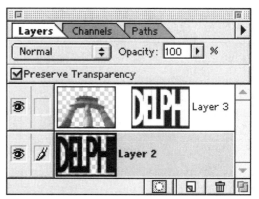

2 *The bottommost layer is the original type layer; the topmost layer was created after pasting into the type selection.*

1 *The separate layers before being joined in a clipping group.*

2 *The layers pulled apart so you can see their stacking order.*

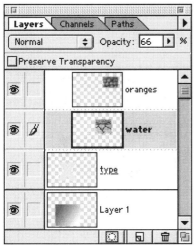

3 *The Layers palette after Alt-clicking/ Option-clicking on the lines above the type layer. The type layer (the underlined name) is the base layer of the clipping group.*

To fill type with imagery using a clipping group of layers:

1. Create type using the Type or Vertical Type tool. It can be editable or rendered.

2. Move the type layer on the Layers palette just below the layer or layers that are to become the type fill **1**–**2**.

3. Alt-click/Option-click on the line between the type layer name and the layer directly above it to create a clipping group. A dotted line will appear and the base (bottommost) layer of the group will be underlined. Only pixels that overlap the letter shapes will be visible **3**–**4**.

4. *Optional:* Activate the type layer and use the Move tool to reposition the letters in the image window.

5. *Optional:* Alt-click/Option-click on the lines between other layers that are directly above the clipping group to add them to the group.

6. *Optional:* Change the mode or opacity for any layer in the clipping group. The blending mode of the base (underlined) layer affects the way the clipping group blends with layers below the group. The blending mode of an indented layer affects only layers in the clipping group.

TIP To release a layer from a clipping group, Alt-click/Option-click again on the dotted line.

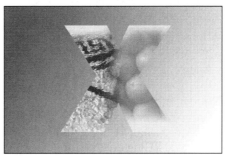

4 *Type filled with imagery using a **clipping group**.*

Fill Type with Imagery using a Clipping Group

To create fading type:

1. Create type on its own layer, and leave the type layer active. The type can be editable or rendered.

2. Click the Add layer mask button on the Layers palette. A layer mask thumbnail will appear next to the layer name **1**.

3. Choose the Linear Gradient tool (G or Shift-G). ▢

4. On the Linear Gradient Options palette, choose 100% Opacity, Normal mode, and Foreground to Background.

5. Choose black as the Foreground color.

6. Drag in the image window from top to bottom or left to right, at least halfway across the type. The type layer mask will fill with a black-to-white gradient. Type will be hidden where there is black in the layer mask **2**.

TIP Click on the layer thumbnail or name on the Layers palette to modify the layer; click on the layer mask thumbnail to modify the layer mask. (Read more about layer masks in Chapter 13.)

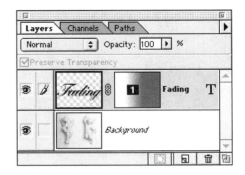

2 *Fading type.*

To apply layer effects to semi-transparent type:

1. To make the layer effect more pronounced, lighten the image using Image menu > Adjust > Levels. If you create an Adjustment Layer, Type: Levels, be sure to merge the adjustment layer with the background before proceeding.

2. Create type on an editable type layer.

3. Choose the Background (image) layer.

4. Choose Select menu > Select All, then choose Edit menu > Copy.

5. Choose the type layer, then Ctrl-click/ ⌘-click the type layer name to select only the type characters.

6. Choose Edit menu > Paste Into (Ctrl-Shift-V/⌘-Shift-V). A new layer will be created **3** and the type will "disappear" because you pasted a perfect

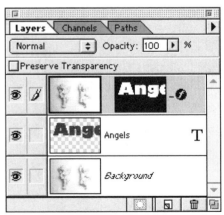

3 *The type layer shapes were used to create the mask for the **Paste Into** layer.*

1 *Outer Bevel and Drop Shadow.*

2 *As a final step for this image, we darkened the type layer slightly via Levels.*

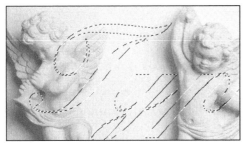

3 *A type mask selection.*

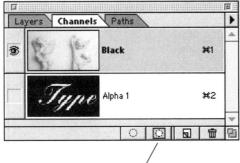

4 *To save a type mask selection to an alpha channel, click the **Save selection as channel** button on the **Channels** palette.*

match of the background. It will reappear after the next step.

7. With the new paste into layer still active, choose from the Layer menu > Effects submenu (we chose Drop Shadow and Bevel & Emboss: Outer Bevel), adjust the settings, then click OK **1**–**2**.

Note: To modify a layer effect, double-click the *f* icon.

TIP To reposition the type effect on the image, hide the original type layer, then click on the mask thumbnail (the rightmost thumbnail) of the paste-into layer. If a link icon displays between the two thumbnails, click the link icon to unlink the mask from the layer image. Then drag the type shapes with the Move tool.

The Type Mask tools create a selection in the shape of type characters. You might want to do this for a variety of reasons: to copy layer imagery in the shape of letters; to mask (limit) an adjustment layer effect to a type selection; to stroke type; or to add a layer mask (Reveal Selection or Hide Selection).

To create a type selection:

1. Activate the layer on which you want the type selection to appear (preferably not a type layer).

2. Choose the Type Mask 🔲 or Vertical Type Mask 🔲 tool (T or Shift-T).

3. Click in the image window where you want the selection to appear.

4. Follow steps 4–9 on pages 228–229 **3**. The selection won't preview on the image.

TIP Double-click the type selection with the Type Mask or Vertical Type Mask tool to reopen the Type Tool dialog box.

TIP Save a type selection to a new channel (click the Save selection as channel button 🔲 on the Channels palette) **4**. It can then be viewed on the Channels palette and loaded onto any layer or layer mask at any time.

To move a type selection:

1. Choose the Type Mask or Vertical Type Mask tool (not the Move tool!).

2. Drag from inside the selection in the image window.
or
Press an arrow key. Hold down Shift and press an arrow key to move the type selection 10 screen pixels at a time.

TIP If you drag a type selection using the Move tool, you'll cut away and move pixels inside the letter shapes from the active layer.

TIP To deselect the selection, choose Select menu > Deselect (Ctrl-D/⌘-D).

TIP To copy pixels from only within a type selection, choose Edit menu > Copy to copy pixels only from the active layer or choose Edit menu > Copy Merged to copy pixels from all visible layers below the selection. Position the type selection over the desired pixels before using either copy command.

TIP To paste imagery into a type selection **1**, select and copy an area of pixels from another layer or another image, create a type selection on the destination image, then choose Edit menu > Paste Into. The type selection will be deselected and a new layer will be created.

To stroke a type selection:

1. Create type with either type mask tool, and leave it selected.

2. Choose Edit menu > Stroke.

3. Choose a stroke Width, Location, Opacity, and Mode **2**.

4. Click OK (Enter/Return) **1**.

To deselect a type selection:

Choose Select menu > Deselect (Ctrl-D/⌘-D). (Don't press Delete or choose Edit menu > Clear—both commands will remove pixels from the selection.)

1 *Imagery pasted into a **type selection**, with a **stroke** added.*

2 *Apply a stroke to a type mask selection via the **Stroke** dialog box.*

1 *Type in a spot channel.*

2 *A type mask selection in a spot channel displays on the image in the current **Ink Characteristics Color** (see **3**, below).*

New Spot Channel

Name: spot channel-type [OK] [Cancel]

Ink Characteristics

Color: ▮   Solidity: 0 %

3 *You can change the **Solidity** value to represent the spot color ink tint.*

To create type in a spot channel:

1. Create an editable type layer (Type tool) so you'll be able to modify it later on.

2. Follow steps 1–6 on page 165 to create a new spot channel.

3. Choose the type layer, then Ctrl-click/⌘-click the type layer name to select only the non-transparent parts of the layer.

4. On the Channels palette, choose the spot color channel name.

5. Choose Edit menu > Fill (Shift-Backspace/Shift-Delete), choose Use: Black, Normal mode, choose the Opacity that you want the spot color ink to have, then click OK.

6. Choose Select menu > Deselect (Ctrl-D/⌘-D) **1**–**3**.

7. *Optional:* Hide the type layer (click the eye icon on the Layers palette).

TIP To move the type in the spot color channel, choose that channel, choose the Move tool, then drag in the image window.

TIP To tint a spot channel, see page 166–167.

TIP If you create a spot channel while a selection is active (as in step 3, above), the selection will fill with the spot channel color at 100%.

To edit type in a spot channel:

1. On the Channels palette, choose a spot channel on which you have created type.

2. Marquee the type.

3. Press Delete to delete the type from the channel.

4. Choose Select menu > Deselect.

5. Double-click the original type layer on the Layers palette, edit the type, then click OK.

6. Follow steps 3–7 from the preceding set of instructions on this page. The spot color channel will now contain the revised type.

Create, Edit Type in Spot Channel

To create a type mask for an adjustment layer:

1. Choose the Type Mask ⬚ or Vertical Type Mask ⬚ tool (T or Shift-T), then click in the image where you want the type to appear.

2. Choose type attributes, enter characters, then click OK. Leave the type selected.

3. Activate the layer above which you want the new adjustment layer to appear.

4. Ctrl-click/⌘-click the Create new layer button on the Layers palette, choose an adjustment type, choose adjustment options, then click OK. The type character shapes will become a mask for the adjustment layer. Only pixels directly under the character shapes will be affected by the adjustment **1**–**2**.

TIP Alt-click/Option-click the adjustment layer thumbnail to display the mask alone. Alt-click/Option-click it again to restore the full image.

TIP With the adjustment layer selected, choose Image menu > Adjust > Invert (Ctrl-I/⌘-I) to swap the black and white areas of the adjustment layer mask.

TIP Use the Move tool (its Auto Select Layer option unchecked) to reposition a type mask on an adjustment layer.

1 *The type selection functions as a mask for the adjustment layer.*

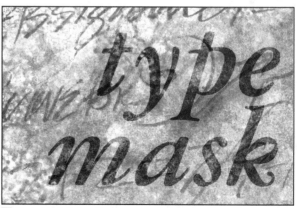

2 *Only pixels below the character shapes are affected by the adjustment layer.*

FILTERS 17

Filter

| Last Filter | ⌘F |
| Fade... | ⇧⌘F |

Artistic ▶	Colored Pencil...
Blur ▶	Cutout...
Brush Strokes ▶	Dry Brush...
Distort ▶	Film Grain...
Noise ▶	Fresco...
Pixelate ▶	Neon Glow...
Render ▶	Paint Daubs...
Sharpen ▶	Palette Knife...
Sketch ▶	Plastic Wrap...
Stylize ▶	Poster Edges...
Texture ▶	Rough Pastels...
Video ▶	Smudge Stick...
Other ▶	Sponge...
	Underpainting...
Digimarc ▶	Watercolor...

1 *Filters are grouped into submenu categories under the **Filter** menu.*

The Groucho filter

PHOTOSHOP'S FILTERS can be used to produce a myriad of special effects, from slight sharpening to wild distortion. Use a filter like Blur or Sharpen for subtle retouching; use a filter like Color Halftone, Find Edges, Emboss, or Wind to stylize an image; use an Artistic, Brush Strokes, Sketch, or Texture filter to make a layer look hand-rendered; or create a wide variety of beautiful lighting illusions using the Lighting Effects filter.

This chapter has three components: techniques for applying filters; an illustrated compendium of all the Photoshop filters; and lastly, a handful of step-by-step exercises that use filters.

Filters are grouped into thirteen submenu categories under the Filter menu **1**. Third-party filters appear on their own submenus. (See the Photoshop User Guide for information about installing third-party filters.)

Filter basics

How filters are applied

A filter can be applied to a whole layer or to a selection on a layer. For a soft transition between the filtered and non-filtered areas, feather the selection before applying a filter.

Some filters are applied in one step (select it from a submenu). Other filters are applied via a dialog box in which one or more variables are specified. Choose Filter menu > Last Filter (Ctrl-F/⌘-F) to reapply the last used filter using the same settings. Choose a filter from its submenu to choose different settings. To open the dialog box for the last used filter with its last used settings, use the Ctrl-Alt-F/⌘-Option-F shortcut.

All the filters are available for an image in RGB Color or Multichannel mode; not all filters are available for an image in CMYK,

(Continued on the following page)

Filter Techniques

Grayscale, or Lab Color mode. None of the filters are available for an image in Bitmap or Indexed Color mode, or to an image that has 16-bits per channel.

Using a filter dialog box

Most filter dialog boxes have a **preview window 1**. Drag in the preview window to move the image inside it. With some filter dialog boxes open, the pointer becomes a square when it's passed over the image window, in which case you can click to preview that area of the image. (Check the Preview box, if there is one, to preview the effect in the dialog box and the image window.)

Click the + button to zoom in on the image in the preview window, or click the – button to zoom out **2**.

A flashing line below the preview percentage indicates the filter effect is taking its sweet time to render in the preview window. A flashing line below the Preview check box means the filter effect is taking its sweet time to preview in the image window.

TIP Press the up arrow on the keyboard to increase the value in a highlighted field by one unit (or .1 unit, if available). Press the down arrow to reduce.

Lessening a filter's overall effect

The **Fade** command lessens a filter effect or an Image menu > Adjust effect (no other commands). After applying a filter, choose Filter menu > Fade "[   ]" (Ctrl-Shift-F/ ⌘-Shift-F), choose an opacity amount and a blending mode, then click OK **3**–**5**.

To lessen a filter's effect with the option to test different **blending modes**, do the following:

1. Duplicate the layer to which the filter will be applied.

2. Apply the filter to the duplicate layer.

3. Move the Layers palette Opacity slider to lessen (fade) the effect of the filter.

4. Choose a different blending mode (**1**–**2**, next page) (see also pages 190 and 192).

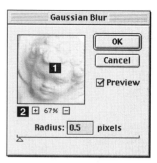

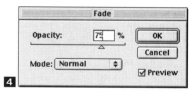

3 *Filter menu > Texture > **Mosaic Tiles** applied to an image.*

5 *After using the **Fade** command in **Overlay** mode to lessen the filter effect on the overall image.*

1 *The original image.*

2 *After applying the **Find Edges** filter to a duplicate of the original layer, lowering the **opacity** of the duplicate layer, and choosing Hard Light blending mode (also try Overlay, Color Dodge, or Difference).*

3 *After applying the **Poster Edges** filter to an image and then using the **History Brush** to restore the angel's face and tummy to its original state.*

Because the filter was applied to a copy of the original layer, later on you can change the blending mode or opacity of the filter effect layer to blend it differently with the original layer, or create a layer mask for the duplicate layer to hide or change the filter effect, or discard the filter layer entirely. When the image is finalized, merge the duplicate layer with the original.

Another way to soften a filter's effect is to modify pixels in only one of an image's color components. To do this, choose a layer, click a **channel** color name on the Channels palette, apply a filter (Add Noise is a nice one to experiment with), then click the top channel on the palette (Ctrl-~/⌘-~) to redisplay the composite image.

You can selectively reduce a filter effect using the **History Brush**. Set the History Brush icon to a prior state on the History palette, and then draw strokes on the image **3**.

Restricting the area a filter affects

Create a **selection** first on a layer to have a filter affect only pixels within the selection. To achieve a soft-edged transition around the filtered area, **feather** the selection before applying the filter.

You can also use a **layer mask** to limit the effect of a filter. The edge between the white and black areas of a layer mask can be soft, hard, or painterly, depending on the type of brush strokes you use to paint the black areas of the mask. By choosing Layer menu > Add Layer Mask > Reveal Selection when a selection is active and then applying a filter to the mask, the filter effect will be visible where the black and white areas of the layer mask meet (try Brush Strokes > Spatter; Pixelate > Pointillize; Stylize > Wind; or Distort > ZigZag or Ripple) (see page 258).

Or create a black-to-white **gradient** in the layer mask and then apply a filter to the layer image (not to the layer mask). The filter will apply fully to the image where the

(Continued on the following page)

Filter Techniques

mask is white and fade to nil in areas where the mask is black **1**–**3**.

Making filter effects look less artificial

Apply **more than one** filter—the effect will look less canned. If the imagery you're creating lends itself to experimentation, try concocting your own formulas. And test different variables in a filter dialog box. If you come up with a sequence that you'd like to reuse, save it in an action.

Maximizing a filter's effect

For some filters, first pumping up a layer's **brightness** and **contrast** values can intensify the filter's effect. To heighten contrast in a layer before applying a filter to it, choose Image menu > Adjust > Levels, move the black Input slider to the right and the white Input slider slightly to the left, then click OK.

To **recolor** a layer after applying a filter that strips color (e.g., the Charcoal filter), use Image menu > Adjust > Hue/Saturation (check the Colorize box).

Texture mapping using a filter

For some filters, like Conté Crayon, Displace, Glass, Lighting Effects, Rough Pastels, Texture Fill, and Texturizer, in lieu of using a preset pattern to create a texture effect, you can load in **another image** to use as the **pattern** for the texture effect. Lights and darks in the loaded-in image will be used to create the peaks and valleys in the texture. The image you're using for the mapping must be saved in the Photoshop file format. In a filter dialog box that contains a Texture drop-down menu with a Load Texture option, select that option, locate a color or grayscale image in the Photoshop format, then click OK.

1 *A radial gradient in the layer mask (see **2**, below) is diminishing the Stamp filter effect in the center of the nest.*

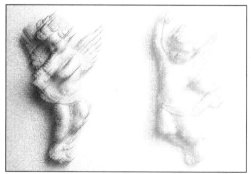

3 *The Rough Pastels filter is applied to the whole layer, but a linear gradient in the layer mask is diminishing the effect on the right side.*

All the filters illustrated

Artistic filters

Original image

Colored Pencil

Cutout

Dry Brush

Film Grain

Fresco

Neon Glow

Paint Daubs

Palette Knife

Artistic Filters

Artistic filters

Artistic Filters

Original image

Plastic Wrap

Poster Edges

Rough Pastels

Smudge Stick

Sponge

Watercolor

Underpainting

Blur filters

Original image

Blur More

Gaussian Blur

Motion Blur

Radial Blur

Smart Blur (Normal)

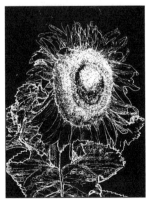

Smart Blur (Edges Only)

Smart Blur (Overlay Edge)

Brush Strokes filters

Original image

Accented Edges

Angled Strokes

Crosshatch

Dark Strokes

Ink Outlines

Spatter

Sprayed Strokes

Sumi-e

Brush Strokes Filters

Distort filters

Original image

Diffuse Glow

Displace

Glass

Ocean Ripple

Pinch

Polar Coordinates

Ripple

Shear

Distort Filters

Distort filters

Spherize

Twirl

Wave (Type: Square)

Wave (Type: Sine)

ZigZag

Noise filters

Original image

Add Noise

Median

Pixelate filters

Original image

Color Halftone

Crystallize

Facet

Fragment

Mezzotint (Short Strokes)

Mezzotint (Medium Dots)

Mosaic

Pointillize

Render filters

Original image

Clouds

Difference Clouds

Lens Flare

For the 3D Transform filter, see pages 197–200.
For the Lighting Effects filter, see pages 262–264.

Sharpen filters

Sharpen Edges

Sharpen More

Unsharp Mask

Sketch filters

Original image

Bas Relief

Chalk & Charcoal

Charcoal

Chrome

Conté Crayon

Graphic Pen

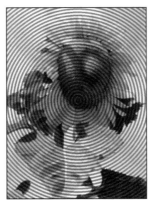

Halftone Pattern (Circle)

Halftone Pattern (Dot)

Sketch Filters

Sketch filters

Original image

Note Paper

Photocopy

Plaster

Reticulation

Stamp

Torn Edges

Water Paper

Sketch Filters

Filters

Stylize filters

Original image

Diffuse

Emboss

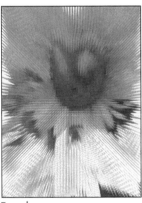

Extrude

Find Edges

Glowing Edges

Solarize

Tiles

Tiles, then Fade (Overlay mode)

Stylize Filters

Stylize filters

Original image

Trace Contour

Wind

Texture filters

Craquelure

Grain (Horizontal)

Mosaic Tiles

Patchwork

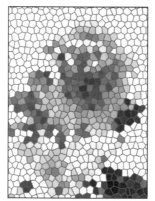

Stained Glass

Texturizer

Stylize Filters; Texture Filters

Added canvas pixels.

1

Selected area.

A few filter exercises

Apply the Ripple, Twirl, or Zigzag filter to a target layer with a white border to produce a warped paper texture.

To create a wrinkled edge:

1. Choose white as the Background color.

2. Use Image menu > Canvas Size to add a border (use a one-layer image).

3. Choose the Rectangular Marquee tool (M or Shift-M).

4. Enter 8 in the Feather field on the Marquee Options palette.

5. Drag a selection marquee across about three quarters of the image (not the border).

6. Choose Select menu > Inverse (Ctrl-Shift-I/⌘-Shift-I). The active selection will now include the added canvas area and part of the image **1**.

7. Apply Filter menu > Distort > Ripple **2**, Twirl, or ZigZag, or a combination thereof. Click the zoom out button (–) in the filter dialog box to preview the whole image.

PHOTO: PAUL PETROFF

2 *A wrinkled edge produced using the **Ripple** filter.*

Take the easy way out:

Use one of the canned frame effects from Extensis' PhotoFrame **3**–**4**, or combine a couple of their effects together. Auto F/X Corporation has a frame package, too.

3 *A **Camera** edge from **Photoframe**.*

4 *A **Watercolor** edge from **Photoframe**.*

Artistic Edges and Frames

In these instructions, you will add a black or gray texture to a layer mask via a filter. Black areas in the layer mask will hide pixels in that layer and reveal imagery from the layer below it.

To apply a texture using a layer mask:

1. Open an image.

2. Create a new layer, and fill it with white.

3. Create layer mask for the new layer by clicking the Add layer mask button on the Layers palette 📷, and leave the layer mask thumbnail active.

4. Apply the Add Noise filter to the layer mask.

5. Apply another filter or series of filters to the layer mask **1**–**2**. Try a Texture filter (Craquelure, Grain, Mosaic Tiles, Patchwork, and Texturizer). Or try Artistic > Dry Brush (small brush size), Palette Knife (small stroke size), Plastic Wrap (use Levels to increase contrast), Sponge, or Watercolor.

   To intensify a filter's effect, apply the Distort > Twirl or Ripple, or Stylize > Wind filter afterward. To fade a filter effect, use Filter menu > Fade.

6. Adjust the opacity of the layer that has the layer mask.

Turn a photograph into a painting or a drawing:

1. Choose Duplicate Layer from the Layers palette command menu, then click OK.

2. Choose Filter menu > Stylize > Find Edges.

3. With the duplicate layer active, click the Add layer mask button. 📷

4. Paint with black at below 100% opacity on the layer mask to reveal parts of the layer below **3**–**4**.

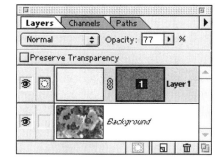

2 *A filter applied via a **layer mask**.*

3 *The original image.*

4 *The final image.*

5. *Optional:* Lower the opacity of the duplicate layer.

6. *Optional:* For a dramatic effect of colors on a dark background, click the layer thumbnail, then choose Image menu > Adjust > Invert (Ctrl-I/⌘-I).

TIP To produce a magic marker drawing, apply the Trace Contour filter, and apply Filter menu > Other > Minimum (Radius of 1 or 2) in lieu of step 2.

1 *The original image.*

2 *Theirs.*

3 *Ours.*

We've come up with a way to turn a photograph into a watercolor using the Median Noise and Minimum filters. Compare it to Photoshop's Watercolor filter.

Our watercolor filter:

1. Duplicate the layer that you want to turn into a watercolor.

2. With the duplicate layer active, choose Filter menu > Noise > Median.

3. Move the Radius slider to a number between 2 and 8.

4. Click OK (Enter/Return).

5. Choose Filter menu > Other > Minimum.

6. Move the Radius the slider to 1, 2, or 3.

7. Click OK (Enter/Return) **1**–**3**.

8. *Optional:* Apply the Sharpen More filter.

Our Watercolor Filter

In the following instructions, the Mosaic filter is applied using progressive values to a series of rectangular selections, so the mosaic tiles gradually enlarge as the effect travels across the image. (Using a gradient in a layer mask instead would gradually fade the Mosaic effect without changing the size of the mosaic tiles **1**.)

To apply the Mosaic filter using graduated values:

1. Choose a layer.

2. Choose the Rectangular Marquee tool.

3. Marquee about one-quarter or one-fifth of the layer, where you want the mosaic tiles to begin.

4. Choose Filter menu > Pixelate > Mosaic.

5. Enter 6 in the Cell Size field **2**.

6. Click OK or press Enter/Return.

7. With the selection still active and the Rectangular Marquee tool still chosen, Shift-drag the marquee to the next adjacent quadrant **3**.

8. Repeat steps 4–7 until you've finished the whole image, entering 12, then 24, then 30 in the Cell Size field. Or to create larger pixel blocks, enter higher numbers—like 8, 16, 28, and 34—in the Cell Size field.

9. Deselect (Ctrl-D/⌘-D) **4**.

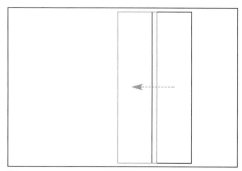

1 *This is the Mosaic filter applied using a **gradient** in a **layer mask**.*

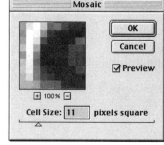

2 *Enter a number in the **Cell Size** field in the **Mosaic** dialog box. Enter progressively higher numbers each time you repeat step 5.*

3 *Apply the Mosaic filter to a rectangular selection, move the marquee, then reapply the filter, etc.*

4 *A **graduated mosaic**.*

Mosaic Filter

PHOTO: CARA WOOD

1 *Select an object.*

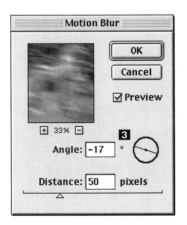

To create an illusion of motion, you will select an object that you want to remain stationary, copy it to a new layer, and then apply the Motion Blur filter to the original background.

To motion blur part of an image:

1. Select the imagery that you want to remain stationary **1**.

2. Choose Select menu > Feather (Ctrl-Alt-D/⌘-Option-D).

3. Enter 5 in the Feather Radius field, then click OK (Enter/Return).

4. Ctrl-J/⌘-J to copy the selection to a new layer **2**.

5. Activate the original layer that contains the background imagery.

6. Choose Filter menu > Blur > Motion Blur.

7. Choose an Angle between -360 and 360 **3**. (We entered -17 for our image.)
   and
   Choose a Distance (1–999) for the amount of blur. (We entered 50 for our image.)
   and
   Click OK (Enter/Return) **4**.

4 *The completed Motion Blur.*

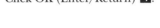

Motion Blur Part of an Image

The Lighting Effects filter produces a tremendous variety of lighting effects. You can choose from up to 17 different light sources and you can assign to each light source a different color, intensity, and angle.

Note: To use this filter, a minimum of 20MB of RAM must be allocated to Photoshop.

To cast a light on an image:

1. Make sure your image is in RGB Color mode **1**.

2. Choose a layer. *Optional:* Select an area on the layer to limit the filter effect.

3. Choose Filter menu > Render > Lighting Effects.

4. From the Style drop-down menu, choose Default or a preset lighting effect **2**.

5. *For Light Type* **3**:

Check the **On** box to preview the lighting effect in the dialog box.

Choose from the **Light Type** drop-down menu. Choose Spotlight if you want a narrow, elliptical light.

Move the **Intensity** slider to adjust the brightness of the light. Full creates the brightest light **4**. Negative creates a black light effect.

For the Spotlight Light Type, you can move the **Focus** slider to adjust the size of the beam of light that fills the ellipse shape (**5**a–b, next page). The light source starts from where the radius touches the edge of the ellipse.

To change the **color** of the light, click on the color swatch, then choose a color from the Color Picker.

6. *Do any of the following in the preview area:*

Drag the center point to move the entire light.

Drag either endpoint toward the center point to increase the intensity of the light (**6**, next page).

For an ellipse, drag either side point to change the angle of the light or to widen or narrow it (**7**a–b, next page).

1 *The original RGB image.*

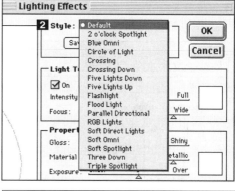

4 *The default spotlight ellipse at **Full Intensity**.*

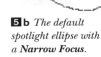

5a *The default spotlight ellipse with a **Wide Focus**. The light is strongest at the sides of the ellipse.*

5b *The default spotlight ellipse with a **Narrow Focus**.*

6 *The default spotlight ellipse after dragging the **end points** inward to narrow the light beam.*

7a *The spotlight ellipse **rotated** to the left by dragging a side point.*

7b *The spotlight ellipse after dragging the **radius** inward to make the light beam more round.*

7. *Move the Properties sliders to adjust the surrounding light conditions on the active layer:*

Gloss controls the amount of surface reflectance on the lighted surfaces.

Material controls which parts of the image reflect the light source color—Plastic (the light source color is like a glare) or Metallic (the object surface glows).

Exposure lightens or darkens the whole layer **8** **a–b**.

Ambience controls the balance between the light source and the overall light in the image **9** **a–b**. Move this slider in small increments.

Click the Properties color swatch to choose a different **color** from the Color Picker for the ambient light around the spotlight.

8. *Do any of these optional steps:*

To add the current settings to the Style drop-down menu, click **Save**.

To **add** another light source, drag the light bulb icon into the preview window (**1**, next page).

To **delete** a light source, drag its center point over the trash icon.

To **duplicate** a light source, Alt-drag/ Option-drag its center point.

9. Click OK (Enter/Return).

(Continued on the following page)

8a *The spotlight ellipse with the **Exposure** Property set to **Over**.*

8b *The spotlight ellipse with the **Exposure** Property set to **Under**.*

9a *The spotlight ellipse with a **Positive** Ambience Property.*

9b *The spotlight ellipse with a **Negative** Ambience Property.*

Lighting Effects Filter

Note: The last used settings of the Lighting Effects filter will remain in the dialog box until you change them or exit/quit Photoshop. To restore the default settings, choose a different style from the Style drop-down menu, then choose Default from the same menu. Click Delete to remove the currently selected style from the drop-down menu.

TIP To create a textured lighting effect, choose a channel, an alpha channel, or another Photoshop file name from the Texture Channel drop-down menu. Move the Height slider to adjust the height of the texture. This works best with the Spotlight Light Type.

TIP An Omni light creates a circular light source **2**. Drag an edge point to adjust its size.

TIP Shift-drag the side points on an ellipse change the size of the ellipse, but keep its angle constant. Ctrl-drag/⌘-drag the angle line to change the angle or direction of the ellipse, but keep its size constant.

TIP To create a pin spot, choose Light Type: Spotlight, move the Intensity slider to about 55, move the Focus slider to about 30, and drag the side points of the ellipse inward to narrow the ellipse. To cast light on a different area of the image, move the whole ellipse by dragging its center point.

TIP If the background of an image was darkened too much from a previous application of the Lighting Effects filter, apply the filter again to add another light to shine into the dark area and recover some detail. Move the Properties: Exposure and Ambience sliders a little to the right.

1 *Dragging a* **new light source** *onto the preview box.*

2 *The default Omni light is round, like a flashlight shining perpendicular to the image.*

Lighting effects in action

To produce **3**, we used a Spotlight with a wide Focus, rotated and reshaped the ellipse, moved the Exposure Property slider slightly toward Over to brighten the light source, and moved the Ambience Property slider slightly to the left to darken the background of the image. Then we Alt-dragged/Option-dragged the ellipse to duplicate the light and illuminate the face on the right. And finally, we created a new, low intensity light to illuminate the background **4**.

3 *The final image.*

4 *These three ellipses were used to produce the image above.*

Lighting Effects Filter

ACTIONS 18

An **included** command has a black check mark; an excluded command has none.

An **action**

Toggle dialog pause   **Stop**   **Play**   **New action**

Record   **New Set**

1 *With the **Actions** palette in **list** (edit) mode, you can exclude a command, toggle a dialog box pause on or off, rearrange the order of commands, record additional commands, rerecord a command, delete a command, or save actions and or sets to an actions file. This is the default (start-up) mode.*

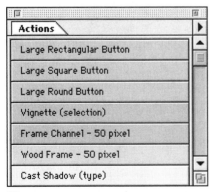

2 *The **Actions** palette in **button mode**. To turn Button mode on or off, choose Button Mode from the Actions palette command menu. The button colors and functions keys chosen in the Action Options dialog box are displayed here.*

AN ACTION IS A recorded sequence of menu commands, tool operations, or other image editing functions that can be played back on a single file or on a group of files. Actions are especially useful for producing consistent editing results on multiple images. For example, you could use an action to apply a series of Adjust submenu commands or a sequence of filters. You could also save a sequence of concise steps into an action to prepare multiple images for print output or to convert multiple images to a different file format or image mode.

An action can be anything from a simple keyboard shortcut to an incredibly complex series of commands that trigger still other actions or that process a whole batch of images. Actions can help you can save seconds or hours of work time, depending on how they're used. Start by recording a few simple actions. You'll be programming more complex processes and boosting your productivity in no time.

The Actions palette is used to record, play back, edit, delete, save, and load actions **1**–**2**. Each action can be assigned its own keyboard shortcut for quick access.

TIP Make a snapshot of the image before running an action on it. That way, you can quickly revert, if necessary, to the pre-action state of the image, and you won't have to undo any action steps.

Actions

Actions are stored in sets on the Actions palette. Sets are a convenient way of organizing task-related actions.

To create a new actions set:

1. Click on the New Set button at the bottom of the Actions palette **1**.

2. Enter a name for the set **2**, then click OK (Enter/Return).

As you create an action, the commands you use are recorded. When you're finished recording, the commands will appear as a list in outline style on the Actions palette.

Note: Some operations, such as Paintbrush tool strokes, can't be recorded.

To record an action:

1. Open an image or create a new one. Just to be safe, experiment by recording and playing back the action on a copy of the file.

2. Click the New Action button at the bottom of the Actions palette **3** or choose New Action from the Actions palette command menu.

3. Enter a name for the action **4**.

4. *Optional:* Assign a keyboard shortcut Function Key and/or display Color to the action. The color you choose will only be displayed in button mode.

5. Click Record.

6. Execute the commands that you want to record as you would normally apply them to any image. When you enter values in a dialog box and then click OK, those settings will record (except if you click Cancel).

7. Click the Stop button to stop recording.

8. The action will now be listed on the Actions palette. Click on the triangular button (list mode) to collapse the Actions list.

TIP Double-click an action name on the palette to open the Action Options

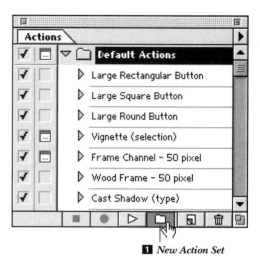

1 *New Action Set*

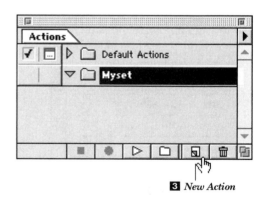

3 *New Action*

Newly recordable features

Here is a list of commands, tools, and functions which can be incorporated into a recorded action. These items are in addition to those already supported by Photoshop 4.0:

Paths palette	Lasso tools	Calculations
Layers palette	Line tool	Apply Image
History palette	Move tool	File Info
Gradient tools	Magic Wand tool	Switching and
Marquee tools	Paint Bucket tool	selecting
Crop tool	Type tool	documents
Polygon tool	Lighting Effects	Free transform

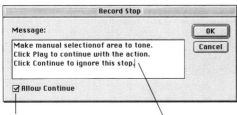

2 *Check the* ***Allow Continue*** *box to create a Continue button which the person replaying the action can press to bypass the stop command and resume playback.*

1 *Enter a* ***message*** *in the* ***Record Stop*** *dialog box to guide the user during playback.*

It's all relative

The recording of any selection-related operation using a selection tool or the Move tool is based on the current ruler units. The units can be actual (e.g., inches or picas) or relative (e.g., percent). An action that is recorded when an actual measurement unit is chosen cannot be played back on an image that is smaller than the original that was used for recording, whereas an action recorded when a relative unit is chosen will work in any other relative space and on an image of any dimensions.

dialog box, where you can rename the action or reset its shortcut key or color.

TIP Include the Save command in an action with caution. An included Save command will be useful if the action will be used for batch processing, but less useful if you're working on individual files. You may want to make the action pause at the Save dialog box to prevent the existing files from being overwritten (see page 271). To delete a Save or any other command from an action, see page 270.

You can insert a stop into an action that will interrupt the playback, at which point you can manually perform a non-recordable (and only a non-recordable) operation, such as drawing brush strokes or spotting dust specs. When the manual operation is finished, you resume the playback by clicking on the play button a second time. A stop can also be used to display an informative alert message at the pause.

To insert a stop in an action:

1. As you're creating an action, pause at the point at which you want the stop to appear. For an existing action, click the command name after which you want the stop to appear.

2. Choose Insert Stop from the Actions palette command menu.

3. Type an instruction or an alert message for the person who's going to replay the action **1**. It's a good idea to specify in your stop message that after performing a manual step, the user should click the Play button on the Actions palette to resume playback. The message will only appear while the stop dialog box is open.

4. *Optional:* Check the Allow Continue box **2** to include a Continue button in the stop alert box **3**. *Note:* With Allow Continue unchecked, you will still be able to click Stop at that point in the action playback and then click the

(Continued on the following page)

Insert a Stop

play icon on the palette to resume the action playback.

5. Click OK (Enter/Return).

6. The stop will be inserted below the previously highlighted command in the action **1**.

TIP If an action is replayed while the Actions palette is in button mode, the Play icon won't be accessible for resuming the playback after a stop. Click the action name again to resume play instead. Choose list mode for the palette when you're using stops.

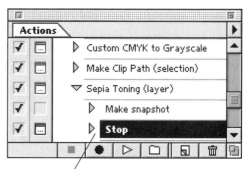

1 A **Stop** command.

To exclude or include a command from playback:

1. Make sure the Actions palette is in list— not button—mode. (In button mode, you can only execute the whole action, and any previously excluded commands won't play back.)

2. On the Actions palette, click the right-pointing triangle next to an action name to expand the list, if it isn't already expanded.

3. Click in the leftmost column to remove the check mark and exclude that command from playback **2**. (Click in the same spot again to restore the check mark and include the command.)

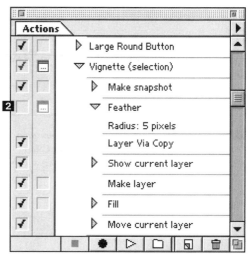

The "Vignette" action is **expanded** *on the Actions palette. The Feather step is unchecked to* **exclude** *it from playback.*

To play back an action on an image:

1. Open the image on which you want to play back the action.

2. Choose list mode for the Actions palette (uncheck button mode).

3. Click an action name on the palette **3**.

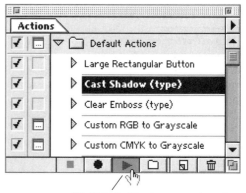

3 *Click the* **Play** *button on the palette.*

```
                    Batch
  ┌─ Play ──────────────────────────┐
  │   Set: [Database Project  ⬍]     │  [   OK   ]
  │ Action: [Add Pict Resoucs ⬍] 🔳1 │  [ Cancel ]
  │                                   │
  │  Source: [Folder  ⬍] 🔳2          │
  │  [ Choose... ] Macintosh HD 2Meg:...: Picts for database: │
  │  ☐ Override Action "Open" Commands│
  │  ☐ Include All Subfolders         │
  │                                   │
  │  Destination: [Folder  ⬍] 🔳3     │
  │  [ Choose... ] Macintosh HD:Desktop Folder:dbPicts: │
  │  ☑ Override Action "Save In" Commands│
  │                                   │
  │  Errors: [Stop For Errors  ⬍]     │
  │  [ Save As... ]                   │
  └───────────────────────────────────┘
```

Playback options

Three new options for playback control are available on the Actions palette command menu—but only when the palette is in list mode.

Accelerated: The fastest option.

Step by Step: When this option is chosen, the action's list expands on the Actions palette. Each step applies to the image as the commands in the action list highlight and execute.

Pause for [   ] seconds: This option works like Step by Step, but with an additional user-defined pause inserted at each step.

More playback options

■ To play an action starting from a specific command within the action, click that command name, then click the Play button or choose Play from the Actions palette command menu.

■ To play one command in a multi-command action, click the command name, then Ctrl-click/⌘-click the Play button.

4. Click the Play button on the palette 🔳4.

The ability to replay an action using the Batch method is one of the most powerful features of actions. The Batch command is found under the File menu > Automate.

Note: Batch processing will end at a stop command in an action. You should remove any inserted stops from an action if you're going to use it for batch playback.

To replay an action on a batch of images:

1. Choose List mode for the Actions palette.

2. Make sure all the files for batch processing are located in the same folder.

3. Choose File menu > Automate > Batch.

4. Choose a set from the Set drop-down menu and choose an action from the Action drop-down menu 🔳1.

5. Choose Source: Folder 🔳2.
and
Click Choose, then locate the folder that contains the files that you want to process.

6. Choose Destination: None to leave the files open after processing 🔳3; or choose Save and Close to save the files over their originals; or choose Folder to save the files to a new folder (click Choose to specify the destination folder).

7. *Optional:* If you chose Folder for the previous steps and checked the Override Action "Save In" Commands box, the image will save to the folder designated in step 5 during playback when a Save command occurs in the action.

8. Click OK (Enter/Return). The batch processing will begin.

TIP For efficient batching, organize your files and folders ahead of time. Make sure all your source files are in the same folder—and make sure the destination folder exists.

Note: A command that is available only under certain conditions (e.g., the Feather command requires an active selection) can't be added to an action unless you also set up or add in that condition.

To add a command (or commands) to an action:

1. On the Actions palette, click the right-pointing triangle next to an action's name to expand the list, if it's not already expanded, then click the command name after which you want the new command to appear.

2. Choose Start Recording from the Actions palette command menu or click the Record button **1**.

3. Perform the steps to record the command(s) that you want to add.

4. Click the Stop button **2** to stop recording.

TIP To copy a command from one action to another, expand both action lists, then Alt-drag/Option-drag the command you want to copy from one to the other. If you don't hold down Alt/Option while dragging, you'll cut the command from the original action. Be careful if you copy any Save commands—they may contain info specifically for the original action.

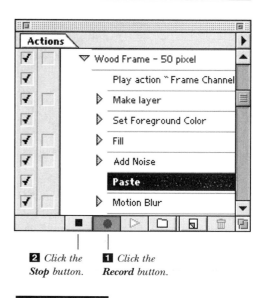

2 *Click the Stop button.*   **1** *Click the Record button.*

Record redux?

A command can be inserted into an existing action using Insert Menu Item. Dialog box settings, however, won't be recorded using this command. Instead, the action will open the dialog box, wait for user input, and then resume. We recommend using the Recording Command instead as a means to insert a controllable pause for any dialog box.

Note: To save the current list of actions as a set for later use, follow the instructions on page 273 **before** you clear any item from the Actions palette.

To delete a command from an action:

1. Click on the name of the command that you want to delete **3**. Shift-click to highlight additonal commands, if desired.

2. Click the trash button at the bottom of the Actions palette, then click OK **4**.
or
Drag the command to the trash icon.

3 *Click on the command that you want to delete.*

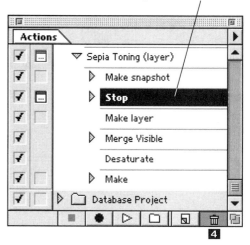

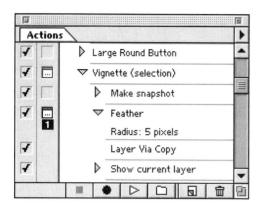

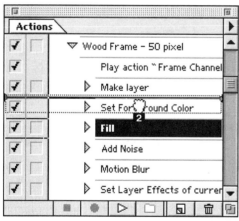

*The Fill command being **moved upward** on the list.*

A modal control is a pause in an action. A modal control can be turned on for any command that uses a dialog box or tool that requires pressing Enter/Return to apply the effect. If you encounter a modal control upon playing back an action, you can either enter different settings in the dialog box or click OK to proceed with the settings that were originally recorded for the action.

To activate/deactivate a modal control in an action:

1. Make sure the Actions palette is in list mode (not button mode).

2. On the Actions palette, click the right-pointing triangle (list toggle button) next to the action name to expand the list, if it's not already expanded.

3. Click in the second column from the left to display the dialog box icon **■**. (Click again in the same spot if you want to remove the modal control.) The action will pause and display this command's dialog box when the modal control is encountered, at which point you can enter new values, or accept the existing values, or cancel. The playback will resume after you close the dialog box.

Note: If commands have been reordered, the action may produce a different overall effect on the image on which it is played.

To change the order of commands:

1. On the Actions palette, click the right-pointing triangle next to an action name to expand the list, if it's not already expanded.

2. Drag a command upward or downward on the list **2**.

To rerecord an entire action using different dialog box settings:

1. Click on the name of the action that you want to revise.

2. Choose Record Again from the Actions palette command menu. The action will

(Continued on the following page)

Modal Control; Rerecord Action

play back, stopping at commands that use dialog boxes.

3. When each dialog box opens, enter new settings, if desired, then click OK. When the dialog box closes, the rerecording will continue.

4. To stop the rerecording, click Cancel in a dialog box or click the Stop button on the Actions palette.

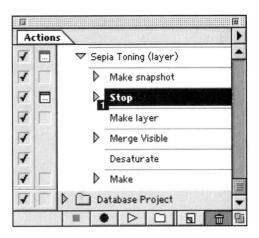

To rerecord a single command in an action:

1. On the Actions palette, double-click the command that you want to rerecord **1**.

2. Enter new settings.

3. Click OK. Click Cancel to have any revisions be disregarded.

Note: You can duplicate an action if you want to experiment with it or add to it without messing around with the original.

To duplicate an action:

Click on the name of the action that you want to duplicate, then choose Duplicate from the Actions palette command menu.

or

Drag the name of the action that you want to duplicate over the New action button at the bottom of the Actions palette **2**.

TIP To duplicate a command in an action, click on the command name, then choose Duplicate from the palette command menu. Or drag the command over the New action button at the bottom of the Actions palette.

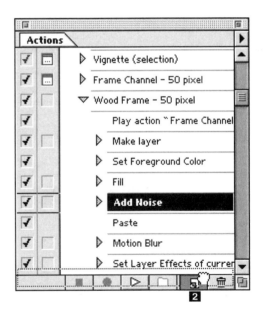

To delete an entire action:

1. Highlight the action that you want to delete.

2. Click the trash button at the bottom of the Actions palette, then click OK.

or

Alt-click/Option-click the trash button.

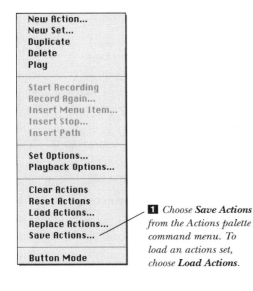

1 Choose *Save Actions* from the Actions palette command menu. To load an actions set, choose *Load Actions*.

Actions are stored automatically in actions sets (a set can contain one or more actions). Follow these instructions to save an actions set to a separate file for use on another computer or as a backup to prevent accidental or inadvertent loss.

To save an actions set to a file:

1. Click on the actions set that you want to save.

2. Choose Save Actions from the Actions palette command menu **1**.

3. Type a name for the actions set file.

4. Choose a location in which to save the actions set file.

5. Click Save. The new file will be regarded as one set, regardless of the number of actions it contains.

TIP You can Alt-drag/Option-drag an action into another actions set (it will copy automatically). Use this technique to reorganize your actions sets.

To load an additional actions set onto the Actions palette:

1. Click the set name below which you want the loaded set to appear.

2. Choose Load Actions from the Actions palette command menu **1**.

3. Locate and highlight the actions set file that you want to append.

4. Click Load/Open.

To replace the current actions set with a different actions set:

1. Choose Replace Actions from the Actions palette command menu.

2. Locate and highlight the actions set file with which you want to replace the existing sets.

3. Click Load/Open.

Where are actions stored?

All actions that are visible on the Actions palette list are stored in the Actions Palette.psp (Win) or Actions Palette (Mac) file in the Adobe Photoshop Settings folder. They live there until they are replaced or the file is trashed. To keep a set from being inadvertently removed, save it as a separate file!

Actions and AppleScript

Macintosh: An action can be controlled from another scriptable application, such as AppleScript. AppleScript is a relatively easy scripting language to learn. A scriptable application like Filemaker Pro, QuarkXPress, or Hypercard lets you drive actions externally using the AppleScript do-script command.

Save, Load, Replace Actions Set

You can make an action run within another action.

Note: The action that will be added will run through all of its commands, and thus will affect the currently open image. So, make sure that you perform this recording on a **duplicate** image.

To run one action in another action:

1. Open a file.

2. On the Actions palette, click the right-pointing triangle (list toggle button) next to the action name to expand the list, if it's not already expanded, then select the command after which you want the original action to appear ▇.

3. Click Record ▇.

4. Choose the action to be added ▇.

5. Click the Play Button ▇ to record it into the other action (you can't double-click on the action). The added action will run through its commands. The new command on the actions list will have this name: "Play Action [action name]."

6. Click the Stop button when the original action is finished ▇.

TIP An action can include multiple actions, but be careful, planning ahead is essential. An action may have been moved or modified or may be unavailable the next time you call upon it. Spend some time organizing your actions and sets, and back up often.

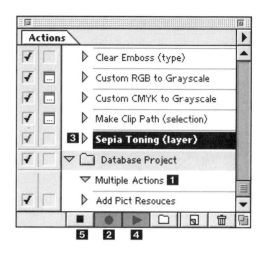

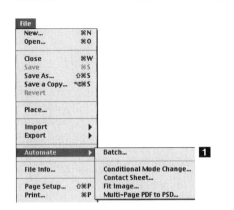

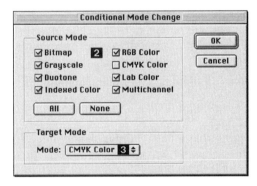

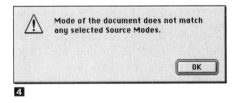

The other Automate commands

In addition to the Batch command on the Automate submenu, there are four additional commands that work like actions on steroids: Conditional Mode Change, Contact Sheet, Fit Image, and Multi-Page PDF to PSD . These commands combine many complex command sequences into one dialog box setting. Adobe will more than likely offer more of these pumped-up actions in the future and surely third-party developers will supply even more. It's a computer doing what a computer does best.

By adding this command to an action, you can ensure that all the files being processed end up in the desired image mode.

To perform a conditional image mode change:

1. Choose File menu > Automate > Conditional Mode Change.

2. Select the source file image mode that you want to convert ②.

3. Choose the desired image mode from the Target Mode: Mode drop-down menu ③. If the image mode of the processed file does not match any of the selected Source Modes, an error alert will appear (click OK) ④.

4. Click OK (Enter/Return).

Automate: Mode Change

Note: Be forewarned, the Fit Image changes an image's dimensions via resampling (by adding or deleting pixels). The image resolution will remain constant.

To fit an image to width and/or height dimensions:

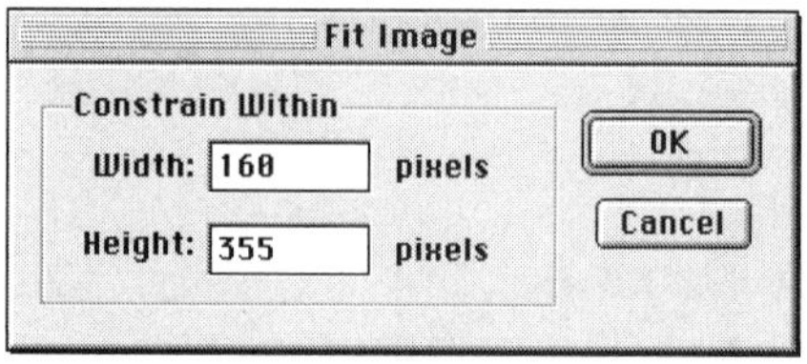

1. Open a file.

2. Choose Edit menu > Automate > Fit Image.

3. Enter the desired Width and Height dimensions. The smaller of the numbers will be used for the fit.

For example, say your source image is 210 x 237 and you enter 275 in the Height field and 1500 in the Width field. The image will be fit to the 275 dimension at the original aspect ratio (with a long dimension of 310).

4. Click OK (Enter/Return).

Fit Image

Constrain Within

Width: 160 pixels

Height: 355 pixels

OK

Cancel

Fit Image

The Contact Sheet commands creates a flattened, miniaturized copy of every image in a designated folder and arranges the copies onto the contact sheet in a user-defined matrix.

To make a contact sheet index of the contents of a folder:

1. Place all the files that you want to appear on the contact sheets in the same folder, and make sure none of the files are open. The files can be saved in any mix of file formats that Photoshop can open.

2. Choose File menu > Automate > Contact Sheet.

3. Click Choose, then locate and select the folder that contains the images that you want to appear on the contact sheet **1**.

4. Choose Contact Sheet Options: Width, Height, Resolution, and image Mode **2**. The width and height dimensions are for the overall sheet.

5. Click Place Across First to create thumbnails that run from left to right in horizontal rows or click Place Down First to create thumbnails that run downward in vertical columns.

6. Enter the total desired number of Columns and Rows in the Layout area of the dialog box.

The Width and Height of the individual image thumbnails will be listed in the lower right corner of the dialog box.

7. Click OK (Enter/Return) **3**. If there are more files in the source folder than can fit onto one sheet, new sheets will be created automatically until all the files have been used.

8. Save the new, untitled contact sheet file.

Contact Sheet Index

A multi-page Acrobat PDF file can be imported into Photoshop. See page 52 for more information on PDF. ("PSD" is the extension for the Photoshop file format.)

To convert a multi-page PDF to Photoshop format:

1. Choose File menu > Automate > Multi-Page PDF to PSD.

2. Under Source PDF, click Choose, and then locate and select the PDF file that you want to convert ■.

3. Choose a Page Range: All or choose From and enter a page range. It's a good idea to be familiar with the source file, because there is no preview of the PDF file ■.

4. Enter a Resolution. For a PDF that contains type for print output, enter a minimum resolution of 250 ppi so the type will rasterize well. 72 ppi is sufficient for a PDF for Web output. Checking the Anti-aliased option slightly softens the edges of type characters and also makes them slightly thinner.

5. Choose a Mode (you can change the image mode later in Photoshop).

6. Under Destination, leave the Base Name as is or enter a new name for the converted file ■. The name will be followed by 0001.psd, 0002.psd, and so on, to identify the source pages.

7. Click Choose, then locate and select a destination folder for the converted files.

8. Click OK (Enter/Return). Image windows will quickly display and close on screen while the conversion process is happening. When it's completed, all the converted files will be located in the folder you designated in step 7, and they can be opened and edited like any other Photoshop files.

Illustrator does it better

Try using Adobe Illustrator 7.0.1 or later to rasterize PDF pages, and then drag the images into Photoshop 5.0. The fonts will convert better and you will also have an opportunity to edit the text, which will become an editable object in Illustrator.

PDF to PSD

PREFERENCES 19

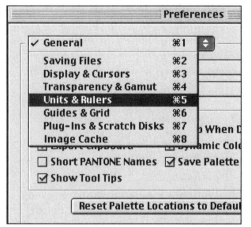

REFERENCES ARE default settings that apply to the application as a whole, such as which ruler units are used, or if channels display in color. Most preference changes take effect immediately; a few take effect on re-launching. All are saved when you exit/quit Photoshop. To access the preferences dialog boxes the fast-and-easy way, see the illustration at left. (Or use the File menu > Preferences submenu.)

Note: To reset all the default preferences:

Windows: In My Computer, open the Adobe Photoshop Settings folder inside the Adobe Photoshop 5 folder, then drag the Adobe Photoshop 5.psp and/or the Color Settings.psp file into the trash.

Macintosh: At the Finder, open the Adobe Photoshop Settings folder inside the Adobe Photoshop 5 folder, then drag the Adobe Photoshop 5 Prefs file and/or the Color Settings file into the trash.

*To access the preferences dialog boxes quickly, use the **Ctrl-K**/⌘-**K** shortcut to open the General Preferences dialog box, then use any of the shortcuts illustrated above to access other dialog boxes, or click **Next** or **Prev** on the right side of the dialog box to cycle through them.*

Windows: Memory & Image Cache Preferences

Macintosh: Image Cache Preferences

Memory & Image Cache Preferences (Win)
Image Cache Preferences (Mac)

1 The image cache is designed to help speed up screen redraw when you're editing or color adjusting high resolution images. Low-resolution versions of the image are saved in individual cache buffers and are used to update the on-screen image. The higher the **Cache Levels** value (1–8), the more buffers are used, and the speedier the redraw.

2 Check **Use cache for histograms** for faster, but slightly less accurate, histogram display in the Levels and Histogram dialog boxes.

279

General Preferences

1 Choose the Photoshop **Color Picker** to access the application's own Color Picker. If you're trying to mix a color in Photoshop to match a color in Macromedia Director or a browser, use the Windows or Apple Color Picker.

2 Choose an **Interpolation** option for reinterpretation of an image as a result of resampling or transforming. Bicubic is slowest, but the highest quality. Nearest Neighbor is the fastest, but the poorest quality.

3 Check **Anti-alias PostScript** to optimize the rendering of EPS images into Photoshop.

4 Check **Export Clipboard** to have the current Clipboard contents stay on the Clipboard when you exit/quit Photoshop.

5 Check **Short PANTONE Names** if your image contains Pantone colors and you are exporting it to another application.

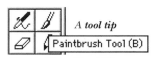
A tool tip

6 Check **Show Tool Tips** to see an onscreen display of the name of the tool or icon currently under the pointer.

7 Check **Beep When Done** for a beep to sound after any command, for which a progress bar displays, is completed.

8 With **Dynamic Color Sliders** checked, colors above the sliders on the Color palette will update as the sliders are moved. Turn this option off to speed performance.

9 With **Save Palette Locations** checked, palettes that are open when you exit/quit Photoshop will appear in their same location when you re-launch.

10 To restore the palettes' default groupings, click **Reset Palette Locations to Default**.

Saving Files Preferences

1 Choose **Image Previews:** Never Save to save files without previews, choose Always Save to save files with the specified previews, or choose Ask When Saving to assign previews for each individual file when it's saved for the first time.

Mac OS: Click **Icon** to display a thumbnail of the image in its file icon on the desktop **1**. Click **Full Size** to include a 72-ppi PICT preview for applications which require this option when importing a non-EPS file. Click **Macintosh Thumbnail** and/or **Windows Thumbnail** to display a thumbnail of an image when its name is highlighted in the Open dialog box **2**.

2 *Mac OS:* Choose **Append File Extension** Always or Ask When Saving to include a three-letter abbreviation of the file format type (i.e., "tif" for TIFF) when you save a Macintosh file for conversion to Windows.

Win and Mac: Choose/check Use Lower Case if you want the extension to appear in lowercase characters.

3 Check **File Compatibility: Include Composited Image With Layered FIles** to automatically save a flattened copy in every document. Use this option for importing Photoshop layered files into a multimedia program (e.g., After Effects or Director). This option will increase a file's storage size, so turn it off if you

ANGELS original

Display & Cursors Preferences

1 Check **Color Channels in Color** to display individual RGB or CMYK channels in color on the Channels palette. Otherwise, they will display as grayscale.

2 Check **Use System Palette** to have the Windows or Apple System Palette be used rather than the document's own color palette. Turn this option on to correct the display of erratic colors on an 8-bit monitor.

3 Check **Use Diffusion Dither** to have Photoshop simulate transitions between colors that are absent from the limited palette of an 8-bit, 256 color monitor.

4 Uncheck **Video LUT Animation** (video lookup table animation) to disable the interactive screen preview if your video card is causing Photoshop to display images incorrectly. With this option unchecked, you will still be able to check the Preview box in a dialog box to preview changes in the image window.

5 For the **Painting Cursors** (Gradient, Line, Eraser, Pencil, Airbrush, Paintbrush, Rubber Stamp, Pattern Stamp, Smudge, Blur, Sharpen, Dodge, Burn, and Sponge tools) choose **Standard** to see the icon of the tool being used, or choose **Precise** to see a crosshair icon, or choose **Brush Size** to see a round icon the exact size of the brush tip (up to 300 pixels). For the non-painting tools (Marquee, Lasso, Polygon Lasso, Magic Wand, Crop, Eyedropper, Pen, Gradient, Line, Paint Bucket, Magnetic Lasso, Magnetic Pen, Measure, and Color Sampler), choose Other Cursors: Standard or Precise.

TIP Depending on the current Preferences setting, depressing the Caps Lock key will turn Standard cursors to Precise, Precise to Brush Size, or Brush Size to Precise.

Standard cursor   **Precise** cursor   **Brush Size** cursor

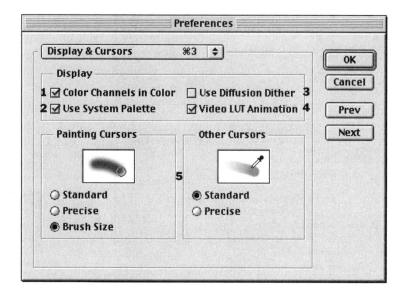

Transparency & Gamut Preferences

1 A checkerboard grid is used to represent transparent areas on a layer (areas that don't contain pixels). You can choose a different **Grid Size**.

2 Change the **Grid Colors** for the transparency checkerboard by choosing Light, Medium, Dark, Red, Orange, Green, Blue, or Purple.

3 Check **Use video alpha (requires hard-ward support)** if you do video editing and use a 32-bit video card that allows chroma keying. You will be able to see through certain parts of the video image.

4 To change the color used to mark out-of-gamut colors on an image if you're using the **Gamut Warning** command, click the Color square, then choose a color from the Color Picker. You can lower the Gamut Warning color Opacity to make it easier to see the image color underneath.

Grid Size: Large; Grid Colors: Medium

Transparency & Gamut Preferences

Units & Rulers Preferences

1 Choose a unit of measure from the **Rulers Units:** drop-down menu for the horizontal and vertical rulers that display in the image window. (Choose View menu > Show Rulers to display the rulers.)

2 To create multiple column guides, enter a **Column Size: Width** and a **Gutter** width.

TIP If you change the measurement units for the Info palette **1**, the ruler units will change in this dialog box also, and vice versa.

TIP You can also open this dialog box by double-clicking either ruler in the image window.

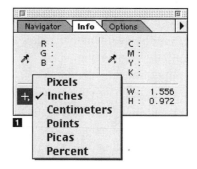

Guides & Grid Preferences

Note: Changes in this dialog preview immediately in the image window.

1 Choose a preset color for the removable ruler **Guides** from the **Color** drop-down menu. Click the color square to choose a color from the Color Picker.

2 Choose Lines or Dashed Lines for the **Guides Style**.

3 Choose a preset color for the non-printing **Grid** from the **Color** drop-down menu.

Click the color square to choose a color from the Color Picker.

4 Choose Lines or Dashed Lines for the **Grid Style**.

5 To have grid lines appear at specific unit-of-measure intervals, choose a unit of measurement from the drop-down menu, then enter a new value in the **Gridline every** field. If you choose **percent** from the drop-down menu, grid lines will appear at those percentage intervals, starting from the left edge of the image.

6 To add grid lines between the thicker grid line increments chosen in the Gridline every field, enter a number in the **Subdivisions** field.

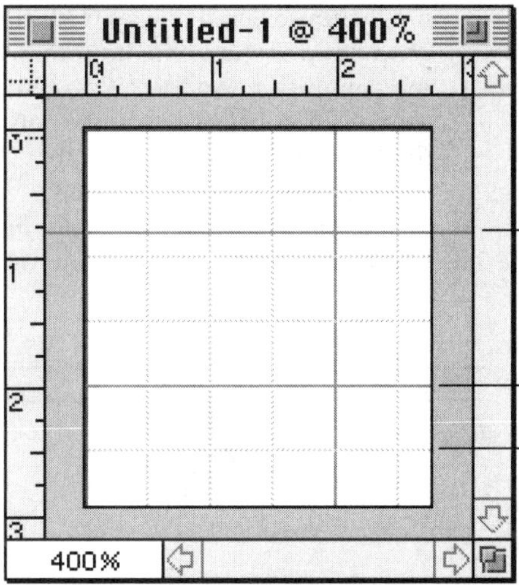

*A **guide** line pulled down from the horizontal ruler.*

*A **grid** line.*

*A grid **subdivision**.*

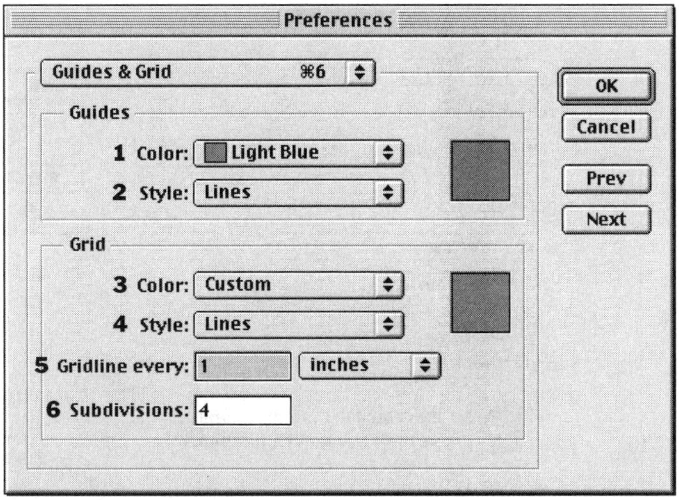

Plug-ins & Scratch Disk Preferences

Note: For changes made in this dialog box to take effect, you must exit/quit and re-launch Photoshop.

1 Click **Plug-Ins Folder: Choose** if you need to relocate or use another plug-ins folder. Photoshop needs to know where to find this folder in order to access the plug-in contents. Photoshop's internal Plug-Ins module shouldn't be moved out of the Photoshop folder unless you have a specific reason for doing so (we're not talking about third-party plug-ins here). Moving it could inhibit access to filters, the Import-Export and Effects commands, and some file formats under the save commands.

2 The **First** (and optional Second, Third, or Fourth) **Scratch Disk** is used when available RAM is insufficient for processing or storage. Choose an available hard drive from the First drop-down menu. Startup is the default.

3 As an optional step, choose an alternative **Second, Third,** or **Fourth** hard drive to be used as extra work space when necessary. If you have only one hard drive, of course you'll have only one scratch disk.

TIP If your scratch disk is a removable cartridge, removing the cartridge while Photoshop is running may cause the program to crash.

TIP To see how much RAM is currently being used while Photoshop is running, choose Scratch Sizes from the drop-down menu at the bottom of the application window (Win)/image window (Mac) **1**. The number on the left is the amount of memory required for all currently open images and the Clipboard. The number on the right is the total amount of RAM available to Photoshop.

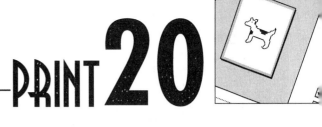

Resolution of output devices

Hewlett Packard LaserJet	600 or 1200 dpi
Apple LaserWriter	600 dpi
IRIS SmartJet	300 dpi (looks like 1600 dpi)
3M Rainbow	300 dpi
Canon Color Laser/Fiery	400 dpi
Epson Stylus Color Pro ink-jet	1440 x 720 dpi
Linotronic imagesetter	1200–4000 dpi

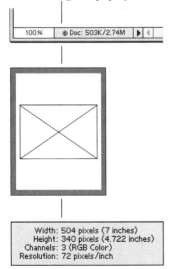

*Press and hold on the **Status** bar in the lower left corner of the application window (Win)/image window (Mac) to display the **page preview**—a thumbnail of the image in relationship to the paper size and other Page Setup specifications.*

*Alt-press/Option-press and hold on the Status bar to display **file information**.*

AN IMAGE CAN be printed from Photoshop to a laser printer, to a color printer (ink-jet, dye sublimation, etc.), or to an imagesetter. A Photoshop image can also be imported into and then printed from a drawing application, like FreeHand or Illustrator; a layout application, like QuarkXPress or PageMaker; a multimedia application, like Director or After Effects; or prepared for viewing online. (For online issues, see the next chapter.)

This chapter contains instructions for outputting to various types of printers, applying trapping, preparing an image for another application, saving a file in the EPS, DCS, TIFF, PICT, or BMP format, creating a duotone, and creating a percentage tint of a Pantone color. The last part of the chapter is devoted to color reproduction basics.

To print a spot color channel, see page 167.

Print

Note: Only currently visible layers and channels will print.

To print to a black-and-white laser printer (Windows):

1. Choose File menu > Print (Ctrl-P).

2. Choose Encoding: Binary **1**.

3. Choose the color space to which you are outputting (usually this is the file's image mode) from the Space drop-down menu **2**.

4. Click Setup, click Properties, click Color Appearance: Grayscale **3**, then click OK.

5. In Print dialog box, make sure the Print to File box is unchecked.

6. Click OK (Enter).

TIP To print only a portion of an image, select that area with the Rectangular Marquee tool. Then, in the Print dialog box, click Print Range: Selection.

Resolution overkill?

If your image resolution is greater than two and a half times the screen frequency—way higher than you need—you'll get a warning prompt when you send the image to print. If this occurs, copy the file using File menu > Save a Copy, then lower the image resolution using Image menu > Image Size.

Note: Only currently visible layers and channels will print.

To print to a black-and-white laser printer (Macintosh):

1. Choose File menu > Print ($\mathcal{H}$-P).

2. Choose Adobe Photoshop 5.0 from the drop-down menu **1**.

3. Choose Encoding: Binary.

4. Choose the color space to which you are outputting (usually the file's image mode) from the Space drop-down menu **2**.

5. Choose Color Matching from the drop-down menu.

6. Choose Print Color: Color/Grayscale **3**.

7. Make sure Destination: Printer is chosen **4**.

8. Click Print (Return).

TIP If your image doesn't print and you have a print spooler or a file that contains JPEG-encoding, try printing with ASCII Encoding. ASCII printing takes longer, so it shouldn't be your first choice.

TIP To print only a portion of an image, select that area with the Rectangular Marquee tool. Then, in the Print dialog box, choose Adobe Photoshop 5.0 from the drop-down menu and check the Print Selected Area box.

TIP Click Save Settings in the Print dialog box to save the current settings—they'll become the new default settings.

Laser Printer: Macintosh

To print to a PostScript color printer:

1. To print to a PostScript Level 2 printer, choose Image menu > Mode > Lab Color (or choose Space: Lab Color in the Print dialog box for step 6, below).
   or
   To print to a PostScript Level 3 printer, choose Image menu > Mode > CMYK Color (or choose Space: CMYK Color in the Print dialog box for step 6, below).

   If you change the mode via the Image menu, you'll be able to see how the image looks in Photoshop before you print it.

2. Choose File menu > Page Setup (Ctrl-Alt-P/⌘-Shift-P).

   Macintosh: Choose Page Attributes from the drop-down menu.

3. Choose the correct color printer option from the Name (Win)/Format for (Mac) drop-down menu. (A printer driver must be installed in your system for its name to appear on this menu.) Click OK (Enter/Return).

4. Choose File menu > Print (Ctrl-P/⌘-P).

5. *Macintosh:* Choose Adobe Photoshop 5.0 from the drop-down menu.

6. Choose Encoding: Binary and choose a color space from the Space drop-down menu, if you didn't already do so for step 1. See the sidebar on this page.

7. *Windows:* Click Setup, click Properties, choose Color Appearance: Color, then click OK.

8. *Macintosh:* Choose Color Matching from the drop-down menu that now says "Adobe Photoshop 5.0."

   Choose Print Color: Color/Grayscale.

9. Click OK (Win)/Print (Mac).

TIP To print an individual layer or channel, make that the sole visible layer or channel before choosing File menu > Print.

PostScript color management

The PostScript Color Management option tells the printer to convert your file's data to the printer's color space. When is this necessary? If you're printing to an RGB printer or if the file's image mode has not yet been converted to the printer's color space.

You also have the option to convert your file at the time of printing via the Space drop-down menu in the Print dialog box, but you won't see a screen preview if you do it this way. If you print a CMYK Color mode image to a PostScript Level 2 printer using the PostScript Color Management option, choose Space: Lab Color. To print a CMYK Color mode image to a PostScript Level 3 printer using the PostScript Color Management option, choose Space: CMYK Color.

*For a PostScript Level 2 printer, click Screens in the Page Setup dialog box (Mac: Adobe Photoshop 5.0 menu option), uncheck Use Printer's Default Screens, then check the **Use Accurate Screens** box ∎, but don't change the Ink angles. The **Halftone Screens** options will take effect if you print from Photoshop or save the file as an EPS or DCS 2 and then print to a PostScript printer.*

How to color separate an image

Convert the image to CMYK Color mode, choose File menu > Print (Mac: choose Adobe Photoshop 5.0 from the drop-down menu), choose Space: Separations, choose any other options, then click Print.

Note: Before printing your file, save your image at the resolution that your prepress house says is appropriate for the color printer or imagesetter you're going to use.

To prepare a file for an IRIS or dye sublimation printer or an imagesetter:

1. To print on a PostScript Level 2 printer, choose File menu > Page Setup, (Mac: choose Adobe Photoshop 5.0 from the drop-down menu), click Screens, uncheck Use Printer's Default Screens, check the Use Accurate Screens box, then click OK twice. Ask your service bureau whether the file should be in CMYK Color or Lab Color mode before saving as EPS.

2. Choose File menu > Save a Copy (Ctrl-Alt-S/⌘-Option-S).

3. Choose a location in which to save the file.

4. *Windows:* Choose Save As: Photoshop EPS, then click Save.

   Macintosh: Choose Format: Photoshop EPS, then click Save.

5. Choose a Preview option **1** and choose Encoding: Binary.

6. If you've changed the screen settings in the Halftone Screens dialog box (as per your service bureau's instructions), then check the Include Halftone Screen box.

   See the "PostScript color management" sidebar on the previous page.

7. Click OK (Enter/Return).

TIP If your image is wider than it is tall, ask your service bureau if it will print more quickly if you rotate it first using Photoshop's Rotate Canvas command.

```
                    None
                    TIFF  (1 bit/pixel)
                    TIFF  (8 bits/pixel)
          ┌─────────────────────────────────┐
          │       Macintosh  (1 bit/pixel)   │
  [1]     │ ✓   Macintosh  (8 bits/pixel)    │   ┌──────────┐
Preview:  │     Macintosh  (JPEG)            │   │    OK    │
Encoding: │ Binary                        ▼  │   └──────────┘
          └─────────────────────────────────┘   ┌──────────┐
                                                 │  Cancel  │
          ☐ Include Halftone Screen              └──────────┘

          ☐ Include Transfer Function

          ☐ PostScript Color Management
```

The Page Setup dialog box

Choose Adobe Photoshop 5.0 from the drop-down menu to access the following options.

1 To print a colored background around the image, click **Background**, then choose a color.

2 To print a black border around an image, click **Border**, choose a measurement unit, then enter a width.

3 **Bleed** prints crop marks inside the image at a specified distance from the edge of the image.

4 **Calibration Bars** creates a grayscale and/or color calibration strip outside the image area.

5 **Registration Marks** creates marks a print shop uses to align color separations.

6 **Corner Crop Marks** and **Center Crop Marks** creates short little lines that a print shop uses to trim the final printed page.

7 **Labels** prints the image's title and the names of its channels.

8 For film output, ask your print shop which to choose, **Negative** or **Emulsion Down**.

9 **Interpolation** reduces jaggies when outputting to some PostScript Level 2 (or higher) printers.

The Page Setup options illustrated

Arizona.gray ←*File and channel name* **label**

Crop *mark*

Registration *mark*

Calibration bar →

Caption → image w/ print options

Photoshop's Trap command slightly overlaps solid color areas in an image to help prevent gaps that may occur due to plate misregistration or paper shift. Trapping is only necessary when two distinct, adjacent color areas share less than two of the four process colors. You don't need to trap a continuous-tone or photographic image.

Note: Photoshop's Trap command flattens all layers and it uses only the spread technique, unlike other applications which may also use the choke method. Consult with your press shop before using this command, and apply it to a copy of your image; store your original image without traps.

To apply trapping:

1. Open the image to which you want to apply trapping, and make sure it's in CMYK Color mode.
2. Choose Image menu > Trap.
3. If a prompt appears, click OK.
4. Enter the Width that your press shop recommends **1**.
5. Click OK (Enter/Return).

293

Preparing a file for another application

Photoshop to QuarkXPress

To color separate a Photoshop image in QuarkXPress, convert it to CMYK Color mode before importing it into XPress. Different imagesetters require different formats, so ask your prepress house whether to save your image in the TIFF (see page 299) or EPS file format (see page 297) or in either of the two DCS formats (see page 298). Use the TIFF format if you're going to apply color management features to the image in QuarkXPress 4.

Photoshop to PageMaker

Convert the file to CMYK mode and save your image in the EPS or TIFF format. Use the TIFF format if you want to apply color management features to the image in PageMaker 6.5.

Photoshop to a film recorder

Color transparencies, also called chromes, are widely used as a source for high quality images in the publishing industry. A Photoshop file can be output to a film recorder to produce a chrome. Though the output settings for each film recorder may vary, to output to any film recorder, the pixel count for the height and width of the image file must conform to the pixel count the film recorder requires for each line it images.

If the image originates as a scan, the pixel count should be taken into consideration when setting the scan's resolution, dimensions, and file storage size.

For example, let's say you need to produce a 4 x 5-inch chrome on a Solitaire film recorder. Your service bureau advises you that to output on the Solitaire, the 5-inch side of your image should measure 2000 pixels and the file storage size should be at least 10 megabytes. (Other film recorders may require higher resolutions.) Choose File menu > New, enter 2000 for the Print Size: Width (in pixels) and 4 inches for the Height, enter a Resolution value to produce

To keep a background transparent

To import a Photoshop image into a drawing or page layout application and maintain its transparent background, save the image with a clipping path (see page 225).

Check your preferences

Before saving a file for use in another application, find out if the target application requires the Include Composited Image With Layered Files box to be checked in Photoshop's Saving Files Preferences in order to open a Photoshop format file 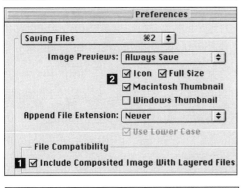. This option saves a composited image for preview along with the layered version. Adobe Illustrator and Macromedia Director both have this requirement. Figure **3** shows the message that will appear if you try to export a Photoshop file with this option off. Most applications also require the Image Previews options to be checked **2**. For a Web file, however, uncheck Image Previews to save a few extra bytes of storage size and speed up the transfer time.

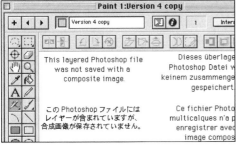

3 *A Director cast member will display this message if you import a layered Photoshop file without having checked the **Include Composited Image With Layered Files** option in Photoshop.*

an Image Size of at least 10MB, and choose RGB Color Mode. Click OK to produce the image entirely within Photoshop. Or note the resolution and dimensions and ask your service bureau to match those values when they scan your image.

If the image is smaller than 4 x 5 inches and you want it to have a colored background, click Background in the Page Setup dialog box, then choose the color your service bureau recommends.

Photoshop to Illustrator

To export a **layer**, choose the Move tool, then drag a layer from the Photoshop image window into an Illustrator 7 image window. The layer will arrive as an RGB image, 72 ppi, in an outlined box. Any layer mask effect will be ignored. You can drag a flattened version of all visible layers into Illustrator 8. Layer effects and layer masks are applied.

Macintosh: You cannot use the Clipboard to copy and paste from Photoshop to Illustrator because Illustrator cannot paste in PICT data. Maybe Illustrator 8 will do it.

To export a Photoshop **path**, use Export > Path to Illustrator (see page 226). The path does not have to be selected, though it should be a saved path—not a work path. In Illustrator, use File > Open to open the saved Photoshop path file. You can use it like any other Illustrator path object. It will import without a stroke (use Artwork View to see it) and with its own crop marks. If you don't change the crops, you can save the file in the Illustrator 7 format, then Place the file back into Photoshop. Don't rescale or reposition its bounding box, or you'll mess up the registration in Photoshop.

To place a Photoshop image as a **bitmap object** in Illustrator, save it in RGB or CMYK image mode in the Photoshop EPS or TIFF file format in Photoshop, and use File menu > Open or File menu > Place in Illustrator. Either way, the image will appear in an outlined box, and it can be

(Continued on the following page)

Photoshop to Illustrator

transformed. And in either format, the original Photoshop image's resolution and image mode will remain the same. The effect of a clipping path can only be displayed for an EPS, however. If, on the other hand, you want to include an embedded profile in an image that Illustrator's color management features recognize, you must save it as TIFF. You can apply a color filter (including Adjust Colors or Invert Colors), the Object Mosaic filter, or a raster filter to the opened or placed object.

To ensure that Photoshop 5 files display properly in Illustrator 7, check the Include Composited Image with Layered Files box in Photoshop's File menu > Preferences > Saving Files dialog box.

Photoshop to CorelDRAW

Windows version 8 or Macintosh version 6 or 8: Save the file as EPS, TIFF, JPEG, BMP, or PSD (Photoshop format), and in RGB Color or CMYK Color mode. In CorelDRAW, use File menu > Import to open the file. Alternatively, you could drag-and-drop a layer or copy-and-paste a layer or a selection from Photoshop into a CorelDRAW window. CorelDRAW 8 will read a layered Photoshop image, with each layer becoming a separate object. You can use the Export Paths to Illustrator command to export a Photoshop path to a file, and then open that file in CorelDRAW.

Once it's imported into CorelDRAW, the bitmap image can be moved around; you can perform bitmap-type edits on it; you can convert it to a different color mode or color depth; or you can resample it by changing its image size and/or resolution. You could even edit the bitmap in Corel PhotoPaint. You could also create a color mask in CorelDRAW in order to mask out portions of the bitmap image or you can apply a 2D or 3D bitmap effect to the image.

To prepare a CorelDRAW illustration for export to Photoshop, save it as EPS or TIFF using File > Export.

The clipping path won't print?

If a Limitcheck error occurs when your high-end printer tries to print a document that contains a clipping path, it may be because the path contains too many points. Follow these steps to reduce the number of points on a path:

1. Activate the clipping path on the Paths palette.

2. Convert the path into a selection.

3. Delete the original clipping path, but leave the selection active.

4. Choose Make Work path from the Paths palette command menu (enter a Tolerance value between 4–6 pixels) to turn the selection into a path.

5. Save the path, then save it as a clipping path (see page 225).

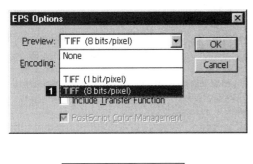

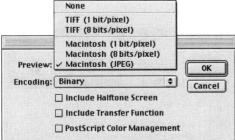

2 *The EPS format is available for an image in any image mode except Multichannel. Alpha channels and spot channels are discarded when you save in this format.*

PostScript color management revisited

The PostScript Color Management option tells the printer to convert your file's data to the printer's color space. This option is necessary only if your file has not already been converted to the printer's color space. You can change the image mode yourself before saving.

To print a CMYK Color mode image to a PostScript Level 2 printer using the PostScript Color Management option, convert the image to Lab Color mode before saving as EPS.

A PostScript Level 3 printer can print a CMYK Color image using the PostScript Color Management option.

The EPS format is a good choice for importing a Photoshop image into an illustration program or into a page layout program (e.g., QuarkXPress or PageMaker). Printing an EPS file requires a PostScript printer.

To save an image as an EPS:

1. If the image is going to be color separated by another application, choose Image menu > Mode > CMYK Color.

2. Choose File menu > Save a Copy (Ctrl-Alt-S/⌘-Option-S). This command saves a flattened version of the image.

3. Enter a name and choose a location in which to save the file.

4. *Windows:* Choose Save As: Photoshop EPS, then click Save.

   Macintosh: Choose Format: Photoshop EPS, then click Save.

5. From the Preview drop-down menu, choose a 1-bit/pixel option to save the file with a grayscale preview or choose an 8-bits/pixel option to save the file with a color preview (Win) **1**/(Mac) **2**.

   Macintosh: Choose either TIFF preview option if you're planning to open the file in a Windows application.

6. For most purposes, you should choose Encoding: Binary, since Binary encoded files are smaller and process more quickly than ASCII files. However, for some applications, PostScript clone printers, or printing utilities that cannot handle Binary files, you'll have to choose ASCII. JPEG is the fastest encoding method, but it causes some data loss. A JPEG file can only print on PostScript Level 2 or higher printer. Read the sidebar on page 304 before choosing JPEG.

7. If you've changed the frequency, angle, or dot shape settings in the Halftone Screens dialog box, then check the Include Halftone Screen box.

8. Read the "PostScript color management revisited" sidebar on this page.

9. Click OK (Enter/Return).

The DCS format is a relative of the EPS format. The DCS 1.0 (Desktop Color Separation) format pre-separates the image in Photoshop, and it produces five related files, one for each CMYK channel and one for the combined, composite CMYK channel. The newer DCS 2.0 format preserves any alpha and spot color channels along with the color channels, and also offers the option to save the combined channels into one file or as multiple files. A DCS file can be printed only on a PostScript printer.

To save an image as a DCS 2.0:

1. Follow steps 1–3 on the previous page.

2. *Windows:* Choose Save As: Photoshop DCS 2.0, then click Save.

   Macintosh: Choose Format: Photoshop DCS 2.0, then click Save.

3. From the Preview drop-down menu, choose the 1 bit/pixel option to save the file with a grayscale preview or choose an 8 bits/pixel option to save the file with a color preview.

4. Choose a DCS option: Single File (all separations together in one file) or Multiple File (one file for each separation), and with No Composite, a Grayscale Composite, or a Color Composite preview **1** (Win)/**2** (Mac).

5. Choose an Encoding option: Binary or ASCII or JPEG (with compression).

6. Leave the Include Halftone Screens and Include Transfer Functions boxes unchecked. Let your prepress shop choose settings for these options.

7. Click OK.

Multichannel

You can save a Multichannel image in the Photoshop DCS 2.0 format as a single file or multiple files. DCS preserves channels. A Multichannel image cannot be saved as a Photoshop EPS for composite (single-page) printing. Converting an image to Multichannel mode flattens all layers.

DCS 2.0 Format

Preview: TIFF (8 bits/pixel)

DCS: Single File with Color Composite (72 pixel/inch) **1**

Single File DCS, No Composite
Multiple File DCS, No Composite
Encoding: Single File with Grayscale Composite (72 pixel/inch)
Multiple File with Grayscale Composite (72 pixel/inch)
☐ Include Single File with Color Composite (72 pixel/inch)
☐ Include Multiple File with Color Composite (72 pixel/inch)

DCS 2.0 Format

Preview: Macintosh (8 bits/pixel) **2**

DCS: ✓ Single File DCS, No Composite
Multiple File DCS, No Composite
Encoding: Single File with Grayscale Composite (72 pixel/inch)
Multiple File with Grayscale Composite (72 pixel/inch)
☐ Include Single File with Color Composite (72 pixel/inch)
☐ Include Multiple File with Color Composite (72 pixel/inch)

Save as DCS

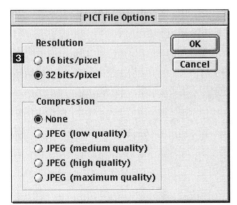

*Windows: Choose a **File Format** option and a **Depth** option.*

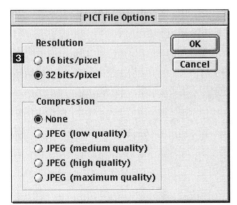

*Macintosh: The **JPEG** compression options are only available for an image that has a 32-bit resolution. The lower the quality, the greater the compression. If the image is going to be outut to a multimedia application, click Resolution: 16 bits/pixel.*

A TIFF file can be imported by most applications, including QuarkXPress and PageMaker. Color profiles are recognized by, and color management options are available for, this format. QuarkXPress can color separate a CMYK TIFF.

To save an image as a TIFF:

1. Follow the first three steps on page 297.

2. *Windows:* Choose Save As: TIFF, then click Save.

   Macintosh: Choose Format: TIFF, then click Save.

3. *Optional:* Not all programs can import a TIFF with an alpha channel. If your target application does not do so, check the "Exclude Alpha Channels" box to discard any alpha channels.

4. Choose IBM PC or Macintosh for the platform the file will be worked on **1**.

5. *Optional:* Check the LZW Compression box to reduce the file's storage size. No image data will be lost.

6. Click OK (Enter/Return).

A BMP or PICT file can be opened or placed as a bitmap image in Adobe Illustrator. Both of these file types can also be imported into most multimedia applications.

Macintosh: The PICT format is not available for an image in CMYK Color mode.

To save an RGB image as a BMP or PICT:

1. Follow steps 2–3 on page 297.

2. *Windows:* Choose Save As: BMP, click Save, then choose a File Format option.

   Macintosh: Choose Format: PICT File, then click Save.

3. Choose a Depth (Win) **2**/Resolution (Mac) **3** option. For an image in Grayscale mode, check 4 bits/pixel or 8 bits/pixel.

4. Read the sidebar on page 304 before choosing any Compression setting.

5. Click OK (Enter/Return).

Save as TIFF; Save as BMP or PICT

Only about 50 shades of an ink color can be printed from one plate, so print shops are sometimes asked to print a grayscale image using two or more plates instead of one to extend the image's tonal range. The additional plates can be gray or a color tint, and are usually used to print midtones and highlights. You can convert an image to Duotone mode in Photoshop to create a duotone (two plates), tritone (three plates), or quadtone (four plates).

The Goodies folder in the Photoshop application folder contains preset dutone, tritone, and quadtone curves that you can load in to use as is or adapt for your own needs (click Load in the Duotone Options box).

Note: Duotone printing is tricky, so ask your print shop for advice. A duotone effect (as seen on screen) can't be proofed on a PostScript color printer. In fact, you can rely only on a press proof.

To produce a duotone:

1. Choose Image menu > Mode > Grayscale. An image with good contrast will work best.

2. Choose Image menu > Mode > Duotone.

3. Check Preview to see your color and curves changes immediately.

4. Choose Type: Duotone **1**.

5. Click the Ink 2 color square **2**. (Ink 1 will be the darkest ink; the higher ink number should be the lightest ink.)

6. To choose a matching system color, like a Pantone color, choose from the Book pop-up menu, then type a color number or click a swatch. Subtle colors generally look better in a duotone than bright colors.
   or
   To choose a process color, click Picker, then enter C, M, Y, and K percentages.

7. Click OK (Enter/Return).

8. For a process color, enter a name next to the color square. For a custom color, leave the name as is.

Threes and fours

Printing a **tritone** (three inks) or a **quadtone** (four inks) requires specifying the order in which the inks will print on press. You can use the Overprint Colors dialog box to adjust the on-screen representation of various ink printing orders, but these settings won't affect how the image actually prints. Ask your print shop for advice about printing.

2 *Click a color square to choose a color.*

3 *Click a curve to modify it.*

Don't change a spot color name.

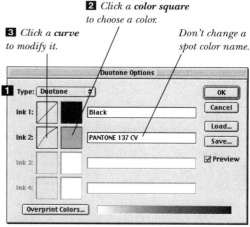

*In the **Duotone Options** dialog box, choose Type: **Duotone**, then click the **Ink 2** color square.*

Produce a Duotone

The image's highlights The image's midtones The image's shadows

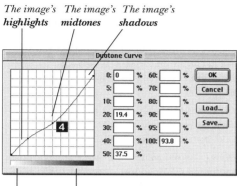

Highlights   Shadows

Nice curves

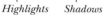

Reshaping the duotone curve for an ink color affects how that color is distributed among an image's highlights, midtones, and shadows. With the curve shape shown in the screenshot above, Ink 2 will tint the image's midtones. To produce a pleasing duotone, try to distribute Ink 1 and Ink 2 in different tonal ranges.

Here's an example. Use black as Ink 1 in the shadow areas, somewhat in the midtones, and a little bit in the highlights. Then use an Ink 2 color in the remaining tonal ranges—more in the midtones and light areas and less in the darks.

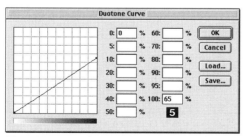

*This is the **Duotone Curve** dialog box for a monotone print. The 100% field value has been lowered to the desired Pantone tint percentage.*

9. Click the Ink 2 curve **3**.

10. Drag the curve upward or downward in the Duotone Curve dialog box **4**. To achieve a duotone effect, the Ink 1 curve must be different from the Ink 2 curve.

11. Click OK (Enter/Return).

12. Click the Ink 1 curve, then repeat steps 10 and 11.

13. *Optional:* Click Save to save the current settings to use with other images.

TIP To reduce black ink in the highlights, lower the black ink (Ink 1) curve 5 percent setting to zero. To reduce color in the shadows, lower the color ink (Ink 2) curve 100 percent setting to around 85 percent.

TIP If you're using a Pantone color and you're going to output the image from an illustration or page layout program, turn on Short Pantone Names in File menu > Preferences > General.

Here's a low-budget—but effective—way to expand the tonal range of a grayscale image. It's printed as a monotone (using one plate).

To print a grayscale image using a Pantone tint:

1. Open a grayscale image.

2. Choose Image menu > Mode > Duotone.

3. Choose Monotone from the Type drop-down menu.

4. Click the Ink 1 color square, then click Custom.

5. Choose the desired Pantone color, then click OK.

6. In the Duotone Options dialog box, click on the Ink 1 curve.

7. In the 100% field, enter the desired tint percentage value **5**. Leave the 0% field at 0 and all other fields blank. Click OK.

8. Click OK to close the dialog box.

9. Save the file in EPS format (see page 297).

Color reproduction basics

A computer monitor displays additive colors by projecting red, green, and blue (RGB) light, whereas an offset press prints subtractive colors using CMYK or spot color inks. Obtaining good CMYK color reproduction on an offset press is an art. The output image will resemble the on-screen image only if the monitor is carefully calibrated for that output device. *Note:* In this section we're discussing offset press output. For online imaging issues, see the next chapter.

Photoshop determines how to convert an RGB image to CMYK mode and how to display a CMYK mode preview based on the current settings in the File menu > Color Settings dialog boxes. Some of these dialogs are discussed on the following pages.

These are the major steps in color separation:

■ Calibrate the monitor (see page 31)

■ Enter CMYK Setup options

■ Obtain a color proof using those settings

■ Match the on-screen preview to the proof

To enter CMYK Setup settings:

1. Choose File menu > Color Settings > CMYK Setup.

2. For **CMYK Model**: Built-in, enter the Ink characteristics for the offset press **1**, such as the **Ink Colors** and **Dot Gain**. Ask your print shop which settings to use.

3. Other characteristics of the offset press are entered in the **Separation Options** area **2**, but since these settings are particular for each press, you must ask your print shop for this information. In short, the **Separation Type** tells Photoshop about the type of press used: Does the press use the **GCR** (gray component replacement) or **UCR** (undercolor removal) method, and how does the print shop handle black ink?

The **Black Generation** amount controls how much black ink is used when the RGB components of light are translated

Ask your print shop at the outset

Color separating is an art. As a starting point, ask your print shop the following questions so you'll be able to choose the correct scan resolution and settings in the Printer Inks Setup and Separation Setup dialog boxes.

What lines-per-inch setting is going to be used on the press for my job? This will help you choose the appropriate scanning resolution.

What is the dot gain for my choice of paper stock on that press? Allowances for dot gain can be made using the Printer Inks Setup dialog box.

Which printing method will be used on press— UCR or GCR? GCR produces better color printing and is the default choice in the Separations Setup box. (GCR stands for Gray Component Replacement, UCR stands for Undercolor Removal.)

What is the total ink limit and the black ink limit for the press? These values can also be adjusted in the Separations Setup box.

Note: Change the dot gain, GCR or UCR method, and ink limits before you convert your image from RGB Color mode to CMYK Color mode. If you change any of these values after conversion, you must convert the image back to RGB Color mode, readjust the values, then reconvert to CMYK Color mode.

In which file format should the file be saved? Ask the print shop what file format it needs.

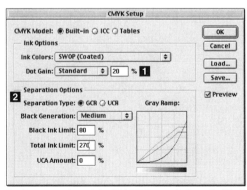

In this screenshot of the CMYK Setup dialog, the Black Ink Limit and the Total Ink Limit values have been changed to values suggested by a print shop. The graph maps the current values.

Total readout

To display total ink coverage percentages on the Info palette for the pixels currently under the pointer, choose **Total Ink** from the pop-up menu next to the leftmost eyedropper on the palette **3**. This readout is based on the current Separation Setup settings.

*In the **CMYK Setup** dialog box, click **Tables**, then click **Save** to save your custom table with specific Ink and Separation Options settings.*

into CMY inks. Black is substituted for a percentage of CMY inks to prevent inks from becoming muddy when they're mixed together. How much black is substituted is determined by the Black Generation amount.

Finally, each press shop uses its own amount of ink coverage on each separation plate. Some shops use less than 100% maximum ink coverage for each plate. Ask your press shop for its **Total Ink Limit** percentage settings.

Once you're satisfied with a set of color proofs from a particular print shop, rather than reenter this information every time you need to do a RGB-to-CMYK conversion for that shop, you can build a reusable table that contains your custom CMYK Setup settings.

To save a separation table:

1. Choose File menu > Color Settings > CMYK Setup.

2. Click CMYK Model: Tables **4**.

3. Click Save, name the file, choose a location for the file, then click Save again. Next time you output in that particular press situation, open the CMYK Setup dialog box, click CMYK Model: Table, and load in the custom table you created and saved for that press.

Note: These settings affect RGB-to-CMYK image mode conversion. If you subsequently readjust any settings in the CMYK Setup dialog box, you will have to reconvert your image from RGB to CMYK mode again using the new settings. Keep a copy of your image in RGB Color mode so you'll have the option to readjust and reconvert it.

(Continued on the following page)

After converting your image to CMYK Color mode, ask your output service or press shop to produce a color proof of the image using the Color Settings you just entered.

You'll adjust the CMYK Setup Dot Gain setting to match the CMYK preview of an on-screen image to a proof. By matching the two images—the on-screen image and the printed proof—you can then rely more confidently on the accuracy of Photoshop's CMYK Color preview.

To match the on-screen image to a color proof:

1. Open the CMYK Color mode image.

2. Choose File menu > Color Settings > CMYK Setup.

3. Load in any custom CMYK Setup settings or reenter all the individual Setup dialog box settings that were used to produce the proof.

4. To match only the overall light and dark values of the on-screen preview to the proof, choose Dot Gain: Standard, then increase or decrease the Dot Gain percentage. Increase the Dot Gain to darken the on-screen preview; decrease the Dot Gain to lighten the on-screen preview.

5. If the on-screen preview has an undesirable color cast—as compared with the proof—choose Dot Gain: Curves. Then choose an individual ink color and move its 50% point value on the curve upward or downward or enter a new value in the 50% field to add or remove amounts of that ink color from the preview, resulting in a better color match between the two images 5. Repeat this step, if necessary, for the remaining individual ink colors. (Using the Curves option for Dot Gain will cause the Dot Gain field to become blank.)

Note: The preview of every CMYK mode image will now reflect the new Ink Options settings, but the actual image information will be changed only if the image is converted to RGB Color mode and then back to CMYK Color mode.

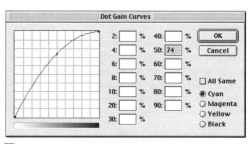

5 *Color balance adjustments are made to individual ink curves (Cyan, in this case) using the **Dot Gain Curves** dialog box. The 50% point value on the curve is moved to achieve a better color match between the on-screen image and a proof.*

File compression

To reduce the storage size of an image, use a compression program like WinZip or PKZip (Win) or DiskDoubler or Stuffit (Mac). Compression using this kind of software is non-lossy, which means the compression doesn't cause data loss.

If you don't have compression software, choose File menu > Save a Copy, choose TIFF from the Format drop-down menu, and check the LZW Compression box in the TIFF Options dialog box. If you want to save the file without alpha channels, also check the Exclude Alpha Channels box. LZW compression is non-lossy. Not all applications will import an LZW TIFF, though. And some applications will import an LZW TIFF only if it doesn't contain an alpha channel.

If you're saving an image for print output, we don't recommend using the JPEG file format, since JPEG compression is lossy, and additional image data is lost with each compression. The data loss may not be noticeable on screen, but it may be quite noticeable on high resolution output. JPEG is more suitable for Web output.

Desaturate another way

You can use Image menu > Adjust > Hue/Saturation instead of the Sponge tool to correct out-of-gamut colors in particular color categories. Move the Saturation slider to the left to desaturate.

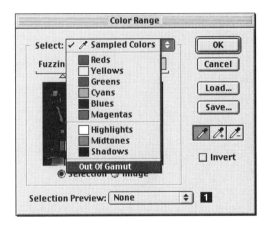

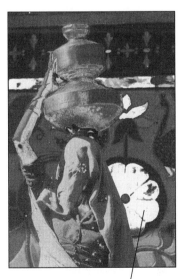

2 *For illustration purposes,* **out-of-gamut** *colors in this image are shown in white instead of the usual gray.*

If you convert an image to CMYK Color mode, its colors are automatically forced into printable gamut. In certain cases, however, you may want to see which areas are out-of-gamut (non-printable) in RGB first, and then change some of them manually. In the following instructions, you'll display out-of-gamut colors in gray using the Gamut Warning command and then use the Sponge tool to desaturate those areas to bring them into printable gamut.

Note: CMYK color equivalents are generated based on the current CMYK Setup dialog box settings, so enter those values first (see page 302).

To correct out-of-gamut colors:

1. Convert your image to RGB Color or Lab Color mode.

2. Choose View menu > Gamut Warning.

3. *Optional:* To select and restrict color changes to only the out-of-gamut areas, choose Select menu > Color Range, choose Select: Out of Gamut **1**, then click OK.

4. Choose the Sponge tool (O, Shift-O).

5. On the Sponge Options palette, choose Desaturate from the drop-down menu and choose a Pressure percentage.

6. Choose a tip on the Brushes palette.

7. Choose a layer.

8. Drag across the gray, out-of-gamut areas **2**. As they become desaturated, they will redisplay in color. Don't desaturate colors too much, though, or they'll become dull. (To turn off the Gamut Warning, choose View menu > Gamut Warning again.)

TIP To preview the image in CMYK in a second window, choose View menu > New View. With the new window active, choose View menu > Preview > CMYK. Make sure both windows are visible.

TIP If the pointer is over an out-of-gamut pixel, exclamation points will appear on the Info palette CMYK readout.

Correct Out-of-Gamut Colors

Color correction: First glance

Such a complex topic as color correction is beyond the scope of this QuickStart Guide. It involves using many commands, including Levels, Curves, Color Balance, and Unsharp Mask. You can get some assistance from the resources listed in the sidebar at right. Just by way of introduction, though, these are the basic steps in the color correction process:

- Calibrate your monitor.
- Scan or acquire a PhotoCD image into Photoshop.
- Limit tonal values to determine where the darkest shadow and lightest highlight areas are in the image, and then limit the highest and lowest tonal values to the range that your print shop specifies. (Areas outside this range won't print well.)
- Color balance to correct any undesirable color cast in the image. You can correct the overall color balance or the neutral gray component of the image.
- Unsharp Mask to resharpen the image.
- Print a CMYK proof, and then analyze the proof with color-reading instruments to determine the exact color characteristics of the output.
- Readjust the Photoshop image, then print and analyze another proof.

On-screen output: Do all your color correction in RGB Color mode. Proof it by viewing it on other monitors or through a browser.

Print output: If you're working with a CMYK scan, do all your correction in CMYK Color mode. For an image that's going to be color separated, Adobe recommends using RGB Color mode and then converting the image to CMYK Color mode using the proper Color Settings options.

TIP Use adjustment layers for your color adjustments so you'll be able to easily readjust the image on a non-flattened copy of the image later on.

Resources

Understanding Desktop Color
   by Michael Kieran

Real World Photoshop 5
   by David Blatner and Bruce Fraser

Using Color Management Systems for Push-Button Color
   by Bruce Fraser

Photoshop in 4 Colors, Second Edition
   by Mattias Nyman

Proof it

To fine-tune your settings, it's a good idea to print a CMYK proof. Use the CMYK test image called Olé No Moire (Testpict.jpg for Windows) that Photoshop provides for this purpose. It's on the CD, in Goodies > Calibrate (Win) or Other Goodies > Calibration (Mac). Before opening it, however, choose File menu > Color Settings > Profile Setup, and in the Profile Mismatch Handling for CMYK, choose Ask When Opening. Open the image and click Don't Convert in the Profile Mismatch alert box.

Color Correction: First Glance

WEB & MULTIMEDIA 21

Welcome to Peachpit's Home Page

Home | Back | Forward | Load Images | Stop | Load Original

Current URL: http://www.peachpit.com/peachpit/welcome.html

Page complete   Image: 25553 of 37873 bytes

Welcome to Peachpit Press

Search

Features | Titles | Meet Us | Order Info | Ask/Tell | Forums

Visit Peachpit Press's web site: http://www.peachpit.com.

THIS CHAPTER covers the preparation of Photoshop images for use in multimedia (on-screen) and on the World Wide Web (online). Conversion to Indexed Color mode is covered first, then using Photoshop images in Director or After Effects, and finally, preparing images for viewing on the Web.

Some multimedia and video programs and some computer systems will not import a Photoshop image that contains more than 256 colors (8-bit color). By converting an image to Indexed Color mode, you can reduce the number of colors in its color table and thus optimize its display on the Web.

Note: Converting a multi-layer image to Indexed Color mode will cause its layers to be flattened. Use the Save As command to work on a copy of the image.

To convert an image to Indexed Color mode:

1. Make sure the image is in RGB Color mode.

2. Choose Image menu > Mode > Indexed Color.

3. Check the Preview box, if desired, then choose a Palette **1**:

You can choose Exact if the image contains 256 or fewer colors. No colors will be eliminated.

Choose Adaptive for the best color substitution.

Choose System (Macintosh) if you're going to export the file to an application that accepts only the Macintosh default palette.

Choose System (Windows) if you're planning to export the image to the Windows platform.

(Continued on the followimg page)

1

Exact
System (Macintosh)
System (Windows)
Web
Uniform
✓ Adaptive
Custom...
Previous

Palette: Adaptive

Color Depth:

Colors: 256

OK
Cancel

Options

Dither: Diffusion

Color Matching: ○ Faster ● Best
☑ Preserve Exact Colors

☑ Preview

ARTWORK BY JOHN GRIMES

Convert to Indexed Color Mode

Choose Web if the image is intended for Web viewing. This option limits the Color Table to only those colors that are available in the most popular Web browsers.

Choose Uniform for a dithered blending of only 216 colors. The Color Table will then be similar to the Web palette table. To create your own palette, choose Custom, then click OK, and edit the Color Table, if desired. (Click Save if you want to save the table for later use. Click Load to load in a previously saved table.) Click OK and skip the remaining steps.

Choose Previous to use the custom palette used in the previous conversion.

4. If you chose the Adaptive or Uniform palette, you can choose a Color Depth to specify the number of colors in the table **1**. If you choose 4 bits/pixel, the table will contain 16 colors; if you choose 8 bits/pixel, the table will contain 256 colors. The fewer bits/pixel in the image, the more dithered it will be. Choose Other if you want to enter your own value in the Colors field.

5. Choose Dither: None, Diffusion, or Pattern. Dithering simulates additional colors that are not in the table. None will cause areas that contain sharp color transitions to look like they're posterized, so it's an option that's best suited for use with flat-color images or the Exact palette. Diffusion may produce the closest color substitution, but it can also produce a dotty effect in those areas. The Pattern option, which adds pixels in a more structured arrangement, is available only when the System (Macintosh), Web palette, or Uniform palette is used (see step 3).

6. Choose Color Matching: Faster for a faster, but less accurate, color conversion, or choose Better for a more accurate, but slower, color conversion. The difference between the two may be more noticeable if the Dither option is turned off (None). The Best option won't

Painting in Indexed Color mode

In Indexed Color mode, the Pencil, Airbrush, and Paintbrush tools produce only fully opaque strokes. For those tools, leave the Opacity slider on the Options palette at 100%. Dissolve is the only tool mode that will produce a different stroke at a lower opacity.

Shrink it down

To reduce an Indexed Color table to two colors and the shades between them, first, choose Image menu > Mode > Color Table, and drag across the Color Table from the first swatch in the upper left corner to the last swatch in the lower right corner. Next, choose a first color from the Color Picker: move the slider up or down on the vertical bar to choose a hue **2**, then click a variation of that hue in the large rectangle **3**, then click OK. Next, choose a last color from the Color Picker. For the best results, choose a warm first color and a cool last color, or vice versa. Click OK to exit the Color Picker, then click OK.

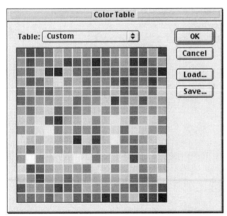

1 *Click a color or drag across a series of colors in the* **Color Table** *dialog box.*

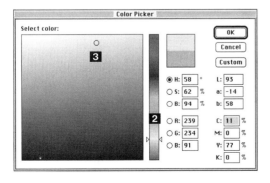

be available if you chose the Dither: Pattern option.

If you chose the Diffusion Dither option, you can also check the Preserve Exact Colors box. Dithering will then be turned off for any color in the image that exactly matches a color on the color palette. Use this option for flat color areas. But don't try to proof this on screen—you probably won't see much of a difference.

7. Click OK (Enter/Return).

TIP If you want to have some control over which colors will be chosen for the palette, create a selection or selections that contain the colors you want to appear on the palette before converting your image to Indexed Color mode, then choose the Adaptive palette for step 3 on page 307.

TIP View your image at 100% to see the effect of the Color Matching option.

To edit an Indexed Color image's Color table:

1. Choose Image menu > Mode > Color Table. The Color Table will display all the picture's colors.

2. Click on a color to be replaced **1**.
or
Select a bunch of colors by dragging across them.

3. Move the slider up or down on the vertical bar to choose a hue **2**, then click a variation of that hue in the large rectangle **3**.

4. Click OK twice.

TIP You can convert a Grayscale picture directly to Indexed Color mode and then modify its color table to add arbitrary color to the image. Try the Black Body or Spectrum table.

Macromedia Director works most efficiently when the cast members are 8-bit bitmap images. In the past, generating a custom palette from a series of images was a tedious process. Here's a simple procedure for creating a palette that can be applied to an individual image or to a group of images. This means that only one palette will have to be imported into Director.

To create a custom palette for indexed images:

1. Create a folder to contain a set of RGB images that you want to contribute to the custom palette. You can add a grayscale file to the folder to assure a good range of tonal values in the custom palette.

2. Choose File menu > Automate > Contact Sheet. Click Choose, then open the folder that you created in step 1. Enter Layout: Columns and Rows values to accommodate all the files in the folder 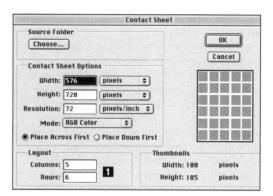. Set the resolution to 72 dpi and the Mode to RGB. Click OK to build the contact sheet, then save the contact sheet. See page 277 for more information about creating a contact sheet.

3. Choose Image > Mode > Indexed Color to change the file to an 8-bit image. Choose Palette: Adaptive 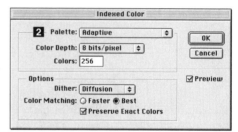, Color Depth: 8-bits/pixel, and choose Dither and Color Matching options. Click OK.

4. Choose Image menu > Mode > Color Table. Examine the palette, click Save ■, and save it in a convenient folder. *Windows:* Use the ".pal" extension. Click Cancel.

To index a 24-bit RGB image to an 8-bit custom palette:

1. Open one of the RGB (24-bit) images that contributed to the contact sheet. Choose Image menu > Mode > Indexed Color.

2. Choose Palette: Custom ■. Click Load, locate the custom palette, then click Open. Click OK twice. The image will map its colors to the colors in the palette.

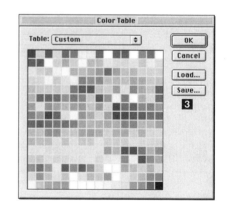

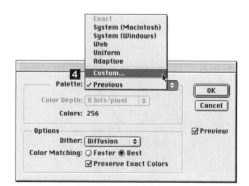

Create a Custom Palette

👁	🖊	type	
👁		flower	
👁		statue	
👁		building corner	
👁		back color	
👁		*Background*	

*The initial composition of the Director frame in the illustration below was developed using Photoshop's layers (left). Each Photoshop **layer** became a separate **cast member** in Director.*

A frame from a Director movie of an interactive map. Each street name is a button link to another point in the movie.

Layers	Channels	Paths
Normal ⇕	Opacity: 100 ▶ %	
☐ Preserve Transparency		
👁 🖊	Layer 6	
👁	Layer 5	
👁	Layer 4	
👁	Layer 3	
👁	Layer 2	
👁	Layer 1	

This Layers palette shows a Motion Blur filter sequence. Each layer was copy/pasted into Director as a separate cast member.

From Photoshop to Director

Imagery, button shapes, bitmapped type, and even some transitions can be developed in Photoshop to use in Director, Macromedia's multimedia application. You can use Photoshop's Layers palette like a storyboard to develop an image sequence. Stack, hide, and show picture elements on individual layers, then use each layer as an individual cast member in Director. Assembling an image via layers in Photoshop is like using the Score in Director to assemble cast members on the Stage.

Ways to use the Layers palette as a storyboard

- Show and hide layers in a sequence to preview how those objects will appear or disappear in Director.

- Move layers in the image window via the Move tool to test animated motion.

- Lower or increase a layer's opacity to preview a fade-out/fade-in effect.

- Select the various elements of a one-layer image and then copy-and-paste them onto individual layers to maximize your animation flexibility. Each element could potentially become a separate cast member in Director.

- Use a layer's imagery as a separate cast member in Director. Ctrl-click/⌘-click on a layer name (not the Background) to select all the pixels on that layer, and use Edit menu > Copy to copy the pixels to the Clipboard. In Director, choose a cast member window on the Cast palette, then choose Edit menu > Paste Bitmap. The Photoshop pixel imagery will become a cast member in Director, but its color transitions and edges may be slightly less smooth.

Macintosh: To preserve better color fidelity and softer edges for objects and type, choose Paste Special > As PICT. This command also produces a smaller file size, but you can't edit or apply Xtras filters to the cast member.

Photoshop to Director

You could also save the Photoshop file in the BMP (Win)/PICT (Mac) or Photoshop format and use Director's Import command to load it onto the Cast palette. But a major disadvantage of this method is that it flattens all the layers.

RGB vs. Indexed Color images

Either method you use to import imagery from Photoshop into Director—using the copy-and-paste method or saving a file in Photoshop and importing it in Director—will produce an RGB file with a 16-bit or greater color depth, which is overly large. To find out the file size of a selected cast member, click the info icon on the Cast palette in Director. Use Transform Bitmap to reduce the size of the cast member to 8-bit to shorten the movie's playback time.

To reduce the size of the Director cast member, in Photoshop you can convert the RGB file to Indexed Color mode using the System palette and an 8-bit or lower color depth resolution.

If you use the Adaptive palette, each Photoshop Indexed Color file that you import into Director will arrive with its own color palette. Loading multiple cast members with assorted palettes can slow the movie playback. Use the copy-and-paste option when you have a small number of Indexed Color files to import; use Director's File menu > Import option if you have a large number of Indexed Color files to import.

While you can use Director to transform a bitmap RGB image from Photoshop and lower its color depth, you'll achieve better results if you do this in Photoshop via Indexed Color mode **1**–**2** (and **3**, next page).

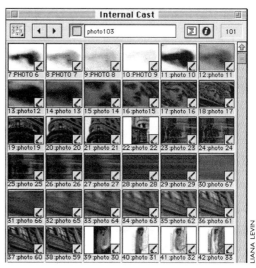

A Director Cast palette. Image and filter sequences were composed using Photoshop layers and then copy-and-pasted onto Director's Internal Cast palette.

1 *This 50K image was saved as an RGB file in Photoshop, pasted as Bitmap into Director, and then reduced to 8-bit depth in Director. Note the graininess in the sky.*

2 *This 150K image was pasted Special > As PICT and kept at a 16-bit depth. It has smooth tone transitions, but it has a larger file size than the image above.*

3 *This 50K image was converted to Indexed Color mode (8-bit depth) in Photoshop and then pasted into Director as Bitmap. The sky is smooth in this smaller-size image, like the 150K image on the previous page.*

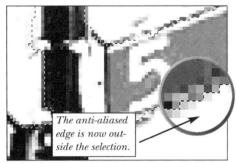

The anti-aliased edge is now outside the selection.

4 *After using the Magic Wand tool to select the white background around the signpost and then inversing the selection, some of the original anti-aliased edge remained. Select menu > Modify > Contract (by one pixel) was used to shrink the selection inward.*

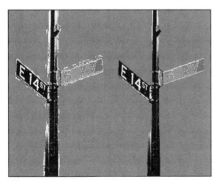

5 *Two bitmap cast members that were pasted into Director. The member on the left was copied without contracting the selection in Photoshop. The member on the right was copied after contracting the selection in Photoshop to remove its halo.*

How to copy a pixel object with an anti-aliased edge into Director

Director displays an object's anti-aliased edges with a white or dotted halo, which will be noticeable if the background behind the object is any color other than white. The halo will also be noticeable if the object moves across a background that isn't uniform or that changes gradually.

This halo problem shouldn't arise if you copy and paste to Director using Paste Special > As PICT for type or shapes created in Photoshop. To avoid this problem when Paste Special isn't available, select an object in Photoshop without its anti-aliased edge, Ctrl-click/⌘-click on a layer name to select the object, then zoom in to at least 200% view so you can see the object's edge clearly. Choose Select menu > Modify > Contract and contract the selection by 1 or 2 pixels to remove the anti-aliased edge **4**–**5**. Finally, copy the object selection and paste it into Director. A soft-edged shape, like a shadow, will have a dotty dissolve along its edge when it's pasted as Bitmap in Director.

Director and Photoshop filters

Photoshop compatible plug-in filters are now accessible from within Director. To use them, make an alias (if possible) of the Filters folder (Photoshop 5 folder > Plug-ins > Filters) or just copy the folder, then place it in the Xtras folder within the Director folder.

The filters are accessed via Director's Xtras menu > Filter Bitmap and/or Xtras menu > Auto Filter, and only work on Bitmap cast members.

Photoshop to Director

Photoshop to After Effects

You can import a layered Photoshop image into Adobe After Effects and position it in the Time Layout window to create animated effects over time for Video or QuickTime output. A layered Photoshop file can be imported as an After Effects composition file. Individual layers and groups will remain intact. Alternatively, a layered Photoshop image can be flattened and imported into After Effects as a pre-composited image.

Render any layer effects in the image before you save the Photoshop file, otherwise the effects will be *eliminated* in After Effects. An un-rendered (editable) type layer, on the other hand, will render correctly in After Effects—there's no need to render it first. Layer masks will import into and render correctly in After Effects.

A Photoshop clipping group will import into After Effects as a pre-composition. To help keep things simple, you can merge a clipping group down to a single layer in Photoshop before saving the file (choose Merge Group from the Layers palette command menu).

An alpha channel in a Photoshop file will be available for matting using After Effects' Set Matte Effect command. Any other channels will be ignored.

If you're using an Avid video production system, use these image dimensions: 720 x 486 pixels (D-1 NTSC). For a QuickTime movie, the image can have any dimensions. For both Avid and QuickTime, the minimum image resolution is 72 ppi. Don't bother using a higher resolution than that.

Sometimes the same image is used in both a print-related project (in which 250 ppi or higher resolution is commonplace) and an After Effects project. Don't use the hi-res file in After Effects. Instead, downsample a copy of it to the correct dimension and resolution for that application using Photoshop's File menu > Image Size command.

Four golden rules for Web image creation

■ Let the content of the image—whether it's flat color or continuous-tone—determine which file format you use.

■ Use an image as low in pixel size as is practical, balancing the file size with aesthetics (number of colors). And remember the fail-safe option for flat-color images for viewing on both Windows and Mac browsers: Load the Web Safe Colors palette onto the Swatches palette.

■ Try reducing the image's color depth.

■ View your Web image through a Web browser on computers other than your own so you can see how quickly it actually downloads and how good (or bad) it looks.

Photoshop to the World Wide Web

The basic formula for outputting a Photoshop image for on-line viewing may seem straightforward: Design the image in RGB mode and save it in the file format used by Web browsers (the applications that combine text, images, and HTML code into a viewable page on the World Wide Web). However, when you load and view an image via a Web browser, you may be disappointed to find that not all colors or blends display well on the Web, and your image may take an unacceptably long time to download and render, which is a function of its storage size. If an image looks overly dithered (grainy and dotty), or was subject to unexpected color substitutions, or takes too long to view on a Web page, it means your design is not outputting well.

Four important issues that you'll need to address for on-line output are discussed on the following pages: the pixel size of the image, the color palette, the color depth, and the file format (GIF or JPEG).

Image size

In order to calculate the appropriate image size, you must know beforehand your intended viewers' monitor size and modem speed. In most cases, you should be designing your image for a 640 x 480 pixel viewing area, the most common monitor size, and a 28.8 Kbps modem, the most common modem speed. By mid-1999, modem speeds of 56 Kbps and faster will be the norm.

The Web browser window will display within these parameters, so your maximum image size will occupy only a portion of the browser window—about 8 inches high (570 pixels) by 7 inches wide (500 pixels). The image resolution need only be the standard resolution of the monitor.

Assuming dimensions of, say, 500 by 400 pixels (7 by 6 inches), a flattened image will be about 600K, according to its Document Sizes reading on the Status bar in the lower left corner of the Application window (Win)/

image window (Mac) in Photoshop. This figure, however, reflects how much RAM is occupied when the image is opened in Photoshop. The same file saved in the GIF or JPEG file format will be much smaller due to the compression schemes built into these formats.

To determine a file's actual storage size:

Windows: Right-click on the file in Windows Explorer and choose Properties from the pop-up menu.

Macintosh: Highlight the file name in the Finder, then choose File menu > Get Info.

If you know the exact compressed file size, you can then calculate how long the file will take to transmit over the Web.

The degree to which the GIF or JPEG file format compresses depends on how compressable the image is. Both formats cause a small reduction in image quality, but it's worth the size-reduction tradeoff, because your image will download faster on the Web. A file size of about 50K traveling on a 28.8 Kbps modem with a half-second per kilobyte download rate will take about 30 seconds to download. (Is this a test question?)

A document with a flat background color and a few flat color shapes will compress a great deal (expect a file size in the range of 20 to 50K). A large document (over 100K) with many color areas, textures, or patterns (an Add Noise texture covering most of the image, for example) won't compress nearly as much. Continuous-tone, photographic images may compress less than flat color images when you use the GIF format. If you posterize a continuous-tone image down to somewhere between four and eight levels, the resulting file size will be similar to that of a flat color image, but you will have lost the continuous color transitions in the bargain. JPEG is the better format choice for a photographic-type image.

To summarize, if an image must be large (500 x 400 pixels or larger), ideally it should contain large areas of only a handful of flat

Create a browser window layer

Take a screen shot of your browser window, open the file in Photoshop, and paste it into a Web design document as your bottommost layer. Now you can design for that specific browser window's dimensions.

Size comparisons of GIFs

20K GIF, *from a 5-level posterized image.*

120K GIF, *from a continuous-tone image.*

colors. If you want the image to be more intricate in color and shape, restrict its size to only a section of the Web browser window.

By the way, patterned imagery that completely fills the background of the browser window is usually created using a tiling method in a Web page creation program or using HTML code.

GIF: the great compromise

GIF is an 8-bit file format, which means a GIF image can contain a maximum of 256 colors. Since a majority of Web users have 8-bit monitors—which can display a maximum of 256 colors, not the thousands or millions of colors that make images look pleasing to the eye—GIF is the standard format to use. It's a good choice for images that contain flat color areas and shapes with well-defined edges, such as type.

To prepare an image for the GIF format and to see how the image will truly look when viewed via the browser, set your monitor's bit depth to 256 colors (not any higher), choose File menu > Preferences > Display and Cursors, check the Use Diffusion Dither box, then click OK.

Your color choices for a GIF image should be based on what a Web browser palette can display. Most browser palettes are 8-bit, which means they can display only 256 colors. Colors that aren't on the palette are simulated by dithering, a display technique that intermixes color pixels to simulate other colors. To prevent unexpected color substitutions or dithering, make sure you use the browser palette for your image. Color substitutions are particularly noticeable in flat color areas, and can make you want to disown an image.

Using the GIF89a Export command, you can create an adaptive palette using the most common colors in the image, instead of just the colors in the system palette. This concentrates the range of 256 colors to those that are most needed in the image, which helps preserve image quality. Unfortunately,

GIF

this adaptive palette probably won't match the browser's palette exactly. What to do? Read on.

Photoshop's Web palette

A more fail-safe approach is to use Photoshop's Web palette, which you can choose if you convert an image to Indexed Color mode. Here's the Web palette's built-in guarantee: Colors in the image will display properly on the current browsers on both the Windows and Macintosh platforms. Here's the rub: In order to create a palette that works on both platforms, since the Windows and Mac browser palettes share only 216 out of 256 possible colors, your image will be reduced to 216 colors, even less than in the GIF format. Don't despair—this is a small loss in a continuous-tone image, and it will actually reduce its file size. Ready to try it?

To create a Web palette for an existing image:

1. Open an image, and if it's not already in RGB Color mode, convert it now.

2. Choose Image menu > Mode > Indexed Color.

3. Choose Palette: Web **1**.

4. Click OK.

5. Choose Image menu > Mode > Color Table.

6. Click Save, then click OK.

To put the Web colors onto the Swatches palette:

1. Choose Replace Swatches from the Swatches palette command menu.

2. Choose the Web Safe Colors Palette inside the Color palettes folder in the Photoshop 5 folder > Goodies > Color Palettes.

3. Click Open. The swatches will now be the 216 colors common to both the Windows and Macintosh Web browsers. Use only those swatches when you choose flat colors for your Web image.

Color depth

If you lower an image's color depth, you will reduce the actual number of colors it contains, which will in turn reduce its file size and speed up its download time on the Web. You can reduce the number of colors in an 8-bit image to fewer than the 256 colors it originally contained via either the Indexed Color or GIF89a Export dialog box. By choosing the Adaptive palette option, you'll have the ability to reduce the number of colors in the palette, and thus in the image.

Photoshop provides previews for both Indexed Color and GIF89a exports so you can test how an image will look with fewer available colors. Color reduction may produce dithered edges and duller colors, but you'll get the reduction in file size that you need. Always preview the image at 100% view to evaluate color quality, by the way.

Color depth (and file size) can also be greatly reduced by first using the Hue/Saturation command to colorize the image and make it monotone and then reducing the number of colors substantially (to as low as 4-bit). This won't diminish the quality of the already monotone image.

GIF89a Export

Use the GIF89a format if you require transparency (you want to mask out the image's background or a portion of the image itself) and interlacing (the image displays in progressively greater detail as it downloads onto the Web page). Transparent GIF is a good choice for an image that will display on a Web page that has a non-uniform background pattern.

Color depth

Number of colors	Bit depth
256	8
128	7
64	6
32	5
16	4
8	3
4	2
2	1

Color Depth; GIF89a Export

To prepare an RGB image for the Web using GIF89a Export:

1. Choose File menu > Export > GIF89a Export.

2. Choose Palette: Adaptive ▉.
   and
   Choose the number of colors (color depth) from the Colors drop-down menu, or enter a specific number.

3. Click Preview to preview the image using the present palette and color depth settings. You can drag the image in the preview window, if you like, and you can also zoom in or out using the zoom tool in the dialog box. Click to zoom in, Alt-click/Option-click to zoom out.

4. Click OK to close the preview window.

5. Try to further lower the color depth level, previewing the results, to see if a lower color depth is tolerable.

6. Leave the Interlaced box checked if you want to display the image in progressively greater detail on the Web page. Uncheck this option if the image contains small type, because interlacing can cause a longer wait for the type to become sharp enough to read.

7. If you're dissatisfied with the image quality, hold down Alt/Option and click Reset to restore the original export settings, then readjust the settings.

8. Click OK when you're satisfied (or as satisfied as you're gonna get) with the GIF export preview.

9. Choose a location in which to save the file, enter a name for the file, then click Save.

GIF9a Export

The original image.

The cake copied and pasted into its own layer. We hid all the other layers before saving in the GIF format.

To create a transparent GIF:

Note: For a one-layer image, perform all of the following steps. For an image on its own transparent layer, start with step 4.

1. Select the part of the image you want to preserve as non-transparent. If you want to produce a soft-edged transition to transparency, feather the selection using a low value (1 to 3 pixels). Feathering will prevent the fringe of pixels on the edges of areas next to the selection from appearing on the background of your Web page. Don't use feathering if you're selecting hard-edged, flat-color imagery. A high feathering value will produce noticeable halos along the edge of the image when it's viewed through a browser.

2. Choose Edit menu > Copy.

3. Choose Edit menu > Paste. The imagery will appear on its own layer.

4. Hide any layers that you don't want to be visible in the final GIF image, and also hide the Background, even if it's all white.

5. Choose File menu > Export > GIF89a Export.

6. Choose Palette: Adaptive, and click Preview to preview the GIF file.

7. Try lowering the number of colors via the Colors drop-down menu or by entering a value.

8. Preview again to evaluate the image quality with a lower color depth.

9. The Transparency Index Color—which is the color for transparent areas—is set to the Netscape background color by default. To choose your own color for the transparent areas, click on the Transparency Index Color box, choose a new color, then click OK. This color will only be visible on a large feathered edge when the image is viewed in the browser.

GIF89a Export

If you want your image to fade or to appear as an irregular shape on a flat background, create two layers in your Photoshop document, one that contains a flat color chosen with the Web palette loaded into the Swatches palette, and one that contains the image with a soft, feathered edge or that has an irregular shape. Hide all the other layers except these two. Use the GIF89a Export command, but don't change the default Transparency color, since transparency isn't created with this type of GIF.

If you're planning to change the background on your Web page using a large flat color background image or via HTML code, you must make the Transparency Index Color box match the background the GIF will appear on top of. Otherwise, default gray will display in the soft edge areas of a large feathered edge (yech).

JPEG: the sometimes solution

The JPEG format may be a better choice for preserving color fidelity if your image is continuous tone (contains gradations of color or is photographic) and it's intended for viewers who have 24-bit monitors, which have the capacity to display millions of colors.

A JPEG plus: It can take a 24-bit image and make it as small as the GIF format can make an 8-bit image.

JPEG's shortcomings: First, a JPEG file has to be decompressed when it's downloaded for viewing on a Web page, which takes time.

Secondly, JPEG is not a good choice for flat-color images or type, because its compression methods tend to produce artifacts along the well-defined edges of these kinds of images.

And third, not all Web viewers use 24-bit monitors. A JPEG image will be dithered on an 8-bit monitor, though dithering in a continuous-tone image is less noticeable than in an image that contains flat colors. You can lower your monitor's setting to 8-bit to preview what the image will look like in an 8-bit setting. If it doesn't contain type or objects

To match colors between Photoshop and another application

If you try to mix a color in Photoshop using the same RGB values as a particular color used in Director or Netscape Navigator, you probably won't be able to achieve an exact match, because Director and Navigator use the Windows or Apple Color Picker (depending on your platform) to determine RGB color values (the number attached to each R, G, and B component), whereas Photoshop, by default, uses its own color picker.

To be able to mix colors using the RGB sliders on the Color palette in Photoshop to match colors used in Director, you should use the Windows/Apple color picker rather than Photoshop's own color picker. Choose Preferences > General, choose Color Picker: Windows/Apple, then click OK. Remember to reset this preference back to the Photoshop color picker when you're finished.

with sharp edges, then the JPEG image will probably survive the 8-bit setting conversion.

JPEG format files can now be saved as progressive JPEG, which is supported by the Netscape Navigator browser, and which displays the image in increasing detail as it downloads onto the Web page.

If you choose JPEG as your output format, you can experiment by creating and saving several versions of the image using varying degrees of compression. Open the JPEG versions of the image in Photoshop and view them at 100% or a more magnified view. Decide which degree of compression is acceptable by weighing the file size versus diminished image quality. Be sure to leave the original image intact to allow for potential future revisions.

Each time an image is resaved as a JPEG, some original image data is destroyed, and the more the image is degraded. The greater the degree of compression, the greater the data loss. To prevent this data loss, edit your image in Photoshop format and then save a JPEG copy when the image is finalized.

To save a copy of an image in JPEG format:

1. Choose File menu > Save a Copy.

2. Choose a location and enter a name for the file.

3. *Windows:* Choose Save As: JPEG, then click Save.

   Macintosh: Choose Format: JPEG, then click Save.

4. Enter an Image Options: Quality value (0–10) or choose from the four drop-down menu options.
   or
   Move the slider to choose from the quality options.

   A Maximum setting will compress the image the least (between 5:1 and 15:1), and preserve image quality the most, but

(Continued on the following page)

Save Copy of Image in JPEG Format

the resulting file size from this setting will be larger than with any other setting.

Try all four settings on different versions of the original, and then reopen the JPEGs in Photoshop to weigh the image-quality versus file-size question.

5. Choose Format Options **1**: Baseline ("Standard") to minimize the amount of data loss during compression.
or
Choose Format Options: Baseline Optimized to optimize image quality during compression.
or
Choose Progressive to produce a progressive JPEG file. This type of file will display in the Web browser in several passes, with more detail revealed with each pass. Choose the desired number of passes (scans) from the Scans drop-down menu.

6. Click OK (Enter/Return).

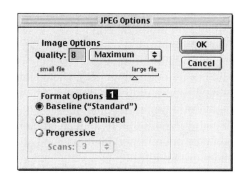

PNG: the future solution?

PNG is a patent-free file format. It supports 24-bit color images; it has an interlacing option; and it offers even more impressive compression than the present JPEG format. PNG also supports alpha channels of 256 levels of gray that can be used to define areas of transparency. With 256 levels of masking gray, you can create a very soft fade to transparency, which means you'll be able to display soft shadows and glowing shapes on the Web.

To save an image in the PNG format:

1. In Photoshop, choose File menu > Save a Copy.

2. Choose a location in which to save the file, and enter a name for the file.

3. *Windows:* Choose Save As: PNG, then click Save.

Macintosh: Choose Format: PNG, then click Save.

4. Choose Interlace: None or Adam7.

5. Choose a filter option for the method

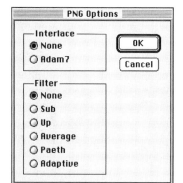

*The **PNG Options** dialog box. **Tip:** Choose Filter: Adaptive to have Photoshop choose the compression filter that best suits the image.*

by which the file will be compressed. (See the Adobe Photoshop User Guide for information on filter options.)

6. Click OK.

Dithering about

Dithering is a technique in which pixels from two palette colors are intermixed to give the impression of a third color. It's used to make images that contain a limited number of colors (256 or fewer) appear to have a greater range of colors and shades. Dithering is usually applied to continuous-tone images to increase their tonal range, but—argh, life is full of compromises—it can also make them look a little dotty.

Dithering usually doesn't produce aesthetically pleasing results in flat color images. This is because the browser palette will dither pixels to recreate any color that the palette doesn't contain. For a flat-color image, turn off the dither option and work with colors from the Web palette loaded into the Swatches palette.

Continuous-tone imagery is, in a way, already dithered. Some continuous-tone imagery looks fine on a Web page with no dithering and 256 colors. The fewer colors the palette of a non-dithered continuous-tone image contains, the more banding will occur in its color transitions. If dithering is turned on, the more dithering you'll see. You can decide which of these two evils appears lesser to your eye.

One more consideration: Dithering adds noise to the file, so compression is not as effective when dithering is turned on as when it's off. So, with dithering on, you may not be able to achieve your desired degree of file compression. As is the case with most Web output, you'll have to strike an acceptable balance between aesthetics and file size.

In Photoshop, you can access a dithering option when you convert an image to Indexed Color mode. You can't control dithering with the GIF89a Export option; this

Dithering

command dithers an image automatically.

On the fringe: to alias or anti-alias

To make an object anti-aliased, pixels with progressively less opacity are added along its edge to smooth the transition between the object and its background. An object with an aliased edge is sharp, with no extra pixels along its edge.

When images are composited in Photoshop, anti-aliasing produces smooth transitions between existing shapes and added shapes. Along the edge of a selection created using a tool with an anti-aliased edge, though, there may be a leftover fringe from the color of the former surrounding pixels. If you copy and paste this type of shape onto a flat color background, the fringe may become evident, and it can look mighty peculiar. To eliminate the fringe, before you create your selection, uncheck the Anti-aliased box on the Options palette for the Marquee or Lasso tool. You'll create a hard-edged selection, with no extra pixels along its edge.

To select imagery on its own layer without selecting semi-transparent pixels on its anti-aliased edge, Ctrl-click/⌘-click the layer name.

When you're initially selecting a shape on a flat color background (all on one layer), use the Magic Wand tool with a low Tolerance setting (1-5). Click on the flat background with Anti-aliased unchecked, zoom in (400-500%) to see the edge of the shape, then choose Select menu > Inverse to select the shape (not its background). If the edge of the selection still includes too many soft-edged pixels, choose Select menu > Modify > Contract, and enter a 1 or 2 pixel value for the amount by which the selection edge will contract. Reapply the command until the soft edge is eliminated.

Defringe

With the GIF89a Export's ability to export a shape on its own layer with a transparent background, the fringe problem is diminished, provided a careful selection was made on the shape initially. If you still detect a fringe using the GIF preview, click Cancel, activate the shape's layer, then apply Layer menu > Matting > Defringe using a value of 1 or 2 pixels.

Using layers for Web design

Since you can use Photoshop to create both imagery and special display text effects, it's a good application for designing Web pages. You can use Photoshop's Layers palette to preview and compose the elements of your Web page design. Create separate layers for such items as a particular background color, a tiled pattern, or imagery. Create aliased or anti-aliased headline text in Photoshop, and enhance it using layer effects or filters. Photoshop text is rasterized, so unlike PostScript text, you don't need to worry about whether the desired fonts are installed in the viewer's system. With elements on separate layers, you can restack, reposition, scale down, color adjust (for a screened back effect, for example), or show/hide different elements of the Web page. You can save the layered version of the page and decide later which layer elements to use.

In a layered document, the Copy Merged command will allow you to copy a selection that includes pixels from all visible layers that fall within the selection. This is a great way to create a "flattened" area of an image. Create a new document, then paste. That flattened area will be on its own new layer. You can duplicate layers to try out different design ideas on the same image, then show/hide individual layers to judge the duplicates.

If you really want to get serious about working with layers for Web design—use Adobe's **ImageReady**. This program helps you optimize an image for size and color quality, and uses layers to view elements and create GIF animations.

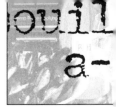

Alpha channel
A special 8-bit grayscale channel that is used for saving a selection.

Anti-alias
The blending of pixel colors on the perimeter of hard-edged shapes, like type, to smoooth undesirable stair-stepping (jaggies).

ASCII
(American Standard Code for Information Interchange) A standard editable format for encoding data.

Background color
The color applied when the Eraser tool is used, the canvas size is enlarged, or a selection is moved on the Background of an image.

Bézier curve
A curved line segment drawn using the Pen tool that can be reshaped by manipulating its anchor points or direction lines.

Binary
In Photoshop, a method for encoding data. Binary encoding is more compact than ASCII encoding.

Bit
(Binary digit) The smallest unit of information on a computer. Eight bits equal one byte.

Bit depth
The number of bits that are used to store a pixel's color information for display.

Bitmap
The display of an image on a computer screen via the geometric mapping of a single layer of pixels on a rectangular grid. In Photoshop, Bitmap is also a one-channel mode consisting of only black and white pixels.

Burn
To darken an area of an image.

Byte
The basic unit of storage memory. One byte equals eight bits. One kilobyte (K, Kb) equals 1,024 bytes. One megabyte (M, MB) equals 1,024 kilobytes. One gigabyte (G, Gb) equals 1,024 megabytes.

Canvas size
The full editable area of an image.

Channel
An image component that contains the pixel information for an individual color. A grayscale image has one color channel, an RGB image has three color channels, and a CMYK image has four color channels.

Clipboard
An area of memory used to temporarily store selection pixels. The Clipboard is accessed via the Cut, Copy, and Paste commands.

Clipping
In Photoshop, the automatic adjustment of colors to bring them into printable gamut.

CMYK
(Cyan, Magenta, Yellow, and Black) The four ink colors used in process printing. Cyan, magenta, and yellow are the three subtractive primaries. CMYK colors are simulated on a computer monitor using additive red, green, and blue light. To color separate an image from Photoshop, convert it to CMYK Color mode.

Color correction
The adjustment of color in an image to match original artwork or a photograph. Color correction is usually done in CMYK Color mode in preparation for process printing.

Color separation
The production of a separate printing plate for each ink color that will be used to print an image. Four plates are used in process color separation, one each for Cyan, Magenta, Yellow, and Black. An addition plate is used for each spot color.

Color table
The color palette of up to 256 colors of an image in Indexed Color mode.

Glossary

Continuous-tone image
An image, such as a photograph, in which there are gradual transitions between shades or colors.

Crop
To trim away part of an image.

Crop marks
Short, fine lines that are placed around the edges of a page to designate where the paper is to be trimmed at a print shop.

DCS 2.0
(Desktop Color Separation) A file format for saving a CMYK image for color separation, with the option for saving spot color channels and alpha channels, and an optional low resolution file for previewing and laser printing.

Dither
The mixing of adjacent pixels to simulate additional colors when available colors are limited, such as on an 8-bit monitor or an 8-bit palette.

Dodge
To bleach (lighten) an area of an image. Also, a so-so car model.

Dot gain
The undesirable spreading and enlarging of ink dots on paper, which causes colors or shades to look darker.

Dpi
(dots per inch) A unit that is used to measure the resolution of a printer or imagesetter. Dpi is sometimes used to describe the input resolution of a scanner, but "ppi" is the more accurate term.

Duotone
A grayscale image that is printed using two plates to enhance its tonal depth. A tritone is printed using three plates. A quadtone is printed using four plates.

Dye sublimation
A continuous-tone printing process in which a solid printing medium is converted into a gas before it hits paper.

8-bit monitor
A monitor in which each pixel stores eight bits of information and represents one of only 256

available colors. Dithering is used to simulate additional colors.

EPS
(Encapsulated PostScript) An image file format that contains PostScript code and, in the case of Photoshop, an optional PICT or TIFF image for screen display. EPS is a commonly used format for moving files from one application to another and also for color separation.

Foreground color
The color that is applied when a painting tool is used, type is created, or the stroke command is applied.

Gradient fill
In Photoshop, a graduated blend between the Foreground and Background colors that is produced using the Gradient tool.

Grayscale
An image that contains black, white, and up to 256 shades of gray, but no color. In Photoshop, Grayscale is a one-channel image mode.

Halftone screen
A pattern of tiny dots that is used for printing an image to simulate continuous tones.

Histogram
A graph showing the number of pixels at each level of brightness in an image.

HSB
See Hue, Saturation, and Brightness.

Hue
The wavelength of light of a pure color that gives a color its name—such as red or blue—independent of its saturation or brightness.

Imagesetter
A high-resolution printer (usually between 1,270 and 4,000 dpi) that generates paper or film output from a computer file.

Indexed color
In Photoshop, an image mode in which there is only one channel and a color table that can contain up to 256 colors. All the colors in an Indexed Color image are displayed on its table—unlike an image in any other mode.

Interpolation
The recoloring of pixels as a result of changing an image's dimensions or resolution or

applying a transform command. Interpolation may cause an image to look blurry when it's printed. You can choose an interpolation method in Photoshop—from slower, but better, to faster but lower quality.

Invert
To reverse an image's light and dark values and/or colors.

JPEG compression
(Joint Photographic Experts Group) A compression method in Photoshop that shrinks a file's storage size, but which can also cause image degradation as a result of data loss.

Kern
To adjust the horizontal spacing between a pair of characters.

Lab
A mode in which colors are related to the CIE color reference system. In Photoshop, an image in Lab Color mode is composed of three channels: one for lightness, one for green-to-red colors, and one blue-to-yellow colors.

Leading
The spacing between lines of type, measured from baseline to baseline.

Lightness
The lightness (or brightness) of a color, independent of its hue and saturation.

LPI
(lines per inch/halftone frequency/screen frequency) The unit that is used to measure the frequency of rows of dots on a halftone screen.

Luminosity
The distribution of an image's light and dark values.

Mode
A method for specifying how color information is to be interpreted. An image can be converted to a different image mode (RGB to Indexed Color, for example). A blending mode can be chosen for a tool or a layer to control how it affects underlying pixels.

Moiré
An undesirable pattern that can result from the use of improper halftone screen angles

during printing. Moirés can also occur if the pattern in an image conflicts with proper halftone patterns.

Object-oriented
A software method (also known as vector) that is used for describing and processing computer files. Object-oriented graphics and PostScript type are defined by mathematics and geometry. Bitmapped images, such as Photoshop images, are defined by pixels on a rectangular grid.

Opacity
The density of a color or shade, ranging from transparent to opaque. In Photoshop, you can choose an opacity for a tool or a layer.

Path
A shape that is comprised of straight and/or curved segments that are joined by anchor points.

PICT
A Macintosh file format that is used to display and save images. Save a Photoshop image as a PICT to open it in a video or animation program (but not for color separation).

Pixels
(image elements) The individual dots that are used to display an image on a computer monitor.

PPI
(pixels per inch) The unit that is used to measure the resolution of a bitmapped image.

Plug-in module
Third-party software that is loaded into the Photoshop Plug-ins folder so it can be accessed from a Photoshop menu. Or, a plug-in module that comes with Photoshop that is used to facilitate Import, Export, file format conversion, or other operations.

Point
A unit of measure that is used to describe type size (measured from ascender to descender), leading (measured from baseline to baseline), and line width.

Posterize
Produce a special effect in an image by reducing the number of shades of gray or colors to a specified—usually low—number.

PostScript
The page description language created and licensed by Adobe Systems Inc. that is used to display and print fonts and images.

Process color
Inks that are used to print an image from four separate plates, one each for Cyan (C), Magenta (M), Yellow (Y), and Black (K). In combination, they produce an illusion of an even wider range of colors.

Quick Mask
In Photoshop, a screen display mode in which a translucent colored mask covers selected or unselected areas of an image. Painting tools can be used to reshape a Quick Mask.

RAM
(Random Access Memory) The system memory of a computer that is used for running an application and processing information, and for temporary storage.

Rasterize
The conversion of an object-oriented image into a bitmapped image. When an Adobe Illustrator graphic is placed or opened in Photoshop, it is rasterized. All computer files are rasterized when they're printed.

Resample
Change an image's resolution while keeping its pixel count constant.

Resolution
The fineness of detail of a digital image (measured in pixels per inch), a monitor (measured in pixels per inch—usually 72 ppi), a printer (measured in dots per inch), or a halftone screen (measured in lines per inch).

RGB
Red, Green, and Blue transmitted light are used to project color on a computer monitor. When pure Red, Green, and Blue light (known as the additive primaries) are combined, they produce white light. In Photoshop, RGB Color is a three-color-channel image mode.

Saturation
The purity of a color, independent of its hue and brightness. The more gray a color contains, the lower is its saturation.

Scan
To digitize a slide, a photograph, or other artwork on a scanner using scanning software so that it can be displayed and edited on a computer.

Scratch disk
(also known as virtual memory) Hard drive storage space that is designated as work space for processing operations and for temporarily storing part of an image and a backup version of the image when there is insufficient RAM available for those functions.

Screen angles
Angles used for positioning halftone screens when producing film to minimize undesirable dot patterns (moirés).

Screen frequency
(screen ruling) The resolution (density of dots) on a halftone screen, measured in lines per inch.

Selection
An area of an image that is isolated so it can be modified while the rest of the image is protected. The moving marquee that denotes the boundary of a selection can be moved independently of its pixel content.

Spot color
A custom mixed ink color used in printing. A separate plate is used to print each spot color. Pantone is a commonly used spot color matching system. (see *Process color*) Each spot channel holds data for an individual custom color.

TIFF
(Tagged Image File Format) A common file format that is used for saving a bitmapped image, such as a scan. A TIFF image can be color separated and can contain color management profiles.

Tolerance
The range of pixels within which a tool operates, such as the range of shades or colors the Magic Wand tool selects or the Paint Bucket tool fills.

Trap
The overlapping of adjacent colors to prevent undesirable gaps from occurring as a result of the misalignment of printing plates or paper.

APPENDIX B: COPYRIGHT PROTECTION

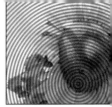

Ten questions and answers about copyright

Written by Tad Crawford

Why is copyright important?

If you are a creator of images (whether Photoshop user, photographer, designer, or fine artist), copyright protects you from having your images stolen by someone else. As the copyright owner, you may either allow or prevent anyone else from making copies of your work, making derivations from your work (such as a poster made from a photograph), or displaying your work publicly. Your copyrights last for your lifetime plus another fifty years, so a successful work may benefit not only you but your heirs as well. If you are a user of images, it is important that you understand the rights and obligations connected with their use so you don't infringe on the copyright of someone else and expose yourself to legal or financial liabilities.

What is an infringement?

Infringement is unauthorized use of someone else's work. The test for infringement is whether an ordinary observer would believe one work was copied from another.

Is it an infringement if I scan an old image into Photoshop and change it?

If the image was created in the United States and is more than 75 years old, it is in the public domain and can be freely copied by you or anyone else. You will have copyright in the new elements of the image that you create.

Is it an infringement if I scan a recent photograph into Photoshop and change it?

The scanning itself is making a copy and so is an infringement. As a practical matter, however, it is unlikely you will be sued for infringement if you change the photograph to the point where an ordinary observer would no longer believe your work was copied from the original photograph.

What does "fair use" mean in terms of copyright?

A fair use is a use of someone else's work that is allowed under the copyright law. For example, newsworthy or educational uses are likely to be fair uses. The factors for whether a use is a fair use or an infringement are: (1) the purpose and character of the use, including whether or not it is for profit (2) the character of the copyrighted work (3) how much of the total work is used and (4) what effect the use will have on the market for or value of the work being copied.

Can I use a recognizable part of a photograph if the entire source photograph is not recognizable?

You would have to apply the fair use factors. Obviously, factor (3) in the previous answer relating to how much of the total work is used would be in your favor, but if the use is to make a profit and will damage the market for the source photograph it might be considered an infringement.

What are the damages for infringement?

The damages are the actual losses of the person infringed plus any profits of the infringer. In some cases (especially if the work was registered before the infringement), the court can simply award between $500 and $20,000 for each work infringed. If the infringement is willful, the court can award as much as $100,000.

Do I have to register my images to obtain my copyright?

No, you have the copyright from the moment you create a work. However, registration with the Copyright Office costs $20 and will help you in the event your work is infringed. To obtain Copyright Application Form VA (for Visual Arts), write to the Copyright Office, Library of Congress, Washington, D.C. 20559 or call (202) 707-9100. Ask for the free Copyright Information Kit for the visual arts and you will receive many helpful circulars developed by the Copyright Office.

Do I need to use copyright notice to obtain or protect my copyright?

It is always wise to place copyright notice on your work, because it is a visible symbol of your rights as copyright owner. Prior to 1989 the absence of copyright notice when the images were published or publicly distributed could, in certain circumstances, cause the loss of the copyright. Since March 1, 1989, the absence of copyright notice cannot cause the loss of the copyright but may give infringers a loophole to try and lessen their damages. Copyright notice has three elements: (1) "Copyright" or "Copr" or "©" (2) your name and (3) the year of first publication.

How do I get permission to reproduce an image?

A simple permission form will suffice. It should set forth what kind of project you are doing, what materials you want to use, what rights you need in the material, what credit line and copyright notice will be given, and what payment, if any, will be made. The person giving permission should sign the permission form. If you are using an image of a person for purposes of advertising or trade, you should have them sign a model release. If the person's image is to be altered or placed in a situation that didn't occur, you would want the release to cover this. Otherwise you may face a libel or invasion of privacy lawsuit.

Digital watermarking

The Embed Digimarc filter embeds nearly invisible copyright information and a contact address into a Photoshop image. This watermark cannot easily be removed by reworking the image in Photoshop. It will be present in any copy or any printout of the image and will even be retained if the printed piece is redigitized by scanning.

Note: To create a valid copyright, you must register with and pay a fee to Digimarc Corporation. They will enter your personal information into their database and issue you a unique creator ID, so your watermark will contain your personal contact and copyright information.

To embed a watermark:

1. Open a flattened version of the image to be watermarked.

2. Choose Filter > Digimarc > Embed Watermark.

3. If you don't yet have a personal Creator ID, click Personalize **1**, then click Register to connect to the Digimarc Web site or phone Digimarc at the number listed in the dialog box.

4. Enter your Creator ID number **2**, then click OK.

5. Enter a date in the Copyright Year field.

6. Check Image Attributes: Restricted, for limited use of the image.

Optional: Check the Adult Content box (this option is not yet functional).

7. Choose the intended final output option—Monitor, Web, or Print—from the Target Output drop-down menu.

or

Enter a Watermark Durability value, or move the slider. If the image is intended for high-resolution printing, enter 1 or 2 to create a nearly invisible mark. If the image is intended for multimedia or Web output, enter 3 or 4 to create a

(Continued on the following page)

Digital Watermarking

333

more visible and more durable water-mark. (This is recommended due to the file conversion, compression, and decompression that typically occurs when such files are prepared for export.) The lower the Watermark Durability, the greater the potential for the watermark to be ruined by image editing.

8. Check Verify to view a scale that describes the durability of the watermark after it's embedded. *Note:* This option involves using the signal strength meter. See Photoshop's online Help for more information about this feature.

9. Click OK.

The Digimarc filter must be available in order view a watermark symbol that's already embedded in an image. The title bar of an image that contains a watermark will display a copyright symbol ©.

To read information about a watermark:

1. With the image containing the water-mark open, choose Filter > Digimarc > Read Watermark. A dialog box display-ing Creator ID and other information will open.

2. *Optional:* Use this information to get in touch with the creator of the image. If you're currently hooked up to the Web via a browser, you can click Web Lookup to open the browser and then navigate to the Digimarc Web site. The creator information will be listed there.

3. Click OK to close the Watermark Information dialog box.

Alicia Buelow
336 Arkansas St.
San Francisco, CA 94107
415-642-8083
e-mail: buelow@adobe.com

Jeff Brice
2416 NW 60th Street
Seattle, WA 98107
206-706-0406
e-mail: cyspy@aol.com

Diane Fenster
287 Reichling Ave.
Pacifica, CA 94044
415-355-5007
e-mail: fenster@sfsu.edu
http://www.sirius.com/~fenster

Louis Fishauf
Creative Director
Reactor Art + Design Limited
51 Camden Street
Toronto, Ontario
Canada M5V1V2
416-703-1913 x241
e-mail: fishauf@reactor.ca
http://www.magic.ca/~fishauf/
http://www.reactor.ca

Wendy Grossman
355 West 51st Street
New York, NY 10019
212-262-4497
http://www.renard
represents.com
(pages 54, 181 and color section)

John Hersey
546 Magnolia Avenue
Larkspur, CA 94939
Voice 415-927-2091
Fax 415-927-2092
http://www.hersey.com
e-mail: ultraduc@hersey.com

David Humphrey
439 Lafayette Street
New York, NY 10003
212-780-0512
e-mail: humphrey@is2.nyu.edu
(page 101)

Liana Levin
105-40 63rd Avenue
Forest Hills, NY 11375
718-459-7313
(pages 311, 312)

Min Wang
795 Coastland Drive
Palo Alto, CA 94303
Voice 415-321-4294
Fax 415-321-6246
e-mail: mwang@adobe.com

Annette Weintraub
Professor
Department of Art
City College of New York
138th St. and Convent Avenue
New York, NY 10031
Voice 212-650-7410
Fax 212-650-7438
e-mail: anwcc@cunyvm.cuny.edu
http://www.artnetweb.com/art-
netweb/projects/realms/notes.html

Seasonal Specialties
Jennifer Sheeler, Creative Director
Barbara Roth, Art Director
Lisa Milan, Senior Designer (1997
    catalog)
Seasonal Specialties LLC (@1996
    All Rights Reserved)
11455 Valley View Road
Eden Prairie, MN 55344
Voice 612-942-6555
Fax 612-942-1801
jen.sheeler@seasonalspecialties.com
barb.roth@seasonalspecialties.com
lisa.milan@seasonalspecialties.com

Directory of Artists

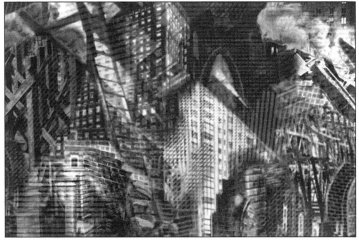

Lifeline, ©1996 Annette Weintraub

Thank you

Nancy Aldrich-Ruenzel, Publisher; *Corbin Collins,* our editor; *Kate Reber,* production coordinator; *Gary-Paul Prince,* publicist; *Keasley Jones,* foreign rights manager; and the rest of the gang at Peachpit Press, for always being helpful and on the ball.

Victor Gavenda, at Peachpit Press, for his meticulous testing—start to finish.

Rebecca Gulick, Senior Writer for MacWEEK and eMediaweekly of San Francisco, for writing the section on color management.

Jim Kingston, of Kingston Design/New Media Productions, Macintosh guide and outfitter, for his contributions to the pages on actions, the Web, and multimedia.

Gregory Little, electronic media artist and assistant professor of art, Kent State University, for contributing the images and first draft of the 3D Transform filter instructions.

Adam Hausman, Macintosh systems specialist, for his layout services.

Judy Susman, Jane Taylor Starwood, and *Susan Hallock,* for proofreading.

Adobe Systems, Inc., for their technical support, and Don Day in particular.

Extensis Corporation, for the PhotoFrame plug-in.

Tad Crawford, attorney, author, and Allworth Press publisher, for contributing the *Ten Questions and Answers About Copyright.*

Photo credits

Nadine Markova (Mexico City), pages 21, 131.

Paul Petroff (Seattle, Washington), pages 77, 130, 132, 257.

John Stuart (New York City), page 293.

Cara Wood (New York City), page 204.

PhotoDisc, pages iii, 4, 26, 41, 58, 60, 61, 62, 79, 80, 85, 106, 124, 125, 132, 139, 147, 148, 155, 161, 163, 186, 210, 223, 225, 229, 243, 245, 259, 312, 316, 321.

All other images are owned by the authors.

Thank Yous

Excaved, ©1996 Annette Weintraub

Index

Index

Want more?

If we write a sequel to this book, what topics would you like us to cover? Drop us a line at **Pixbill@aol.com**.